The Study of World Politics

The Study of World Politics is a two-volume set that presents forty of some two hundred essays authored by Professor James N. Rosenau, a renowned international political theorist. Included are articles recently published and those that have not previously been published. All focus on the study of world politics, with the twenty-three articles in this volume devoted to probing theoretical and methodological challenges.

This volume is divided into five parts and addresses such issues as:

* the challenge of world politics
* the professional political scientist
* methods
* concepts and theories
* the analysis of foreign policy

Included in this collection is perhaps James N. Rosenau's most widely-read essay, "Pre-Theories and Theories of Foreign Policy", as well as several essays that articulate various dimensions of global governance and how they are shaped by the dynamics of globalization. These articles are marked by unique and imaginative formulations which break with a number of conventional approaches employed in the fields of international relations and foreign policy.

The Study of World Politics provides the reader with access for the first time to a collection of James N. Rosenau's outstanding scholarship, making this an invaluable book to students and academics with an interest in politics.

James N. Rosenau is University Professor of International Affairs at The George Washington University, USA, having previously been affiliated with three other universities. He is a former President of the International Studies Association (1984–5) and a holder of a Guggenheim Fellowship (1987–8). His books include *Turbulence in World Politics: A theory of change and continuity* (1990), *Along the Domestic-Foreign Frontier: Exploring governance in a turbulent world* (1997), and *Distant Proximities: Dynamics beyond globalization* (2003).

The Study of World Politics

Volume 1: theoretical and
methodological challenges

James N. Rosenau

 Routledge
Taylor & Francis Group

LONDON AND NEW YORK

First published 2006
by Routledge
2 Park Square, Milton Park, Abingdon, Oxon OX14 4RN

Simultaneously published in the USA and Canada
by Routledge
270 Madison Ave, New York, NY 10016

Routledge is an imprint of the Taylor & Francis Group

© 2006 James N. Rosenau

Typeset in Baskerville by
RefineCatch Ltd, Bungay, Suffolk
Printed and bound in Great Britain by
TJ International Ltd, Padstow, Cornwall

British Library Cataloguing in Publication Data
A catalogue record for this book is available from the British Library

Library of Congress Cataloging in Publication Data
A catalog record for this book has been requested

ISBN10: 0–415–36337–3 (hbk)
ISBN10: 0–415–36338–1 (pbk)

ISBN13: 9–78–0–415–36337–2 (hbk)
ISBN13: 9–78–0–415–36338–9 (pbk)

Contents

Volume 1

List of illustrations   ix
Acknowledgments   x

1 Introduction   1

PART I
The challenge   5

2 The future of politics   7

3 Building blocks of a new paradigm for studying world politics   11

4 Rigid boundaries: states, societies, and international relations   20

5 Powerful tendencies, startling discrepancies, and elusive
   dynamics: the challenge of studying world politics in a turbulent era 26

6 Political science and political processes: narrowing the gap?   34

PART II
The professional   47

7 The birth of a political scientist   49

8 Intellectual identity and the study of international relations, or
   coming to terms with mathematics as a tool of inquiry   53

9 Courage versus caution: a dialogue on entering and prospering
   in IR (co-authored with Ersel Aydinli)   59

PART III
Methods   79

10   Comparison is a state of mind   81

11   CFP and IPE: the anomaly of mutual boredom   84

PART IV
Concepts and theories   95

12   The theoretical imperative: unavoidable explication   97

13   Many damn things simultaneously – at least for awhile:
     complexity theory and world affairs   107

14   Muddling, meddling, and modeling: alternative approaches to
     the study of world politics in an era of rapid change   120

15   Territorial affiliations and emergent roles: the shifting nature of
     identity in a globalizing world   133

16   Capabilities and control in an interdependent world   140

17   The skill revolution as a dynamic process   154

18   Generational change and Internet literacy   159

PART V
The analysis of foreign policy   169

19   Pre-theories and theories of foreign policy   171

20   Pre-theorizing about foreign policy in a globalized world   200

21   China in a bifurcated world: competing theoretical perspectives   206

22   Toward single-country theories of foreign policy: the case of the USSR   229

23   National interest   246

     Notes   255
     Index of subjects   281
     Index of authors   297

Volume 2

List of illustrations   ix
Acknowledgments   x

 1 Introduction   1

PART I
The challenge   5

 2 The new global order: underpinnings and outcomes   7

 3 Ominous tensions in a globalizing world   13

 4 Aging agendas and ambiguous anomalies: tensions and
    contradictions of an emergent epoch   19

 5 Global affairs in an epochal transformation   31

PART II
The profession   47

 6 Material and imagined communities in globalized space   49

 7 Many globalizations, one international relations   63

 8 The globalization of globalization   72

PART III
Globalization   81

 9 The complexities and contradictions of globalization   83

10 Toward a viable theory of globalization   91

11 Democracy and globalization   96

12 Think globally, pray locally   104

PART IV
Governance   109

13 Toward an ontology for global governance   111

14 Governance in the twenty-first century   121

15 Global governance as disaggregated complexity   147

16 Change, complexity, and governance in globalizing space   161

17 Strong demand, huge supply: governance in an emergent epoch   180

   Notes   197
   Appendix: Publications of James N. Rosenau   221
   Index of subjects   240
   Index of authors   256

Illustrations

Figures

21.1   The two worlds of world politics   220
21.2   China in a bifurcated world   221

Tables

 6.1   Some possible sources of fragmegration at four levels of aggregation   41
19.1   An abbreviated presentation of the author's pre-theory of
       foreign policy, in which five sets of variables underlying the
       external behavior of societies are ranked according to their
       relative potencies in eight types of societies   176
19.2   Examples of vertical systems in each of the four issue-areas   194
19.3   Matrix of means and ends   195
19.4   A further elaboration of the author's pre-theory of foreign
       policy, in which five sets of variables underlying the external
       behavior of societies are ranked according to their relative
       potencies in sixteen types of societies and three types of issue-areas   198
21.1   Four models of the international system   214
21.2   Three models of decision-making   223
21.3   The responsiveness of five global structures to three different Chinas   225
22.1   Factors central to a theory of the USSR   240

Acknowledgments

Needless to say, a long career of writing incurs a number of intellectual and administrative debts. In addition to assistants in four universities and my invisible college – those colleagues and students in the field who have provided suggestions and criticisms on panels and in correspondence and who are too numerous to list – I am especially grateful to Hongying Wang for her advice and support in the process of completing this two-volume project.

*   *   *

A number of the chapters in this book were originally published in other works. Although some have been revised, I am nonetheless grateful to the following publishers for their permission to reprint the indicated materials:

Chapter 2, "The future of politics", was excerpted and reprinted from *Futures*, Vol. 31 James N. Rosenau, "The Future of Politics," pp. 1005–16, Copyright 1999, with permission from Elsevier.

Chapter 4 combines parts of two prior essays. One is excerpted from "Unfulfilled Potential: Sociology and International Relations", a contribution to a symposium published in the *International Review of Sociology*, Vol. 12, No. 3 (November 2002), pp. 543–47, and is reprinted here with permission of Taylor & Francis (www.tandf.co.uk/journals). The other is a paper presented at the Annual Meeting of the International Studies Association, New Orleans, March 26, 2002, devoted to an evaluation of the *Handbook of International Relations*, edited by Walter Carlsnaes, Thomas Risse, and Beth Simmons (Thousand Oaks, CA: Sage Publications, 2002).

Chapter 5, "Powerful Tendencies, Startling Discrepancies, and Elusive Dynamics: The Challenge of Studying World Politics in a Turbulent Era," was first published in the *Australian Journal of International Affairs*, Vol. 50 (April 1996), pp. 23–30, and is reprinted here by permission of Taylor & Francis (www.tandf.co.uk/journals).

Chapter 6, "Political science and political processes: narrowing the gap?" was originally published in Frank H. Fu (ed.), *The Development of Social Sciences in the 21st Century* (Hong Kong: Faculty of Sciences, Hong Kong Baptist University, 2001), pp. 32–47, and is reprinted here by permission.

Chapter 7, "The birth of a political scientist," was originally published in *PROD*, Vol. 3 (January 1960), pp. 19–21. That journal was later renamed *American Behavioral Scientist*, and the article is reprinted here with permission from Sage Publications.

Chapter 8, "Intellectual identity and the study of international relations, or coming to terms with mathematics as a tool of inquiry", was originally published in *Mathematical Models in International Relations*, Dina A. Zinnes and John V. Gillespie (eds.), pp. 3–9, Copyright © 1976 by Praeger Publishers, Inc. Reproduced by permission of Greenwood Publishing Group, Inc., Westport, CT.

Chapter 9, "Courage versus caution: a dialogue on entering and prospering in IR," co-authored by Ersel Aydinli was originally published in the *International Studies Review*, Vol. 6 (2004), pp. 511–26 and is reprinted here with permission from Blackwell Publishing.

Chapter 10, "Comparison as a state of mind," was originally published in *Studies in Comparative Communism* (now called *Communist and Post-Communist Studies*), Vol. III (Spring/Summer 1975), pp. 57–61, and is reprinted here by permission.

Chapter 11, "CFP and IPE: the anomaly of mutual boredom", was originally published as "CFP and IPE: The Anomaly of Boredom," Copyright 1988 from *International Interactions*, Vol. 14, No. 1. Reproduced by permission of Taylor and Francis, Inc., http://www.taylorandfrancis.com.

Chapter 12, "The theoretical imperative: unavoidable explication," was originally published in the *Asian Journal of Political Science*, Vol. 11 (December 2003), pp. 7–20, and is reprinted here by permission.

Chapter 13, "Many damn things simultaneously – at least for a while," was originally published in *Theoria: A Journal of Social and Political Theory*, No. 93 (December 1999). Copyright Faculty of Human and Management Sciences, University of KwaZulu-Natal, Pietermaritzburg.

Sections of Chapter 14, "Muddling, meddling and modeling: alternative approaches to the study of world politics in an era of rapid change," first appeared in *Millenium: Journal of International Studies*, Vol. 8, No. 2 (1979), pp. 499–523, and are reproduced here with substantial alternations with the permission of the publisher.

Chapter 16, "Capabilities and control in an interdependent world," was originally published in *International Security*, Vol. 1, No. 2 (Fall, 1976), pp. 32–49, © 1976 by the President and Fellows of Harvard College and the Massachusetts Institute of Technology. Reprinted here by permission.

Chapter 19, "Pre-theories and theories of foreign policy," was originally published in R. Barry Farrell (ed.), *Approaches to Comparative and International Politics* (Evanston, IL: Northwestern University Press, 1966), pp. 27–92, and is reprinted here by permission.

Chapter 21, "China in a bifurcated world: competing theoretical perspectives," was originally published in Thomas Robinson and David Shambaugh (eds.), *Chinese Foreign Policy: Theory and Practice* (Oxford, 1995), pp. 524–51, and is reprinted here by permission of Oxford University Press.

Chapter 22, "Toward single-country theories of foreign policy: the case of the USSR," was originally published in C. F. Hermann, C. W. Kegley, Jnr., and J. N. Rosenau (eds.), *New Directions in the Study of Foreign Policy* (Boston, MA: Allen and Unwin, 1987) pp. 53–74, and is reprinted here with permission of the Thomson Corporation.

Chapter 23, "National interest," is reproduced from *International Encyclopedia of the Social Sciences*, edited by David Sills and Robert Merton, Macmillan © 1968, Macmillan, and is reprinted here by permission of The Gale Group.

Lastly, I could not end these acknowledgements without mentioning my research assistant, Miles Townes, to whom fell the task of acquiring these permissions from the various publishers and otherwise helping to prepare the manuscript for publication. I am very grateful to him. I am also grateful to my publisher, Craig Fowlie, for his support in generating and supporting this project.

1 Introduction

To bring together into two volumes a selection of one's prior writings is not as easy a task as it might seem. Quite aside from space limitations, the difficulty of achieving a coherent group of essays, and the need to edit out unnecessary duplication, one is compelled to confront some tough questions: What is the larger meaning of revisiting and publishing these essays? Am I deceiving myself? In the guise of tracing intellectual development and contributing to knowledge in the field, am I doing little more than servicing my ego? Was a lifetime of probing the dynamics of world politics worth the effort? Will making these essays available have any lasting value for those who follow? Would it be better to heed the advice of an undergraduate who once reacted to a book of mine that I had assigned to his class by announcing, "You should have left it in the trees!"?

In short, compiling these essays has been a humiliating task, and I like to think that I have undertaken it only out of a long-standing commitment to the idea that the name of the game we play is circulating ideas and thereby contributing to the enlargement of knowledge. Idealistic? Perhaps. Rationalization? No, a lifetime of social science, of trying to capture the underlying dynamics that sustain, undermine, or transform social, political, and economic systems, has reinforced a long-standing conviction – call it an article of faith – that teaching and writing about world politics is a way of circulating ideas to unknown others and that, somehow, maybe, the ideas will be received and prove to be meaningful and influential. It is this article of faith that underlies the preparing of these volumes and the essays of which they consist. One doesn't know how far the ideas will circulate or how consequential they may be, but my article of faith drives me to believe that circulating them will matter. More accurately, my ideas and writings are among those of many others who seek to fathom world affairs and who, collectively, will circuitously as well as directly make their way into policy-making circles and debate in the public arena.

All told, my article of faith as well as (early on) career considerations have resulted in the writing or editing of more than forty books and monographs and some 200 papers, some unpublished, some published in obscure journals, and some as part of the syntheses developed in my three most recent and important books that I have come to regard as a trilogy.[1] Notwithstanding this extensive output, however, writing is for me a lonely and difficult task. One interacts with colleagues and critics, thrives on collegiality, and hears from and reacts to unknown others through e-mail, but nonetheless at its core the task of puzzling through and writing up the challenges confronting humankind is a lonely and humbling endeavor. It is a matter of one's analytic and normative self against all the ambiguities and complexities of the human condition, all the competing interpretations of how and why events and trends unfold as they do.

Criteria of selection

In looking back over all the articles I have written, wincing at some of them and pleased with others, it is clear that they all focus on the challenge of understanding one or another aspect of world politics and that they are marked by two central and recurring themes. Hence the common title of the two volumes is *The Study of World Politics* and their different subtitles reflect the two recurrent themes. In this volume I have included articles and papers concerned with theory and method, whereas the essays in the other volume focus on the challenges of globalization and global governance. Of course, the main foci of the two volumes are not mutually exclusive. Several of the chapters in this volume anticipate or take note of the processes of globalization, just as theory and method are necessarily relevant to the chapters of Volume 2. On balance, however, the overlap of the two volumes is not nearly so salient as the distinctions between them.

In selecting the essays that follow I have sought to strike a balance between unpublished and previously published papers that are not well known either because they appeared in foreign journals or in books that have not been widely read. In addition, in this volume I have sought to strike a balance between recent papers and those written earlier in my career.[2] Such a balance does not mark the other volume because it is only relatively recently that globalization and global governance have climbed high on research agendas.

Since all but two of the essays in this volume were previously published in one or another of the last four decades, there is a sense in which they reflect my intellectual development. The development is perhaps especially discernible in the narrowing of my interests from the general problems of theory and method presented here to the more specific foci of globalization and governance probed in the second volume. It must be emphasized, however, that tracing intellectual development is not a main purpose of the endeavor. Pieces of my intellectual autobiography can be found in several different sources[3] and there is no need to elaborate it further here beyond the inclusion of Chapters 7 and 9. To repeat, the prime purpose is to provoke thought through the circulation of ideas.

Organization of this volume

The distinction between theory and method cannot be clear-cut. It is difficult to focus on theoretical challenges without touching upon their methodological implications, and vice versa. Still, the two are sufficiently different to warrant treating them as separate subsections of this book. In addition, an earlier but now largely abandoned focus of my work, the challenge posed by the analysis of how foreign policy is made and conducted, serves as the prime concern of a third subsection.

Conceptual foci

Throughout most of the ensuing chapters a restlessness is expressed with conventional approaches to the theories and methodologies used in the study of world politics. As will be seen, underlying the discontent is a conviction that the world is undergoing enormous changes and that therefore both our theories and our methods must be adjusted accordingly. Analyzing change poses problems that are not easily resolved – and in some respects they may not be resolvable – but I feel strongly that fear of failure is a poor reason to avoid seeking to trace the dynamics of transformation, that one must make the effort even if it falls short. Thus more than a few of the ensuing chapters address the problem of change in one way or another. It should be noted, however, that despite this recurrent focus I am far from satisfied that extensive progress is being made in unraveling the dynamics that sustain change in social systems.[4]

A preoccupation with change and transformation sensitizes one to the rapidity with which events and trends become obsolete. To tool up on a current situation, teach students about its intricacies, and write up analyses of its underpinnings without locating it in a larger and more enduring context is to be only momentarily up-to-date. It is not to acquire concepts, perspectives, or information that enables one to grasp the dynamics of the new situations that evolve subsequently. This is why most of my essays do not focus on particular issues or countries. Chapters 21 and 22 are exceptions, but their analyses seek to generalize beyond the immediate circumstances that occasioned the writing of them.

Another intense conviction underlies more than a few of the chapters, namely, that objective analysis is not possible and that thus objective findings cannot be generated. One can never tell the whole story about an individual, event, situation, trend, country, or international system, thus forcing one to select some of its aspects as important and to dismiss other aspects as trivial, a process of selection that perforce renders the resulting analysis other than objective. To the extent that others do not subscribe to the resulting analysis it can be viewed as a subjective interpretation, whereas if the result is shared by like-minded others it becomes intersubjective. And it is intersubjective understandings created through further investigation, verification, and revision by others that serve as the foundations of knowledge in any field. In effect, these understandings are consensuses that continuously change as new formulations and findings lead to their revision or, indeed, to rival consensuses. In short, there are no ultimate truths about world politics, but rather competing consensuses about how the world works.

Although the various essays are marked by theoretical concerns, these are never far removed from the question of evidence, of what phenomena are empirically relevant. For it is data and evidence that renders theories credible. But data and evidence have to be credible too, and herein lies a difficult set of choices. A single instance or case can be illustrative and compelling, but can it serve as evidence? Or must the single case be included with many others to form a central tendency for it to be part of an interpretation that supports or negates a theory? And what about the outlier, the deviant case, the exception? Are these not potentially revealing of a theory's worth or falsity? My response to such questions has undergone alteration across time. Early on it seemed clear that only central tendencies were relevant to the knowledge-building process, that any other form of empirical observation could not hold up as a meaningful insight into the human condition. Such was the presumption of my long-time commitment to the generation of quantitative, scientific findings. At that time the outlier, deviant case, and exception were viewed simply as noise in the system, as phenomena that did not require careful examination. More recently, however, I have come to realize that unique phenomena that deviate from central tendencies can be useful in the theory-building process if they are treated as instances of some larger pattern that may be at work. Obviously, one cannot devote time to pursuing the implications of every deviant case. That would be an endless process with little payoff. Instead one should pay attention only to those deviant cases that involve important actors or countries, as they might point to patterns that had not previously been appreciated.

   Still another theme that recurs throughout the ensuing chapters concerns the rigidity of disciplinary or sub-disciplinary boundaries and the difficulty of spanning the boundaries through multidisciplinary inquiries. Put more positively, several of the essays seek to bridge the boundaries by highlighting the ways in which the concepts and methods on opposite sides of the boundaries are not nearly as antithetical as may be thought by those who champion them. The tendency of those committed to a particular paradigm to reject alternative perspectives or even to make minor modifications is, regrettably, widespread. Analysts become so wedded to their own formulations that the temptations to downplay the utility of alternative schemes are considerable and continuously reinforce the preferred paradigm. Yet, to be locked tightly in a conceptual jail is to run the risk of ignoring insights or data that may be relevant to the problems the investigator seeks to clarify.

Part I
The challenge

2 The future of politics[1]

To reflect seriously on the future of politics in the coming decades is to proceed from several basic premises that we all hold but that we normally do not explicate. One concerns our presumptions relative to the nature of change and the capacity of human systems to undergo transformation. A second involves our assumptions about the location of causation in human affairs, whether it originates and is sustained by agents or structures. A third derives from our premises concerning the role of individuals and their vulnerabilities to change, their readiness to engage in collective action, and their capacity for adapting to new conditions.

It follows that to the extent we hold different premises about change, agents, structures, and individuals, then to that extent our understandings of the future of politics are bound to be discrepant. In the ensuing chapters I undertake to explicate my premises along these lines as a means of suggesting what the long-term future of politics is likely to be. To anticipate the central thrusts of my analysis, I believe we are well into a period of profound transformations in which such deep changes are occurring in both the agents and structures and the relationship between them that world affairs in the future will be substantially different than it is today. More specifically, I argue that new technologies have facilitated four simultaneous and interrelated revolutions – what I shall call an organizational explosion, a skill revolution, a mobility upheaval, and a major rearrangement of global structures – that are generating differences in kind rather than simply differences in degree and that, as a result, we are entering a new epoch.

Before outlining this new epoch, let me repeat that my understanding of it stems from my basic premises about change and causal dynamics and that those who proceed from very different premises are likely to anticipate a different future for politics. More than that, because our differences stem from divergent assumptions, they are not subject to empirical proof. We can articulate the logic of our initial premises and we can marshal evidence in support of them, but our conclusions are bound to be a function of our points of departure. Thus, even if we agree on the empirics of the human condition, we may still differ enormously on what they signify because we proceed from different ontological and epistemological premises. Accordingly, rather than attempt to demonstrate that my analysis is sound and accurate, all I can do is articulate my basic premises and hope that they serve to alert others to the need to explicate their underlying assumptions and the interpretations to which they give rise.

An emergent epoch

A key to grasping the emergent epoch lies in the contradictions that pervade the course of events. Each day brings word of a world inching slowly toward sanity even as it moves toward breakdown. And not only do these integrative and disintegrative events occur simultaneously, but more often than not they are causally related. More than that, the causal links tend to cumulate and generate a momentum such that every integrative increment tends to give rise to a disintegrative increment, and vice versa. The simultaneity of the good and the bad, the global and local, the coherent and incoherent – to mention only a few of the interactive polarities that dominate world affairs – underlies the emergence of a new epoch in human affairs and the differences in kind that distinguish it. Indeed, I would argue that the best way to grasp world affairs today is to view them as an endless series of tensions in which the forces pressing for greater globalization and those inducing greater localization interactively play themselves out. To do otherwise, to focus only on globalizing dynamics, or only on localizing dynamics, is to risk overlooking what makes events unfold as they do.

But it would be erroneous to view the emergent epoch as comprised of simple interrelationships, readily discernible, and easily understood. They encompass the tensions between core and periphery, between national and transnational systems, between communitarianism and cosmopolitanism, between cultures and subcultures, between states and markets, between patriots and urbanites, between decentralization and centralization, between universalism and particularism, between the global and the local – to note only the more conspicuous links between opposites that presently underlie the course of events and the development or decline of institutions. And each of these tensions are marked by numerous variants; they take different forms in different parts of the world, in different countries, in different markets, in different communities, in different professions, and in different cyberspaces, with the result that there is enormous diversity in the way people experience the tensions that beset their lives.

At the core of the emergent epoch and the tensions that sustain it are interactions between new technologies and the uses made of them by people and their collectivities. The acceleration of the microelectronic revolution in recent decades offers an obvious example. It has brought words and pictures, ideas and philosophies, statistical data and detailed scenarios, into homes and offices most places in the world from most other places in the world, and it has done so with a speed that renders the transmission and reception of the messages virtually simultaneous. Global television, the Internet, the fax machine, and the fiber optic cable are only the more conspicuous of the many electronic technologies that have reduced communication distances to milliseconds. Similarly, the jet aircraft has reduced geographic distances to less than twenty-four hours in the sense that every city in the world is less than a day away from any other city. Stated more succinctly, the emergent epoch is marked by accelerating processes in which global spaces are moving into local places and local repercussions are occurring on a global scale.

By themselves, however, these technological innovations do not fully explain the advent of a new epoch. Neither globalizing nor localizing dynamics are amorphous forces that somehow drive the course of events. They consist of processes as well as structures, processes that are initiated, expanded, contracted, disrupted, or otherwise sustained by human agency, by people acting individually or collectively to cope with challenges and move toward goals. To be sure, at times it may seem as if the processes are structural and independent of agency – as, for example, when reference is made to market forces or to the influence of American norms as sources of behavior elsewhere in the world – but even the most all-encompassing of these processes are nonetheless founded on human agency, on huge multitudes of people – say, in the market – concurrently acting in the same way. Put differently, it is a gross mistake to posit or imply an inevitablism at work in world affairs, to "reason that globalization . . . refers to very large scale matters, in contrast to the 'small-scale' status of individuals." Rather, "individuals are as much a part of the globalization process as any other basic category of social-theoretical discourse" – or, more accurately perhaps, "globalization has involved and continues to involve the *institutionalized construction* of the individual."[2]

Among the major human transformations that can be traced to interactions with the technological innovations, three have unfolded at the micro level of individuals and a fourth pervades the macro level of collectivities and global structures. As indicated, one involves a transformation in the competence of individuals in every country and corner of the world, the transformation that I call a "skill revolution" wherein the analytical, emotional, and imaginative skills of healthy adults everywhere have become increasingly refined and now exceed those possessed by earlier generations. Another transformation has occurred with respect to the readiness of people to form and join associations, a transformation I call the "organizational explosion" wherein staggering numbers of new organizations, some tightly hierarchical and some more loosely structured, have sprung up in and across all the world's communities. And still another transformation consists of the vast movement of people from every country and corner of the world to other countries and corners, what I call the "mobility upheaval." The macro transformation involves the authority relationships between individuals at the micro level and their collectivities at the macro level, relationships that have led to the bifurcation of global structures into a state-centric world of states and a multi-centric world of diverse other kinds of collective agents.

Put in another way, the emergent epoch derives from a multiplicity of causal factors, each reinforcing the others in ways that defy reduction to an overarching theory. This means there can be no easy or overriding answer to the question of what drives the course of events. Power is too disaggregated, and feedback loops are too pervasive, to assert that global affairs are now driven by the United States, or by globalization, or by capitalism, or by whatever grand scheme may seem most compelling. No, what drives the emergent epoch consists of complex dynamics that spring, in turn, from numerous sources and cannot be traced to a singular origin.

Each of these transformations and their links to the new technologies is assessed in one or another of the chapters that follow, but suffice it to assert here that taken together they have irrevocably altered the way in which world affairs are conducted. They underlie the globalization of national economies, the weakening of states, the erosion of sovereignty, the decentralization of governments, and the growing influence of nongovernmental organizations (NGOs) – to mention only a few of the transformed structural features of the emergent epoch.

The future of politics

If the foregoing analysis of the underlying dynamics of the emergent epoch is reasonably accurate, a broad outline of the nature and direction of politics in the future can be readily derived. With ever more skillful publics converging into ever greater numbers of networks and organizations, with people on the move ever more extensively, and with global structures increasingly bifurcated, it seems likely that the contradictory trends toward greater integration and greater fragmentation will continue to accelerate. Perhaps most notably, this means that authority at all levels of community throughout the world is likely to be increasingly decentralized and, in many cases, weakened. Despite its resources and history, even the authority of the United States is likely to undergo continuous decentralization and fragmentation.[3] It follows, too, that the level of conflict within countries is likely to intensify, sometimes culminating in violence but perhaps more often in a diminution of community cohesion.

At the same time as the dynamics of localization unfold, so will those of globalization continue to accelerate, especially at regional levels. If the European Union makes it as a coherent entity, its successes are likely to spur similar tendencies in other regions of the world. On the other hand, the bifurcation of global structures makes it seem highly improbable that formal governmental institutions will evolve on a worldwide scale. A much greater likelihood is that cooperation between like-minded actors in the state- and multi-centric worlds will result in issue-based regimes that acquire some authority to cope with problems that arise in their issue-areas.

While the twenty-first century may well be marked by less interstate war than the twentieth, it seems likely to be as pervaded by as much commotion, change, and upheaval as its predecessor. The emergent epoch, in short, is still very much in its infancy.

3 Building blocks of a new paradigm for studying world politics[1]

Cast in terms of the conference and panel for which this chapter was written, it is not difficult to presume the existence of "new international realities" that call for a "new paradigm." In my judgment the so-called "war on terror" is not among the new realities. Terrorist activities have long been a part of the international scene. The attacks of September 11, 2001, have certainly added to the salience of terrorism, but they are neither the vanguard of new realities nor the foundations of a new paradigm. Rather, as elaborated below, the realities and paradigm derive from the advent of an acceleration of pervasive processes wherein several inter-related dynamics have generated a vast, global disaggregation of authority that, in turn, has given rise to new global structures.

Locating disaggregating processes at the center of the new paradigm will not be easy. Indeed, for two reasons it will prove wrenching for many analysts and perhaps too difficult to manage for more than a few observers. One of the obstacles is inherent in us as analysts, while the other is inherent in the nature of the new realities. We are obstacles to the necessary paradigmatic innovation because we are so fully ensconced in the conceptual jails that comprise our present paradigms that negotiating a jailbreak poses both intellectual and emotional challenges that cannot readily be overcome. Any paradigm is a conceptual jail because its coherence derives from a structure that provides an answer to any developments that might nullify its validity. Just as a Marxist can offset any challenge by asking, "And in what socio-economic class did you grow up?" and just as Freudians can preserve their paradigm by responding to any question by asking, "And what did your mother do to you when you were three?" so are the paradigms of realists, liberals, and constructivists in the field of international relations (IR) structured in such a way as to negate any line of reasoning that undermines their coherence. And the more our paradigms are challenged, the more are we likely to dig in and assert their utility in coping with new aspects that emerge on the world scene.[2]

And even if somehow we manage to recognize the need to undertake a jail-break, we have to face the new realities and confront the need to fashion new premises about how the world works. For the structure of world politics has undergone enormous changes in recent decades, changes that continue to unfold and become increasingly discrepant with our conventional paradigms. Put simply, profound complexities with which we have little familiarity presently mark the world scene as the number and variety of actors that crowd the global stage proliferate and as new means of communication expand their capacity to interact. No longer is it possible simply to ascribe developments as the consequence of state actions and the exercise of state sovereignty. A plethora of other dynamics are now at work that raise serious doubts about the viability of states and the conditions under which their actions are relevant to the course of events. To be sure, complexities have always marked world affairs, but those at work today are an order of magnitude greater than earlier ones. Or perhaps more accurately, our analytic antennae today are significantly more sensitive than those we had in the past and thus enable us to recognize complexities that previously went unseen.

A post-international perspective

Like most of us, I undertake to overcome these problems by falling back on concepts that I developed previously and that serve to organize my inquiry into the nature of a turbulent world.[3] Noted briefly in the previous chapter, four conceptual dynamics – the skill revolution, the organizational explosion, the pervasive disaggregation of authority, and the bifurcation of world politics – are especially relevant inasmuch as they anticipated the new complexities and can serve as key foundations for a new paradigm. The four dynamics are so thoroughly interrelated, with each serving as a building block for the others, that the ensuing presentation should not be interpreted as a ranking of their importance.

The skill revolution

For a host of reasons, some derived from the Internet, global television, and other new technologies, some from diverse forms and sources of travel, some from the need to cope with ever-greater complexity, and some from the other dynamics noted below, people the world over have evolved new capacities to render distant events proximate through enhanced analytic, emotional, and imaginative talents. The new capacities and talents amount to what I have elsewhere labeled a "skill revolution" that is worldwide in scope and that consists less of people being more informed and more of them having added to their working knowledge about how human affairs are structured.[4] Whatever an IQ may reflect, people in diverse countries have been recording higher IQ scores for some six decades[5] and measures of the capacity for integrative complexity of elites have been rising for eight decades[6] – to mention only some of the data indicative of the skill revolution. Put differently, increasingly people at all levels of community and in every part of the world have undergone empowerment, a sense that they know when, where, and how to engage in collective action and thus contribute to the course of events. Stated in still another way, the ranks of individuals who can have an impact on how issues evolve, are sustained, and get resolved is growing. From the tourist to the terrorist, from the Internet user to the protester, from the aid worker to the disk jockey, from local activists to global elites, from the technical specialist to the suicide bomber – to mention only a few of the innumerable types of persons who may shape daily events – individuals have joined collectivities as central actors on the world stage.

This is not to say that all individuals are becoming equally skilled and empowered. Far from it: those connected to the Internet are doubtless more skillful in relating to world affairs than the vast majority who do not have a connection. Nor is it to imply that people are converging around common values as a consequence of their enhanced skilled. On the contrary, people remain ensconced in the values of their cultures even as their greater skills extend their understanding of these values and their relevance to issues. Nevertheless, despite the differences that mark individuals and societies, it seems clear to me that any paradigm appropriate as a tool for understanding the new complexities of our time must allow for a trend toward people everywhere becoming more skillful and empowered in the context of their own cultures and circumstances.

The organizational explosion

Due in good measure to the skill revolution and the more empowered people it is generating as well as swollen by the networking capacities fostered by the Internet, but also because of the salience of environmental and human rights issues and a widespread felt need in an ever more complex world to reach out to like-minded others, organizations are being formed at every level of community and through-out the world. Indeed, with the advent of the Internet the rate of organizational formation is sufficient to warrant the label of an "explosion." Trend lines descriptive of this phenomenon are difficult to compile because many organizations do not report to record-keeping centers, but such data as have been collected as well as numerous anecdotal materials all point to a continuing growth pattern.[7] Although the pattern may be less pronounced in the United States,[8] the organizational explosion is so intense that it needs to be treated as the basis for key parameters of any paradigm designed to account for the new international realities.

The disaggregation of authority

The skill revolution and the organizational explosion are major building blocks for one parameter of any new paradigm designed to analyze the emergent world scene, namely, the continuing and extensive process whereby authority is undergoing disaggregation at every level of community, in every walk of life, and in all parts of the world. No longer concentrated in large, hierarchical organizations, authority is continually emerging along more horizontal lines in small associations, extensive networks, and the fragments of splintered organizations. Even some individuals now can act authoritatively under certain circumstances. As a consequence, the global stage is ever more crowded with diverse authorities that sometimes cooperate, often conflict, and endlessly interact. The days in which states dominated the course of world politics are long gone. Their leadership today requires mobilizing support among the many other actors that share the global stage with them, a fact that has led to the bifurcation of the central structures that have sustained world politics for several centuries.

The bifurcation of world politics

Any new paradigm must acknowledge, it seems to me, that the proliferation of global actors and the dispersion of their authority have resulted in the transformation and not the breakdown of global structures. Disaggregated authority and the proliferation of actors has led to the emergence of the multi-centric world as a sometime partner, sometime rival, and sometime co-equal of the long-standing state-centric world, a process that I have called the bifurcation of world politics[9] and that some analysts have treated as the emergence of a global civil society.[10] Virtually every analyst designates the members of the multi-centric world as "non-state" actors, but I have resisted this nomenclature on the grounds that it privileges states by clustering all the other collectivities on the global stage in a residual category.[11] To refer continuously to "non-state" actors is to presume that they are outliers and that their multi-centric world is thus subordinate to the state-centric world. This may be the case in many issue areas, but in more than a few areas it is also the case that collectivities in the multi-centric world often shape issue outcomes and on occasion they even prevail. In short, the emergent global structure does not posit one of the two worlds as more central than the other. It is illustrative, for example, that unofficial Israeli and Palestinian "peace teams" negotiated a symbolic Middle East peace plan called the "Geneva Accord" that upset the Israeli government, encouraged the Palestinian Authority, and evoked praise from the United States that further agitated the Israeli government.[12]

The bifurcation of global structures is a central foundation on which a jailbreak from existing paradigms must rest. But in this case a jailbreak is especially difficult precisely because the concept of a bifurcated world necessitates a downgrading of the importance of states as actors – not a dismissal of them by any means, but simply a downgrading that allows for recognition of the centrality of the numerous collectivities in the multi-centric world that can have consequence as shapers of issue outcomes.

The difficulties of negotiating a jailbreak in this respect are somewhat eased by the fact that the bifurcation of world politics has become institutionalized. Since the summer of 1992 in Rio de Janeiro, when the state-centric world convened to address environmental problems and more than 3,000 organizations of the multi-centric world gathered nearby to debate the issues and submit resolutions and recommendations to the state-centric delegates, and then subsequently when the pattern was repeated in Vienna on human rights issues, in Cairo on population questions, in Copenhagen on quality of life issues, in Beijing on the rights of women, and in many locales whenever the boards of the World Bank, IMF, and WTO convened, it has become clear that meetings of representatives of the state-centric world are very likely to be accompanied by counterparts from the multi-centric world. Clearly, the regularity of these occasions amounts to an institutionalization of the bifurcated structure. It is difficult to imagine future meetings of the state-centric world on major issues that do not generate the nearby presence of representatives of the multi-centric world. The latter has generated an organization to speak and act on behalf of those groups most distressed about the neo-liberal economic policies that prevail in the state-centric world. The World Social Forum holds annual meetings at which its members criticize and offer alternatives to its neo-liberal counterpart, the World Economic Forum.[13] In effect, the institutionalization of bifurcated global structures has facilitated the emergence of left- and right-wings in the multi-centric world that contest each other for influence, or at least headlines, on a number of issues.

The challenge of analyzing the multi-centric world

Multiple challenges confront analysts seeking to comprehend the role the multi-centric world plays in shaping and sustaining the "new international realities." Here four challenges are confronted and, hopefully, clarified. All of them are derivatives of the premise that the overall structure of world politics has become one of institutionalized bifurcation. To anticipate the core problems inherent in each of the four challenges, one is the need to break free of the premise that the state-centric world is the predominant structure through which world affairs unfold, a conceptual jailbreak that in turn involves recasting our understanding of the nature of states, their capacities, and the roles they play on the world stage. The second involves the definitional need for clarity on the characteristics of the actors that comprise the multi-centric world. The third focuses on the internal structure of the multi-centric world, its coherence, conflicts, and potentials. The fourth challenge concerns the need to comprehend the conflicts that can occur within the multi-centric world as well as those that ensue between it and the state-centric world.

Negotiating a jailbreak

As previously indicated, I have found it helpful to break out of the jails of traditional paradigms by resort to the parameters that are the basis of my model of turbulence in world politics. This arduous, even excruciating task was accomplished as a result of having long maintained an "anomaly" file in which I put clippings and articles that were not comprehensible in the context of my earlier training and formulations. The file grew so large in the 1980s that it sent me back to the drawing board to hunt for escape routes out of my conceptual jail. The technique worked: by pondering accounts that could not be easily understood, and thus made no sense in terms of my prevailing grasp of world politics, I pressed myself to frame a new paradigm.[14] Such a procedure is arduous and excruciating because one's present conceptual jail encompasses premises that can offset any and all challenges. Thus the anomaly file must contain materials that seem so outlandish at first that even one's existing paradigm cannot readily cope with them. In my case, to cite one example, a newspaper story that reported the "hotline" established to facilitate quick communications between the White

House and the Kremlin after the Cuban missile crisis in 1962 was sold; yes, it was sold to the Swiss, a development so startling at the time that one could only pause in an effort to try to find a context into which to put it.[15]

The definitional challenge

The literature on actors that are neither individuals nor agencies of governments is pervaded with formulations and labels with which to draw distinctions among them and, in so doing, to define them. Are corporations and other profit-making organizations members of civil society? Or does civil society exclude governments and for-profit organizations? What about nongovernmental organizations (NGOs) that enjoy financial support from their governments? Different analysts, each of whom offers a rationale consistent with the purposes of their inquiry, answer such questions differently.[16] Here, given an effort to lay the building blocks of a new paradigm, an all-inclusive conception is employed: rather than making fine distinctions among the various types of actors that are not governments, transnational civil society is equated with the multi-centric world and is conceived to be comprised of collectivities that are largely autonomous with respect to governments and that have mechanisms for exercising authority over the persons of which they are comprised.[17] Thus corporations as well as advocacy groups, professional societies as well as labor unions, churches as well as universities, Internet-generated networks as well as crime syndicates – to cite just a few of many possible examples – are considered actors on the global stage as long as on occasion their actions transgress the boundaries of one or more states. Diverse as they may be, these actors have one common characteristic: they are not governments. In short, here the definitional challenge is met by treating the multi-centric world as consisting of NGOs in the literal sense of the label. Of course, this formulation also encompasses the individuals who exercise or respond to each NGO's authority.

The conceptual challenge

Two related problems confront any effort to conceptualize the nature and role of the multi-centric world in a global bifurcated structure. One has already been implied, namely, that of rethinking the nature of the state and recognizing that it is no longer the predominant actor in world politics. It is, to be sure, still very much a key player and it still can give direction to the course of events in a number of ways. One does not have to presume the eventual demise of the state as a meaningful actor in order to undertake a jailbreak.[18] But it appears imperative that the state concept be revised to allow for its diminished capacity to push its way around on the global stage. Most states no longer control the flow of money, goods, pollution, drugs, crime, and people across their borders to the same extent as they did in the past. To a large extent these controls have either been taken over by actors in the multi-centric world or states have shared them with the other actors. Given the huge extent to which states have been regarded not as the first among equals but as the first presiding over subordinates, a major reorganization of thought will be required to treat them as one of many actors on an ever more crowded global stage. Yes, states still control the flow of currencies through their central banks and, yes, they still can mobilize armies and resort to massive coercion under some conditions; but the complexities, size, and scope of the multi-centric world serve to limit their capacities to frame and implement their goals.

Put differently, unfortunately it is exceedingly comfortable to presume the pre-dominance of states. It is relatively easy to trace both the positive and negative developments in world politics to the ways in which states conduct themselves. Such a perspective enables one to readily ascribe causation rather than having to account for the multiplicity of diverse dynamics that contribute to outcomes in global affairs today.

Perhaps even more difficult is a second conceptual challenge: that of assessing and delineating the structures of the multi-centric world, composed as it is of myriad organizations with myriad purposes, interests, and capabilities that are undergoing a continuing disaggregation of authority. Are the structures coherent, or are they no more than diverse, unrelated, spheres of authority (SOAs)?[19] Does the very diversity have structural features that derive from common goals, methods, and procedures? Are there some codified or (more likely) informal rules comparable to those that underlie interactions in the state-centric world? Does the literature on transnational civil society offer any clues as to the structures and coherence of the multi-centric world?

The answers to these questions must perforce be tentative. The multi-centric world is still very much in an early stage of its evolution. Its actors have had a chance to form and multiply on a large scale only since the end of the Cold War, hardly enough time to manifest the outlines of coherent structures and codify regulations designed to govern their conduct. Still, certain preliminary answers can reasonably be offered. First, given the extensive disaggregation and diversity of its actors, it is doubtful that a coherent set of structures, even a minimal system-wide consensus, will ever evolve that prevails throughout the multi-centric world. Rather, it is likely that pockets of regulations will develop in diverse issue areas through coordination among NGOs that have comparable purposes, engage in similar behavior, and thus have good reasons to regulate themselves. Evidence of developments along this line is already available.[20] Second, both within and between issue-area clusters it seems likely that conflict will be as pervasive as cooperation. As indicated by the competition between its left- and right-wings, the multi-centric world is no less marked by tensions than its state-centric counterpart. Indeed, given its much larger size and scope, the multi-centric world is likely to be a site of continuing friction and endless competition, some of which may well be cut-throat and brutal. Third, the various segments are likely to establish different kinds of relationships with collectivities in the state-centric world. Some of these relationships will surely be founded on cooperative efforts to move toward com-mon goals, while others will surely be rooted in conflict and virulent competition.

Given these characteristics of the multi-centric world, the question arises as to whether it is accurate to depict it as a "world," a term that implies coherence around shared values and structures that are at least minimally integrated into a larger whole. Would it not be more appropriate to label it as a congeries of NGOs that go their own way and have little in common? Indeed, given the diversity and highly disaggregated nature of the multi-centric world, is it reasonable to speak of overall global structures as having undergone bifurcation? Are these structures not best summarized as "nfurcation," with the "n" standing for any number of divides that separate the NGOs from the state-centric world?

While it is probably more accurate to refer to an nfurcated than a bifurcated world, there are two good reasons to retain the bifurcation label for overall global structures. One is that despite their diversity and disaggregation, all the actors in the multi-centric world are apart from the state-centric world, an emphasis that may be undermined if they are not summarized in terms of this common characteristic. Second, and much more important, to describe global structures as nfurcated is to downplay the relevance of states and the coherent structures of their world. An nfurcation label implies states are just one of many actors, none of which can exercise much authority because of the weight of numbers. Such an implication is clearly misleading. States remain central actors even if their capabilities have been diminished with the advent of the skill revolution and the organizational explosion. By retaining the notion of the overall global structure as bifurcated, the centrality of states is not underestimated even as the concept of bifurcation makes clear that they are now faced with formidable foes as well as assisted by helpful partners in the multi-centric world. By maintaining the concept of bifurcation the emergence of new global structures is highlighted even as the relevance of states is acknowledged.

Comprehending the range of conflict within the multi-centric world

It goes without saying that the multi-centric world is marked by intense competition among the actors within its various issue areas. Corporations vie for markets; nonprofit organizations compete for funds and other forms of support; entertainment companies and sports teams compete for audiences; crime syndicates wrangle over their territories; and so on across the full range of transnational activities, with each NGO seeking to establish and enhance their relationships with various governments. All of these rivalries are established features of the political process that renders the multi-centric world one of continuing commotion and upheaval.

What is perhaps less fully recognized, however, is the competition and rivalry that unfolds within NGOs as well as between them. Many of them sustain large bureaucracies that are marked by internal squabbles that can have significant repercussions. This may especially be the case for transnational NGOs that have branches in different countries. A good, troubling case in point is that of Save the Children, a humanitarian organization that has done its share of good work in the past but that recently was wracked by a conflict between its branches in the

United States and the United Kingdom. The former, eager to avoid offending its corporate and government donors, ordered the latter to end its criticism of US military action in Iraq. "Save the Children UK came under enormous pressure after it accused coalition forces of breaching the Geneva Convention by blocking humanitarian aid. . . . Within hours of the statement appearing, the US wing was demanding . . . withdrawal [of the criticism]. . . ."[21] Given the nature of bureaucracies, it is hardly surprising that such squabbles are not infrequent in Save the Children and, presumably, in a number of other transnational NGOs.[22]

A brief summing up

Conceiving of a bifurcated world marked by a continuing skill revolution and organizational explosion facilitates an understanding of the large degree to which global affairs have become marked by complexity. Such a formulation (dare I say paradigm) highlights the messiness of the world scene and the degree to which it is prone to ambiguity and contradiction even as it offers building blocks for a paradigm that serves cogent analysis.

4   Rigid boundaries

States, societies, and international relations[1]

The study of international relations (IR) in the West has a long, occasionally distinguished history. Dominated initially in the years after World War I by scholars in England, after World War II by counterparts in the United States, and since the end of the Cold War joined by colleagues in Germany, Scandinavia, Japan, and a host of other countries, IR has gained momentum as technology has reduced time and distance and rendered world affairs ever more salient and threatening. And increasingly it has become an enterprise administered separately from the other established social science disciplines. More than a few IR specialists explain this evolution as an instance of IR becoming a discipline unto itself – part political science, part history, part economics, part sociology, part psychology, part anthropology, and even a small part biology and other hard sciences – a huge umbrella that encompasses all phases of human experience because its scope is global and its foci as diverse as the values, preoccupations, and practices of people everywhere.

For the most part, however, it is an umbrella that has failed to open: most IR specialists throughout the world are political scientists.[2] For all the interdisciplinary verbiage and potential, only a limited number of scholars in other fields of inquiry have applied their disciplinary concepts and methods to the issues, processes, and structures of IR. To be sure, one can readily note distinguished IR investigators from other disciplines – Kenneth Boulding in economics, Herbert Kelman in social psychology, Raymond Aron in history come immediately to mind – who have devoted their disciplinary skills to problems of IR. Even a few such as Susan Strange whose background was not clearly located in any discipline, have devoted a lifetime to assessing diverse dimensions of IR. But the scarcity of such exceptions tends to affirm the assertion that a preponderance of those in the field had their formal training in political science.

It could be argued that this observation is misleading, that it overlooks more selective approaches to IR phenomena undertaken outside political science. In economics, for example, international trade, investment, and finance are major foci and they are surely an aspect of IR. Likewise, sociologists who specialize in conflict resolution can be viewed as concerned with IR, as can philosophers who ruminate about war and justice. Such reasoning is compelling in the sense that selective approaches within various disciplines do come under the umbrella. But their presence there is more a matter of their special interests having international ramifications than pursuing IR as a central focus of their inquiries. Economists who specialize in trade issues, for example, usually work within the confines of their discipline and departments rather than reaching out to and collaborating with colleagues in other disciplines whose work has implications for trade patterns and negotiations.

Whatever may be the degree to which other than political scientists come under the umbrella – and, to repeat, I think they are solitary figures – the interesting question is why they are relatively scarce? Why, for example, have not sociologists formed an IR subfield and become as preoccupied with the subject as their political science colleagues? IR is not inherently founded on inquiries into political matters. On the contrary, being global in scope, IR spans virtually every aspect of human endeavor even though most research and writing in the field is confined to political issues. And so does sociology embrace a very broad spectrum of experience – from medical sociology to family sociology, from the sociology of emotions to the sociology of religion, and so on through 43 formal subfields listed by the American Sociological Association (ASA). Indeed, it logically follows that practitioners in the IR discipline or (more cautiously) field should be predominantly comprised of sociologists who have compiled a rich literature on diverse dimensions of the human condition. To my knowledge, however, such is not the case,[3] and thus one again returns to the puzzling question of why so few sociologists are to be found in the ranks of IR scholars?[4]

I think the answer to the question stems from the same roots that explain why the concerns of many political scientists in the IR field are excessively oriented toward the nation-state and the international system, thereby overlooking a vast array of issues and problems in which the roles states play is matched by, if not secondary to, those of other actors and systems. Just as political scientists are trained to treat the state as the terminal entity that stands above and supersedes all other political actors in its claim on the loyalties of people, so are sociologists taught early that society is the terminal entity with respect to which organizations, groups, and individuals conduct their affairs. Yes, the boundaries that separate states and societies have become increasingly porous in an age of globalization. And yes, loyalties and identities have proliferated to the point of undermining commitments to states and societies. And yes, the Internet and other microelectronic technologies have considerably lessened the relevance of time and distance, thereby further weakening the ties that bind states and societies. And yes, the vast movement of people of all kinds around the world has led to multicultural and sub-cultural bonds that weaken the competence of states and societies. And yes, the huge proliferation of transnational advocacy groups, corporations, and professional societies has served to highlight a vast array of interactions that circumvent the authority of states and societies. But, no, with the exception of the ASA's section on the Political Economy of the World Systems, such developments are not sufficient to alter the notion that the state and society are the terminal entities on which analyses should be founded.

And what underlies the prevailing resistance to re-conceptualizing terminal entities in the face of such dynamic transformations? Why are able scholars in both disciplines still mired in long-standing and conventional perspectives? Partly habit, both on the part of analysts and the orientations of citizens, who are seen as so locked into historical and habitual ways that their ultimate identities and loyalties are never treated as problematic. Partly, too, notions of power in which both the society and the state are seen as so fully ensconced on the high moral ground and so fully endowed with the physical instruments of coercion that their attenuation as a terminal entity is viewed as highly improbable, if not impossible. No matter that in many parts of the world private security forces outnumber those of their state. No matter that increasingly noticeable numbers of young men avoid military service in different parts of the world or that, in Israel, a substantial group refused to remain on duty in Palestine. No matter that multicultural communities have replaced either the dominant ethnic or the melting-pot society. No matter that the Internet has stimulated the emergence of vast numbers of transnational networks not subject to the authority of any states. Such developments are seen as aberrations rather than possible signs of emergent central tendencies. As aberrations they preserve the state and society as terminal entities.

Nonetheless, strong and powerful as the state and society premises may be, I am inclined to anticipate that this conceptual orientation will ultimately give way to new formulations of terminal entities, probably to diverse schemes in which a multiplicity of entities are conceived to be terminal. As the age of globalization continues to shrink time and distance, and as reactions against globalization continue to stress the local community and its values, so eventually is sociology (and political science, too) likely to relax its long-standing boundaries and allow for transnational and sub-national perspectives that are not cast in the shadow of the national society and the nation-state.

To be sure, getting out from under those shadows will not be easy. Social scientists, like the people they study, are prone to habitual modes of behavior, and thus are more likely to cast their inquiries into habitual frameworks that are taken for granted than to treat their organizing premises as problematic. In the case of political scientists the habitual framework is reinforced by a restless preoccupation with comprehending war, which is viewed as being initiated, sustained, and terminated by states. For sociologists the continuing strength of analytic habits derives from an overriding concern with systems and subsystems, which are seen as marked by endless interactions and frictions that unfold in the context of societies as the ultimate arbiter. Yet, and to repeat, such habits are presently under assault by the dynamics of globalization and are likely to give way eventually to new and different organizing premises. Already, for example, most political scientists posit intrastate wars as much more of a central tendency than interstate wars, a shift that is freeing them up to recognize and assess the degree to which sovereignty is undergoing transformation and the limits within which states can exercise their power. Likewise, I have the impression that sociologists are increasingly focusing on ethnic tensions, a shift that enables them to by-pass the society as the adjudicator of system–subsystem tensions.

IR needs sociologists

Whether the adoption of new premises more suitable to the emergent epoch will lead sociologists to crowd under the IR umbrella remains an open question. Surely some will, especially those who elevate globalization to the top of their concerns and research agendas. But conceivably others, fearing their disciplinary perspectives will be undermined if they broaden their horizons, will alter their organizing premises without doing so in the context of global dynamics.

I would like to see a wholesale shift into IR by sociologists. We need some of their prime conceptual inclinations. Most notably, perhaps, IR can benefit from the micro–macro theories, methods, and approaches that sociologists bring to their inquiries. Their system–subsystem orientations – their premises, hypotheses, and data that seek to draw the links between people at the micro level and collectivities at the macro level – are woefully lacking in the study of IR today. Aside from a few efforts to focus on agent–structure dynamics,[5] most IR practitioners either take them as given or they ignore them altogether, whereas the sociological literature is rich with formulations and studies founded on micro–macro analysis.[6] To be sure, in a political context the problem is especially difficult to resolve,[7] but the need to address it is all the more urgent as globalization accords ever greater consequence to the attitudes and actions of nongovernmental actors, both private individuals and advocacy groups as well as multinational corporations and many other types of organizations.

Equally important, the IR field needs a deeper involvement on the part of sociologists because their discipline is much more flexible and broad-gauged than is political science, history, and economics. Present workers in the IR vineyards need to be pushed by sociologists to look beyond their preoccupations with war, state building, and democracy. They could benefit greatly, for example, from the myriad insights organizational theory has to offer, insights that go well beyond the nuts-and-bolts findings and formulations to be found in the field of public administration.

To some extent, of course, sociologists are still entrapped by old habits even as they also are inclined toward orientations that are appropriate to coming under the IR umbrella. Their entrapment can be seen in their tendency to take note of past sociological treatises and their authors – such as Weber and Parsons – thus suggesting a readiness to abide by the society-as-a-terminal-entity perspective.[8] These major works of the past share a perspective in which global phenomena are posited as exogenous to the operation of social systems. For all their importance as seminal formulations, and for understandable reasons, the writings of earlier sociologists were perforce penned in an era in which globalization was not envisioned as a prime dynamic of social life.

The handbook of international relations: *an open umbrella?*

Much the same analysis can be applied to the *Handbook* – described by the publishers on the jacket as "the first authoritative and comprehensive survey of the field" – as it offers an opportunity to ascertain whether the IR umbrella has opened such that brethren in the other social sciences have joined political scientists under its broadened span. More than that, the advent of new premises suitable to the emergent epoch enables us to assess whether the state is still conceived as the primary, if not the only, terminal entity.

The *Handbook* contains a rich array of insights, concepts, propositions, formulations, and historical accounts, many of which are ensconced in rigorous trenchant and analytic assessments. While the breadth of the field raises doubts as to whether any such compendium can be "authoritative and comprehensive," it can readily be asserted that the editors and authors have compiled an extremely useful and sophisticated introduction to the current foci and concerns of IR scholars. This is not faint praise designed to take the sting out of what follows. It is a good book, one that graduate students are likely to have at the top of the reading lists on which they rely to take their general examinations.

But what about the umbrella? And the treatment of terminal entities? The answer to the former question is clear-cut: the umbrella remains largely unopened. Using the titles of the professional positions occupied by the thirty-four authors and co-authors of the book's twenty-eight chapters as a crude measure of disciplinary affiliations, the IR field is still the province of political scientists. Two have positions in the field of law, two in economics, twelve in IR, and eighteen in political science. Moreover, virtually all of the twelve whose titles connote an IR perspective were trained as political scientists. In addition, the thirteen-page, small-type, two-column index does not include entries for "interdisciplinary," "disciplines," "sociology," "anthropology," or variants of such terms. Perhaps equally telling, the chapters on the roles of history and psychology in IR were both written by political scientists. Such a skewed distribution is not, of course, the fault of the editors. It is, rather, a reflection of the state of the field. For all the lip service paid to the desirability of interdisciplinary approaches to IR, the fact remains that it has yet to attract practitioners from a wide variety of disciplinary perspectives.

The treatment of terminal entities is more ambiguous. Most of the essays implicitly assume the state is the terminal entity for publics and public officials throughout the world. Indeed, in most chapters the authority of states is posited as given, as so unproblematic as not to warrant discussion. The index neither lists any variant of the terminality concept nor refers to hierarchies of loyalties. Yet, several essays do elaborate on ways in which authority in the global system has undergone dispersion at the expense of states. Michael Zürn's chapter on globalization and Thomas Risse's on transnational actors are suggestive of this dispersion. And even more conspicuous in this regard is Thomas J. Biersteker's chapter on "State, Sovereignty, and Territory." He stresses that such concepts are subject to change and that, indeed, they have undergone considerable change in recent decades. He stresses, for example, that "states may cut back on the range of claims of final authority they make," that they "are no longer recognized as legitimate final authorities when it comes to the violation of the human rights of individuals or groups located within their domains," that "competing claims of authority have started to emerge from non-state actors in the world system," that "[t]rad-itional state claims of sovereign authority are increasingly competing with other sources of legitimate authority in the international system," and that "the cumula-tive impact of these incremental changes in practices could lead to a situation in which the authority claims of states become increasingly hollow."[9]

In sum, despite the utility of the *Handbook*, one can only wonder what it might have been like if all the chapters had treated states as variables and cast their analyses on the basis of Biersteker's observations. My own estimate is that such a volume would be much more in touch with what IR is today and what it is likely to become in the decades ahead.

5 Powerful tendencies, startling discrepancies, and elusive dynamics

The challenge of studying world politics in a turbulent era[1]

In recent attempts to analyze world affairs and tease out its central tendencies, I seem increasingly to call attention to contradictions, to discrepancies, to opposites, as if the prime central tendency consists of divergent paths, as if everything regresses to a mean that is bi-modal and better grasped as two separate means. And this presentation is no exception. In an effort to identify the challenges we face in trying to understand the dynamics likely to underlie world politics in the twenty-first century, I shall end up focusing on both huge similarities and big differences – what I once called patterned chaos,[2] then referred to as distant proximities,[3] and now am also inclined to view simply as contradictory patterns that may feed off each other and, as such, are *the* central tendency of our time.

Faced with pervasive contradictions, with fuzzy causal sequences, with powerful tendencies offset by startling discrepancies, with a growing multitude of uniformities and a swelling number of disparities, how do we proceed? Anticipating the thrust of the analysis, five obstacles are posited as inhibiting our capacity to grasp the course of future events:

1 one might be called the "it's-still-a-world-of-states" syndrome, in which a host of factors are cited as eroding the sovereignty and competence of states even as the implications of this erosion are avoided by presuming that somehow states are still so predominant as to determine everything of significance that happens on the world stage;

2 a second obstacle can be called the "yes-but" approach, in which analysts acknowledge the advent of powerful dynamics and then negate the acknowledgment by citing offsetting trends;

3 a third can be called the "you-get-what-you-see" perspective, in which contradictions are regarded as deriving from independent sources and thus as incapable of being causally or dialectically linked;

4 a fourth can be called the "it's-too-early-to-tell" school, in which the contradictory dynamics that sustain the turbulence of our time are considered to be equally powerful, thus inclining observers to avoid assessing the relative primacy of each dynamic on the grounds that it is premature to reach any conclusions about the emergent world order; and

5 a fifth can be called the "insufficient-methodology" premise, in which a

transforming world is seen as too elusive to trace, thus defying systematic inquiry and predisposing analysts to adhere to earlier conceptions of world politics for which appropriate methodologies are deemed to be available.

Taken as a whole, these obstacles share a reluctance to accept the consequences of presuming that fundamental transformations are restructuring the nature of world politics. If one accepts this presumption, if one is ready to affirm that world affairs seem contradictory and elusive precisely because strong currents of change are at work, then one need not cling to traditional conceptions of the role of states or seek theoretical refuge in ambiguous patterns.

In short, we have to learn how to accommodate huge similarities and large differences without throwing up our hands and concluding either that everything is so distinct from everything else that generalization is not possible or that everything is too murky to be subjected to systematic empirical inquiry. The contradictions are enormous; they are glaring; they defy orderly analysis; but still, embedded in the differences are commonalities that cannot be ignored, tensions that are likely to continue to drive the course of events and that thus need to be probed if we are to comprehend the likely course of world politics in the decades ahead.

In the last two years I have had an opportunity to observe one of these contradictions at first-hand. Indeed, leaving aside wartime military service, on only two occasions have I strayed from the ivory tower and had first-hand encounters with an ongoing reality of world affairs. The reality is the pervasive trend toward democratic practices and the opposite, equally pervasive trend toward disenfranchised peoples. One of these encounters stemmed from being on a team of "outside observers" invited to monitor the Paraguayan election in May 1993. It was a moving experience to see people standing in line in the hot sun for hours at a time, waiting to cast their first vote, clearly grateful that they could give voice to their preferences in a country long marked by authoritarian rule. The other encounter occurred a year later at the Immigration Center in Hong Kong, where we had to extend a visa. The very large space that spanned five full floors was jammed with people of all races and colors, but mostly with young Philippine women seeking to extend their stay so that they could continue working as maids. It was a jolting experience to see people waiting anxiously in line, nervous lest their access to a livelihood would be cut off arbitrarily by a faceless clerk behind a window. Having seen widespread hope in Paraguay, I saw widespread resignation in Hong Kong, and in the similarities that differentiate the two situations one gets a sense of the severe challenges we face in trying to make sense of a globalizing world.

World politics in the twenty-first century

In order to analyze the challenges that we face as students of a dynamically changing world scene, it is necessary to start with some understanding of what the underlying dynamics are. Whatever understanding one may have in this regard – and analysts differ considerably – one's conception of the conceptual and research problems to be surmounted is bound to be shaped by what one perceives to be the undercurrents flowing through the global system. The aforementioned five obstacles inhibiting our analyses only make sense if one presumes, as I do, that the transformations at work in every corner of the world are so profound that the politics and polities of the future will, for better or worse, be quite unlike the circumstances that govern international life today. Contrariwise, if one presumes that the continuities currently sustaining world politics far outweigh the change dynamics, then the conceptual and research problems to be faced are familiar, manageable, and present few serious obstacles to further understanding.

So as to proceed, in other words, a brief synopsis is needed that outlines what I regard as the main stirrings leading the world – and us as students of it – into uncharted domains. As previously noted and elaborated at great length elsewhere,[4] three basic parameters of the global system strike me as undergoing transformation. One involves citizens at the micro level who, I would argue, are everywhere experiencing a skill revolution that has enabled them to perceive more clearly where they fit in the course of events and thus to engage more effectively in collective actions designed to serve their interests. A second transformation is occurring at what I call the macro–micro level through which individuals are linked to their collectivities: the argument here is that collectivities everywhere, governments and nongovernmental organizations alike, are undergoing authority crises in which traditional conceptions of legitimacy are being replaced by performance criteria of legitimacy, thus fostering organizational disarray, stalemate, restructuring, and proliferation that, in turn, enhances the readiness of individuals to employ their newly acquired skills on behalf of their perceived self-interests. A third transformation is unfolding at the macro level of global structure, and here I would contend that processes of bifurcation have given rise to two worlds of world politics that are still working out their respective domains as the foundations of the emergent global order: a multi-centric world comprised of diverse nongovernmental actors who are independent of the state-centric world and who frequently conflict, cooperate or otherwise interact with counterparts in the state-centric world.

These three parametric transformations are conceived as having been underway for some four decades and as likely to continue for the foreseeable future. And they are also seen as both sources and consequences of two other dynamics that are not so much parameters of the system as they are basic processes that fuel and are fueled by each of the parametric transformations. I have in mind here the processes of globalization and localization and the links between them, what some refer to as "globalization" and what I have elsewhere called the processes of "fragmegration" on the grounds that this term nicely captures the simultaneity and interactive basis of those forces propelling collectivities toward integration and those spurring fragmentation. Viewed as a single dynamic, the processes of fragmegration are posited as tapping into the skill revolution by sensitizing people to the possibility that the identity and bases of their citizenship may be changing; as tapping into many authority crises by redirecting loyalties and legitimacy sentiments which, in turn, are altering the support collectivities can command; and as tapping into the bifurcation of global structures by weakening the sovereignty and competence of states and hastening the formation or consolidation of collectivities to the multi-centric world.

Having devoted three books and a number of essays to spelling out this conception of the underlying dynamics driving world politics,[5] the temptation is to elaborate and seek to demonstrate the accuracy of the conception. In the interest of addressing the challenges we face as students of world politics, however, I shall resist this temptation and simply ask you to play my game and temporarily assume that the foregoing is an accurate assessment of the paths that are leading the world into the future.

It's still a world of states

Perhaps the most difficult challenge analysts face in adjusting their thinking to the fast pace of change concerns the role, competence, and sovereignty of states. Few quarrel with the notion that the electronic revolution, the global division of labor, the transnationalization of production and finance, and the heightened sensitivity to ecological processes – to mention only some of the more conspicuous globalizing dynamics – are rendering boundaries more porous, jurisdictions more ambiguous, identities more murky, state sovereignty less meaningful, and governmental authority less effective. Most observers would also agree that these trends are not momentary deviations from the historic path long traveled by states and their governments. Somehow, on the other hand, many analysts are unable to live with the implications of the assumption that increasingly nation-states are sharing power with other authorities at the subnational, transnational, and supranational levels. On numerous occasions I have heard thoughtful observers concur that power-sharing lies ahead and that sovereignty is in decline, only then to back away and insist that, after all, states still retain exclusive authority to resort to coercion, that they still are more powerful than any nongovernmental organization, that they can still prevail when push comes to shove, that they can still reject policies and actions undertaken in the multi-centric world, and that for a number of additional reasons they are still the dominant actors on the global stage.[6]

No matter that more often than not states avoid exercising their exclusive authority to resort to coercion; no matter that they are more inclined to heed special interests than to use the greater power they are alleged to have over nongovernmental organizations; no matter that push rarely comes to shove and results in the reversal of policies and actions undertaken in the multi-centric world.

And, put more empirically, no matter that the state of Zaire is unraveling, as have Rwanda and Somalia before it; no matter that Algeria and Egypt have come close to civil war; no matter that the European Union is increasingly making decisions to which member countries must adhere; no matter that multicultural regimes are emerging in the US and Canada; no matter that many directives of China's central government are ignored by its provincial governments; no matter that the G-7 are essentially helpless in the face of severe currency crises; no matter that the Mafia and drug lords have the force and support to control major segments of cities and countries around the world; and so on down a long list of indicators which point to transformative processes that are relocating authority and diminishing the role of states.

It is as if to acknowledge such changes is to necessitate returning to Square One and reconceptualizing the nature of politics. This would mean trying to grasp a world in which disarray marks the long-standing order of things, a world in which no class of actors predominate, in which unfamiliar patterns keep recurring and make it increasingly difficult to rely on theoretical formulations and analytic habits with which we have long been comfortable. Better to insist that it's still a world of states. This syndrome allows one to avoid rethinking fundamental premises while at the same time accepting and affirming the presence of change dynamics. I dare to say that if more of us were ready to return to Square One insofar as the distribution of authority around the world is concerned, our collective efforts to comprehend the course of events would be advanced immeasurably.

Yes, but

Many analysts also have considerable difficulty adjusting to the dynamics of globalization. The seeming contradictions between the forces spreading people, goods, and ideas around the world and those that are impelling the contraction of people, goods, and ideas within narrowed geographic spaces often appear to encourage needlessly qualified acknowledgements that robust changes are at work on a global scale. All too often, I would argue, observers will agree that industries and economies are undergoing extensive globalization and that comparable processes are at work with respect to the spread of the values on which consumer cultures rest, but instead of accepting the full significance of these patterns, they then feel the need to stress that the times are also witness to localizing processes, to implosions of societies, and the mushrooming of exclusionary nationalisms. "Yes, but," the refrain seems to be – yes, globalization is a powerful tendency, but so is localization; or at least the localizing forces amount to such a startling discrepancy that they are bound to slow down and even redirect the pace of globalizing transformations. It is almost as if the two dynamics are seen as canceling each other out, thus allowing analysts to cling to a view that the world is not undergoing nearly as much change as might seem to be the case. To recur to an earlier metaphor, it is as if they prefer to average out the globalizing and localizing dynamics in order to conclude that only incremental changes are at work, that all is well and stable, rather than living with the complications of a bi-modal distribution of the changes that lends itself to two very different averages.

The main danger of this "yes, but" approach is that one runs the risk of underestimating the dynamics of globalization. If in several decades political, economic, and social structures are going to be very differently configured than they are today – as I feel is likely – it will be because the powerful tendencies toward globalization will have produced new norms, practices, and institutions that are virtually unimaginable from our present vantage point. Without downgrading the importance of localizing dynamics, in other words, these are not the prime forces driving the course of events. However the contradictory pressures toward expansion and contraction may be linked, it is the processes of globalization that are setting the terms and shaping the structures of the emergent global order. For better or worse – and there is much that will surely be worse by most normative standards – the peoples, economies, and polities of the world are caught up in long-term processes of overlap and convergence. Or at least this proposition needs to be kept constantly in mind if we are to appreciate fully the dynamism of our times.

You-get-what-you-see

Closely related to and reinforcing of the "yes, but" approach is a posture that treats the contradictions for what they seem to be, separate dynamics that derive from independent sources and have independent consequences. Perplexed by the simultaneity of the opposing forces of centralization and decentralization, many analysts appear to find it simpler to stick with observables and not probe beyond what they see, thus enabling them to hold constant what seem like confounding variables. And there is, of course, much to be said for such a perspective. Trends do stem from unique circumstances that have a logic of their own. Considered in a short time perspective, globalizing and localizing dynamics do derive in part from different sources. At any moment in time the growth of similar institutions, the expansion of markets, the onset of pervasive environmental problems, the spread of new technologies for the transfer of money, ideas, and pictures, and a host of other factors sustain the processes of globalization irrespective of the historical precedents designed to maintain local and national controls over the pace and direction of change. Likewise, at that same moment in time the psychic comfort derived from close-at-hand activities and loyalties, the habits inherent in long-standing native cultures, and the unique features of the immediate neighborhood, and many other factors propel the processes of localization without regard to the processes that may be unfolding in globalizing directions. Leaving aside their long-term consequences, in other words, globalizing and localizing dynamics may evolve irrespective of any counter pressures exerted by the other.

Yet, this "you-get-what-you-see" perspective can be profoundly misleading and result in a failure to consider the possibility that the two dynamics may be causally or dialectically linked. If allowance is made for a longer time perspective, what appear at first to be independent sources may emerge as part and parcel of the same underlying historical sequences. It is possible, in other words, to distinguish between independent dynamics that give rise to true polarizations and interdependent dynamics that only appear to be polarizing. The latter seem different because at one moment in time they are moving in different directions, but across time the seemingly opposite moves may be functions of each other. A good example here is the simultaneity of the dispersal of production facilities by multinational corporations and their concentration of banking, accounting, and other functions in major global centers. Contradictory as these patterns may seem, however, they emerge as anything but a true polarization with the passage of time. The geographic dispersal could not occur very efficiently if the corporations did not bring together to one place those activities common to all their branch facilities, with the result that decentralizing and centralizing processes are part and parcel of the same globalizing dynamic.[7]

In a like manner, the dynamics of globalization which underlie the spread of Western norms associated with a consumer culture and the dynamics of localization which underlie xenophobic retreats to particularistic cultures may not be as true a set of polarizations as they appear to be at first glance. Behaviors on each side of the contradiction do go in strikingly opposite directions, but analyzed across long stretches of time they emerge as inextricably linked, with the latter being a reaction against the former, a sense that dearly held cultural and community values are threatened by the spread of Western norms. Thus often you do not get what you see; often localization is best viewed as a reaction to rather than a negation of globalization.

It's-too-early-to-tell

Yet, it strikes me as a mistake to let the need to allow for the passage of time to serve as an excuse for not assessing the relative primacy of globalizing and localizing dynamics. It is all too easy to avoid making these theoretical estimates by treating the various dynamics as so powerful as to be more or less equal in their causal consequences. Subsequent inquiry may demonstrate that one's estimates are erroneous, but that is no reason not to rely on one's analytic skills and training as a basis for asserting the estimates at the outset. Even if they are shown to be wrong, understanding will have been advanced by virtue of the original reasoning having gone astray. To resist making the foregoing assessment that primacy attaches to globalizing rather localizing tendencies on the grounds that it is too early to tell which initiates the fragmegrative sequences is to deprive ourselves of possibly rich insights into the underlying dialectics that may be steering the course of events.

Insufficient methodology

Finally, we face enormous challenges in developing methodologies appropriate to comprehending a world in which dynamic transformations and pervasive contradictions are commonplace. How to trace the dialectics that link globalizing and localizing tendencies? How to test for whether loyalties and conceptions of citizenship are changing? How to assess the extent of the skill revolution? How to uncover transformations in authority structures? How to evaluate the degree to which sovereignty is eroding and states are undergoing a diminution of their competencies? Based as they are on huge big structures, large processes, and huge comparisons,[8] these are mind-boggling questions if one is an empiricist committed to supporting general observations with hard and systematic data. Indeed, they are so daunting as to tempt one into basing one's research strategy on hermeneutic rather than scientific methods or, alternatively, into denying the extent of the transformations so that one can focus on problems that lend themselves to familiar methodological treatments.

Conclusion

Clearly, a number and variety of empirical inquiries will be needed to probe the transformations of these turbulent times. In one sense, however, there is plenty of time: the transformations are likely to continue well into the future and, in so doing, to reveal other projects worthy of investigation. In another sense, of course, time is scarce: an understanding of these new and complex dynamics is urgently needed if sound policies are to be framed. Even as systematic inquiries are undertaken, therefore, so must policy-oriented studies proceed, using whatever crude research techniques may be available, on the presumption that profound changes are altering the global landscape. Not to do so is, in my judgment, to forego the chance of meeting the challenges posed by the powerful tendencies, startling discrepancies, and elusive dynamics that mark this swift-moving era of global history.

6 Political science and political processes

Narrowing the gap?[1]

I was trained as a political scientist, but I am finding it increasingly difficult to remain within the confines of the discipline. Politics, government, governance, and all the other phenomena that fall under the political science umbrella are surely important in all kinds of ways, but somehow for me the umbrella is not broad enough to encompass adequate explanations for what shapes the course of events at any level of community. So I have come to think of myself as a social scientist with a readiness to explore political processes and institutions when they are relevant to the more encompassing puzzles that pique my curiosity.

All my puzzles are essentially conceptual and they all have considerable implications for the study of politics. So I remain within the scope of my assigned task in this conference by addressing here five of the most perplexing puzzles and indicating their relevance for political scientists. But you should know at the outset that my puzzlement has taken me out of the political science mainstream in my country. For reasons that I think I understand and that I'll note shortly, lately I find myself much more comfortable among colleagues and journals outside the United States.

To make such a distinction, of course, is to presume that political science (and perhaps other social sciences, too) varies across countries and regions, that it is not rooted in universal principles and procedures, that it matters who we are, where we come from, and where we were trained. And by this I mean more, much more, than simply variability in the issues that colleagues probe in different countries or regions. Obviously political scientists in Hong Kong are going to focus on Asian problems much more extensively than those affiliated with institutions in the United States or Europe. No, the variability springs from deeper roots than geography. It involves ontological, epistemological, conceptual, and methodological differences that stem from varying personal temperaments and cultural premises. Only to the degree that personality and culture are conditioned by configurations of land and water can it be said that geography underlies the intellectual differences among political scientists.[2]

In short, whatever may be the mix of temperament and culture, there is no one right way to do political science. We differ on the methodologies we employ, on whom we regard as the key actors on the political stage, on what motivates them, on the extent to which they act rationally, on the dynamics that sustain and shape their interactions, on whether agency underlies structure or vice versa, and so on across the vast spectrum that comprises the world of politics. The central (though by no means the only) trend in American political science today amounts to a groundswell favoring rational-choice models that explain the behavior of officials, publics, countries, and institutions in terms of calculations in which gains are to be maximized and costs minimized. Many political science departments in the US are dominated by colleagues who adhere to such models and who train their graduate students to follow their lead. Indeed, it is not far-fetched to observe that more than a few departments are deeply divided by the issues that swirl around the wisdom of proceeding from an assumption of rationality.[3] There are, of course, rational-choice devotees elsewhere in the world, but I have the impression that their numbers and influence are much less than is the case in the United States. Put differently, and to return to an earlier theme, it is the rational-choice models that comprise the mainstream in my country and that leads me to be more comfortable with work going on elsewhere. That I have written nine papers for conferences in Europe and Asia in the last three years and only one for an occasion in the US is a good measure of how far I appear to have strayed from my intellectual heritage.

Before discussing the puzzles that presently pique my curiosity, let me say a few words as to why I think the mainstream in the US is flowing so swiftly in the one direction or, perhaps more accurately, why it is by-passing those who choose to swim in different tributaries. To put it bluntly, I think the world is undergoing enormous change even as many, if not most, American political scientists, perhaps for diverse reasons, tend to downplay, even to ignore, the larger forces underlying the fundamental transformations in their professional analyses. Their colleagues elsewhere, on the other hand, feeling very much more ensconced in the changes and much less beholden to superpower leadership, have begun to make major adjustments in their conceptual and methodological equipment to account for the changes. This strikes me as particularly the case with respect to the acceleration of globalization and its de-territorializing consequences, dynamics that pervade journals and conferences outside the US but are relatively scarce among my countrymen and women, many of whom continue to treat the boundaries between the domestic and the foreign as firm and durable. There may be a growing awareness that these boundaries are increasingly porous and this awareness has even been articulated through bargaining strategies based on rational-choice analyses;[4] but when push comes to shove the awareness is not carried to the point where the degree of porosity is taken into account. The bargaining is posited as occurring across the boundaries and not through or around them. My own interpretation is that globalization is founded on such complex and unfamiliar processes that many colleagues find it easier to remain firmly within their long-standing fields and subfields. To allow for the transformations that are presently at work within and among societies, to work around and through the domestic–foreign boundaries rather than across them, is to become involved in extraordinarily complex phenomena for which existing conceptual and methodological equipment is insufficient.

Put differently, the luxuries of a superpower – the feeling that no problems are so urgent as to require a relaxation of disciplinary boundaries and practices – encourage American political scientists to refine their discipline and practices rather than confront the challenges posed by the transformative dynamics. No matter that what is foreign is also domestic, and vice versa. No matter that emotion, impulse, and erratic behavior often underlie the conduct of voters, officials, and institutions. No matter that increasingly nonlinear processes are more central to the course of events than linear sequences. No matter that these characteristics are operative in every subfield – whether it be local, comparative, American, or international politics. What matters is that the discipline must be preserved in each subfield, that its boundaries remain intact, and that those entering the profession be inculcated with the premises, skills, and values that sustain the subfield.[5]

Five puzzles

If this critique of American political science seems like sour grapes, let me articulate my out-of-the-mainstream perspectives not in terms of others having gone astray, but in terms of five major dimensions of globalization that strike me as urgently needing to be addressed. There are, of course, a number of other dimensions that should command focused attention, but these five can be seen as prerequisites to focusing on the others. Put differently, whether or not my characterization of American political science is applicable elsewhere – as it may well be since so many non-American members of the profession were trained in the United States – the five puzzles of special interest to me are, I believe, relevant to any present-day political inquiry in any subfield of the discipline. All five puzzles derive from the dynamics and complexity of the epoch that has emerged subsequent to the Cold War and its immediate aftermath. Some of the puzzles have been briefly mentioned in previous chapters, but here they are elaborated at greater length in the hope of enlisting help in addressing them. What follows is not so much a set of conclusions as a congeries of questions I think we collectively need to ponder.

Terminal entities

One of the puzzles concerns the weakening of states as the terminal entities for the loyalties and affiliations of citizens. With the death of distance, time, and sequentiality, it seems clear, people are developing new identities and rethinking old ones. The rapidly growing literature on identity tells us that globalization is loosening ties to the home states, to national heritage, even as new entities emerge as candidates to which people may attach their highest loyalties. Put differently, authority everywhere is tending toward disaggregation, upwards to supranational entities, sidewards to social movements and NGOs, and downwards to subnational associations and governments. Thus we are confronted with the puzzle of how to conceptualize the basic units of analysis in politics, those collectivities that have the capacity to exercise authority, informally as well as formally, and in so doing to enjoy the support of they who heed their directives. Elsewhere I have sought to resolve this puzzle by conceiving of world affairs as consisting of innumerable spheres of authority (SOAs) that are founded on new social contracts that specify how their affairs are conducted.[6] I am far from sure that my SOA scheme resolves the puzzle posed by the erosion of state competencies, but it does have the virtue of provoking thought about possible solutions.

In other words, and to repeat, I think all of us, Asians and non-Asians alike, need to abandon the domestic–foreign boundary in our analyses, or at the very least allow for it being extremely porous and often ineffective.[7] Admittedly, the erosion of national boundaries in Asia is occurring at a much slower pace than elsewhere, and there are more than a few countries in the region where borders remain high and fixed; but it is also the case that many dimensions of globalization span all national boundaries. Information, currency, crime, drugs, pollution, and often people readily transgress even the most deeply entrenched politically constructed boundaries, thus posing in another way the puzzle of how to conceptualize terminal entities if states are increasingly unable to maintain the effectiveness of their borders.

Change

If one assumes, as I do, that the world, its societies and its people are undergoing transformations so profound as not to be fully appreciated, then a major conceptual challenge needs to be faced: how do we know change when we see it? How do we differentiate between evolutionary and breakpoint change? At what levels of aggregation are deep and enduring changes most likely? Do changes at, say, micro levels necessitate comparable changes at macro levels, and vice versa? Are some forms of change illusory, amounting to no more than brief disruptions of underlying patterns? With few exceptions, such questions have not been the focus of conceptual inquiries by political scientists.[8] Most of us tend to take for granted that salient changes in the actors and structures of world affairs will be manifest as they unfold. Sure, when a regime collapses or an alliance breaks up, when markets decline precipitously, or when situations deteriorate abruptly, we have little difficulty discerning the end of one historical sequence and the onset of another. Ascribing change to such developments is easy, but in assessing the durability of the changes, or discerning the early indicators of regime, alliance, situational, or market collapses, our conceptual equipment is rudimentary, if not altogether lacking. This is why all too often we are surprised by the turn of events.

There are, of course, no magic formulas for understanding and anticipating different forms of change. Still, there are ways of maximizing our ability to assess when transformations may ensue. One is to assume that systems are always on the edge of collapse, an assumption which compels us to be sensitive to, even in awe of, the capacity of systems to get from one moment, week, year, or decade in time to the next. To proceed from the opposite assumption – that systems are likely to persist – is to limit our readiness to recognize the formation and early stages of change dynamics. Another way of coping with the challenge of change is to allow our variables to vary – that is, to mentally imagine a wide range of possible shifts in the values of all the variables relevant to our concerns. Most of us, for example, did not allow for the possibility that the Cold War and the Soviet Union would come to abrupt ends. In retrospect, such failures border on the inexcusable.[9] Or at least if we had been more sensitive to the susceptibility of systemic collapse and thus been alert to variations in the two structures expressive of such tendencies, it may have been less surprising.

Fragmegration

Of the numerous change dynamics presently shaping world affairs, two clusters stand out as paramount – those that foster globalization, centralization, and integration on the one hand and those that promote localization, decentralization, and fragmentation on the other. While these polarities move the course of events in opposite directions, they are continuously, simultaneously, and often causally interactive, giving rise to the prime tensions with which individuals and their collectivities must contend. In order to capture the inextricable and pervasive character of these interactions, I use the concept of "fragmegration," which is admittedly awkward and grating but at the same time reminds us that the processes of globalization and localization tend to be one and the same.[10] Indeed, it can readily be argued that the emergent epoch is one of fragmegration and not simply one of globalization. The so-called "battle of Seattle" in late November, 1999, offers a quintessential illustration of fragmegrative dynamics: as the representatives of states gathered for the integrative purpose of negotiating new trade agreements, so did various NGOs and individuals take to the streets in order to demonstrate their opposition and to highlight the fragmenting nature of such agreements.

While anthropologists, sociologists, journalists and business executives have recognized the importance of fragmegrative processes[11] and even coined their own labels for them,[12] these crucial dynamics have not been accorded centrality by the IR community. To the extent that globalizing or localizing forces are examined, they tend to be explored and traced separately, with only passing attention being paid to the ways in which each set of forces impacts on the other. One reason for this conceptual gap probably concerns the simultaneity of fragmegrative dynamics. The processes whereby the several polarities are linked to each other are comprised largely of feedback mechanisms, of nonlinear sequences that present enormous methodological dilemmas (see below). Most of us are accustomed to linear analysis, to discerning how dependent variables vary in response to the operation of various independent variables. The idea that each dependent variable becomes instantaneously an independent variable tends to be too mind-boggling to acknowledge, much less serving as the basis for inquiry. So fragmegrative studies languish for want of an effective methodology.

Equally important, the conceptual gap is by-passed because of the number and variety of sources that contribute to and sustain the processes of fragmegration. One of these sources consists of what I have elsewhere labeled "the skill revolution" wherein people everywhere are increasingly able to construct scenarios that trace the course of distant events back into their homes and pocketbooks.[13] A second source involves the large degree to which collectivities around the world are undergoing authority crises, by which is meant the paralysis and stalemates that prevent them from framing and moving toward their goals. A third focuses on the bifurcation of global structures whereby the long-standing state-centric world now has a rival in an emergent multi-centric world of diverse actors such as ethnic minorities, NGOs, professional societies, transnational corporations, and the many other types of private collectivities that now crowd the global stage. A fourth is what I call the "organizational explosion" that has witnessed a huge proliferation of associations and networks at every level of community. A fifth I call the "mobility upheaval," by which is meant the vast and ever-growing movement of people around the world, a movement that includes everyone from the tourist to the terrorist and from the jet-setter to the immigrant. A sixth consists of the many microelectronic and transportation technologies that have collapsed time and space. A seventh involves the complex processes through which territoriality, states, and sovereignty have weakened to the point where it can be reasonably asserted that landscapes have been supplemented – and in some cases replaced – by mediascapes, financescapes, technoscapes, ethnoscapes, and ideoscapes.[14] An eighth concerns the large degree to which national economies have been globalized.

How these eight major sources (and doubtless others could be identified) interactively generate and sustain the dynamics of fragmegration is an enormous analytic challenge, but it is a challenge with which I believe political scientists are going to have to grapple hard and long if our discipline is to progress in comprehending politics at all levels in the decades ahead. And along with probing the interaction of the various fragmegrative dynamics, we will also have to investigate each of them separately in order to tease out their fragmegrative content and consequences.[15] Our research agenda, in short, is huge and virtually endless. More than that, it offers many opportunities for those in any subfield of the discipline who seek to identify important dissertation topics. They will not be easy to research and write, but each and every one of them is bound to break new ground and push our understanding of politics into new realms.

Micro–macro links

Still another critical aspect of fragmegrative dynamics involves the links between individuals at the micro level and collectivities at the macro level. Like change and fragmegration, these links have not been the focus of extensive conceptualization and investigation. While few analysts would deny that the flow between the two levels is central to how collectivities come into being and sustain themselves through time, how their micro–macro relationships are configured, and how people are shaped by the collectivities to which they belong, the interaction across these levels has been largely taken for granted or, in one well-known case, assessed to be beyond systematic comprehension.[16] As indicated in Chapter 5, we simply do not have any viable theory that anticipates how individuals will vary in response to varying macro inputs or how the structures and policies of macro collectivities might be undermined, redirected, sustained, or otherwise affected by new patterns at the micro level. Again, this is a preoccupation in some of the social sciences,[17] but IR scholars have essentially ignored the puzzles posed by the links among the levels of aggregation. Indeed, a major paradigm in the field, realism, proceeds from the premise that the only relevant action is that of states at the macro level, that individuals at the micro level can be assumed to follow the lead of their states.

The reasons for this seeming obliviousness to micro–macro links are not difficult to identify. Tracing such links is extremely difficult theoretically and thus even more challenging empirically. Those of us who do not subscribe to realist formulations intuitively know that the links are endlessly operative, that what collectivities and individuals do on the global stage are in part reactions to each other, but faced with the task of tracing their interactions, we tend to find it easier to take them for granted than to wrestle with the puzzles they pose. I do not claim to have made any progress in solving the puzzles,[18] but I do contend that comprehension of world affairs increasingly requires us to address the challenge and frame models that offer a chance to fit some of the pieces of the puzzles together. As the skill revolution, authority crises, structural bifurcation, the organization explosion, the mobility upheaval, microelectronic technologies, the weakening of territoriality, states, and sovereignty, and the globalization of national economies accelerate and extend their impact on fragmegrative dynamics, so does it become all the more urgent that we collectively confront the causal interactions thereby established. Table 6.1 is an effort to highlight the vast domain across which such theorizing must roam. The entries in its cells are no more than impressionistic hypotheses as to how the sources of fragmegration may play out at the micro, macro, macro–macro, and micro–macro levels, but hopefully they are suggestive of some of the paths inquiry into such relationships should follow.

Perhaps most notably, the skill revolution has highlighted the importance and urgency of micro–macro theorizing. If it is the case that people everywhere are ever more skilled at linking distant events to close-at-hand circumstances and then, through their enlarged networking capacities facilitated by the Internet and the organizational explosion, knowing when, where, and how to engage in collective action, it seems likely that the course of events will be shaped by developments at the micro level having an impact on actors and institutions at the macro level. The emergent pattern represented by the "battle of Seattle" and other protests against international economic institutions can readily be interpreted as an indicator of how issues will climb to the top of the global agenda in the future. Furthermore, collective action may not be the only consequence of micro inputs, as is illustrated by the increasing frequency of individual hackers breaking into and paralyzing computer systems.

Table 6.1 Some possible sources of fragmegration at four levels of aggregation

Levels of aggregation → / Sources of fragmegration ↓	MICRO	MACRO	MACRO–MACRO	MICRO–MACRO
Skill revolution	expands people's horizons on a global scale; sensitizes them to the relevance of distant events; facilitates a reversion to local concerns	enlarges the capacity of government agencies to think "out of the box," seize opportunities, and analyze challenges	multiplies quantity and enhances quality of links among states; solidifies their alliances and enmities	constrains policy making through increased capacity of individuals to know when, where, and how to engage in collective action
Authority crises	redirect loyalties; encourage individuals to replace traditional criteria of legitimacy with performance criteria	weaken ability of both governments and other organizations to frame and implement policies	enlarge the competence of some IGOs and NGOs; encourage diplomatic wariness in negotiations	facilitate the capacity of publics to press and/or paralyze their governments, the WTO, and other organizations
Bifurcation of global structures	adds to role conflicts, divides loyalties, and foments tensions among individuals; orients people toward local spheres of authority	facilitates formation of new spheres of authority and consolidation of existing spheres in the multi-centric world	generates institutional arrangements for cooperation on major global issues such as trade, human rights, the environment, etc.	empowers transnational advocacy groups and special interests to pursue influence through diverse channels
Organizational explosion	facilitates multiple identities, subgroupism, and affiliation with transnational networks	increases capacity of opposition groups to form and press for altered policies; divides publics from their elites	renders the global stage ever more transnational and dense with non-governmental actors	contributes to the pluralism and dispersion of authority; heightens the probability of authority crises

Continued

Table 6.1 continued

Levels of aggregation → Sources of fragmegration →	MICRO	MACRO	MACRO–MACRO	MICRO–MACRO
Mobility upheaval	stimulates imaginations and provides more extensive contacts with foreign cultures; heightens salience of the outsider	enlarges the size and relevance of sub-cultures, diasporas, and ethnic conflicts as people seek new opportunities abroad	heightens need for international cooperation to control the flow of drugs, money, immigrants, and terrorists	increases movement across borders that lessens capacity of governments to control national boundaries
Microelectronic technologies	enable like-minded people to be in touch with each other anywhere in the world	empower governments to mobilize support; renders their secrets vulnerable to spying	accelerate diplomatic processes; facilitate electronic surveillance and intelligence work	constrain governments by enabling opposition groups to mobilize more effectively
Weakening of territoriality, states, and sovereignty	undermines national loyalties and increases distrust of governments and other institutions	adds to the porosity of national boundaries and the difficulty of framing national policies	increases need for interstate cooperation on global issues; lessens control over cascading events	lessens confidence in governments; renders nationwide consensus difficult to achieve and maintain
Globalization of national economies	swells ranks of consumers; promotes uniform tastes; heightens concern for jobs	complicates tasks of state governments vis-à-vis markets; promotes business alliances	intensifies trade and investment conflicts; generates incentives for building global financial institutions	increases efforts to protect local cultures and industries; facilitates vigor of protest movements

Methodology

The conceptual challenges posed by the dynamics of change, fragmegration and micro–macro interactions share two major methodological dilemmas. One concerns our long-standing, virtually unconscious habit of probing problems in a broad geographic or spatial context, a habit that has been aptly called "methodological territorialism."[19] This habit poses an acute problem: as indicated by the ever-growing porosity of domestic–foreign boundaries, territoriality is much less pervasive than it used to be, and yet all the social sciences construct their inquiries, develop their concepts, formulate their hypotheses, and frame their evidence-gathering procedures through spatial lenses. Nor are officials immune from the problem: as one analyst put it, "Trapped by the territoriality of their power, policy makers in traditional settings often have little choice but to address the symptoms rather than the causes of public problems."[20] Putting this problem in empirical terms, the weaknesses of methodological territorialism become glaring when confronted with data such as these:

- some 300 million mobile telephones
- about 900 million telephone lines
- two billion radio sets
- one billion television receivers
- 180 million Internet users
- thousands of global products
- several hundred million global credit cards
- yearly foreign exchange turnovers of US$450 trillion
- several trillion US dollars' worth of offshore bank deposits
- US$35 million in annual transborder movements of securitized funds
- 44,500 transborder companies with collective annual sales of US$7 trillion
- over 250 multilateral regulatory institutions
- 16,500 noncommercial, nonofficial transborder associations
- accelerated global warming
- enormous reductions in biological diversity[21]

And the upward trend of all these figures is such that they were all out of date within minutes of having been counted. From 2000 to mid-2004, for example, the number of mobile phones nearly doubled to 1.5 billion.[22]

   The other methodological problem I have already alluded to, and it is no less severe: the dynamics of change, fragmegration and micro–macro interactions are pervaded with feedback processes and thus they pose the difficult question of how to explore them systematically. In other words, we are increasingly confronted by events that unfold virtually simultaneously, making it fruitless to cast analyses in terms of the interaction of independent and dependent variables. More accurately, analyses cast in a conventional linear framework seem bound to fall short in terms of capturing the interactive, high-speed nature of the phenomena of interest. How, then, to proceed? What methodologies might be available for probing nonlinear sequences of interaction? Are we bound to rely exclusively on case studies that, hopefully, somehow reveal the underlying tendencies that drive the transformative impacts of fragmegration and micro–macro links and are at the same time free of methodological territorialism? Can nonlinear methodologies drawn from mathematics and statistics be adapted to the needs of the political inquiry? If we are not ourselves adept at such methods, how do we make an effective case for students employing them?

Never having been very sophisticated as a methodologist, I do not have very precise answers to these questions. I know they are important and I presume there are colleagues who can answer them with some authority. Still, ignorance is no excuse. If the mysteries of a fragmegrative world are to be fathomed, we cannot shy away from the methodological questions on the grounds of inexperience. Herewith, then, a partial, somewhat informed response to the methodological challenge: while case studies can surely be of value, there are also nonlinear procedures that have become more feasible as a result of advances in computer technologies. As I understand it, there is now the prospect of computer chips that will be 10 billion (yes, 10 billion) times faster than those in use today.[23] This heightens the potential of using computer simulations based on complexity theory, of building nonlinear feedback mechanisms into models that simulate the dynamics of change, fragmegration, and micro–macro interactions. To recur to points made earlier, conceptualizations of these three sets of dynamics are in short supply and obviously need to be refined before computer models can be applied. If it is assumed that such refinements will eventually be developed, however, then computer simulations may prove to be a useful methodology in unraveling the mysteries of a fragmegrative world.

As for the problem of motivating and equipping students to take advantage of the technological advances that lie ahead, let me report on a teaching aid that I have found highly effective semester after semester for the last several years. It is a book entitled *Complexity: The Emerging Science at the Edge of Order and Chaos* by M. Mitchell Waldrop.[24] In all my years of teaching I have never given an assignment that has had such pervasive consequences. Each semester the first week's assignment is to read the entire book and write a five-page evaluation of it. The reactions are consistently impressive. Even though the book refers only occasionally and peripherally to the relevance of complexity theory for world affairs, and even though much of the book is about matters far removed from the concerns of social science – it is the story of the Santa Fe Institute in New Mexico – the students find the outlines of complexity theory eye-opening and virtually every week of the semester one or another student mentions the book and voices an idea they picked up from it. No book I have ever assigned lingers so persistently in the memory banks of students. In the last few years several students have rethought their study plans in the direction of tooling up in computer science.

Conclusion

In sum, I find myself persuaded that the future of our discipline, its capacity to confront the huge conceptual and methodological challenges that have eluded our generation, lies in the training of those who will enter the field in the future. We need to acknowledge our own limitations and alert those we train to the virtues of breaking with past paradigmatic assumptions and finding new ways of understanding and probing the enormous challenges posed by the dynamics of disaggregated authority, change, fragmegration, micro–macro interactions, and complexity.

The incentives to confront such challenges are considerable, but there remain the obstacles posed by rational-choice approaches and the premises associated with a firm and durable domestic–foreign boundary. The very simplicity of these approaches and premises seem to lure the faint-hearted into accepting narrow goal definitions, well-established boundaries, and elegant methodologies. We cannot hope to probe the dynamics of fragmegration equipped with a definition of goals that is profoundly Western and focuses on the accumulation of wealth while not allowing for goals that, say, maximize glory to ancestors. We cannot hope to account for change without accounting for the porosity of boundaries. We cannot hope to explore the underpinnings of the emergent epoch with approaches that drive us back to reliance on the positivist enterprise, to only studying propositions that are testable. To be sure, there is plenty of room for conventional political science – my own vita is littered with it as a consequence of my having been an early behavioralist – but I would argue that at least the venturesome among us ought to suspend the commitment to rational-choice models, rigid boundaries, and conventional methods until we can more fully grasp the deep and profound transformations that are at work in every community and at every level of analysis. If some of us can truly commit ourselves to such a suspension, if we can appreciate the joys of being venturesome, if we can feel free to study the big issues with crude methodologies, and – most important – if we can orient some of our students along these lines, political science as a discipline will begin to catch up with the way the world is and, in so doing, will have moved on to a higher and more secure analytic plane.

Part II
The professional

7 The birth of a political scientist[1]

Here, on a quiet lakefront in Maine, recurring thoughts about a dissertation just completed intrude rudely upon a vacation that was expected to be wonderfully free of that which hung so heavily for five long years. But at least this is an ideal spot for reflection: across the water, where the nearby woods blend into the distant mountains, one can see both the trees and the forest, an unaccustomed sight to the tired possessor of a new Ph.D.

In retrospect, it is astonishing how much psychic energy can be invested in a doctoral candidacy. One hears a great deal about the long hours, the stiff exams, and the intense competition which mark the training of medical and law students. But who has ever heard of a fledgling doctor or lawyer who postponed taking his exams or dawdled over completing his requirements? Yet such behavior seems to be commonplace among aspiring academicians. The number of graduate students who sail easily and quickly through their graduate career is probably very small compared to those who either fail to complete their studies or who do so after considerable procrastination, hesitation, and self-laceration. Moreover, the fears and frustrations of graduate students are ordinarily impervious to the friendly assurances of their teachers and advisers. I doubt whether the elders of any profession provide new recruits with as much encouragement and sympathy as do instructors of graduate courses. Indeed, one occasionally hears of an adviser who practically guarantees passage of prelims in order to get a gifted and troubled student over the hurdle. Some graduate programs have even adopted institutional devices intended to reduce the tensions that hinder effective study. More than a few now require new students to attend a series of lectures that acquaint them with the psychological hazards as well as the formal requirements which lie ahead.

But, alas, the difficulties lie in the students and not in a heartless system that makes rigorous and excessive demands. Considerate and kindly paternalism is apparently no match for the self-doubt (and perhaps self-pity) that the graduate student thrusts in his own way. Why is this? And why is it so unique to an academic career? Some psychoanalysts contend that acquiring a Ph.D. stands for the attainment of adulthood, a condition of life that the troubled graduate student subconsciously wishes to avoid for a variety of reasons. To be an adult is to be on a par with his parents, to possess status, to have a title, to incur obligations –

circumstances that are all very awesome and threatening to the person whose childhood fostered fears of competition and responsibility. And these are the very circumstances that attend the earning of a doctorate. The new Ph.D. can no longer fall back on the security of being a student, of having others determine how he should spend his time and what he should learn. Henceforth others will view him as a grown-up, as learned and responsible, and sometimes they may even call him "doctor." Even worse, his professors will no longer be his seniors, becoming instead his colleagues (brothers rather than fathers), and it could be that someday he will find himself surpassing them. It is successful competition against one's father: an exciting thought, and a dreadful thought ("Better not take prelims this time – I might pass them").

It might be argued that this interpretation does not explain why the graduate student seems so much more susceptible to psychological difficulties than his medical and legal counterparts. Surely the M.D. and the LL.B. also symbolize adulthood and entrance upon a professional life. Why, then, do not unresolved childhood fears haunt the schools of medicine and law? I imagine the psychoanalyst would reply that the latter provide much more definite and precise channels to a career, that the medical or law student has already made the transition to adulthood and thus defines himself as acquiring technical training pursuant to the fulfillment of goals already decided upon. The graduate student, on the other hand, has not had to decide what he will be doing ten or fifteen years later. Thus he may still possess those childhood fears that certainty about the future could resolve. And, if he wants, he can further postpone adulthood by reminding himself that despite his age, he is still attending school, just as he always has since the age of five.

There is still another, equally crucial, factor that renders preparation for an academic career psychologically more hazardous than the training for any other profession: namely, the dissertation. To take courses is to *consume* knowledge, which is then inventoried through examinations. Although it varies in pace and skill from student to student, this consumption process is essentially a technical matter, involving the mastery of new data and patterns of thought. To write a thesis, on the other hand, is to *produce* knowledge. Even if it is based on secondary sources or is merely a translation or interpretation of someone else's work, a dissertation is a creation that derives its substance from within the student. Unlike his contemporaries in medical or law school, then, the graduate student is thrust back upon his own resources. He is a producer as well as a consumer. He is required to contribute, to originate, to create. Little wonder that he becomes so intimately and emotionally involved in his dissertation, viewing it with the same ambivalent mixture of tenderness and awe that mark parental attitudes toward children. And little wonder that no amount of advice or encouragement can get him to finish and submit his thesis if he is not satisfied with every dimension of the product he has fashioned. For, in a fundamental sense, the graduate student posits himself as the major judge of his thesis. He is his own worst critic, demanding of himself a perfection that neither his adviser nor his dissertation committee would dare ask of even a senior colleague in the field.

The meaning of a dissertation for its creator is also wide open to psychoanalytic interpretation. Some might even say that it represents the ninth month in the birth of an adult. (Perhaps more than random imagery was operative when a colleague, upon hearing that I had been granted a degree, congratulated me for "having emerged from the long, dark tunnel.") Whatever its deeper psychological meanings, however, surely the dissertation constitutes a unique experience. Aside from the arts, what other profession requires of its new recruits a creative innovation as the mark of fitness to enter the field? Businessmen are expected to be innovative and productive in their forties and fifties, as are doctors, lawyers, engineers, civil servants, and so on. But the scholar is required, in his early twenties, to make an original contribution to his profession. Whatever the wisdom of such an arrangement (and I do not question it), surely the graduate student is entitled to founder a bit, to doubt himself, to advance at an uneven pace. I rather suspect that the medical or law schools would have a considerably higher proportion of troubled students if an original contribution to medical or legal studies were a prerequisite of graduation.

There are, of course, concrete intellectual consequences of the emotional energy that is invested in a dissertation. One of the most important results is the persistency of the question, "How do I know this?" At least in my case all the fears of completing a successful thesis forced me to challenge and re-challenge the validity of each sentence I wrote. I became acutely sensitive to the nature of proof, to tests of reliability, to the distinctions between fact and inference, and to the impossibility of obtaining neat and final conclusions about complex phenomena. It is one thing to comprehend in a general fashion the necessity of employing sound procedures. All graduate students develop a certain sophistication along these lines, and derive not a little excitement from a newly found capacity to demonstrate the methodological flows of major works in their field. But it is quite another thing to experience at first hand the dilemma of accumulating reliable knowledge – that is, knowledge which, within its own limits, facilitates accurate prediction. A dissertation not only provides such an experience, but, given its deeper meaning for the graduate student, it also compels a kind of soul-searching about reliability that, I am certain, leaves a permanent mark upon the course of subsequent research.

This is not to ignore the considerable falderal that accompanies each day's bout with the thesis. It is impossible to be unaffected by the warnings and rumors, real or imagined, that each generation of graduate students passes on to its successors and upon which so many coffee breaks thrive. Thus one is ever alert to the idiosyncrasies, real or imagined, of his adviser, just as the predilections of key members of the dissertation committee are an ever-present consideration. Thus one is ever aware of the "Department" and its unwritten regulations about the length, format, and subject matter of an acceptable thesis. And thus one pays respect to a variety of traditions which are said to lessen the risks of non-acceptance – an appropriate number of footnotes, perhaps a table or two of imposing statistics, not to mention an elaborate bibliography that lists the standard works in the field regardless of their utility.

But even as one makes all the necessary obeisances to the folklore of dissertation writing, the large question of "how do I know this" persists. And it does so not only because of a gnawing fear that somehow a member of the orals board might ask precisely such a question; it also endures because the graduate student has to live with himself. His thesis is too important to him to permit of a casual approach to the question of reliability. It is a matter of earning, rather than falsifying, his way into adulthood. Even if others are impressed by imaginative insights, varied footnotes, elaborate graphs, and tight organization, he knows that this is only the appearance of reliability, not the substance of it. And so he embarks on a search for certainty, only to find that it lies in such phrases as "apparently," "presumably," and "it would seem as if." It turns out, however, that these phrases are even more meaningful possessions than the three new letters that will soon follow his name. For these phrases reflect a self-discipline, a modesty, and an integrity that are not easily achieved – traits that, in effect, separate the man from the boy and thereby signify his coming of age.

8 Intellectual identity and the study of international relations, or coming to terms with mathematics as a tool of inquiry[1]

It may be wondered how a person whose work in the IR field is not of a mathematical nature can dare to write about applying mathematics to international relations. I do so because I have long pondered various approaches to the field and, in the process, have come to terms with mathematics as a tool of inquiry. One does not have to be skilled at mathematics to appreciate its uses. One can be a consumer as well as a producer of mathematical findings. Choosing the consumer role, however, is not much easier than opting for the producer role. There are a number of obstacles to overcome in making either choice, and it is in regard to these obstacles that perhaps some remarks by a nonmathematical investigator can be useful.

Some insight into the obstacles involved is provided by the experience of a good friend of mine. Forty years old, married with two children, and living on an inadequate professor's salary, he recently decided to go further into debt because he found himself unable to undertake the kind of inquiry into politics that he deemed necessary. Prior to this decision he had acquired considerable skills as a generator and analyst of quantified data, skills that resulted in a number of important studies and a growing reputation as one of the nation's most competent political scientists. Despite the success, however, he concluded that he was ill-equipped to carry on his work, that only by tooling up in mathematics could he begin to address and (hopefully) resolve the questions about the underlying dynamics of politics that plagued him. So he took a year's leave of absence from his university, borrowed $9,000 from a credit union, reassured his family that somehow they would make ends meet, and set out to learn mathematics, first at the simple levels presented in high school, then on to the more advanced levels to be found in college and postgraduate curricula.

My friend's choice illustrates two points that need to be appreciated if one is to benefit from tooling up in mathematics. One is that mathematics can be seen as a powerful tool with which to probe the dynamics of international politics. The second is that the availability of mathematical approaches to the study of human affairs can serve as a catalyst for confronting important questions about one's own intellectual identity.

Indeed, the power of mathematical tools can hardly be appreciated unless one has first pondered one's approach to the study of world affairs. This question of intellectual identity has to be confronted because the facts and trends of inter-national relations are not self-evident. They do not simply present themselves for any observer to comprehend. The observer must interpret them, give them coherence so that patterns can be discerned in the welter of events and under-standing thereby developed. To interpret is to derive meaning, and to derive meaning is to employ one or another tool of analysis. Since different tools of analysis can yield different interpretations of the same phenomena, one's choice of analytic tools can be deeply personal. At stake is nothing less than one's grasp of, posture toward, and commitment to one's subject, the rigor, skill, and imagin-ation with which one probes the mysteries of the past and the likelihoods of the future.

The availability of mathematical tools highlights the need to establish an intel-lectual identity with respect to one's subject because such tools are widely felt to be inappropriate to the study of IR. Hence, normally those who use them must overcome both the inhibitions against mathematics that are frequently instilled early in life and the gaps in training that widen as the inhibitions deepen. Unfortunately, the prejudices against the application of mathematical reasoning are especially strong in the IR field. Those who enter the field tend to come out of a tradition of legal or historical scholarship, where the notion of reducing human experience to mathematical formulas and analysis is considered to be misguided and absurd at best and degrading and blasphemous at worst. Claiming that such an approach overlooks, even undermines, the spirit and dignity with which people conduct their affairs, many assert that human feelings and aspirations are too varied and too private to be subject to mathematization. In addition, many of those who enter the field do so less out of intellectual curiosity and more out of a commitment to improving the human condition and lessening the chances of war, a priority that is certainly commendable but that also tends to foster impatience with tools of analysis that subject values to the strict rigors of logic.

There are, in short, many intellectual postures one can take toward the field, each with philosophical assumptions and rules of procedures that set it apart from the others. One cannot say that any of these approaches is superior to the others. Much depends on the types of problems that one seeks to solve, the kinds of knowledge one wants to see cumulate, and the criteria of evidence with which one is most comfortable. Mathematical tools are not suitable to every problem and they do not yield empirical findings to which statistical criteria of evidence can be applied. But they do provide powerful instruments with which to probe certain kinds of problems.

While mathematical tools are not inherently superior to any others, and while their use does not necessarily preclude reliance on other modes of inquiry, they are distinctive. As noted below, they require explicit premises and procedures that clearly differentiate them from historical, case-study, quantitative, and journalistic forms of investigation. This is why their availability tends to pose especially intense personal questions of intellectual identity. To be sure, such questions arise with respect to any approach one may follow, but they seem particularly acute in the case of mathematics because the language and procedures on which it rests are so different. Impelled to seek solutions to immediate problems and trained to approach world affairs inductively, most observers must confront the questions of who they are intellectually and what kind of knowledge they want to uncover before they can commit themselves to the style and language that mathematical analysis requires. By the time they become enamored of the potential of mathematics, moreover, many have become so accustomed to one or another form of inquiry that they feel awe for mathematical formulas and inadequate about their capacity to comprehend them. So, unlike my friend, most conclude it is too late to retool and either fall back on a humanistic rejection of the utility of mathematical applications or rationalize that they never have been able to master the intricacies of algebra and calculus, much less even more advanced mathematical tools.

Much the same can be said about the potential consumers of mathematical analyses. Potential producers may have to make excruciating choices that require the reorientation of careers and the disruption of family life in order to be able to engage in mathematical inquiry, but those who simply want to use and apply the results of such inquiries also have to assess who they are and what they regard as valid knowledge. To pick one's way slowly through a mathematical formulation is no easy task if one has had little recent training in mathematics. It requires patience with oneself, respect for alternative ways of generating knowledge, and tolerance for insights that are derived more from logic than from observation. All the biases that inhibit the acquisition of mathematical skills operate even more powerfully on those who might have occasion to employ the findings uncovered through their application. Not choosing to learn the intricacies of advanced mathematics, consumers can, if they are so disposed, readily attempt to compensate for their sense of inadequacy about mathematics by stressing the uniqueness of people and the inviolability of the human spirit. Indeed, those who are most resistant to the idea of using mathematics in the study of international relations are likely to be those who know least about it and who cling fearfully to a narrowly defined intellectual identity they perceive as threatened by an obscure methodology.

Chances are that most readers of articles or books dedicated to mathematical analysis have puzzled through their intellectual identity to the point where such inquiries are not threatening, else they would long since quit reading this chapter. However, lest some who got this far still have open minds in their quest for identity and in the event that a few plan to read on because they intend, perhaps unknowingly, to rely on my argument as further proof of the wisdom of their prejudices, it is useful to note why mathematics can serve as a powerful tool for unraveling the mysteries of international life. The key lies in the fact that mathematical analysis proceeds deductively and logically from a set of axioms about a problem of concern to the analyst. The axioms are derived either systematically or impressionistically from observation, but however they are derived, once they are linked together in a model rigorous logic takes over and the ensuing analysis is governed by relationships inherent in the mathematics employed rather than by those perceived to be operating empirically. The power of the tool springs from the dynamics of the problem that are thereby revealed – that is, the way in which the variables subsumed by the axioms logically interrelate as the analyst relaxes one or another original condition or builds in one or another new parameter. Unfolding events in the real world may not conform to the logic inherent in the model (indeed, they are unlikely to be very consistent, since the axioms of the model are not designed to cover all the deviations and exceptions that prevail in the real world), but the underlying tendencies and interrelationships from which particular situations deviate are laid bare by tracing deductively the interaction that logically follows from the conditions treated as axiomatic. Precisely because the welter of cross-currents and exceptions that render the real world complex are excluded, the mathematical analyst can uncover the basic tendencies that are at work. A major source of the power of mathematical tools is their capacity to uncover relationships that might not otherwise be discerned or might be so obscured as to be only dimly perceived.

All of this is the case, of course, only if the axioms and model are sound, creative, and relevant and the analyst knowledgeable and skillful as a mathematician. As in everything else, mathematical analysis is no more cogent than the creativity with which it is used. There can be poor mathematics, just as there can be poor history or poor quantitative interpretation. In addition to mastering the discipline of mathematics, the analysts must have a feel for the substantive problems to which the discipline is applied, if the full power of the mathematical tools is to be realized. To apply mathematics creatively one must creatively grasp one's chosen problem, else the logic derived from the axioms one develops will yield barren results. Insight, imagination, wild hunches, and intuitive formulations are as central to the mathematical analyst as to the humanistic scholar. They differ only in the procedures they employ once their minds creatively delineate their respective problems.

This is not to say, or even to imply subtly, that mathematical tools are a panacea. Such tools do have limits and there are many kinds of problems for which they are unsuited. Most notably, being a deductive rather than an inductive science, mathematical tools cannot be employed to solve empirical problems. They can clarify relationships and point to possible outcomes, but they cannot facilitate analysis of what in fact happened or is happening in a real-world situation. Nor do they allow one to trace the impact or sources of deviant cases. Their scope is general and not specific, and one has to turn to empirical methods whenever specificity is a primary characteristic of the problem under investigation.

But to acknowledge that mathematical tools offer no panacea is not to justify rejecting their use. Some are quick to reject them on these grounds, as if to admit that such tools have some utility is to run the risk that they will be obliged to follow my friend's example and make personal sacrifices in order to establish a new intellectual identity. Admirable as my friend's choice may be, it is not the only one available. For a variety of reasons one can make the choice not to engage in extensive retooling and to remain essentially a consumer of mathematically derived analyses. I myself feel inept in this regard and am quite convinced that no amount of diligence could fully retool me as a skilled producer of mathematical studies of international phenomena. My identity, the result of much soul-searching and realistic attempts to assess my interests and talents, lies in a readiness to entertain and ponder insights into world politics, however they may be derived. Because one is untrained in and insecure about mathematical procedures one need not be suspicious of the results they generate. The test is not whether one can follow the progression from one equation to the next, but rather whether one is impressed with the insights to which the application of mathematical reasoning inexorably gives rise. Despite my skimpy knowledge of mathematics, I am impressed with the variety, importance, and incisiveness of the conclusions that pervade much of the mathematical literature in IR. They deal with questions of war and peace, with alliances and coalitions, with choices that are rational and those that are not, topics that surely can benefit from further investigation from a multiplicity of perspectives.

For non-specialists to come to terms with mathematical studies, in short, they need merely give up defensiveness about their own identity and recognize that mathematical inquiries are a supplement and not a threat to their own modes of investigation. To make acceptance of this perspective easier they may find it useful to think of mathematics as they do of foreign languages. Few would dismiss an analysis written in German or Arabic because they lack knowledge of these languages. On the contrary, the tendency is to assume it is sound and valuable (why else would it be available?) and to seek help in getting a translation of its essential thrust. Why should we take any less constructive an attitude toward mathematics. It too is a language and thus it too lends itself to translation. Non-specialists are likely to find their mathematical colleagues cooperative, even flattered, when they ask for help in translating the central points of a mathematical analysis, so that they need merely be clear on the substantive questions around which they seek to initiate a dialogue with specialists in mathematics.

There is a quid pro quo for the non-specialist's tolerance of mathematical analyses. If those who undertake such analyses want to enlarge their capacity to frame sound and creative axioms through dialogues with those of us who develop IR knowledge in nonmathematical ways, it is reasonable to expect that they will conclude their analyses with non-technical summaries of their substantive findings. These need not be full translations, which are an undue burden and which, in any event, can never be as precise as the mathematical analysis itself. But succinct synopses do seem both feasible and warranted, ones that highlight the general (if not the precise) nature of the relationships derived from the parameters posited as axiomatic at the outset.

In each case the summary should also include a notation of how the analysis differs from others developed mathematically, thereby giving non-specialists a basis for assessing both the merits of an analysis and its utility. The burden for sustaining a dialogue, in other words, must necessarily fall on those who use mathematical methods. If they want to maximize their contribution to understanding they will have to maintain and extend their contacts with the much larger community of nonmathematical students of world politics, a task that requires them to be continuously aware that their mode of inquiry is a form of language that needs to be translated if their ideas and findings are to circulate widely.

I would argue that this translation burden is one that those who have found their intellectual identity through mathematics should happily shoulder. Since mathematical analyses are no sounder than the understandings of world politics on which they rest, and since the larger IR community has a great deal to offer by way of penetrating knowledge on the subject, those who employ mathematics have good reason to initiate and maintain communications with their nonmathematical colleagues. We may often be obstinate and impatient, but we are not lacking in valuable insights and findings that can inform and guide the process of formal model building.

In sum, all concerned have much to gain from a continuous dialogue. There are many roads to IR knowledge and those who traverse them need each other's assistance when their paths cross if their shared goal of enlarged understanding is to be realized.

9 Courage versus caution

A dialogue on entering and prospering in IR[1]
(co-authored with Ersel Aydinli)

Introduction

AYDINLI: As a newcomer with a recent Ph.D. trying to make my way in the community of international relations (IR) scholars, I sometimes feel like a juggler with too many balls in the air. How can I possibly keep aloft the many different roles I see for myself in this community? I feel I must be a good teacher and guide students in gaining disciplinary knowledge, yet I believe I should also be a thoughtful and well-informed intellectual who can possibly positively influence political developments in my local Turkish environment as well as internationally. Moreover, it is obvious that I must be a researcher, produce quality scholarship, and hope in doing so that I contribute to the accumulation and progression of disciplinary knowledge. Finding an appropriate balance between these roles, or deciding whether one or more should take precedence, presents me, and no doubt other young scholars, with very difficult choices.

Furthermore, within each of these roles that I see for myself, I am faced with additional choices concerning not only the messages I present, but also the ways that I want to get these messages across. If I consider only the role of researcher, I need to ask whether I want to try to forge my way alone or whether I would be better served by clearly identifying myself as part of a particular research community. And if I choose the latter, then which research community should it be? Should I pay homage to the most traditional ideas so that I remain a part of the core of the IR community? How do I act so as to retain my own perspectives while at the same time become an accepted member of this community and survive? In other words, how do I build up my professional identity?

We emergent scholars seem to be picking our way through if not treacherous then at least problem-ridden territory on our journey to building up our professional identities. We are faced with choices between various theoretical identities – from the broadest epistemological and paradigmatic questions (for example, should we take the positivist or post-positivist route?) to more disciplinary specific positions (are we a realist? a neo-liberal? or perhaps a constructivist?). There are also the practical elements of one's identity. In other words, should we locate ourselves firmly in the academic world of the university, in think-tanks, or in policy centers? Should we choose to emphasize our teaching or our research? There arises a whole set of different choices if we happen to be a foreigner trained in the West, for then we must also decide, among other things, whether to try and locate ourselves professionally in our native "local" IR circles or in the greater international IR community.

It is hardly unreasonable for an emergent scholar – to the extent s/he is conscious of these choices and the stakes they involve – to find this socialization journey into the discipline a daunting one. The journey takes on added complexities when we begin to consider other questions such as how much we are in control of making these choices and how much they are determined for us by restrictions that range from the more concrete (for example, language abilities, institutional requirements, access to technology) to the more abstract (for example, the limits of one's disciplinary training, one's personal tendencies when considering group membership, one's intellectual inclinations).

For myself, I felt it would be an interesting exercise to seek out the ideas and guidance of someone who had not only made this journey but who had done so in what might be called an adventurous manner and in the process given evidence of a willingness to reflect upon his journey. From both his published literature and from personal contact with him, I have an impression of James N. Rosenau as a scholar without rigid fixations on certain concepts or ideas and as a scholar who has been open about his professional journey. It was when I read the final chapter of his book *Distant Proximities*, in which he presented a critical self-reflection of his own academic journey,[2] that I became fully convinced that he would be an ideal person from whom to seek insights about various issues and dilemmas puzzling and troubling me in my professional life.

In that chapter, "A Transformed Observer in a Transforming World: Confessions of a Pre-post-modernist," I was deeply struck by Rosenau's forthright discussion of personal and intellectual traits that he believes have shaped his professional life, including his apparent major shift from doing research in a "scientific" tradition to one he calls "relaxed-science." In explaining his own professional development, he notes his openness – or perhaps need – to seek new and different approaches, his methodological conviction as to the inseparability of individuals from the larger contexts in which they participate, and finally his observations over the latter part of the twentieth century that states have been losing control and therefore his deepening commitment to focusing his scholarly inquiry on the "frontier" between domestic and foreign affairs. I found myself also intrigued by the case he builds at the end of this chapter for methodological and theoretical bridge-building, which he bases on his belief that we can and must seek consensual understandings if we are to accumulate knowledge.

The following dialogue thus began in a sense as I read Rosenau's confessional chapter and filled the margins with questions and comments, which I subsequently communicated to him. We went on to exchange ideas on various aspects of the processes of newcomer socialization and professional identity formation. Very much in relation to these processes, we spoke as well on issues of change (for example, how open can a scholar be to change in his/her identity, research agenda, or perspectives? What are the costs of such changes?) and methodology (for example, how and why do some scholars attempt so-called "jailbreaks" from firmly entrenched methodological identities?). The resulting dialogue, presented here, is therefore structured broadly along these themes of socialization, methodology, and change. Since this dialogue includes various references to passages or ideas in the "confessions" chapter of Professor Rosenau's *Distant Proximities*, the interested reader may find benefit in reading his book as well.

On becoming an IR scholar

AYDINLI: The epigraph to your autobiographical chapter in *Distant Proximities* says that "the forward-moving are doomed to be misunderstood." As such, it distinguishes only between so-called "forward-moving" individuals and presumably less progressive types. I wonder whether the truth of the epigraph might be more or less significant for scholars at different stages of their professional development. As a newcomer myself, I have to ask: Can a newcomer in the discipline afford to be unconventional? Can s/he wander innovatively through the "terra incognito," or in doing so will s/he run the risk of being ignored? In point of fact, is the discipline more accepting of the "new" when it comes to the experienced scholar?

ROSENAU: These are good questions. I am far from sure of how to respond. There are, as you imply, orthodoxies that pervade the fields of IR and political science (and perhaps all the social sciences). They consist of standard hurdles that newcomers have to jump over in order to progress further down the track. The hurdles are most conspicuous when it comes to writing an acceptable dissertation, but they can also block the route to tenure by requiring publication in established journals, reference letters written by established scholars located in established universities, etc. Thus it can be difficult for any newcomer to get accepted at the outset. Now and then (but not often) an article or book might be so compelling that the author's fledgling status is ignored and he or she moves ahead quickly. Allison's *Essence of Decision* is a good example in this regard.[3] To repeat, however, few newcomers make a mark with their first publications.

It follows that the "new" is more likely to gain acceptance when it is authored by more experienced scholars. But for more experienced scholars to break out of their long-existing mold is extremely difficult. They develop a deep stake in what they have done for which they have won praise and approval. As a result, they tend to be unable and unwilling to dare to try new approaches, and to probe unexplored questions.

AYDINLI: This seems to spell a dilemma for the discipline in that those most poised to make changes (the newcomers) are in the worst position to do so because they lack widespread legitimacy or name-recognition. Those in the best position to make changes and have these arrest attention are the least likely to do so. The question, of course, comes to mind: how did you manage to make the changes you note in your chapter when you were at the time an experienced scholar?

ROSENAU: Exactly how I managed to move beyond my work in comparative foreign policy and the rigorous (today I am inclined to use the word "rigid") approach to scientific inquiry that I was espousing at the time is not clear to me. It is certainly not the case that I always planned to move in new directions once I got tenure. Indeed, it was not until more than two decades after I got tenure that I began to move in new directions with the writing of *Turbulence in World Politics*.[4] In the last, autobiographical, chapter of *Distant Proximities*, I offer an explanation for the move, but it is far from a thorough explanation. The main reason set forth in that chapter is that I had become restless over the discrepancy between the way world politics seemed to be evolving and what I understood to be its foundations. A number of events seemed so contrary to my training in and grasp of the field that I started an "anomaly" file in which I put clippings about events for which I had no ready explanation. The anomaly file grew rapidly as the 1980s wore on and I decided it was time to go back to the drawing board and develop a new theoretical perspective that was not negated by the anomalies.

But this set of statements is hardly a full explanation. I can think of numerous reasons not mentioned in that chapter. A major one concerned a sense that I did not have the methodological skills – or was it fortitude? – to empirically implement the theoretical framework I had developed in the 1960s for comparing the foreign policies of different countries.[5] Several colleagues around the country were implementing the framework through the compilation of event data sets that, in turn, allowed for sophisticated quantitative analyses. In a sense, therefore, I felt free to follow the dictates of the anomaly file. In short, I experienced considerable intellectual growth.

AYDINLI: Would you say that there were any costs to this change to a non-mainstream position?

ROSENAU: Yes, I suppose you can say there were "costs" that attached to having broken with the orthodoxy and gone off in unexplored directions. I see myself as increasingly marginalized in the US political science and IR communities, as a bit too far out to be sought for conferences, speeches, papers, etc. I sense that my work is now appreciated more by people elsewhere in the world than in the United States. It would seem that colleagues abroad are less bound by our American orthodoxies and thus more ready to find merit in my explorations. The same might also be said about the work of Richard Ashley at Arizona State. I have the impression that his work is more often pondered abroad than here at home.

AYDINLI: As someone from elsewhere in the world, I might suggest that in the mainstream of North America, IR still tends to be exclusive of "other worlds" (the periphery as well as peripheral images of world politics). Since you do not represent that mainstream, you also do not fall into the trap of American-centrism. For this reason, among others, you are appreciated abroad where people seem to try and look at things in a more global perspective, or at least not in a US-centric one.

Going back to the first part of your comment, I wonder what you think are the primary reasons for your marginalization. Might it not come in part from the fact that your work in the 1990s does not seem to fall into a single, prominent, and clearly identifiable theoretical path? As students of IR, when we are introduced to IR theory we are presented generally with a categorized list that, with some variations, basically goes from realism to liberalism to Marxism, constructivism, and critical theory. We also see names of certain scholars clearly identified with these primary categories, the obvious ones being people like Waltz, Keohane, Wendt, and so on. But I wonder where you fit in these categories? Since you do not seem to clearly fall into any single one, it is perhaps to be expected that you would be less likely to be familiar to students. I also suspect that this instructional method of introducing these set categories and certain individuals within them provides a strong push for students to position themselves explicitly within a single theoretical category.

When I say that you do not seem to fit into any single category, I seem to be going along with your concluding self-assessment in the confessions chapter of being a bridge-builder, a position you say was reached after passing through an earlier position of single-minded "feistiness" (which we could equate with the newcomer's desire or feeling of being pressured to fit into a single category). You say that you are not sure whether it is possible for someone to skip the earlier stage. Which raises the question, is such a transformation purely a matter of socialization (you have to live it to experience it) or can mentoring ease or speed it along – essentially, can we guide students in a way that they can skip over the "single-minded" period and the need to find a niche? Should we? It seems like the beginning of an answer may lie in asking what the purpose of the "single-minded" period is; arguably, it is the emergent scholar's attempt to carve out a niche for him/herself. Perhaps the problem does stem in part from our training, which seems to teach that finding a niche (or even just discovering a gap in a literature review) is a process with a confrontational logic, involving the discrediting of others and the putting forth of something new and different.

ROSENAU: Once again you ask penetrating questions, though in some ways they are the same questions with the added dimension of whether a break with orthodoxy can be taught, whether it is possible to encourage and mentor one's students to be independent and venturesome. It is an excruciating question because, on the one hand, encouraging one's students to conform to the established orthodoxy is an anathema for me, but, on the other hand, one is reluctant to have them risk their careers because they listened to you and got set back because they broke with the prevailing orthodoxy prematurely. I had one very bright graduate student who came to the conclusion on his own that he could not and would not write the standard dissertation, with the result that he left graduate school. I regretted his decision because he was very gifted, but I also understood and did not try to talk him out of it. Conceivably, he might have stayed on, swallowed his pride (or, as a favorite colleague used to say, "risen above his principles"), and written a dissertation that minimally met the orthodox standards. I suppose that is always an alternative, but it is risky because one is never quite sure what the minimal standards are or whether they will still be in place when it is time to defend the dissertation.

AYDINLI: Perhaps the idea of bridging, synthesizing, and recognizing value in old ideas only comes as scholars themselves grow older!

ROSENAU: Does aging have anything to do with moving on? Probably so, though I do not recommend feeling constrained until one reaches their fifties or sixties. The process of moving on occurs subtly and slowly, perhaps facilitated by some positive feedback one gets after the initial move, as I did as a consequence of publishing my *Turbulence* book in 1990 when I was 66 years old. That work caused a stir because it offered a new systematic approach to grasping the underlying dynamics of world politics and seemed so relevant to the changes that followed the end of the Cold War. For a while it led to invitations to write papers that applied the turbulence model to particular situations. Encouraged by the favorable response to this book and building on the papers I subsequently wrote that extended the model, I was then led to writing *Along the Domestic–Foreign Frontier*, which came out in 1997.[6] So, looking back, in my case, it does seem that I became more innovative as I aged, though let me repeat that I do not recommend waiting until later in life before daring to depart from established modes of inquiry. If one has, as I like to put it, "a fire in one's belly" that can only be stoked by efforts to push back the frontiers of knowledge, there is every reason to rekindle or add fuel to it as one gains a sense of intellectual identity and security (and tenure!) in his or her thirties.

AYDINLI: Going back to the idea of developing a clear, single theoretical identity, I find it interesting to consider how one goes about doing this; obviously the act of citing others in our works is a clear way of identifying where we stand. As newcomers, it is like registering ourselves in a new neighborhood – citations acting as the code for the language among the members of that community. They not only tell others where you belong, but they may have practical implications as well since, for example, referees of journals, conferences, and grant submissions might look at them. We could assume that if a referee falls into the same community, your submission is more likely to get accepted. Or from the opposite side, I have seen in my recent experience as co-editor of a journal that some authors request their manuscripts not be sent to particular scholars – presumably those from other "communities."

ROSENAU: I did go through a confrontational stage with paragraphs and articles criticizing the proponents of the approaches and concepts that I found wanting. However, today I no longer need to confront other schools of thought and their devotees. In IR, for example, it has become standard to cite Kenneth Waltz either favorably or critically. I no longer cite him at all. Neither he nor Robert Keohane is in the list of authors in the index of the *Distant Proximities* book. I may be wrong in responding in this way, but my new perspectives have simply not yielded to a need to build on or reject earlier works. Of course, whenever earlier works contain findings or concepts that serve to enlarge what I am trying to say, I do cite and expand on them. Such citations, however, range widely beyond the IR mainstream as my grasp of the field has expanded to include work being done in the social sciences other than IR and political science.

AYDINLI: These last comments seem to support the idea that you are not a part of a single theoretical brotherhood. As a result, you do not need to "take an oath of membership" via citing certain works or ideas or trying to discredit others. Which brings me back to the bridge-builder identity. Why is it so hard to have a bridge-builder identity? Why do scholars seem to cling to a particular theoretical/methodological disciplinary identity and how can we free ourselves from these? Even those who oppose established dichotomies in IR seem themselves to have just created an alternative identity to emphatically espouse. It seems like there is a great deal of talk about building, consensus, compromise, yet very little action in that direction.

Examining my own experience, I always felt that the questions/issues I observed in real life experiences led me to the inquiries I pursued and that the nature of these inquiries determined the ways in which I would conduct them. Now I am feeling increasingly pushed into defending certain positions that I am not even sure I fully espouse, simply because they seem to be under an excessive reactionary attack. For example, consider certain broad theoretical positions. In my current work context, I find myself defending positivism against increasing numbers of colleagues who rather fervently expound post-modernist or post-positivist approaches.

Somewhat similar to this general theory-related dilemma is another that I find myself confronting particularly as an IR scholar from the periphery, namely, am I to be an importer of theories or should I strive to be a creator of theories out of my indigenous context? Predominantly I see colleagues taking the first route – an issue that has received some discussion in the literature, including in an article I co-authored.[7] These colleagues basically adopt the latest or most fashionable theoretical trend and set up a local franchise. It seems to be a pragmatic choice – the ingredients and menu are set, so to speak, as are the customers. Choosing the indigenous theory-creation route seems the more challenging – both intellectually and practically. It rules out the ease of having an obvious starting literature from which to proceed methodologically or of having obvious journals to which to send your works, and therefore seems to render you less competitive against the importers. Perhaps the most distressing aspect of this problem, both personally and from the perspective of knowledge accumulation in the discipline, is that I know there are scholars throughout the periphery who are choosing not to join the franchisers. I have met people like this from India, Russia, China, and Finland just to name a few. But they, we, are too dispersed, or perhaps simply too unaware of each other's existence, to recognize the possibility of coming together in a collectivity which might have more influence. For now, the importing route remains the dominant one, and, at least in the Turkish case, this trend seems unlikely to change in the short run. There are the practical reasons for importing theories, but there are also socially related issues for doing so in the periphery such as the dominance of the elite in the local IR discipline and their familiarity – and subsequent attraction – with things foreign.

In considering these various dilemmas and how ultimately I will choose my way among them, I, of course, wonder whether you have ever experienced unease with the routes you chose or the positions you chose to assume, and have you ever felt any pressures to go a certain way?

ROSENAU: Since I turned away from orthodoxy I have not once experienced unease about the turn. The pressures are all now within me. The fire in my belly burns too furiously to be anxious about the departure from orthodoxy. Indeed, it is that very fire that allows me to resist pressures to, as you put it, "go a certain way."

AYDINLI: Let me interrupt for a second. I wonder if this attributing of all the pressures to coming from within is because of your position as a senior scholar. It seems that for the newcomer the pressures come from outside. The more senior scholar may have a greater freedom to no longer care about the outside.

ROSENAU: As I have already indicated, you are correct: being older and more secure provides a freedom to go one's own way, or at least a freedom not to adhere to established ways. But there is more to it than that. This process also involves the development of some basic intellectual convictions that evolve with time and experience. In my case these convictions, this fire in my belly, add up to a desire, perhaps even a compulsion, to demonstrate that it is possible to clarify the human condition through social scientific analysis. Social scientists share this conviction, but a broad swath of publics everywhere is either not familiar with or antagonistic to the notion that people can be studied systematically. My social science is not conventional, but it is social science and not merely naval gazing. I see myself as a theorist who values empirical materials and their validation. For me, theory involves generalization about one or another process or institution that sustains one or another aspect of world politics; by empirical materials I mean what I call "observables," those data that are descriptive of how the processes or institutions operate.

With regard to building bridges, let me say that it is hard to do and rarely happens because most scholars are so fully rooted in their paradigms that, in effect, they are incarcerated in conceptual jails and have no interest in finding escape routes (see Chapter 2 in my *Turbulence* book for an elaboration of this point; it is called "Justifying Jailbreaks"). A good example is evident in my occasional involvement in efforts to collaborate with economists. Most of them seem to have no or little interest in collaboration because (a) they have their own paradigm that lacks a need for political variables and (b) they cannot advance (or at least they think they are unable to) in their fields by going outside and working and publishing with colleagues in the other social sciences.

But despite these problems I have managed to build a few bridges. In addition to forming close working relationships with sociologists and psychologists, early in my career I edited a large book of readings (some fifty reprinted articles and a few original pieces) that served as a bridge by drawing widely on the social sciences and that for years enjoyed considerable success.[8] It can fairly be said, I think, that a whole generation of IR graduate students were assigned this reader in their first year of graduate study and I still encounter people high in government and academe who say, in effect, "I am glad to meet you and put a face to a memory. I read (and suffered with) your reader way back in graduate school." Unfortunately three decades later the publisher let the book go out of print and thus most of those in today's generation do not know of its existence. More recently, I was among the founders of the Globalization Studies Network, which is, in effect, a consortium of globalization centers and which encompasses some thirty-five centers from a wide variety of countries in all parts of the world. The Network is an excellent example of a bridge!

In sum, it follows that while you may still be a newcomer, I urge you to resist the pressures of colleagues, either the pressures that push you to yield to their ways or those that encourage you to opt for approaches which need defense. It sounds trite, but the best way is to be yourself intellectually, wherever that may lead you.

On being a "pre-post modernist"

AYDINLI: Turning to more specific elements of your own personal journey in the formation of methodological identity – an aspect of our overall professional development that I think is extremely important – I would like to ask about your self definition as a pre-post modernist in your most recent book. First, correct me if I am wrong, but in trying to understand your conceptualization of pre-post modernism, it seems to involve:

a relaxing the structures of parsimony (a step away from a "scientific" or what we could call a positivist approach),

b a commitment to moving from subjective to intersubjective understandings that can allow for consensus (a step away from post-modernists), and

c the idea that all research is value-laden so we must be explicit about the values that guide what we are doing.

I should admit from the start that I am somewhat uneasy with the title of the chapter that says it is the "confessions of a pre-post modernist." To me this gives the impression that you have changed dramatically, crossing (somewhat ashamedly) from a "positivist" position to a "nearly" post-modernist one (with the implication that you may someday move on to the "full" post-modernist position). This understanding is further encouraged when you say that you went through a "major transformation" – the presumption being that said transformation was from a positivist/scientific position to an almost post-modernist one. But as I was reading the chapter – and as I read more about your calls for bridge-building – I began to wonder whether it might not be misleading to apply a label to yourself that implies you are at least moving toward a particular (post-modernist) position rather than finding a term that either (a) more directly reflects how you have developed the old position or (b) reflects something truly new (bridging).

The bridging you speak of appears to be built on two primary concepts: explicitness (which is undervalued by many positivists) and intersubjectivity (which is undervalued or dismissed by many post-modernists/positivists). Given that this new position seems to truly identify the key strengths and weaknesses of both primary approaches (and thus proposes a bridging), do you feel the terminology you use to define pre-post modernism adequately expresses this bridging ideal?

Overall you provide enough critical comments about post-modernism (for example, your description of post-modernists becoming "rigid and ideological" in their rejection of behavioral approaches) and you do not reject positivistic, "scientific" ideals (for example, when you seem to argue that one can remain scientific while still recognizing that there is no such thing as purely objective inquiry), leading the reader to question your "pre-post modernism" title. Is it really reflective of who you are? And, do you think that post-modernists would accept this title for you? Do you think they might consider you a wolf in sheep's clothing?

ROSENAU: Your insights are well taken, except that your comments tend to be overreactions to the label I used. In my mind I used the "pre-post modern" label as a spoof, as a way of suggesting that I fall shy of being a post-modernist without dismissing their insights entirely. More than that, I suppose I wanted to resort to spoof in order to imply that some observers were too quick to pick up on new labels. The speed with which many analysts dismissed "positivism" bothered me because it seemed so anti-empirical. In retrospect, my spoofing only compounded the problem and thus it is NOT an approach I would use again. If my label is misleading, I do regret it, as I certainly do not see myself as moving toward post-modern perspectives.

But you are right in highlighting my commitment to explicitness and intersubjectivity. For me, focusing on these is what the game of research is all about. There is no other if one wants to comprehend the human condition. Knowledge in the social sciences cumulates as investigators make explicit the values, concepts, and methods that underlie their formulations and findings, thus enabling others to evaluate the formulations and findings and serving either as the basis of an emergent intersubjective consensus or as results that are not widely accepted and fail to enlarge understanding. That is the main reason that I included my confessions chapter in *Distant Proximities*. Some might see the chapter as overly egotistic, but I see it as living by the commitment to explicitness. It is true that all too few analysts proceed in this way. One is hard pressed to find a book, or even a paragraph, in which the author sets forth the personal background factors underlying his or her work. Come to think of it, I cannot think of any that do this, though it should be a standard procedure to have at least a paragraph in a preface that tells the reader where the author is coming from.

Put differently, I am convinced that intersubjectivity is the only way knowledge accumulates because we do not want subjective interpretations and we cannot obtain objective ones. So we have to settle for those findings, insights, and formulations that thoughtful observers buy into, thus giving rise to a consensus about the ideas or findings involved. This is the reason why we do research and publish: to contribute to the ongoing research on a subject, or to revise it with our findings, or to demonstrate it is erroneous. Knowledge-building is in this sense fundamentally a social process. (As J. Robert Oppenheimer once said, "gossip is the life blood of physics!") Of course, a field can have competing intersubjective consensuses, and in fact most fields do. Such is the nature of knowledge, an ever-evolving series of competing consensuses. To be sure, the adherents of the various paradigms aspire to enlarging their ranks by winning over adherents of the competing paradigms. In this sense the competition among the various consensuses can, at best, be a constructive method of knowledge-building even as it can also, at worst, get vicious and counterproductive.

AYDINLI: I could not agree more. Indeed, I would wager that if such an understanding were the most widespread or common one in our discipline, newcomers would feel a great deal more secure in the face of the many difficult choices I cited earlier. Your definition of intersubjectivity is inclusive enough to allow for the further growth of a sensible mainstream, yet exclusive enough not to let marginal elements confuse the general principles of scholarship and inquiry. I would say that for newcomers it is a tremendously useful image of social science inquiry in general.

Also, in terms of your attempts at explicitness in your confessions chapter, I firmly believe in its value. I think it is worthwhile for us all to take a moment to consider the effect explicitness has on our reading of a particular scholar's works when we first get the opportunity to meet that scholar in person. I was very much influenced during my graduate studies when, for example, Alexander Wendt and Stephen Krasner joined in as guests at our graduate seminars at McGill. After listening to and meeting them, there was no doubt but that our classroom discussions of their works went in different and, I believe, more insightful directions. For better or for worse, it became virtually impossible to read those scholars' works again in the same way as we did when they were just a name, affiliation, and a list of research interests or previous publications. Of course, the latter may provide us with subtle clues about certain aspects of the author's identity, but nothing on the scale of a face-to-face meeting or an explicit attempt by the author at open self-reflection or self-identification.

This experience suggests to me that perhaps we should consider a disciplinary movement to encourage our members to develop and expand the currently accepted genre of the "author's bio note" into something more revealing and explicit than simply affiliation and research interests. I would like to see, for example, some indication of the author's past history, such as where they have worked and lived. Has the author remained all of his or her life in one place? Did s/he take a break along the educational path to join the Peace Corps, live abroad, or work in a different field? I think it would also be valuable to know about some of the author's non-professional affiliations or interests. Of course, it would be up to the individual author to determine how many or which of these affiliations to provide, but even that choice would be revealing to the readers and help them interpret the content of the text. In other words, reading that someone belongs to Amnesty International or the Nature Conservancy may not reveal the full "truth" about that person if they also choose to omit that they are a member of a more conservative political party, but it does at least provide us insights into the identity the author likes to put forth to others. Going beyond the author bio could provide valuable information if the authors were encouraged in their texts to indicate how they came to choose the research topic or particular questions they investigate. Was it simply a personal interest or were there pragmatic issues involved such as a possible future grant? Was the topic of global or current scholarly interest or something sparked by a dinner table conversation?

Returning once more to your confessions chapter, you ultimately conclude that all groups' methodologies are essentially the same – they all "share a readiness to proceed explicitly as they probe whatever problems of world politics they deem significant."[9] Do you think this belief in everyone's readiness to be explicit could be an over-optimistic one?

ROSENAU: You are right, I was overly optimistic, as can be readily inferred from my previous comment. I suppose my bridge-building impulses underlay the optimism, as if one can focus on the areas of convergence and avoid those of divergence. Clearly, however, I am wrong in this regard. As I understand some post-modernists, for example, the background of the author is irrelevant. Indeed, so is the author, since according to this perspective what counts is the text.

Personal and disciplinary transformations

AYDINLI: I have always seen you as a scholar of change who happens to specialize in world politics. It strikes me as a pity that we do not even have a subsection in the International Studies Association (ISA) with a focus on change. Do you think such a section would be useful? Would you find such a labeling of yourself an appropriate one, or could you recommend a better one?

ROSENAU: Yes, I accept the label. Change is the central condition of our times and, thus, it is a more accurate label than any other that I can think of. My faltering memory tells me that there may have once been a proposal for an ISA section that focused on "transformation," but I do not know what came of it. I do know that the American Political Science Association has a section on Ecological and Transformation Politics and I applaud any effort to create such a section in ISA. It would surely help to call attention to the field's prime dynamics.

AYDINLI: On the whole, how accepted a concept do you find transformation to be in IR? How open-minded do you think we are; are we still very much trapped in conceptual jails?

ROSENAU: It is my impression that the concepts of change and transformation are neither widely accepted nor widely used in IR (and political science too). I believe the reason is that many do, indeed, remain trapped in conceptual jails that do not include propositions allowing for change. That is a primary weakness of the realist paradigm, but it is also true of other approaches. So we may be open-minded, but our tools curb our ability to express our imaginations and to become committed to theoretical and empirical innovation.

AYDINLI: I suppose it is important to note that change does occur, but could we also say perhaps that change is slower than it should be? In a discipline like IR, more so than in most other disciplines, we are issue-bound; we need to try and understand things as they happen. Even potentially radical historic changes can happen rapidly. There is, as a result, a heavy burden on the shoulders of IR scholars to develop our scholarly response to these changes in an equally rapid manner. Of course, I am not suggesting that we turn our theoretical analyses entirely into event-based policy discussions, but it seems undeniable that, particularly in the current era, the traditional time lapse between events and the scholarly study of those events has shrunk. When the world around us is rapidly changing, there are bound to be problems if we maintain the basic instinct to stick resolutely to traditional approaches and theories or even issues stemming from our earlier disciplinary socialization. One need only consider the obvious example of recent years: before we had wrapped up conclusively our attempts to understand the end of the Cold War, we had to turn to exploring and debating the significance of September 11.

You, of course, have certainly not been one to shy away from change and transformation. Considering the routes you ultimately have taken, you have identified the need to be different as a key element directing your transformations as a scholar. Related to this "need," at least twice in your confessions chapter you differentiate yourself from the "norm:"

> ... the assumption that turning points in one's intellectual development are largely responses to climactic moments in world affairs does not apply in my case.[10]

From post-modern and post-structural perspectives, scientists deceive themselves as well as their audiences when they cast their results in the language of established facts. There is truth in this line of reasoning – except in my case it does not hold.[11]

I wonder two things. First, do you think this need to be different is unique? I recall a colleague once telling me how she asked a class of Turkish graduate students studying cultural issues whether they considered themselves "typical" Turks; not a single one of them said yes. So, if it is true that there is possibly a common desire to be different (or, at the least, not to be "just another mainstream IR scholar"), how does this relate to the contradictory idea that the vast majority cling to "established ideas"? Second, going back to the issue of a need to be different, do you see any risks in such a self-admitted need when it comes to one's academic inquiry?

ROSENAU: My guess is that the need to be different is confined to a few analysts. And sometimes I think it is a dangerous tendency. To be different for the sake of being different is as rigid as the inclination not to be innovative. On occasion, at those times when I feel insecure about a new formulation, I worry this may be true of me and I try to contest the need to be different by endlessly asking myself whether I am saying or writing this sentence or paragraph just to be different, merely to shock the conventional among us. There is pleasure to be had in challenging and shocking people in the mainstream, but it is essentially a transitory and counterproductive pleasure. It takes one's eyes off the main goal of expanding our understanding of how the world works.

The risks for me personally are not very great, partly because few will probably read my confessions chapter and partly because I am too near the end of my career and too set in my ways for such risks to be relevant. For younger scholars, however, the risks may well be considerable, especially if the need to be different leads them to absurd intellectual perspectives (indeed, this may be the case for some post-modernists).

AYDINLI: I am curious as to which intellectual perspectives you are referring to when you say "absurd," especially with respect to post-modernists.

ROSENAU: I have in mind those who ignore the virtues of being explicit and value merely giving voice to their subjective perspectives without labeling them as such.

AYDINLI: Do you think this need to be different is the major source for your being always "ahead of others" – something I believe John Ruggie once said about you?

ROSENAU: Wow, now there is a tough question! John is very kind, but I am not sure whether I have moved ahead or fallen behind others. If it is the former, I am reluctant to ascribe it to a psychological need rather than a set of intellectual insights – or at least I am reluctant to admit as much. But let me say, doubtless psychological dynamics are at work in all of us. I have just been a little more willing to acknowledge them, or perhaps a little more willing to speak about what underlies my intellectual commitments.

AYDINLI: And do you really accept the assumption that IR scholars' intellectual turning points correspond to turning points in world affairs?

ROSENAU: I know I made such a statement in my intellectual autobiography that is Chapter 19 in *Distant Proximities*, but on second thought that may be inaccurate. Our conceptual jails tend to be too well constructed to allow turning points in world affairs to upend them. Turning points in world affairs do give pause and some (like September 11) may lead to revised thinking about the dynamics that sustain the course of events. But such revisions usually lead to re-affirmations of the existing paradigms with new wrinkles or qualifications. I am really not sure of all the factors that led me to turn in new directions. To revert to the earlier metaphor, I guess the fire in my belly became a wildfire that expanded across new terrain. In addition, as I have already indicated, the anomaly file was surely part of it and a sense that existing paradigms were insufficient was also an important motivator.

AYDINLI: Still on the subject of change, you describe your 1997 book *Along the Domestic–Foreign Frontier* as stressing the idea that a frontier has been created where the domestic and foreign converge; this concept seems a follow up on your earlier linkage politics arguments – so to what extent does that particular move on your part represent continuity or change in your research inquiries?

ROSENAU: I have always felt that the unifying theme of all my work is the overlaps, links, connections – whatever they may be called – between domestic and foreign affairs. My 1969 edited book on *Linkage Politics* may seem to be the origin of this line of thinking,[12] but actually it is first manifest in the 1963 paper I wrote entitled "Pre-Theories and Theories of Foreign Policy" that was published in 1966 in a book edited by R. Barry Farrell. That may be the best essay I have ever written. It still serves to organize my thinking about foreign policy. And I believe it may do the same for more than a few others.

AYDINLI: On the same general issue, why do you think that IR as a discipline remains so insistent on keeping the distinction between domestic and foreign?

ROSENAU: Because the state is still regarded as the prime and dominant entity in world affairs and, thus, the discipline is organized along the lines of that distinguishing feature. Moreover, these are the same lines around which governments are organized. All states have agencies or departments devoted to domestic problems and others devoted to foreign problems, thereby giving rise to interagency committees rather than wholesale governmental reorganization that allows for the overlap of the two central domains of national and societal life. The new US Department of Homeland Security may be a portent of change in the direction of agencies that embrace both domestic and foreign challenges.

AYDINLI: Your writings, by being rooted in transformation and in the "proposition that these transformations continue to unfold," give the impression of work with an unending, unreachable destination. We are left to trace the paths of these transformations, but by the time we catch a glimpse of some result, the "current reality" has already changed. It is like looking at a star and knowing that the light we are seeing left the star so many years ago that in fact the star itself may no longer even exist. So, what do you see as the biggest challenges for one who focuses his/her research agenda on transformation?

ROSENAU: Yes, our endeavors involve striving for unreachable goals. But that ought not be off-putting. There is pleasure to be derived from continuing the quest even if one knows it can never be adequately realized. In the nature of things, knowledge is transitory, endlessly evolving, endlessly shifting emphases, as the intersubjective consensuses undergo transformation; for me, that is a major reason why its pursuit is so exciting. The biggest challenge of such a commitment is conceding that the task has no end and realizing that the quick obsolescence of knowledge means our contributions will be fleeting and only briefly meaningful. Few are the scholars whose contributions continue to have consequence once they are no longer probing and their lives come to an end. Karl Deutsch, for example, was a major figure in IR because his publications were so innovative, but he is rarely cited today and doubtless few in the younger generation have even heard of him, much less read his writings.

AYDINLI: On the same topic, but going back to your decision to label yourself as a "pre-post modernist," I wonder if you see any relation between your inquiries focusing on issues that are constantly in the process of taking shape and a possible frustration with observation methods that seem incapable – due perhaps to conceptual time lags or even just practical problems such as dissemination procedures – of keeping up with the pace of change. Could such a potential clash have led you to feel that you can never really catch up with the transformations you seek to understand, and thus post-modernism expresses better the frustrated feeling that may result? Basically, could the elusiveness of the subject have led you in any way to a certain methodological positioning?

ROSENAU: I have already said that the pre-post modernist label was essentially a spoof. But the elusiveness of the subject does lead me often to ponder the question of how we can develop a methodology capable of capturing the complex, nonlinear nature of IR today. I think the answer lies in agent-based modeling through computer simulations, but I fear I am too old to tool up in this regard. The most I can do – and I do try – is to impress upon students the need to tool up in the computer sciences. Most are reluctant and reject the advice (indeed, many come into IR in order to get away from mathematics and computational science), but a few have bought into the idea in recent years with compelling results.

For years now, in every seminar I teach I have students read M. Mitchell Waldrop's *Complexity* as their first assignment,[13] and I tell them that reading the book will change them!! The book tells a remarkable and provocative story and discussions of it are usually extremely exciting and eye-opening. At one level it tells the story of the Santa Fe Institute and its founders, distinguished leaders in various disciplines who managed to develop a new theory that offers insights into the meaning of life and the underpinnings of our complex world today. In so doing, at another, more abstract level, it raises profound and provocative philosophical issues that bear on world politics as well as many other dimensions of the human condition. Little wonder, then, that each semester a few of the students become so enamored of complexity theory that in fact they do change their orientations and, in some instances, their curriculum!

AYDINLI: The question "of what is this an instance?" which you often raise in your presentations at seminars and conferences seems to be the only constant for you; why do you think that is? Is there a chance that your methodological identity lies in this question and, if so, how would you describe the identity that it suggests?

ROSENAU: Yes, that question is a constant for me. It not only dominates my intellectual inquiries, but it also pervades my personal life – riding elevators, walking streets, eating in restaurants, observing strangers, to mention only some of the settings in which I ask about what I observe "of what is this an instance?" So, yes, it is my methodological identity. Its prime virtue is that in asking the question about whatever one observes one is driven to climb up the ladder of abstraction in order to find a larger category into which to classify what one has just seen. This exercise is the route to theory, a route that I enjoy traversing. I view the higher rungs of the ladder of abstraction as the locations where the interesting questions and phenomena lie, whether they are in our personal or professional life. It is on the higher rungs that the mind comes alive, which is not to denigrate the lower rungs where empirical materials are found. Perhaps some people have their minds come alive at the lower rungs, but I find the rarified air at the top of the ladder exhilarating.

AYDINLI: I know I speak not only for myself but for others who have had the opportunity to work with you, when I say that your question "of what is this an instance?" is a great contribution to teaching and research. It gives a clear starting point in the mess of world politics. It offers us something to cling to. I think that regardless of one's stage of disciplinary socialization, when you're perplexed, asking a good methodological question like this one allows us or guides us to ask good research questions.

Another phrase, or in this case a word, that I often associate with you is "checkableupable." In your confessions chapter you relate being "checkable-upable" to being explicit, which you say is "at the heart of science"[14] Throughout the piece you talk about relaxing your "scientificness" but you remain loyal to "checkableupableness." The latter term seems scientific to me, what does it mean to you?

ROSENAU: There is no contradiction whatever between the two concepts. I argue that we need to relax our criteria of parsimony, not that we should give up on being scientific. The *Turbulence* (1990) book contends that the mounting complexity of world affairs requires us to loosen our criteria rather than cling to just a few (as realism does). Thus, for example, I write about eight major sources of globalization in the *Distant Proximities* book, but I am not prepared to suggest there are hundreds or even a dozen – that would be carrying relaxation too far. An encyclopedic enumeration of variables is as

counterproductive as an excessively parsimonious one. "Checkableupableness" is my way of calling attention to the need for explicitness. That is what
the term means to me.

AYDINLI: What is so magical about eight major sources? Why would a dozen be
too many? How does one know when to stop enumerating relevant variables?

ROSENAU: It may sound evasive, but one stops identifying the crucial variables
when the mind comes to rest, which is another way of saying that one stops
when one is persuaded that the identified variables account for most of the
variance one's theory seeks to explain. Given the complexity of world politics, it is highly doubtful that one's comprehension of IR is so creative and
thorough that one can account for one hundred percent of the variance. So
there is nothing magical or mystical about the number of variables one
comes to regard as crucial. To repeat, one stops when one is confident that
the interaction of the specified major variables account for most of what
drives the course of events.

In attempting to probe the dynamics of globalization, I stopped at eight
variables because each of them is operative in every country of the world.
There are crucial issues high on the global agenda – such as nuclear proliferation – that surely need to be investigated, but they are not relevant to
policymaking in every country. But the eight variables do meet the every-
country criterion. These are fully elaborated in Chapter 3 of my *Distant
Proximities*. They consist of what I call the skill revolution; the organizational
explosion; authority crises; the bifurcation of global structures; technologies
that have shrunk time and distance; the mobility upheaval; the weakening of
states, territory, and sovereignty; and the shift to neo-classical economic policies. Some of these are central to the turbulence formulation that I developed
in the late 1980s, but it was not until I subsequently became preoccupied with
the dynamics of globalization in the mid-1990s that I began to bring the
eight together as the basis for an over-arching theoretical framework.

AYDINLI: Speaking of the *Turbulence in World Politics* book, you once said that you
consider it your most important book. Where were you in your methodological positioning when you were writing this book? Would the result have
been different if you were writing it now? Would it still be your best book?

ROSENAU: By the time I started writing that book I had moved on from a commitment to a very strict scientific approach. Indeed, as I have already said, in
the second chapter of that book I argued for the need to relax our criterion of
parsimony. As for it still being my best book, I think it is for several reasons,
not the least being that *Turbulence* turned out to be the first in a trilogy, though
the second, *Along the Domestic–Foreign Frontier* and the third, *Distant Proximities*,
were not planned to be sequels. Only in retrospect do they loom as a trilogy,
with the continuity being that, unbeknown to me at the time, they succes-
sively narrow in on micro actors and probe the ways in which individuals at
the micro level shape, and are shaped by, collectivities at the macro level. So
Turbulence seems important partly because it turns out to be innovative and
creative through the framing of a variety of new and (I think) important

concepts (such as a bifurcated world, the skill revolution, and the relevance of pervasive authority crises), but also because it paved the way for the two books that followed. There are a couple of lesser points I would change in *Turbulence* if the publishers would agree to a revised edition (which they will not because it still sells fourteen years later). On balance, though, I would not alter the prime thrusts of the book. Indeed, developments since 1990 have more than affirmed the core of the turbulence model. In the last fifteen years, for example, individuals as migrants, terrorists, and mobilized activists have become increasingly conspicuous on the world stage. Likewise, the global stage has become increasingly crowded with a huge number and variety of non-governmental organizations that have pressed governments into adopting new perspectives and policies, thus highlighting the ever-greater relevance of bifurcated global structures, much as the turbulence model anticipated. So yes, I still regard it as my best book, though I am also very proud of those that followed.

AYDINLI: Perhaps one final methodological question, you refer in your confessions chapter in *Distant Proximities* to a paper on the fiftieth anniversary of the UN in which your of what is this an instance question sounds like it emphasizes an historical approach.[15] Yet this is something you do not often do in your work it seems. Have you ever been "accused" of an apparent ahistorical perspective? What do you think about such an argument?

ROSENAU: Yes, I have often been accused of being ahistorical, especially by several of the essays in the book Heidi Hobbs edited entitled *Pondering Postinternationalism*.[16] And there is some truth to the charge. Its reality derives from two sources: (a) my reading of history is limited and (b) I think analysts are much too quick to explain events and trends as part of historical patterns. The second reason may be a function of the first, I suppose, but I have long developed an elaborate conviction that historical analogies (and, after all, that is all that historical explanations of current patterns are) can be very misleading, that the variables at work in previous eras may not be at work in the present or they may operate differently. It has always seemed to me, for example, that the US intervention in Vietnam was founded on the premise that since such an intervention worked in Korea, a similar outcome could be expected in Vietnam, an analogy that clearly proved to be inaccurate. Stated more generally, in order to apply the lessons of history, one needs a theory of when a lesson is applicable and when it is not. But as far as I know, such a theory of history's lessons does not exist, thus inhibiting any attempt to meaningfully ransack history for relevant lessons. Of course, if by chance one develops a theory of history's lessons, its premises should be made explicit, a task that staggers the imagination.

AYDINLI: This conversation has been genuinely fascinating for me, hearing the details about and gaining insights regarding the various stages and turning points in your academic career to date. Even more interesting to me is the impression I have that the changes you have made have been part of a smooth – rather than tumultuous or terribly painful – process of transformation. Your ability to do this perhaps seems smooth because of what I see as one of your remarkable traits, namely, the ability to avoid becoming entrenched in the jails of a single paradigmatic or methodological identity (a trap that proves comforting to so many scholars), but rather to remain open to change and innovation. Your scholarly identity seems directed at an ideal of "good" scholarship that remains unbounded by particular questions, ways of asking them, or ways of answering them. Your example can certainly provide encouragement to newcomers in the discipline who may be feeling pressured into unwanted identities or lost because they do not seem to fit into a singular identity. It seems appropriate to end by asking what we might expect next from you on your never-ending transformative journey?

ROSENAU: That question has been very much on my mind of late. The answer has two dimensions, one practical and the other intensely personal. The practical dimension includes three unfinished projects. One is a quantitative study of how American leaders contribute to and are shaped by the dynamics of globalization that several colleagues and I have undertaken. This topic has yet to be systematically explored. We have written and expect to publish a book entitled *On the Cutting Edge of Globalization: An Inquiry into American Elites.*[17] After finishing *Distant Proximities* I started writing a book entitled *People Count.* I wrote some seven chapters, but then got diverted to other projects and have yet to be moved to return to it. I am also attempting to compile a two-volume collection of my essays that have not been published or have appeared in more obscure journals.

This last project involves looking back and highlights some very personal considerations. At some point one has to face the question of whether what seems like a never-ending journey is, in fact, coming to an end and, if so, when to acknowledge that it is over. I have often said I wanted to follow the example of Ted Williams, perhaps one of the greatest baseball players of the twentieth century. In March of 1960, after a career of 19 years, Williams announced that the coming season would be his last. Most ball players do not stop until their talent declines to the point where their services are no longer sought. But Williams announced that the 1960 season was his last and, then, on the last day of that season at his last at bat hit a home run! That is a model for me because I do not want to keep writing and researching if the quality of my work declines. I want my last paper or book to be the social science equivalent of a home run. Thus, I need to pause and ponder how to proceed from here into the future. I am dominated by the realization that not much time remains even as it would be good to use what is left in the most constructive way I can and that requires some heavy thinking.

Part III

Methods

10 Comparison is a state of mind[1]

Let me start by emphasizing that comparison is as much a state of mind, a predisposition, an impulse, as it is a method. What is involved is an interest in recurring patterns at rather abstract levels. If one has a comparative state of mind, instead of asking how various things converge to produce a certain set of outcomes in a given society, one asks what are the similarities and differences between this outcome and this process in this situation as against an outcome and a process in another situation. The comparative impulse predisposes one to look for similarities and differences across cases. The presence of the comparative impulse is signified by the kinds of questions one considers. If one is only interested in how at a moment in time, or at a place in space, things converge to produce a given outcome, one does not have a comparative state of mind.

Some of us in political science and IR have gone off the deep end in this regard, driven (some might say distracted) by the comparative state of mind to seeking out recurring patterns across 130 nations. Indeed, we have formed one of the more interesting organizations in which I have ever had the pleasure of participating, the Inter-University Comparative Foreign Policy Project, otherwise known as the ICFP. It began early in 1967, has since held five conferences, has consisted of members from ten different universities, and has somehow still managed to persist. ICFP has been the vehicle for two books and some 100 papers.[2] It has yielded some 145 hypotheses for which empirical data are now available. It has even contributed to the advent of a yearbook for foreign policy studies.[3] It has a history recorded through 1972[4] and subsequently continued to grow as a community of scholars interested in comparing foreign policies.

The ICFP is reminiscent of Kuhn's description of a normal science in that this group of scholars spend their time elaborating upon and refuting each others' hypotheses and findings concerning foreign policy behavior across a number of systems. At its heart is a commitment to tough, hard empirical data, especially those types of data that have come to be called events data. Several events-data sets relevant to the comparative study of foreign policy have been created, one at Ohio State, another at USC, another at North Carolina, and still another at Syracuse. All of them involve a reconstruction, on a day-by-day basis, of what nations do with respect to other nations, based upon global sources like *The New York Times* or *The Times* (London) as well as several regional sources. I am not sure whether specialists in Communist systems are aware of these data sets, but if they are not, I commend them to your attention for your own possible use. You will find that all of them contain data on the daily international behavior of a number of Communist countries.

The ICFP is not an empire-building group. Its members do not want to convert colleagues. They long ago came to appreciate that conversion is neither desirable nor possible. They are interested only in unraveling the mysteries of foreign policy and building on each other's studies. There is, however, some annoyance at the progress that the ICFP has enjoyed; it stems from a regrettable tendency toward intellectual conflict between those who tend to be specialists in an area and those who are impelled by a comparative state of mind. To be sure, some area specialists are also comparativists, but many are not. That need not be the case. They can engage in comparisons within their area of specialization. Alternatively, they can undertake case studies in such a way that others can use each case as one among many. Those who write case studies in Communist affairs thus ought to try to converge upon common problems and common variables so that others, either in the area or outside it, can use the variety of case studies for comparative purposes.

I have asked myself what one who thinks of himself as a student of comparative foreign policy can say that might be useful to one who is a student of the Communist world. This, in turn, leads to three questions: Why compare the foreign policies of Communist societies? What variables might a student of comparative foreign policy be interested in if he is also interested in Communist systems? If students of Communist politics have a comparative state of mind, what variables might be of interest to them? I think the answer to all three of these questions is roughly the same. One compares the foreign policy of Communist systems because there are characteristics of such systems that can be clarified by comparing their behavior. That is, certain variables are central to Communist systems which can be better grasped through observing their operation in several such systems, and which, if this is accomplished, can serve the intellectual interests of both the student of comparative Communism and the student of comparative foreign policy. Three such variables come quickly to mind. One is ideology, since it remains static for some countries and varies for others. Another variable is one-party rule, in which one looks for commonalities and differences across different authoritarian systems marked by one-party rule. The third variable could be that of East European culture, wherein one compares the Communist states of that region with other Communist states that do not have a common geographic locale and shared historical experiences. To be sure, East European cultures are marked by diversity, but a distinction can nonetheless be drawn in terms of geography and history compared with Africa or Asia.

It is useful to ask students of the Communist world – even those who do not have a comparative state of mind, but would be interested in seeing where it might lead – what kind of variables are of interest? My test for the appropriateness of a variable would be to play a mental game along the following lines: If you want to test your interest in ideology as a variable, ask yourself whether the idea of comparing, say, Bulgaria and Cuba along other dimensions excites your imagination and whets your theoretical appetite. If your answer is that this is really a dull question, then ideology is not a variable that interests you. At least to an outsider it would seem that if you are interested in the potency of ideological considerations as dynamics in the foreign policy of Communist systems, the idea of comparing Bulgaria and Cuba would be a very legitimate one. If it does not seem very central to you, but if the idea of comparing Bulgaria and Romania *does*, then your interest would seem to be in cultural variables – those having to do with Eastern Europe, making Bulgaria and Rumania more worth comparing than Bulgaria and Cuba. For myself, I would want to find out the relative strengths of different variables in different systems. The advent of a Communist regime in Cuba or China is, from a comparative perspective, a great event. It allows one to see what happens when one relaxes cultural variables.

Such a mental game yields an answer to the question of whether there is more to be gained from comparing the foreign policy systems of Communist states than from comparing Communist states with non-Communist states. My impulse is that it would be preferable to start out, not by comparing Communist and non-Communist systems, but by comparing the inputs and outputs of the former on the grounds that in this way one can hold a number of important variables constant and thus develop more incisive analyses.

11 CFP and IPE

The anomaly of mutual boredom[1]

Anomalies are not always easy to identify. Usually, to be sure, their occurrence is so startling that we immediately sit up and take notice, acknowledging quickly that the anomaly is surprising, that it simply does not fit into our understanding of how things work. Sometimes, however, anomalous dynamics evolve incrementally, creep up on us as it were, and it is only in retrospect that we are surprised to find things have not been unfolding as we thought they did. The anomaly discussed here is of this latter, incremental kind. Stated most succinctly, it is the puzzle of why the rapidly growing emphasis on international political economy (IPE) as an organizing focus for political scientists has had virtually no impact on the systematic or comparative study of foreign policy (CFP) and, indeed, why the latter has apparently been so irrelevant to the former.

This lack of interaction between the two subfields is all the more surprising when one appreciates that both share a focus on the convergence of national and international systems: just as IPE inquires into the dynamics wherein production cycles and trade practices within domestic economies are both sources of and responses to global monetary patterns, so is CFP centrally concerned with how external and internal factors interact to shape the foreign policies of states. Yet their common preoccupation with the overlap of national and international phenomena has not drawn the two subfields together. Why? What keeps the two intellectual traditions so isolated from each other and their practitioners so bored with each other's work? Indeed, why has the isolation and mutual boredom not been recognized as an anomaly worthy of exploration?[2]

Retrospective surprise

One way of breaking into the problem is to look back to the beginnings of CFP in the 1960s and ask what subsequent developments in world affairs would have been surprising to the early practitioners. Five such developments stand out (though doubtless many more could be enumerated) and assuming the reader agrees that we would have rejected, or at least scoffed at, predictions of these developments several decades ago, four of them serve to highlight a growing sensitivity to change even as the fifth calls attention to our continuing insensitivity to IPE phenomena. The five developments that come to mind as seeming both commonplace from a 1980s' perspective and absurd from a 1960s' vantage point can be summarized as follows:

1   Sadat's trip to Israel and speech to the Knesset;
2   the stationing of Cuban troops in Angola;
3   the emergence of Libya as a major world actor;
4   the seizure of the US Embassy in Teheran and the subsequent support and management of the seizure by the Iranian state;
5   the excessively strong US dollar, the debt crises of Third World Countries, the emergence of the IMF's capacity to impose austerity programs on debtor nations in exchange for further loans, and the many other monetary problems that have thrust IPE issues high on the global agenda.

Surprising as the forecast of any of these developments would have been at an earlier time, only the last of the five remains an anomaly today. There is simply no room in any of our CFP models for IPE issues and their links to foreign policy. Or at least one is hard pressed to indicate how our thinking about the way states conduct themselves abroad has been affected by the surge of monetary problems to high places on the global agenda, and their absence from our theoretical drawing boards is conspicuous by virtue of being so anomalous.

The first four of these developments, on the other hand, are no longer puzzling. Quite to the contrary, the ease with which we now accept – and account for – them is a measure of the large extent to which our CFP models have matured in the last twenty years. Indeed, all four of them seem so understandable today that it is hard to imagine our ever being vulnerable to perplexity over such possibilities. But back in that simpler era few, if any, among us would have anticipated Sadat's sudden gesture of reconciliation because our models then did not accord so much leeway to individual variables. Chiefs of State simply do not reverse years of political socialization and commitment, we would have retorted to an obstreperous graduate student who naively suggested that progress in the Middle East might result from some leader breaking with precedent and undertaking to talk directly with his adversaries. Similarly, none of us could have envisioned Cuban troops abroad or the emergence of Libya because our models then posited a one-to-one ratio between size and external consequences. Small states are simply unable to be active and command attention on the world stage, we would have replied knowingly to the same student who persisted in imagining outrageous situations. And perhaps least of all would our early models have allowed for one country using force to take over the embassy of another. Countries simply do not do that to each other, we would have answered the student, raising our voice in exasperation as we stressed that it has long been a well-established custom for all nations to respect the embassies of others as sovereign territory and that, indeed, not even Hitler seized them.

In effect, the hypothetical student (who ever had one so prescient?) was pressing us to let the variables of our models vary as widely as our imaginations would permit. In all four cases the surprising development involved a failure to allow for the extremes of recognized continua. We knew that leaders vary in their capacities for innovation, that superpowers station troops abroad, and that new regimes alter the rules; but we did not extend this logic to seemingly absurd extremes.

Today, however, such extensions have become common practice. Aware of how quickly we tend to impose limits on this variability and also much more sensitive to the realization that the world really is as extraordinarily complex as we have always alleged, we are much more inclined to pause and press ourselves to broaden the range of values across which variation can occur.[3] This is no trivial achievement. It has diminished the probability of puzzling anomalies. Even more important, the ability to allow for greater variance in our main variables signifies a readiness to adjust our thinking and frameworks to the ever accelerating dynamism of world affairs, to recognize that the quickening pace of global interdependence is obscuring old boundaries and forming new linkages, thus rendering both the conduct and study of foreign policy increasingly challenging. To be sure, more surprises probably lie ahead and future hindsight will surely reveal a variety of values across which we presently do not allow our variables to vary. Yet now we know to be on guard against premature closure, a lesson that can only serve well our efforts to clarify sources, processes, and outcomes of foreign policy activities.

There is another common dimension in the first four developments listed above. They all involve actors in the Third World, actors whose decision rules were unfamiliar to our Western sensitivities in the 1960s. But twenty-plus years of experience with the diverse ways of politics in the underdeveloped world has sharpened our analytic skills and empathies with respect to the values, perceptions, motives, and predispositions that underlie foreign policy decision making in that part of the world. To be sure, our capacities in this respect still have a long way to go. Studies of foreign policy in the Third World still lag conspicuously and this may in itself be an important anomaly worth probing.[4] For to grasp fully the norms, priorities, and premises of foreign offices in non-Western countries is to dare to step outside our long-standing Western paradigm in which legitimacy is attached to the decisions of duly constituted authorities and change is initiated and brought about through established and accepted procedures.[5] To repeat, however, First World students of CFP have made enough progress in this regard to help resolve many of the anomalies that might have proved so troubling in earlier decades.

Continuing surprises

But the fifth set of developments listed above – those involving IPE phenomena – remains puzzling. Here extensions of the variance ascribed to key variables yield no solutions. To allow for greater flexibility and innovation on the part of statesmen and states is not to shed greater light on the relevance of foreign policy to currency crises, budget deficits, trade imbalances, monetary regimes, or the many other IPE issues that crowd the global agenda. Such matters simply lie outside the concerns of CFP, so much so that the index of a major work summarizing conceptual and empirical developments in the subfield does not include entries under "aid," "currency," "financing," "foreign aid," "foreign economic policy-making," "international political economy," "political economy," or "trade."[6] Similarly, while the IPE subfield is preoccupied with the role of the state in world affairs, this concept was dismissed long ago by students of foreign policy as being too abstract for analytic purposes.[7] The closest those in the subfield of CFP come to the word "state" is as shorthand for the foreign office of the United States.

It might be argued that it was less our analytic practices and more fundamental changes in the course of events that accounts for the probability of our rejecting some years ago the idea that economic considerations would become so central as dynamics of foreign policy and world politics. It is not that we failed to manipulate our variables properly, or that we did not sensitize them adequately to the vagaries of political economy, but rather that the world underwent transformation, elevating issues of low politics in the 1960s to the realm of high politics in the 1980s. In short, this argument would conclude, our models were insufficient. They focused on diplomatic and military variables and held constant, or dismissed as minor, those pertaining to issues of political economy.

While there may be some truth to this line of reasoning, it fails to explain the continuing gap between the two subfields. Why have CFP analysts not allowed for change and upgraded their models to account more fully for shifts in the global agenda? Why have they not looked again at the concept of the state? Why has the literature of this subfield not yet taken a decisive turn in the direction of seeking to comprehend the processes and policies through which governments cope with IPE issues? Why does the formulation and conduct of foreign economic policy stand apart as a separate form of activity and the focus of large, self-contained volumes[8] to which only passing mention is made in general textbooks?[9] Contrariwise, why have IPE practitioners been so neglectful of decision-making and other foreign policy processes? Why have they been so ready to presume that IPE dynamics unfold apart from diplomatic and foreign policy contexts?

Some analysts, and most notably Starr,[10] respond that in the case of CFP the questions are misleading, that no anomaly exists, that in fact IPE phenomena have long been incorporated into CFP analysis. As long ago as the 1966 "Pre-Theory" article,[11] Starr contends, IPE problems were addressed by CFP practitioners when they focussed on and found a conceptual home for issue-area phenomena and the dynamics through which national systems penetrated one another and became party to each other's political processes. He posits a broad range of IPE concerns – including the impact of multinational corporations, the focus on dependence and dependencia, the structural approaches that probe core–periphery connections in dominant and dependent countries, the efforts to uncover transnational relations, and the evolution of the concept of complex interdependence – as amounting to "a literature which systematically compares the foreign policy activities of states, focusing on economic issues, tools, and consequences, and doing so within terms of reference established in 'Pre-Theories' . . . [and] the concept of penetration."[12]

Maybe so, but Starr does not demonstrate the connections. And in the absence of documentation, he would seem to confuse potential for practice and would thus have difficulty citing any sensitivity to CFP queries or variables in the IPE literature or any sensitivity to IPE foci in the CFP literature. For, to repeat, with few exceptions the two literatures depict very different research traditions.[13] Notwithstanding the logic which Starr sees as inextricably linking them, the two subfields are presently organized around sharply different theoretical problems, analytic concepts, empirical domains, and methodological premises. Where one is linked to states and case histories, the other centers on decision-making organizations and recurring patterns. Where one often presumes rational choices and cost–benefit assessments as sources of action, the other allows for perceptual processes and bureaucratic politics. Where one attributes outcomes and behavioral tendencies to structural imperatives, the other posits action as stemming from goal-oriented aspirations. In some deep sense, then, it is reasonable to observe that a graduate student tooled up in one of the subfields could not prosper in the other without tooling up anew.

And even the exceptions to the bifurcation are suggestive of the gap that separates the subfields. In his search for the sources of change in US monetary policy, for example, Odell subjected a number of domestic and decision-making variables to intensive examination and, in so doing, cited much of the same literature used by CFP analysts;[14] but in the end he concludes that such variables are relatively peripheral and only occasionally operative:

> ... the most powerful sources of change in American foreign monetary policy (during the 1960s and 1970s) are international market conditions, the interstate military and economic power structure, and the circulation of policy ideas through Washington. . . . Additionally, some influence, though clearly weaker, is felt on certain occasions from changing US domestic political conditions and still less from government organization and internal bargaining. *The working assumptions of several schools of analysis are called into question by this study.*[15]

Indeed, Odell affirms the gap between the subfields by indicating that the role of domestic and decision-making variables in IPE is "a subject requiring much study in itself" and that "surprisingly little has been established" by the few IPE scholars who have ventured into this realm of inquiry.[16]

Understanding the anomaly

Two questions arise: why the anomaly of distinctly separate subfields with common concerns? And should the gulf be narrowed (that is, is either subfield likely to benefit if it partakes of the other)? Neither answer to these questions is self-evident. Doubtless there are a multiplicity of reasons keeping the subfields apart, else long ago their separation would have been recognized and efforts begun to engineer their convergence. Mutual boredom is likely to be reinforced by a variety of factors rather than stemming from a single source. Hence the search for an explanation of the anomaly must range widely. And not until the outlines of an explanation is developed can we begin to frame a response to the second question of whether a convergence of the subfields should be promoted.

Since an extensive inquiry into the reasons for the anomaly would require a lengthy probing of the philosophical and methodological foundations of IPE and CFP as foci of research, here we can only suggest some of its more obvious sources. At first glance the most obvious is the fact that most foreign policy analysts lack training in economics and thus shy away from focusing on IPE problems for want of skills with which to handle them. While it is surely accurate to characterize the training of CFP practitioners as woefully insufficient in economics, closer examination reveals this explanation as overly simple. As indicated by their long-standing readiness to tool up in statistics and mathematics, CFP analysts have never hesitated to seek further training when it seem warranted. Yet they have not done so with respect to econometrics, theories of the firm, the writings of Adam Smith, and the many other staples in the IPE storehouse.

Nor does avoidance of new skills seem like an adequate explanation for why IPE practitioners have shied away from further training in the foreign policy domain. If an overlap of the subfields seemed minimally salient to them, at the very least they would insist that their students get exposed to the dynamics of perception and cognitive balance, theories of organizational adaptation, the writings of Max Weber, and the many other implements in the CFP toolshed. Traces of such an overlap appear conspicuously absent in the training of IPE graduate students.

No, the answer must lie more in the content of the subfields than the skills of those who practice them. And a focus on content differences does indeed yield some clues. In the first place, IPE has come to define its domain as one of macro problems sustained by macro processes derived from macro structures in which the controls can only be marginally affected by the intervention of micro actors, whereas CFP proceeds from the initial premise that its domain involves international problems in which micro actors participate in macro processes that can shape and (occasionally) even control other micro actors as well as their macro structures and processes.[17] Both paradigms may be erroneous – in the sense that world politics can be viewed as resulting from the interaction of macro and micro dynamics – but they are nonetheless operative, with the result that the questions and observations which are relevant to one field tend to seem quite mundane to the other.

To be sure, IPE practitioners do not have a common conception of their subfield and they are quick to differentiate themselves as mercantilists, liberals, institutionalists, Marxists, etc. Despite these differences, however, they all share a presumption that trade, production, supply, demand, labor, and investment variables derive from the behavior of large aggregates of individuals whose common activities are responsive to macro structures and processes over which none of them can exercise meaningful control. Accordingly, with all relevant individuals being assumed to found their actions on the same kind of self-interested analyses of costs and benefits, IPE analysts can – and do – focus their attention on the summed results of these system-dominant patterns. Their models do allow for change, but the changes are of the kind – such as new technological break-throughs or labor incentives – that impact commonly on all the individuals involved. That is, they are macro-induced transformations that do not also lead to micro differentiation, changes that alter the fortunes and skills of whole classes of people rather than those of particular individuals.

Stated differently, the changes that preoccupy IPE students are not seen as originating with the talents, perceptions, bargaining, heroism, flaws, or any other attributes of leaders. Indeed, leaders, either as individuals or as groups, are not conspicuous in IPE accounts. They are not posited as anguishing over decisions, conflicted among alternatives, or caught between the tugs of the past and the imperatives of the present. They and their decisions are, rather, treated as out-comes of large-scale processes to which they yield by either reaffirming or shifting a course of action. Thus it is that the IPE literature has no meaningful equivalents of US presidents wandering in the Rose Garden prior to deciding what to do about missiles in Cuba, or small groups of officials working out how to respond to an attack by North Koreans, an embassy-seizure by Iranians, or a strike against the Suez Canal.

Put in still another way, the gulf between the subfields is sustained by the nature of the outcomes that follow from the action each regards as central. Where the focus of IPE analysts on macro processes makes it relatively easy for them to trace the consequences of action (a GNP or trade balance either goes up or down by an observable amount), the concern of their CFP counterparts with more micro dynamics leads them to endless difficulties over the meaning and measurement of outcomes (allies or adversaries may comply incrementally, occasionally, margin-ally, reluctantly, or otherwise partially with a foreign policy effort to modify their behavior). CFP analysts may envy the ease with which IPE colleagues can measure dependent variables, and the latter may be sympathetic to the measurement prob-lems faced by the former, but the difference here is so considerable as to reinforce the sense each has of the other's concerns as secondary, remote, and/or uninteresting.

Even the labels attached to turning points in the histories of CFP and IPE suggest the micro–macro differences: where the accounts of the former are dis-tinguished by the names of concrete individuals – such as, say, the Marshall Plan and the Nixon Doctrine – those of the latter are often marked by places – say, the Tokyo Round or Bretton Woods. Or, to illustrate this crucial difference between the two subfields in still another way, while the CFP literature is pervaded with inquiries into particular roles and how interpretations of them vary among differ-ent occupants, comparable entries in the IPE literature are conspicuous by their rarity. Compare, for example, the availability of sophisticated role analyses of foreign service officers, foreign secretaries, or defense ministers in a number of countries with the literature on treasury ministers, international bankers, or multinational executives. IPE scholars concentrate on banks and not bankers, on corporations and not executives, on treasuries and not ministers, foci which are entirely consistent with their concern for macro institutions and processes.

It follows that formulations like my Pre-Theory are of little value to IPE theorists and cannot be traced in their literature. Where CFP students are concerned with the relative potency of idiosyncratic and role variables, the ways in which operational codes are affected by multiple sources of advice and advocacy in decisional processes, and the diverse channels through which domestic opinion is fed into bureaucratic politics, such matters do not become especially salient for their IPE counterparts because what counts for the latter is what goods are being produced and distributed in what volume under what constraints. They do not need to worry about the circumstances under which the producer, trader, banker, worker, and investor can exercise idiosyncratic discretion, are exposed to a diversity of advice, or are subjected to pressures from publics. Such considerations are quite secondary to profitability and/or survival in the world capitalist economy. Surely, for example, IPE graduate students would be strongly discouraged from undertaking such dissertations as, "The Role of the World Bank President," "A Comparison of Treasury Departments in the First, Second, and Third Worlds," or "Shifting Public Moods Toward the Strength of the Dollar." Such projects would be seen as yielding little payoff, either empirically or theoretically.

It is, of course, true that some IPE analysts, especially those of the institutionalist, mercantilist, and Marxist schools, do posit economies as in need of some controls and thus accord regulating functions to government for which the standard economic models do not allow. To acknowledge that politics can intrude upon economics, however, is not necessarily to invite the possibility of treating micro dynamics as relevant variables. For despite their readiness to accept the presence of controls exogenous to the economy, most IPE scholars are not impelled to focus on the perceptions, motives, roles, and actions of officials, or even to probe the competition among government agencies with conflictful responsibilities.[18] Instead they remain wedded to their macro orientations by subsuming micro processes, structures, and actors under the rubric of the state, as if the decision-making dynamics of states are also the product of economic necessities and thus do not need to be subjected to intensive analysis.

Some might view the foregoing analysis as unnecessarily complex. What you are describing is the distinction between economics and politics, they would say, and there is no need to invest them with more elaborate meaning. Such a distinction is too vague, however. Economics and politics mean different things to different people,[19] so that nothing gets explained by stressing that the boredom of IPE and CFP analysts with each other derives from their respective disciplinary foci. All such an explanation does is pin labels on the differences and, in so doing, it prevents us from evolving an understanding of the many ways in which economics and politics both converge and diverge. This is why it is important to see foreign policy as an activity undertaken by relatively few individuals who seek to stretch across culture and modify or preserve the behavior patterns of others. Elaborating on such a perspective and contrasting it with the multitude of disaggregated activities that sustain the international political economy enables us to discern the dynamics that separate our subfields and inhibit our recognition of common interests. Economies and polities do, after all, nourish each other and we want to be able to see how that happens, rather than being blinded by simplistic labels.

Toward the reduction of Mutual Assured Boredom (MAB)

In sum, the distance between the subfields is complex and extensive. MAB is inherent in their respective foci. It derives from their structural dimensions and is bound to continue until such time as the boundaries between macro and micro dynamics are bridged. The question is whether bridges are desirable in this instance? Or whether MAB inhibits fruitless diversions and thus allows for a division of labor that is appropriate to knowledge building? Having already implied a conviction that empirical reality lies in the interaction of macro and micro processes, my own answer is to regret MAB and to opt for bridges. And I would start building them by noting that the anomaly would seem to be conceptual and not empirical, so that its resolution can be achieved through reconceptualization rather than research.

Students of IPE can begin this task by recognizing that neither the economic patterns nor the macro structures that govern them are integral parts of the state of nature. Both the patterns and the structures are subject to fluctuations and variations that are rooted in political and social needs and wants which, viewed from a strict economic perspective, are nonrational. Oil shortages can become gluts, open markets can become bounded zones, consumers can become patriots, producers can become civic-minded – transitions which may not follow the immutable laws of economics and are thus subject to manipulation and control through private and public decisions made by individuals and groups who experience anguish, conflict, rivalry, and all the other dynamics operative at micro levels. And once IPE analysts begin to make ample conceptual room for micro structures and processes they are likely to find that they use the concept of the state too ambiguously, that structural changes can be induced by human controls as well as by technological innovations, and that market forces are interactive with, rather than determinants of, governmental choices. With such an orientation, in fact, they may even find good reasons to encourage their graduate students to pursue dissertation inquiries into bankers, the role expectations to which bank officials feel responsive and the leeway for idiosyncratic discretion to which they feel entitled.

Put in terms of a concrete agenda for IPE students intent upon reducing MAB, they could usefully begin by focusing on the concepts of control and authority, concepts that are comprised of relational phenomena and are thus bound to orient one's thinking toward micro processes. Control does not occur, nor does authority get sustained, unless they are exercised by some persons and acceded to by others, and in this interaction one is very likely to discern, or at least to question, the micro underpinnings of macro structures. And for the IPE analysts who hesitate, fearful of escaping the comforts of their conceptual jails, let them return to a reading of Dahl and Lindblom's *Politics, Economics, and Welfare*, a work published in 1953 but still a classic formulation that renders the mutual concerns of IPE and CFP anything but boring.[20] Or let them heed the advice of one of their own and tool up on the relevance of such key concepts as security, power, and bargaining to IPE.[21]

Similarly, the reduction of MAB requires students of CFP to pay more attention to how structural constraints underlie the decisions and actions of those who conduct the external relations of states. They need to look again at what the Sprouts termed "probablism" and "possiblism"[22] and how Waltz,[23] Parsons,[24] and similar theorists conceive of structure, a reading exercise which will highlight the considerable extent to which micro decisions are made in response to macro requirements even as they also allow for the negation of structural imperatives. And once they begin to make conceptual room for circumstances in which macro structures may be dominant, they are also likely to find that the motives, perceptions, rivalries, and other micro attributes of individuals and groups are still worthy of analysis, if only because one never knows when such structures are being affirmed or negated.

All of this is not to suggest that both IPE and CFP students need to come to terms with the question of whether economics predominates over politics or vice versa. While this issue is often cited as central to how one assesses IPE problems,[25] and while it does embrace the relative importance of authority and markets as controls, the point here is precisely that of obfuscating the boundaries between economics and politics, of stressing that MAB is best overcome by presuming the two are interactive in any situation.

Part IV
Concepts and theories

12 The theoretical imperative

Unavoidable explication[1]

Among the most glaring discrepancies that pervade the world today is the gap between the ever-greater messiness of the world and the unarticulated ways in which it is assessed. There is, of course, no lack of commentary on the present world scene. The preoccupation with Iraq's weapons of mass destruction, with European–US relations, with North Korea, with the rich–poor gap – to mention only the issues presently at the top of the global agenda – pervades conversations and the press. But there is a shortage of incisive reflections on the sources and consequences of the various situations, a shortage of explicated theory underlying the plethora of observations about the unfolding world scene.

Even worse than the absence of theoretical explication is a widespread attitude that theorizing is at best a luxury and at worst a silly, counterproductive enterprise. Frequent are the comments that theories are wasted effort and misleading, if not downright erroneous. "Come off your high theoretical perch," say the critics, "Come down where the action is and get your hands dirty with real-world data." In government circles those who engage in theorizing about the dynamics underlying the messiness of the world are said to be far-fetched, far removed from any of the "real" problems that have to be confronted. In the academic world, among faculty, administrators, and students alike, theory-oriented teaching and research is viewed as misguided because it is not seen to be "policy relevant." Among journalists the attitude toward theoretically based formulations is often expressed in seven words: "Why don't they write in plain English!"

In short, there is a need to make the case for grounding analysis in explicit theoretical roots. The world's messiness cannot be directly managed or ameliorated by theoreticians, but the path toward management and amelioration can be smoothed if all concerned have a better appreciation of the value of theory and the ways in which it can clarify the policy challenges. Such is the purpose of this article: first, to set forth the underlying nature of the theoretical enterprise and, second, to elaborate an example of how theoretical sensitivities can lead to clarification of the central tendencies at work in the world.

We are all theorists

In the most basic sense policy makers, journalists, academicians – indeed, every-one – who downgrade theory give voice to a profound misunderstanding of the fundamental premises of the enterprise. And they do so without appreciating that they too are theorists, that they bring theory to bear every time they assess one or another aspect of world affairs. Being theoretical is unavoidable! Why? Because the very process of engaging in observation requires sorting out some of the observed phenomena as important and dismissing the others as trivial. There is no alternative. The details of situations do not speak for themselves. Patterns are not self-evident. Observers must give them meaning through the theories they bring to bear. They must, to repeat, select out from everything they observe those aspects that seem significant and discard those they deem as inconsequential.

Put differently, inescapably we live in a world of imperfect information. And even if somehow perfect information was available, we could not make full use of it. The details of any situation are virtually infinite and time is not sufficient to examine each of them. They include, among many other things, what officials consumed for breakfast and whether they ate with their children, or whether the sun was out when diplomats conferred. Such matters are real-world aspects of any situation, but they are far too numerous and trivial to include them in any assess-ment. In short, one cannot proceed to know anything without differentiating between the important and the trivial, and then confining one's analysis to the important and treating the trivial as given or constant.

"Wait a minute," a long-time diplomat might respond, "that's ridiculous, I spent years on the scene and I know what the underlying dynamics are!" Furthermore, another skeptic might contend, "Everything depends on the issue at stake." While the experiences of country or issue specialists can certainly lead to extensive information and a "feel" for the situations that arise in their area of specialization, it can also lead to tunnel vision, to a confidence in their powers of observation that inhibits the recognition of change or the evolution of new dynamics. And it is also precisely the close familiarity with the details that can generate anti-theoretical perspectives on the part of specialists and render them less reliable as observers than would be the case if they were sensitive to the need to differentiate between the important and the trivial. Indeed, it can readily be argued that their indifference or distaste for theory often leads policy makers to give narrow or distorted advice to their superiors and journalists to write stories that exaggerate and mislead. It is no accident that both foreign offices and good newspapers rotate their staffs to new country or issue assignments every few years. Such personnel policies are designed to prevent the kind of atheoretical specialization that can undermine sound observation.

This is not to suggest that policy makers and journalists ought to develop and work with refined theories marked by a special terminology, mathematical formu-lations, or elaborate game theoretical models. Clearly they have neither the time nor the training to engage in advanced theorizing. But they do have the time to be sensitive to the bases for the lines they draw between the important and the trivial.

Such a sensitivity requires a continuous readiness to be explicit about the reasoning that underlies the choices through which they attach salience to some aspects of a situation and dismiss other aspects as irrelevant. Stated much more simply, explication lies at the core of the theoretical enterprise. No matter how crude the explicated premises (i.e. propositions) or insights (i.e. hypotheses) may be, the very fact of explicating them means that the observer is a theorist, much as he or she might reject such a characterization.

To be sure, recognizing and articulating one's underlying premises and the bases of one's insights can be extremely difficult. This is especially the case for those who downgrade the utility of theory and have confidence that their experiences are leading them in the right direction. Under such circumstances it is all too easy to deny that observation derives from more than what is immediately apparent to the senses or what one has experienced in the past. To repeat, however, inevitably the underlying premises are operative. They cannot be avoided even if they are neither self-evident nor consciously grasped.

Much the same can be said about what I call the it-all-depends approach that is used by those who avoid explication because, as they put it, everything depends on the issue they are addressing. It is as if they believe it is possible to be a realist on Monday, a liberal on Tuesday, a constructivist on Wednesday, an institutionalist on Thursday, and a postinternationalist on Friday. Clearly, flexibility of this sort strains the imagination and is virtually impossible. Theories are neither endlessly flexible nor issue-bound. And equally clearly, observers are not so free of habitual ways of thinking that they can bounce easily from one theory to another.

Doubtless one's premises and insights can vary from issue to issue, but what are the underlying criteria that lead to different interpretations of whatever may be the issues at stake? Issues do spring from varying dynamics, but they are also embedded in more encompassing criteria about the motivations and attitudes that lead individual actors to do what they do and the structures that condition the behavior of collective actors. The more encompassing criteria may not be elaborate or sophisticated, but they do exist and they do underlie appraisals of when the observer needs to shift grounds in order to delineate one issue from another. Without such criteria all issues would be intuitively assessed on the basis of a wide array of stimuli, from the professional to the personal, from the prejudicial to the self-serving. Yes, in short, observations need to vary as issues vary, but they also spring from common experiential and intellectual roots that need to be made explicit in order to shift confidently among issues. To settle for stressing that everything depends on the issue is to give vent to anti-theoretical convictions.

End of the Cold War

The failure of most observers to anticipate the events of 1989–91 offers a classic case of the need for explicit theorizing. In retrospect it is hard to believe that so many thoughtful and experienced observers had no inkling that the Cold War and the Soviet Union were on the verge of collapse. Yet, that was the case. One would be hard pressed to find a textbook on international relations (IR) of the 1980s that had a single paragraph, let alone a single sentence, in which allowance was made for the possibility of the Cold War and the Soviet Union coming to an end. Two considerations serve as the most plausible explanation of this failure. One concerns the absence of a readiness to explicate underlying premises, thereby increasing the likelihood that observers merely reaffirmed pre-existing perceptions and thus missed events and patterns that could have been interpreted as moving toward a denouement. But even if the explicated premises merely confirmed the obvious interpretation that no historical breakpoints lay ahead, a second technique for anticipating the unexpected involves treating situations as puzzles rather than as clear-cut certainties, as possibly containing altered circumstances rather than familiar precedents. Put simply, thoughtful observers failed to allow their variables to vary, to be imaginative and ponder unlikely and counterintuitive developments that required revision in their understanding of the Cold War and the Soviet Union.

There is, of course, no guarantee that allowing one's variables to vary will result in an accurate picture of what may lie ahead. Such a procedure can be as faulty as not explicating one's reasoning. Nevertheless, it is a procedure that enables us to probe the richness of our theoretical sensitivities and it can help guard against egregious misperceptions and interpretations. The end of the Cold War and the Soviet Union may never have been widely anticipated, but in retrospect it seems clear that many of us could have done a better job of allowing for the possibility of their collapse.

Coping with complexity

Some might argue that world affairs have become so complex that it is near impossible to differentiate between the important and the trivial, that there is no choice but to "feel" one's way through the welter of nonlinear phenomena that mark the course of events. Such reasoning is far-fetched. Yes, the level of complexity at all levels of community has increased greatly with the collapse of time and distance brought on by new technologies and the advent of a globalizing world. But such circumstances do not relieve observers of needing to select out those features they deem critical and dismissing those they regard as extraneous to whatever situations concern them. On the contrary, if anything, the greater complexity reinforces the necessity of explication, else overly simplistic explanations will seem very inviting. Indeed, to a large extent numerous analysts have fallen back on long-standing concepts that may have been relevant in earlier, less complex epoch but that appear increasingly out of touch with the emergent properties of the global system. To revert – as surprisingly many do – to interpreting the central tendencies at work in the world as expressive of the balance of power is illustrative in this regard. Such linear concepts are not only well worn, but they also serve as analytic crutches and thus inhibit accounting for the growing role of active and skillful publics and their protest movements, for the numerous countries that have entered into authority crises, for the vast movement of people around the world, and for the greater salience of nongovernmental organizations

(NGOs), corporations, professional societies, and the many other new actors now crowding the global stage.

Of course, the intensification of global complexity does complicate the task of differentiating the important from the trivial. Yet, as the offense tends to catch up to the defense in military matters, so do theorists tend to develop new conceptual equipment to cope with ever-greater complexity. A mushrooming literature on complexity has evolved in recent years and it is pervaded with useful concepts with which to probe situations marked by endless nonlinear feedback processes.[2] The insight that actors co-evolve with their environments, that small events can have large consequences, and that a process of emergence is always at work in any system are among the concepts that lie at the core of complexity theory. Another is the notion that strange attractors eventually draw the trajectories of many social systems into the same space, especially the space in which global and local dynamics clash and merge that I have labeled "fragmegration" (see Chapter 6).

The state

Among the substantive foci that have become ever more complex and that thus further heighten the need for explicated theory is the state and its role in world affairs. All too many analysts take for granted – and thereby avoid explication – that the state continues to be the predominant actor on the world stage, the terminal entity for any political loyalties people may have. This may be so, and it may not be; but whatever may empirically be the case, the many, rapid, and deep transformations that mark the present moment in history highlight the urgency of treating the state as problematic rather than as given. This can be a wrenching task, as the concept of the state as the terminal entity around which world affairs are organized is so fully implanted in the minds and memories of most observers as to be an analytic habit that seems anything but problematic. Like the heavy smoker who cannot quit, the academics who write textbooks, the journalists who report on events, the analysts who dissect public situations, the officials who frame policy, and the citizens who ponder events – indeed, virtually everyone – are addicted to the presumption that the course of events originates and culminates with states and the power they bring to situations.

My theoretical orientations run counter to this habit. My explicated understanding of the role played by states focuses on the numerous ways in which their authority has been undermined by the dynamics of globalization and fragmegration. By treating states as problematic, I perceive other entities on the world stage as increasingly influential and thus as narrowing the scope within which states can be effective and serve their historic missions. My theoretical perspective emphasizes the decreasing ability of states to control the flow of information, pollution, drugs, money, crime, goods, and (to a lesser extent) people. As a result, I am impressed by the large extent to which the boundary between domestic and foreign affairs has undergone erosion and become increasingly porous.[3] Given a worldwide collapse of time and space as a consequence of new information and transportation technologies, what was once distant is now proximate, and vice versa.[4]

This is not to assert a pervasive reality. It is only to explicate my theoretical perspective and to argue that others need to do the same, whatever understandings they may evolve when they treat the state as problematic and ponder the various ways in which the authority of states may be undergoing a weakening in the present period. Other observers – perhaps a preponderance of them – may well perceive that a diminution of state power has not occurred, that some states are more powerful and authoritative than ever, and that my explication is profoundly flawed. But that is not the point. I am only contending that the state needs to be viewed as problematic and that viewing it in this way can only be accomplished by explicating one's underlying premises on the matter.

In other words, nuance is needed in theorizing about the state. Given the variability among states, any theoretical explication of their structures and roles should probably be in the form of a continuum that differentiates between those that are failing and those that remain highly competent, with allowance made for locating all states somewhere along the range between these two extremes. Indeed, in order to counter the aforementioned tendencies toward simplistic theoretical formulations induced by the paralyzing complexity that world affairs have become, it is probably advisable to frame our orientations and convictions in the context of one or another continua. In that way we are not only likely to engage in nuanced analyses, but such a mental technique may also enable us to discern relationships and dynamics that otherwise escape our attention. Most of all, it will facilitate treating the state as problematic and may even chart a path that culminates in identifying other terminal entities that have become part of the world scene.

History and change

Another crucial foundation of our theoretical perspectives that needs to be made explicit is the way in which we conceive of history and the changes it does or does not sustain. While few would argue that change in world affairs is anything but problematic, the same cannot be said about the related concept of history. The notion that history is problematic runs counter to a widespread presumption that it contains lessons that can be put to good use today. All too few observers are prepared to allow for the possibility that history may be marked by sharp breakpoints, moments when the course of events turns sharply in new directions for which history has no meaningful analogies. Rather, most proceed with the assumption that hidden (or obvious) in prior epochs or circumstances are developments that correspond sufficiently to contemporary dynamics to warrant probing the earlier sequences of events as guides that can be applied to the current situations.

And even if they acknowledge the possibility of sharp breakpoints, many observers are nonetheless inclined to presume that history is not problematic, that it does offer clues to understanding the course of events. The tendency to treat the sequences of history as self-evident and thus to reason by historical analogy can fairly be regarded as widespread, with the result that the task of questioning which are the relevant analogies is often ignored and analytic and policy decisions are then made without concern for the accuracy of the historical lessons regarded as applicable. To emphasize the problematic nature of historical analogies, I like to describe their use as the process of ransacking history. The way in which American officials assumed that the situation in Vietnam in the early 1960s was similar to Korea in mid-1950 or Europe in 1939 is a classic example of how historical analogies can lead to misguided decisions.

No less instructive is a growing tendency in the early years of the twenty-first century to perceive an analogy between the alleged emergence of the United States as the world's only superpower and the Roman empire. More than a few analysts treat the balance of power of the Cold War as having been replaced, first, by a unipolar system with the US as the single pole and, more recently, by US attitudes, policies, and capabilities that are conceived as comparable to Rome centuries ago. Analyses that proceed from this analogy seem ill-founded and risky if credence is given to the proposition, as I do, that the central tendency in today's world is toward the continued disaggregation of authority rather than its continued consolidation.[5] The US's power may seem preponderant on paper, but when a listing of the number of ways in which its efforts at home and abroad have fallen short – not to mention its inability to control the flow of money, goods, people, pollution, drugs, crime, and ideas – is contrasted with the proliferation of NGOs, the increasing frequency of ever-larger protest marches, and the mushrooming power of multinational corporations, the weaknesses of the analogy to the Roman empire take on a far-fetched appearance. And it is further unmasked by the argument that the disaggregation of authority presently underway is comparable to the processes whereby the Roman empire deteriorated. Such reasoning is faulty because, in effect, those who advance it do not allow for its negation. Either US power is comparable to the Roman empire or its diminished power is comparable to the decline of Rome, an analogy that serves no purpose other than providing a false sense of wisdom and thereby diverting attention from probing beneath the surface of the current scene for the dynamics that are likely to shape the course of events in the years ahead.

In addition to being sensitive to the fallacies of analogical reasoning and the need to treat history and its sharp turns as problematic, it is also essential that we explicate our notions of change in order to distinguish between situations marked by varying degrees of change, by stasis, by slow evolutionary change, and by rapid accelerating change that falls short of a breakpoint. Again, in other words, it is useful to explicate a continuum, in this case one that identifies varying degrees of change and transformation.

The September 11 terrorist attacks on the World Trade Center and the Pentagon are a quintessential example of the need to explicate our underlying concepts of change and history. By a huge margin most observers quickly interpreted the events of that horrific day in 2001 as a profound and enduring historical change. Without pausing, without the caution of waiting for subsequent developments, September 11 was seen as so profoundly different that the world would never be the same again. As one journalist put it, ". . . few veteran foreign policy watchers can remember when a single event has had so instant and so profound an effect on the entire dynamic of world politics."[6] For those analysts who subscribed to theoretical perspectives that ascribed power and authority to NGOs and other actors not formally part of the state system, however, September 11 was essentially more of the same, more an extreme case of postinternational politics. The explication of such a perspective did not treat the terrorist attacks as mundane or ordinary, but neither did it view them as a case of breakpoint change, as a sharp break in the main structural features of world politics. In one case, for example, it was stressed that there could be no denying that "there have been and still are substantial turmoil and changes in the global system; [but that nevertheless] "the events of 9/11 were consistent with the postinternational model and the actual impact of those events *per se* appears in retrospect and a broader postinternational context to have been relatively limited."[7]

Needless to say, this is not to argue that the postinternational perspective on change is the correct one; rather, it is to emphasize the need to explicate one's conception of change and history so that events can be interpreted in a meaningful and incisive context. To repeat, history does not speak to observers; they have to give it voice and the more explicitly they can set forth their bases for doing so, the better and more cogent will be their observations. Stated differently, there is no single correct interpretation of why things happen the way they do. There are as many interpretations as there are theoretical lenses through which to observe the unfolding world scene and there is no sure way to assess which interpretation is the most solid and accurate. But the more explicitly the criteria for rendering an interpretation are set forth, the easier will it be to evaluate its logic and utility.

The agent–structure challenge

While I have never had difficulty explicating my theoretical premises with respect to the state, change, and history, there is one extremely important problem that has always seemed elusive. I refer to the deeply philosophical question of whether the course of events is a response to the activities of human agents or to the structures that are generated by cultures, institutions, and a large array of other endlessly repeated patterns of interaction within and between societies. There is a growing literature and preoccupation with this question in the IR field,[8] and it is not difficult to find both sides of the issue persuasive. Surely everyone is a product of their culture as well as the institutions and aggregate patterns that prevail in their communities. At the same time it has always seemed clear to me that such macro phenomena are also shaped by the individuals of which they are comprised. Consequently, my way of explicating the agent–structure challenge – what I prefer to call the micro–macro problem – is to presume that individuals at the micro level shape and are shaped by their collectivities at the macro level. In other words, agents and structures are so inextricably linked, so endlessly interactive, that each is a product of the other. Sorting out the causal arrows that flow between the two levels is a chicken-and-egg problem, thus suggesting that in some situations the individuals initiate the causal flow while under other circumstances collectivities start the sequence of interaction. Is this another way of asserting that it all depends? No, it is a basis for explicating the numerous hypotheses listed in Table 6.1 of Chapter 6 that allow for both causal flows and that cumulatively suggest an outline of a set of interrelated theories, though perhaps not the basis for a single, integrated theory.

It has been argued that the micro–macro problem is unsolvable, that one cannot explain macro phenomena through analyzing micro actions, and vice versa.[9] But this line of reasoning suffers from the absence of a continuum. Elsewhere I have attempted to solve the problem with respect to the dynamics of fragmegration on the grounds that a solution ought to be feasible since fragmegrative processes are to a large extent rooted in the interaction between individuals and collectivities seeking either to contract/preserve their fragmenting domains or to expand/enlarge their integration with counterparts elsewhere in the world. The effort at a solution may be less than successful, but it does identify a variety of ways and settings in which the micro–macro interactions unfold.[10]

Theorizing about fragmegration

But the task here is not that of solving the agent–structure challenge. Rather, it is to illustrate how one might go about explicating one's theoretical sensitivities. I do so by elucidating a long-standing conviction that globalization and fragmegration are driven mainly by eight main dynamics at work on the world scene today. These are set forth as the rows in Table 6.1, while the columns delineate four levels of aggregation, the micro, macro, macro–macro, and macro–micro levels. An analysis of the phenomena encompassed by each of the eight rows and four columns has been developed elsewhere[11] and is not relevant to the central concern here with illustrating how one engages in theoretical explication. This is accomplished by offering crude hypotheses as entries in the 32 cells of the 4 × 8 matrix that have yet to be tested even as they are suggestive of the theoretical premises that underlie my inquiries into the complexities of a world that is both globalizing and localizing.

Since the eight sources of fragmegration involve phenomena that can be independent of each other, it would be erroneous to contend that the relationships outlined in Table 6.1 are suggestive of a coherent theory. As noted, its hypotheses are more in the nature of a set of interrelated theories. More accurately, to explicate how the various dynamics are interrelated is the next theoretical step that I want to undertake. Such a step not only requires explicating how each dynamic operates to initiate and sustain a causal flow (a difficult task in itself), but it also necessitates explication of the ways in which each does and does not interact with the seven others at the four levels of aggregation (a much more difficult challenge, to say the least). Consider, for example, the interaction between the increasing movement of people around the world (referred to as a "mobility upheaval" in the fifth row) and the authority crises that mark the daily life of many countries (the second row). With rare exceptions, the travel of tourists occurs without posing questions of how authority is exercised in the countries they visit. On the other hand, the increasing flows of legal and illegal immigrants around the world has led to severe authority crises in many countries, with local populations resenting their presence and often acting in ways that are contrary to prevailing practices and established authority.

Once again, in other words, continua are needed – one for each of the rows – so that the theorist is in a position to locate the conditions under which each dynamic may have an impact on the other seven and those circumstances where the impact is nil. Presumably, for example, the more extensive the arrival of immigrants in a country, the more will its authority structures undergo tension and transformation; or put in terms of the columns, the greater the flow of immigrants at the micro level, the greater the consequences for societal authority at the macro level. To develop continua for each dynamic is, however, only a partial solution to the theoretical challenge. Ideally one would need hypotheses that link the continua not only to each of the others, but also how each might link to two of the others, three of the others, and so on, an array of permutations and combinations that totals 85,344.[12]

Obviously, the necessity of explicating 85,344 relationships in a coherent theoretical fashion is likely to exceed the talents of any theorist. Indeed, even if the most advanced high-speed computer was used, it is doubtful whether such a complex theory could be developed, or even if it would be useful and usable if successfully subjected to a vast computer articulation. To be sure, complexity theory could assist the effort when it is recalled that systems co-evolve with their environments and each continua is then treated as co-evolving with the others. Even so, the task is too daunting to undertake, much less to comprehend the import of the findings that are generated. In all likelihood theorists would have to presume there are many globalizations and fragmegrations, a not unreasonable presumption,[13] and then explicate a separate theory for those of the combinations or permutations they consider most interesting and relevant.

Unmanageable as theorizing about 85,344 relationships may be, the absurdity of the task brilliantly illustrates the complexity with which present-day theorists of world affairs must cope. And unfortunately, even scaled down versions of this complexity are such as to lead some theorists to fall back on simple formulations such as realism or liberalism. Unlike these perspectives, approaches that acknowledge the ever-greater complexity that has accompanied the age of the Internet and globalization do not have a few overarching principles under which phenomena can be readily grouped and analyzed. Or at least all-encompassing organizing principles that can be applied to present-day world affairs have yet to be developed, thus exaggerating the felt need to define parsimony in terms of a minimal number of dynamics.

Furthermore, not only does the absurdity of this example illustrate the centrality of explication as a feature of the theoretical enterprise, but it also suggests how explication serves to clarify the task present-day theorists confront. More than that, it highlights the large extent to which we as theorists must play mind games as we juggle and wrestle with the diverse phenomena of which our subject is comprised. At the end of the day useful theory depends on those who construct it being venturesome and letting their minds wander and their variables vary.

13 Many damn things simultaneously – at least for awhile

Complexity theory and world affairs[1]

In this emergent epoch of multiple contradictions that I have labeled "fragmegration" in order to summarily capture the tensions between the fragmenting and integrating forces that sustain world affairs,[2] a little noticed – and yet potentially significant – discrepancy prevails between our intellectual progress toward grasping the underlying complexity of human systems and our emotional expectation that advances in complexity theory may somehow point the way to policies which can ameliorate the uncertainties inherent in a fragmegrative world. The links here are profoundly causal: the more uncertainty has spread since the end of the Cold War, the more are analysts inclined to seek panaceas for instability and thus the more have they latched onto recent strides in complexity theory in the hope that it will yield solutions to the intractable problems that beset us. No less important, all these links – the uncertainty, the search for panaceas, and the strides in complexity theory – are huge, interactive, and still intensifying.

In short, all the circumstances are in place for an eventual disillusionment with complexity theory. For despite the strides, there are severe limits to the extent to which such theory can generate concrete policies that lessen the uncertainties of a fragmegrated world. And as these limits become increasingly evident subsequent to the present period of euphoria over the theory's potential utility, a reaction against it may well set in and encourage a reversion back to simplistic, either/or modes of thought. Such a development would be regrettable. Complexity theory does have insights to offer. It provides a cast of mind that can clarify, that can alert observers to otherwise unrecognized problems, and that can serve as a brake on undue enthusiasm for particular courses of action. But these benefits can be exaggerated and thus disillusioning. Hence the central purpose of this chapter is to offer a layman's appraisal of both the potentials and the limits of complexity theory – to differentiate what range of issues and processes in world affairs it can be reasonably expected to clarify from those that are likely to remain obscure.

Uncertainties

That a deep sense of uncertainty should pervade world affairs since the end of the Cold War is hardly surprising. The US–Soviet rivalry, for all its tensions and susceptibility to collapsing into nuclear holocaust, intruded a stability into the course of events that was comprehensible, reliable, and continuous. The enemy was known. The challenges were clear. The dangers seemed obvious. The appropriate responses could readily be calculated. Quite the opposite is the case today, however. If there are enemies to be contested, challenges to meet, dangers to avoid, and responses to be launched, we are far from sure what they are. So uncertainty is the norm and apprehension the mood. The sweet moments when the wall came down in Berlin, apartheid ended in South Africa, and an aggression was set back in Kuwait seem like fleeting and remote fantasies as the alleged post-Cold War order has emerged as anything but orderly. Whatever may be the arrangements that have replaced the bipolarity of US–Soviet rivalry, they are at best incipient structures and, at worst, they may simply be widespread disarray.

Put differently, a new epoch, a new ontology or common sense of what is important and how it should be valued,[3] can be said to be evolving. As indicated, it is an epoch of multiple contradictions: The international system is less dominant, but it is still powerful. States are changing, but they are not disappearing. State sovereignty has eroded, but it is still vigorously asserted. Governments are weaker, but they can still throw their weight around. At times publics are more demanding, but at other times they are more compliant. Borders still keep out intruders, but they are also more porous. Landscapes are giving way to ethnoscapes, mediascapes, ideoscapes, technoscapes, and financescapes, but territoriality is still a central preoccupation for many people.[4]

Sorting out contradictions such as these poses a number of difficult questions: How do we assess a world pervaded with ambiguities? How do we begin to grasp a political space that is continuously shifting, widening and narrowing, simultaneously undergoing erosion with respect to many issues and reinforcement with respect to other issues? How do we reconceptualize politics so that it connotes identities and affiliations as well as territorialities? How do we trace the new or transformed authorities that occupy the new political spaces created by shifting and porous boundaries?

The cogency of such questions – and the uncertainty they generate – reinforce the conviction that we are deeply immersed in an epochal transformation sustained by a new worldview about the essential nature of human affairs, a new way of thinking about how global politics unfold. At the center of the emergent worldview lies an understanding that the order which sustains families, communities, countries, and the world through time rests on contradictions, ambiguities, and uncertainties. Where earlier epochs were conceived in terms of central tendencies and orderly patterns, the present epoch appears to derive its order from contrary trends and episodic patterns. Where the lives of individuals and societies were once seen as moving along linear and steady trajectories, now their movement seems nonlinear and erratic, with equilibria being momentary and continuously punctuated by sudden accelerations or directional shifts.

Accordingly, the long-standing inclination to think in either/or terms has begun to give way to framing challenges as both/and problems. People now understand, emotionally as well as intellectually, that unexpected events are commonplace, that anomalies are normal occurrences, that minor incidents can mushroom into major outcomes, that fundamental processes trigger opposing forces even as they expand their scope, that what was once transitional may now be enduring, and that the complexities of modern life are so deeply rooted as to infuse ordinariness into the surprising development and the anxieties that attach to it.

To understand that the emergent order is rooted in contradictions and ambiguities, of course, is not to lessen the sense of uncertainty as to where world affairs are headed and how the course of events is likely to impinge on personal affairs. Indeed, the more one appreciates the contradictions and accepts the ambiguities, the greater will be the uncertainty one experiences. And the uncertainty is bound to intensify the more one ponders the multiplicity of reasons why the end of the Cold War has been accompanied by pervasive instabilities. Clearly, the absence of a superpower rivalry is not the only source of complexity. Technological dynamics are also major stimulants, and so are the breakdown of trust, the shrinking of distances, the globalization of economies, the explosive proliferation of organizations, the information revolution, the fragmentation of groups, the integration of regions, the surge of democratic practices, the spread of fundamentalism, the cessation of intense enmities, and the revival of historic animosities – all of which in turn provoke further reactions that add to the complexity and heighten the sense that the uncertainty embedded in nonlinearity has become an enduring way of life.

In some corners of the policy-making community there would appear to be a shared recognition that the intellectual tools presently available to probe the pervasive uncertainty underlying our emergent epoch may not be sufficient to the task. More than a few analysts could be cited who appreciate that our conceptual equipment needs to be enhanced and refined, that under some conditions nonlinear approaches are more suitable than the linear conceptual equipment that has served for so long as the basis of analysis, that the disciplinary boundaries that have separated the social sciences from each other and from the hard sciences are no longer clear-cut, and that the route to understanding and sound policy initiatives has to be traversed through interdisciplinary undertakings.[5]

It is perhaps a measure of this gap between the transformative dynamics and the conceptual equipment available to comprehend them that our vocabulary for understanding the emergent world lags well behind the changes themselves. However messy the world may have been in the waning epoch, at least we felt we had incisive tools to analyze it. But today we still do not have ways of talking about the diminished role of states without at the same time privileging them as superior to all the other actors in the global arena. We lack a means for treating the various contradictions as part and parcel of a more coherent order. We do not have techniques for analyzing the simultaneity of events such that the full array of their interconnections and feedback loops are identified.

Searching for panaceas

So it is understandable that both the academic and policy-making communities are vulnerable to searching for panaceas. Aware they are ensconced in an epoch of contradictions, ambiguities, and uncertainties, and thus sensitive to the insufficiency of their conceptual equipment, officials and thoughtful observers alike may be inclined to seek security through an overall scheme that seems capable of clarifying the challenges posed by the emergent epoch. Complexity theory is compelling in this regard. The very fact that it focuses on complex phenomena and presumes that these are subject to theoretical inquiry, thereby implying that complex systems are patterned and ultimately comprehensible, may encourage undue hope that humankind's problems can be unraveled and effective policies designed to resolve them pursued.

Stirring accounts of the Santa Fe Institute, where complexity theory was nursed into being through the work of economists, statisticians, computer scientists, mathematicians, biologists, physicists, and political scientists in a prolonged and profoundly successful interdisciplinary collaboration, kindled these hopes.[6] The stories of how Brian Arthur evolved the notion of increasing returns in economics, of how John H. Holland developed genetic algorithms that could result in a mathematical theory capable of illuminating a wide range of complex adaptive systems, of how Stuart Kauffman generated computer simulations of abstract, interacting agents that might reveal the inner workings of large, complicated systems such as the United States, of how Per Bak discovered self-organized criticality that allowed for inferences as to how social systems might enter upon critical states that jeopardize their stability, of how Murray Gell-Mann pressed his colleagues to frame the concept of co-evolution wherein agents interact to fashion complex webs of interdependence – these stories suggested that progress toward the comprehension of complex systems was bound to pay off. And to add to the sense of panaceas, expectations were heightened by the titles these scholars gave to their works written to make their investigations meaningful for laymen. Consider, for example, the implications embedded in Holland's *Hidden Order*[7] and Kauffman's *At Home in the Universe*[8] that creative persistence is worth the effort in the sense that eventually underlying patterns, a hidden order, are out there to be discovered.[9]

There are, in short, good reasons to be hopeful: if those on the cutting edge of inquiry can be sure that human affairs rest on knowable foundations, surely there are bases for encouragement that the dilemmas of the real, post-Cold War world are susceptible to clarification and more effective control. Never mind that societies are increasingly less cohesive and boundaries increasingly more porous; never mind that vast numbers of new actors are becoming relevant to the course of events; never mind that money moves instantaneously along the information highway and that ideas swirl instantaneously in cyberspace; and never mind that "connectivity is exploding"[10] such that the feedback loops generated by societal breakdowns, proliferating actors, and boundary-spanning information are greatly intensifying the complexity of life late in the twentieth century. All such transformative dynamics may complicate the task of analysts, but complexity theory tells us that they are not beyond comprehension, that they can be grasped.

I do not say this sarcastically. Rather, I accept the claims made for complexity theory. It has made enormous strides and it does have the potential for clarifying and ultimately ameliorating the human condition. Its progress points to bases for analytically coping with porous boundaries, societal breakdowns, proliferating actors, fast-moving money and ideas, and elaborate feedback loops. But to stress these strides is not to delineate a time line when they will reach fruition in terms of policy payoffs, and it is here, in the discrepancy between the theoretical strides and their policy relevance, that the need to highlight theoretical limits and curb panacean impulses arises.

Strides in complexity theory

Before specifying the limits of complexity theory, let us first acknowledge the claims made for it. This can be accomplished without resort to mathematical models or sophisticated computer simulations. Few of us can comprehend the claims in these terms, but if the theoretical strides that have been made are assessed from the perspective of the philosophical underpinnings of complexity theory, it is possible to identify how the theory can serve the needs of those of us in the academic and policy-making worlds who are not tooled up in mathematics or computer science but who have a felt need for new conceptual equipment. Four underpinnings of the theory are sufficient for this purpose. The four are equally important and closely interrelated, but they are briefly outlined separately here in order to facilitate an assessment of the theory's relevance to the analysis of world affairs.

   As I understand it, at the core of complexity theory is the complex adaptive system – not a cluster of unrelated activities, but a system; not a simple system, but a complex one; and not a static, unchanging set of arrangements, but a complex adaptive system. Such a system is distinguished by a set of interrelated parts, each one of which is potentially capable of being an autonomous agent that, through acting autonomously, can impact on the others, and all of which either engage in patterned behavior as they sustain day-to-day routines or break with the routines when new challenges require new responses and new patterns. The interrelationships of the agents is what makes them a system. The capacity of the agents to break with routines and thus initiate unfamiliar feedback processes is what makes the system complex (since in a simple system all the agents consistently act in prescribed ways). The capacity of the agents to cope collectively with the new challenges is what makes them adaptive systems. Such, then, is the modern urban community, the nation-state, and the international system. Like any complex adaptive system in the natural world, the agents that comprise world affairs are brought together into systemic wholes that consist of patterned structures ever subject to transformation as a result of feedback processes from their external environments or from internal stimuli that provoke the agents to break with their established routines. There may have been long periods of stasis in history where, relatively speaking, each period in the life of a human system was like the one before it, but for a variety of reasons elaborated elsewhere,[11] the present period is one of turbulence, of social systems at all levels undergoing powerful tensions that are in direct contradiction with each other.

These tensions derive from diverse processes whereby the major parameters of the global system no longer serve as boundary conditions and, instead, enter into a period of high complexity and high dynamism.[12] As a result, the contradictory tensions generate clashes between numerous forces that foster tendencies toward integration, globalization, and centralization on the one hand and toward fragmentation, localization, and decentralization on the other – to mention only the most conspicuous of the polarities that comprise the emergent epoch. In order to capture the simultaneity and causal links of these polarities, I use the aforementioned "fragmegration" label to designate the emergent epoch.[13] More importantly, however the epoch may be labeled – and my label is purposefully grating in order to stress the sharpness of the break with past eras – the profound transformations of its parameters and the tensions thus produced exhibit all the characteristics of complex adaptive systems.

The four premises of complexity theory build upon the foregoing conception of a complex adaptive system. They call attention to dimensions of complex adaptive systems that both offer promising insights into world affairs and highlight the difficulties of applying complexity theory to policy problems.

Self-organization and emergent properties

The parts or agents of a complex adaptive system, being related to each other sufficiently to form recurrent patterns, do in fact self-organize their patterned behavior into an orderly whole[14] and, as they do, they begin to acquire new attributes. The essential structures of the system remain intact even as their emergent properties continue to accumulate and mature. Through time the new properties of the system may obscure its original contours, but to treat these processes of emergence as forming a new system is to fail to appreciate a prime dynamic of complexity, namely, the continuities embedded in emergence. As one analyst puts it, the life of any system, "at all levels, is not one damn thing after another, but the result of a common fundamental, internal dynamic."[15] Thus, for example, the NATO of 1996 is very different from the NATO of 1949 and doubtless will be very different from the NATO of 2006, but its emergent properties have not transformed it into an entirely new organization. Rather, its internal dynamic has allowed it to adapt to change even though it is still in fundamental respects the North Atlantic Treaty Organization.

Adaptation and co-evolution

But there is no magic in the processes whereby systems self-organize and develop emergent properties. In the case of human systems, it is presumed they are composed of learning entities,[16] with the result that the dynamics of emergence are steered, so to speak, by a capacity for adaptation, by the ability of complex systems to keep their essential structures within acceptable limits (or, in the case of nonhuman organisms, within physiological limits).[17] Human systems face challenges from within or without, and the adaptive task is to maintain an acceptable balance between their internal needs and the external demands.[18] At the same time, in the process of changing as they adapt, systems co-evolve with their environments. Neither can evolve in response to change without corresponding adjustments on the part of the other. On the other hand, if a system is unable to adjust to its environment's evolutionary dynamics and thus fails to adapt, it collapses into the environment and becomes extinct. To recur to the NATO example, the Organization managed from its inception to co-evolve with the Cold War and post-Cold War environments despite internal developments such as the 1967 defection of France from its military command and external developments such as the demise of the Soviet Union and the superpower rivalry. Indeed, as the environment evolved subsequent to the end of the Cold War, NATO accepted France's decision to rejoin the military command in 1996. The adaptation of NATO stands in sharp contrast to its Cold War rival, the Warsaw Pact. It could not co-evolve with the international environment and failed to adapt; in effect, it collapsed into the environment so fully that its recurrent patterns are no longer discernible.

As the history of France in NATO suggests, the co-evolution of systems and their environments is not a straight-line progression. As systems and their environments become ever more complex, feedback loops proliferate and non-linear dynamics intensify, with the result that it is not necessarily evident how any system evolves from one stage to another. While "no one doubts that a nation-state is more complex than a foraging band," and while the evolution from the latter to the former may include tribal, city-state, and other intermediate forms, the processes of evolution do not follow neat and logical steps.[19] Systems are unalike and thus subject to local variations as well as diverse trajectories through time. Equally important, evolution may not occur continuously or evenly. Even the most complex system can maintain long equilibria before undergoing new adaptive transformations, or what complexity theorists call "phase transitions." Put differently, their progression through time can pass through periods of stasis or extremely slow, infinitesimal changes before lurching into a phase transition, thereby tracing a temporal path referred to as "punctuated equilibrium."

The power of small events

It follows from the vulnerability of complex adaptive systems to punctuations of their equilibria and tumultuous phase transitions that small, seemingly minor events can give rise to large outcomes, that systems are sensitive at any moment in time to the conditions prevailing at that moment and can thus initiate processes of change that are substantial and dramatic. Examples of this so-called "butterfly effect" abound. Perhaps the most obvious concerns the way in which an assassination in 1914 triggered the onset of World War I, but numerous other, more recent illustrations can readily be cited. It is not difficult to reason, for instance, that the end of the Cold War began with the election of a Polish pope more than a decade earlier, just as the release of Nelson Mandela from prison was arguably (and in retrospect) an event that triggered the end of apartheid in South Africa.[20]

Sensitivity to initial conditions

Closely related to the power of small events is the premise that even the slightest change in initial conditions can lead to very different outcomes for a complex adaptive system. This premise can be readily grasped in the case of human systems when it is appreciated that the processes of emergence pass through a number of irreversible choice points that lead down diverse paths and, thus, to diverse outcomes. This is not to imply, however, that changes in initial conditions necessarily result in unwanted outcomes. As the foregoing examples demonstrate, the power of an altered initial condition can lead to desirable as well as noxious results, an insight that highlights the wisdom of paying close attention to detail in the policy-making process.

The limits of complexity theory

Can complexity theory anticipate precisely how a complex adaptive system in world affairs will organize itself and what trajectory its emergence will follow? Can the theory trace exactly how the system will adapt or how it and its environment will co-evolve? Can the theory specify what initial conditions will lead to what large outcomes? No, it cannot perform any of these tasks. Indeed, it cannot even anticipate whether a large outcome will occur or, if it does, the range within which it might fall. Through computer simulations, for example, it has been shown that even the slightest change in an initial condition can result in an enormous deviation from what would have been the outcome in the absence of the change. Two simulations of the solar system are illustrative:

> Both simulations used the same mathematical model on the same computer. Both sought to predict the position of the planets some 850,000,000 years in the future. The first and second simulation differed only in that the second simulation moved the starting position of each planet 0.5 millimeters. With such a small change in the initial conditions, [it is reasonable] to expect that the simulations would yield almost identical outcomes.

> For all but one of the planets this is exactly what happened. Pluto, however, responded differently. The position of Pluto in the second simulation differed from its position in the first by 4 billion miles. Pluto's resting position is, in this mathematical model, extremely sensitive to the initial conditions.[21]

Applying these results metaphorically to the global system of concern here, it could well be presumed that the Pluto outcome is the prototype in world politics, that numerous communities and societies could deviate often from their expected trajectories by the political equivalent of 4 billion miles. The variables comprising human systems at all levels of organizations are so multitudinous, and so susceptible to wide variations when their values shift, that anticipating the movement of planets through space is easy compared to charting the evolution of human systems through time.

In short, there are strict limits within which theorizing based on the premises of complexity theory must be confined. It cannot presently – and is unlikely ever to – provide a method for predicting particular events and specifying the exact shape and nature of developments in the future. As one observer notes, it is a theory "meant for thought experiments rather than for emulation of real systems."[22]

Consequently, it is when our panacean impulses turn us toward complexity theory for guidance in the framing of exact predictions that the policy payoffs are least likely to occur and our disillusionment is most likely to intensify. For the strides that complexity theorists have made with their mathematical models and computer simulations are still a long way from amounting to a science that can be relied upon for precision in charting the course of human affairs that lies ahead. Although their work has demonstrated the existence of an underlying order, it has also called attention to a variety of ways in which the complexity of that order can collapse into pervasive disorder. Put differently, while human affairs have both linear and nonlinear dimensions, and while there is a range of conditions in which the latter dimensions are inoperative or "well-behaved,"[23] it is not known when or where the nonlinear dimensions will appear and trigger inexplicable feedback mechanisms. Such unknowns lead complexity theorists to be as interested in patterns of disorder as those of order, an orientation that is quite contrary to the concerns of policy makers.

At the same time, however, there are some signs of positive institutional developments designed to harness the potentials of complexity theory to the conditions of the epoch of fragmegration that has emerged since the end of the Cold War. One example is the Santa Fe Institute, whose investigators are not unmindful of the need to focus their hard-won perspectives on the uncertainties and contradictions that lie ahead in the twenty-first century.[24] Perhaps an even more fully institutionalized example is that of the Conference on World Regions, which seeks to link complexity theory to the nonlinear dynamics of fragmegration by achieving "a high degree of intellectual resonance between the emerging scientific paradigm of complexity theory and an emerging political paradigm of *global regionalism*: a political model that seeks to catalyze the emergence of a nonhierarchical, self-organizing regime of horizontally linked regions and their leading private-sector actors pursuing a shared vision of ever-intensifying political devolution and ever more convergent economic, regulatory, and political processes."[25]

Theorizing within limits

The limits of complexity theory may thus not be as severe as they seem at first glance. If the search for panaceas is abandoned and replaced with a nuanced approach, it quickly becomes clear that the underlying premises of complexity theory have a great deal to offer as a perspective or worldview with which to assess and anticipate the course of events. Perhaps most notably, they challenge prevailing assumptions in both the academic and policy-making communities that political, economic, and social relationships adhere to patterns traced by linear regressions. Complexity theory asserts that it is not the case, as all too many officials and analysts presume, that "we can get a value for the whole by adding up the values of its parts."[26] In the words of one analyst,

> Look out the nearest window. Is there any straight line out there that wasn't man-made? I've been asking the same question of student and professional groups for several years now, and the most common answer is a grin. Occasionally a philosophical person will comment that even the lines that look like straight lines are not straight lines if we look at them through a microscope. But even if we ignore that level of analysis, we are still stuck with the inevitable observation that natural structures are, at their core, nonlinear. If [this] is true, why do social scientists insist on describing human events as if all the rules that make those events occur are based on straight lines?[27]

A complexity perspective acknowledges the nonlinearity of both natural and human systems. It posits human systems as constantly learning, reacting, adapting, and changing even as they persist, as sustaining continuity and change simultaneously. It is a mental set, a cast of mind that does not specify particular outcomes or solutions but that offers guidelines and lever points that analysts and policy makers alike can employ to more clearly assess the specific problems they seek to comprehend or resolve. Furthermore, the complexity perspective does not neglect the role of history even though it rejects the notion that a single cause has a single effect. Rather, focusing as it does on initial conditions and the paths that they chart for systems, complexity treats the historical context of situations as crucial to comprehension. Equally important, locating complexity theory in a historical context allows us to begin to specify the conditions under which the uncertainties fostered by the complexity of world affairs may last only for "awhile" – to quote from the title of this chapter – and be followed by patterned routines and regularities. I shall return to this point in the section below on the relevance of historical sequences.

The first obstacle to adopting a complexity perspective is to recognize that inevitably we operate with some kind of theory. It is sheer myth to believe that we need merely observe the circumstances of a situation in order to understand them. Facts do not speak for themselves; observers give them voice by sorting out those that are relevant from those that are irrelevant and, in so doing, they bring a theoretical perspective to bear. Whether it be realism, liberalism, or pragmatism, analysts and policy makers alike must have some theoretical orientation if they are to know anything. Theory provides guidelines; it sensitizes observers to alternative possibilities; it highlights where levers might be pulled and influence wielded; it links ends to means and strategies to resources; and perhaps most of all, it infuses context and pattern into a welter of seemingly disarrayed and unrelated phenomena.

It follows that the inability of complexity theory to make specific predictions is not a serious drawback. Understanding and not prediction is the task of theory. It provides a basis for grasping and anticipating the general patterns within which specific events occur. The weather offers a good example. It cannot be precisely predicted at any moment in time, but

> there are building blocks – fronts, highs and lows, jet streams, and so on – and our overall understanding of changes in weather has been much advanced by theory based on these building blocks. . . . We understand the larger patterns and (many of) their causes, though the detailed trajectory through the space of weather possibilities is perpetually novel. As a result, we can do far better than the old standby: predict that "tomorrow's weather will be like today's" and you stand a 60 percent probability of being correct. A relevant theory for [complex adaptive systems] should do at least as well.[28]

Given the necessity of proceeding from a theoretical standpoint, it ought not be difficult to adopt a complexity perspective. Indeed, most of us have in subtle ways already done so. Even if political analysts are not – as I am not – tooled up in computer science and mathematics, the premises of complexity theory and the strides in comprehension they have facilitated are not difficult to grasp. Despite our conceptual insufficiencies, we are not helpless in the face of mounting complexity. Indeed, as the consequences of turbulent change have become more pervasive, so have observers of the global scene become increasingly wiser about the ways of the world and, to a large degree, we have become, each of us in our own way, complexity theorists. Not only are we getting accustomed to a fragmegrative worldview that accepts contradictions, anomalies, and dialectic processes, but we have also learned that situations are multiply caused, that unintended consequences can accompany those that are intended, that seemingly stable situations can topple under the weight of cumulated grievances, that some situations are ripe for accidents waiting to happen, that expectations can be self-fulfilling, that organizational decisions are driven as much by informal as formal rules, that feedback loops can redirect the course of events, and so on through an extensive list of understandings that appear so commonplace as to obscure their origins in the social sciences only a few decades ago.[29] Indeed, we now take for granted that learning occurs in social systems, that systems in crisis are vulnerable to sharp turns of directions precipitated by seemingly trivial incidents, that the difference between times one and two in any situation can often be ascribed to adaptive processes, that the surface appearance of societal tranquillity can mask underlying problems, and that "other things being equal" can be a treacherous phrase if it encourages us to ignore glaring exceptions. In short, we now know that history is not one damn thing after another so much as it is many damn things simultaneously. And if we ever slip in our understanding of these subtle lessons, if we ever unknowingly revert to simplistic formulations, complexity theory serves to remind us there are no panaceas. It tells us that there are limits to how much we can comprehend of the complexity that pervades world affairs, that we have to learn to become comfortable living and acting under conditions of uncertainty.

Historical sequences

As indicated by the qualifying phrase in the paper's title, the limits of this perspective involve the duration of complexity as an underlying global condition. More precisely, complexity theory enables us to identify circumstances under which the emergent fragmegrative epoch may begin to wane and yield to recurring and routinized patterns. To discern such a possibility is to proceed from an understanding of how and why historical sequences move from one epochal phase to another. Put more strongly, to discern major epochal fluctuations one needs a theory of history, a philosophy of when transformative dynamics punctuate equilibria and when new equilibria subsequently evolve, of how historical sequences get compiled out of unique factors and recurrent imperatives, of when unexpected, contingent, or random events make a difference and when they do not, of what conditions allow societies and their institutions to absorb new challenges and what conditions overwhelm them, of when, where, and why the choices made by individuals and their organizations are predetermined and when, where, and why they are freely made.

Following the lead of a philosophical formulation derived from complexity theory,[30] the outlines of an appropriate historical theory that allows for the waning of the emergent epoch involves a two-stage conception of how historical conditions come into being and when they begin to attenuate. In the first, early stage, the three basic parameters experience systemic shock which results in high degrees of uncertainty, contradiction, fluctuation, and unpredictability that border on chaos and thus accentuate the degree to which contingencies can underlie the actions of individuals and collectivities; then in the later stage, with the passage of enough time for habits and orderly patterns to evolve, the parameters begin to settle as fixed boundary conditions that reduce the degree to which contingencies can alter any sequence's trajectory. Once the world passes through a threshold from the previous epoch, in other words, high degrees of complexity and dynamism set in and last for an indeterminate length of time wherein the lessons of history have little relevance for the course of events. Whenever this first stage gives way to lesser degrees of complexity and dynamism – and the time involved here can be variable but is likely to be measured in decades – the pattern of events begin to resemble prior sequences and the lessons of history can once again be pondered to good effect. Put differently, the change in historical sequences from the early to the later stages is gradual and occurs when and where the uncertainties, contradictions, and fluctuations induced by the complexities and dynamism of turbulence begin to yield to imperatives that cannot be readily ignored. As a result, the choices open to individuals and collectivities are much greater in the earlier than in the later stages of historical sequences.

It should be added that these historical sequences unfold unevenly in different parts of the world. For a wide range of cultural, political, and economic reasons, fragmegrative dynamics occur in different ways, at different paces, with diverse degrees of complexity and varying consequences in different regions, countries, and communities. Thus it is erroneous to anticipate worldwide uniformity in the timing of the two-stage sequences. It is more accurate, rather, to conceive of a multiplicity of staggered sequences that ultimately culminate in similar circumstances.[31]

From this theory of historical sequences follows the foregoing assumption that eventually – perhaps in the next fifty or one hundred years – the age of fragmegration will be fully established as the common sense of the prevailing epoch. At that distant time people will have become so accustomed to the contradictions, ambiguities, and uncertainties that, in effect, they will no longer be contradictory, ambiguous, and uncertain. Rather, they will have become regularities, stable patterns in which the parameters-turned-variables once again become boundary conditions – that is, to mention the key parameters of the turbulence model – the skill revolution becomes commonplace, authority structures become institutionalized, and the processes of bifurcation become routinized. At that point, of course, the epoch enters a period of stasis that renders it increasingly vulnerable to the kind of systemic shocks that may induce the onset of yet another period of turbulence. From this broad perspective, a prime analytic challenge of complexity theory is to comprehend the circumstances under which local and global dynamics interact in different parts of the world to initiate shifts that move the historical sequences from one stage to the next.

Conclusion

In sum, while it is understandable that we are vulnerable to the appeal of panaceas, this need not be the case. Our analytic capacities and concepts are not so far removed from complexity theorists that we need be in awe of their accomplishments or be ready to emulate their methods. Few of us have the skills or resources to undertake sophisticated computer simulations – and that may even be an advantage, as greater technical skills might lead us to dismiss complexity theory as inapplicable – but as a philosophical perspective complexity theory is not out of our reach. None of its premises and concepts are alien to our analytic habits. They comprise a perspective that is consistent with our own and with the transformations that appear to be taking the world into unfamiliar realms. Hence, through its explication, the complexity perspective can serve as a guide both to comprehending a fragmegrated world and theorizing within its limits.

14 Muddling, meddling, and modeling

Alternative approaches to the study of world politics in an era of rapid change[1]

When paradigms crumble, they crumble very quickly. The slightest inroad into their coherence opens gaping holes and the collapse of each of their premises raises further doubts about their adequacy. Before long everything seems questionable, and what once seemed so orderly soon looms as sheer chaos. Such a process of paradigm deterioration, I believe, is under way in the study of world affairs. And while this can lead to an exciting sense of venturesomeness, so can it result in enormous difficulties and confusion.

Thus these are hard times for those who theorize about world affairs and foreign policy. No sooner had we successfully come through several decades of enormous theoretical progress than the world that we began to comprehend manifested unmistakable signs of profound change, rendering our hard-won theoretical sophistication increasingly obsolete. No sooner had we replaced the "billiard ball" model of the realists with a differentiated state model that focused on decisional processes and the domestic sources of foreign policy than the competence of governments began to decline and their capacity to sustain effective foreign policies underwent further deterioration. No sooner had we moved significantly forward in understanding the dynamics of arms races and the premises of strategic theory than new problems of interdependence began to rival the older questions of diplomatic and military strategy as issues on the global agenda. No sooner had we started to link the machinery of foreign policy formulation to the external behavior of states than a host of other important entities appeared on the world scene that were neither governments nor conducted foreign policies. And no sooner had we perfected new methodologies for analyzing decisions and tracing the pattern of events than relevant decisions and events began to spring from the behavior of multinational corporations and other types of non-state organizations that could not be readily examined through the application of the hard-won methodologies.

In short, nothing seems to fit. Our great strides in theory and research during the 1950s, 1960s, and 1970s no longer correspond well to the world they were intended to describe. Authority has been too widely decentralized and societies too thoroughly fragmented to be adequately handled by even our most refined concepts. Consider, for example, these 1979 events reported in the Los Angeles press:

The Navahos and 21 other western Indian tribes enter into discussions with the Organization of Petroleum Exporting Countries (OPEC) in an effort to get advice on the development of energy resources.

President Sadat of Egypt takes his case to American Jews through a full-page advertisement in the *Los Angeles Times* and other US newspapers.

How does one analyze such developments? In what niches of the post-realist, differentiated and multipolar state model can they be placed? The answer strikes me as obvious as it is distressing: such events have no home in our current formulations. We could, of course, discuss them as isolated, inconsequential or transitory phenomena, a reaction that would then allow us to treat them as random incidents and to muddle through in spite of them. I doubt, however, whether we will long be able to muddle through our analyses as if basic and profound changes in the structures of world politics were not at work. The evidence that such transformations are under way seems too extensive to ignore. The Navaho may never get the aid they want; Sadat may never get the peace he wants; but aspirations, efforts and activities of this kind seem likely to become more pervasive and salient in world politics.

Another possible reaction to the indicators of underlying change involves acknowledging that structural transformations are at work and attempting to accommodate them by meddling with our current formulations. Indeed, this would seem to be the prevalent analytic posture in the field today. Aware that the dynamics of change are too extensive to dismiss, many analysts have sought to tidy up their conceptual equipment to account for the transformations.[2] Explorations have been sought through emphasis on the mounting interdependence of groups and societies, through stress on the proliferation of non-state actors (hence the Navahos), and through the notion that transnational relations have come to rival interstate relations as dominant features of the world scene (hence Sadat's appeal to American Jews). But such meddling will not do. The tidied up formulations are too ungainly to yield a deeper understanding. To posit greater interdependence is not to explain complexity. To allow for a much greater variety and number of significant international actors is not to account for the direction and pace of decentralization. To conceive of transnational phenomena as more salient is not to grasp what moves the course of events.

A third reaction to the presence of pervasive change is possible. Rather than preserving our current formulations either by dismissing the change or by absorbing it, we could treat it as so fundamental as to welcome the deterioration of existing paradigms and to warrant the construction of entirely new models. Such an analytic posture has been adopted by a few analysts who have gone well beyond tidying up and offered whole substitutes for the post-realist, differentiated and multipolar state model. Most notably, the underlying structural changes have been located in the context either of an issue paradigm that depicts the complexities of a decentralized world[3] or of a global society that subsumes and manages an ever more interdependent world.[4] But these paradigmatic endeavors are also wanting. For the world appears to be both more decentralized and more inter-dependent, thereby requiring a paradigm that posits an overall global structure which imposes coherence on diverse issues without presuming the orderliness of a society.

Putting first things first

The foregoing rests on two basic convictions that can be usefully explicated. One is that no amount of muddling or meddling through can prevent the collapse of a paradigm that has started to go. Thus I see no choice for us but to start afresh with the modeling approach. I shall return to the question of what this choice might involve.

Secondly, I am convinced that neither epistemological nor methodological problems are the source of our difficulties in the field today. The need to develop a new paradigm springs, not from the failure of quantitative techniques or the insufficiency of qualitative modes of analysis, but from the dynamics of change that are rendering the world ever more complex. Whether one is inclined to rest inquiry on scientific practices, on Marxian dialectics, on historical-interpretative approaches, or on the methods of analytic philosophy, one still has to contend with the declining capacity of governments, the rise of new issues, the advent of new actors and the many interactive effects that derive from mounting inter-dependence in an increasingly fragmented world. These substantive dynamics are at work no matter how we proceed.

It is conceivable that some of the substantive dynamics lend themselves to greater clarification through one epistemology or methodology than another, but this would be hard to demonstrate and the energy invested in such a debate does not seem worth any gains that might result. Much more is to be gained by presuming that all the available epistemologies and methodologies have something to offer if more appropriate paradigms can be developed.

The realist–idealist and science–non-science debates have spent themselves and one senses that an acceptance – if not a tolerance – of diversity has set in. Few among us still have a need to assert the importance of such contested method-ological and epistemological issues.

I have long wondered why methodological introspection seemed so much more endemic to the study of international relations than to other fields of political analysis. The answer is to be found, I think, in the elusiveness of international phenomena – in the great distances from which we must observe them and the tough cultural barriers through which our observations must pass.[5] It now seems clear that these very difficulties are also an advantage, since they have inhibited the emergence of orthodoxy and encouraged the perfection of diverse methodologies.

This is not to say there is no need to be methodologically aware or epistemo-logically sensitive. Obviously such matters will continue to be important – if only because the advent of new non-governmental actors may require the develop-ment of new techniques of analysis – and clearly inquiry will be more incisive the more sophisticated it is in these regards. But our hard-won tolerance of diversity does allow us to put methodological concerns in perspective and to converge on the central problem. This is the problem of theory, of constructing paradigms that more adequately account for the changing structures of world politics.

An American distortion?

Reactions to earlier versions of the foregoing reasoning have made me keenly aware that the processes of pervasive change are not self-evident, that many observers do not perceive a need for new paradigms because they view the structures and dynamics of world politics as essentially undifferentiated from the past. The wealthy elites still dominate the working classes (say the Marxists), the superpowers still dominate the international scene (say the power theorists), and nongovernmental actors have always limited the capacities of governments (say the post-realists). The trends and developments that strike me as reflective of basic transformations are seen by others as peripheral, as mere perturbations in long-standing, deeply rooted historic patterns.

This criticism has been voiced primarily by non-Americans, who contend that the perception of pervasive change is not so much an empirical observation as it is a conceptual bias of scholars.[6] The decline of the US role in world affairs, supplemented by an inclination towards pragmatic and non-historical analysis that sometimes amounts to faddism, is said to have predisposed American students of international relations to be much too quick to treat marginal fluctuations as central changes and much too ready to ignore the possibility that things are the same as they have always been except for a substantial lessening of their country's influence over the course of events. It could be. The question of how much change constitutes basic change is more a conceptual than an empirical question; the empirical attempts to measure change have not yielded such clear-cut and convergent findings as to promote widespread agreement on whether fundamental transformations are at work.[7] And surely American scholars have long been biased towards keeping their studies of world affairs consonant with their images of world affairs.[8]

To dismiss the indicators of change as an American bias, however, is to fail to confront the central question of whether world politics is undergoing transformation. Such a dismissal may even be expressive of a non-American bias in which European and Asian scholars presume that nothing basically new can ever develop because comparable events can always be found in history. One can always identify incidents in the past that correspond in some salient ways to any present event. But history also records breakpoints, watersheds, and transformations, with the result that the presumption of historical continuity can be just as prejudiced and self-deceptive as the assumption that profound changes are occurring. Furthermore, it is the very nature of paradigms that they are so encompassing as to be entrapping, preventing us from seeing their increasing inappropriateness because they are founded on premises that can absorb and explain any contradictions. This is why paradigms seem to crumble quickly once they start to crumble: when we finally break free of them enough to get an inkling of their inappropriateness, they are already far gone and thus appear to crumble quickly.

How, then, does one proceed? Assuming the problem is conceptual and not empirical, what presumption does one make as to whether profound changes are transforming world politics or whether deep-seated continuities are preserving the existing structure? I find it safer to proceed as if the changes are occurring than to treat them as peripheral. In this way we can, at least, allow for the evolution of a new paradigm which may, subsequently, prove insufficient because not that much change has occurred. But if we muddle or meddle through by stressing the deep-seated continuities, we run the risk of missing out on the prevailing dynamics of our field. I admit to being insufficiently grounded in history and I acknowledge the possibility that my perspectives are too grounded in American biases. Yet I find the indicators of change to be so impressive and so pervasive that I cannot avoid the conclusion that trying to develop new paradigms is energy well expended.

Some essential components of new paradigms

To recognize the rapidity with which a paradigm crumbles when it starts to go is not to discern the outlines and basic premises of those that might evolve in its place. A long period of disarray and tension may have to ensue before the essential components of a new paradigm are pieced together into a structured and parsimonious whole.

There is an exception to the lengthy process of paradigm replacement. If the reasons for the collapse of the old are consistent with the basic premises of a well-developed, existing paradigm that has not previously seemed competitive, then a ready-made alternative is at hand and the period of disarray can be avoided. If, for example, one became disenchanted with the differentiated state model because the behavior of the new actors and the dynamics of the new issues of interdependence appeared to stem from class conflicts that had not previously seemed so central, one might readily adopt the Marxist perspective. Such a shift to the Marxist paradigm strikes me as likely to be made by increasing numbers of international relations analysts in industrial democracies. Mounting North–South tensions, demands for a New Economic Order and the prominent role multinational corporations have come to play as rivals to governments in world politics can readily be interpreted in a Marxist framework as the differentiated state model seems increasingly inappropriate. Moreover, since "Marx is capable of a wide range of interpretations . . . each perfectly consistent within itself," and since there are thus "many Marxes,"[9] the handling of monetary crises, famine, trade imbalance, and many of the other new interdependence issues, may be just as easily cast in one or another Marxist framework as any fledgling non-Marxist paradigm that may evolve.

I wish it were so simple. Building paradigmatic foundations is so arduous and tenuous that ready-made formulations as incisive as those to be found in Marx are tempting replacements. As I understand the four essential elements that the many

Marxist formulations have in common,[10] however, the fit does not seem sufficient to yield to temptation. Though necessary, this is not the place to undertake an analysis of how the dynamics of change may or may not be shaping a world that conforms to Marxist paradigms. Suffice it to note that I find too much diversity in the fragmentation of authority, as well as in the structures, social bases, and aspirations of the new non-state organizations through which the fragmentation is occurring, to accept the Marxist emphasis on class struggle as the prime motor of historical change.

So I, for one, need to start from scratch and undertake a search for the essential components of a future paradigm that accounts for an overall global structure which imposes coherence on diverse issues without presuming the orderliness of a society. But where to begin? What criteria should we use to select the building blocks of appropriate new models? My answer to these key questions is twofold. First, we need to develop concepts that focus on dynamic rather than static phenomena, that are organized around the processes of interacting entities rather than their attributes. If we can construct the outlines of a world in which the course of events is sustained by processes rather than actors, our paradigm will not be rendered obsolete by the declining capacities of governments, the advent of new issues initiated by new organizations, the fragmentation of authority, or the evolution of interdependence. For all these tendencies are processes and they ought to be subject to investigation irrespective of whether they are maintained by states, bureaucracies, nongovernmental entities, or transnational bodies. Second, it follows that we need to begin with building blocks that are developed at such a high level of abstraction that they enable us to analyze the processes presently at work and any that may unfold in the future. Highly abstract concepts, moreover, can help free us from the differentiated state paradigm to the extent that they involve new words, labels, and ideas that may inhibit our inclination to fall back into old analytic habits.

But what processes should be the focus of our modeling effort? Here I derive the answer from what strikes me as the most elemental dynamic common to both the changes and the continuities at work in world politics, namely, that dynamic or set of dynamics whereby individual actions are summed and thereby converted into collectivities and then, at subsequent points in time, converted over and over again into more or less encompassing collectivities. Such dynamics underlie the emergence of new issues and actors, both those that result from the fragmentation of authority and those that stem from cooperative integration. They also undergird the decline of old issues and actors as well as those that remain unaltered by changing circumstances. I shall refer to these most elemental dynamics as aggregative or disaggregative processes, since the summing of actions into more or less encompassing collectivities can be readily seen as transformations through which behavior is more or less widely aggregated.

This line of reasoning leads to a world populated by a great variety of aggregations that are macro wholes summed out of micro parts. Some of the aggregations are formal organizations, others are loose coalitions; and still others comprise unorganized individuals whose actions sum to recognizable wholes; but all of them are subject to events or trends that alter their parts and thus the sums to which they cumulate. As a result, all of the aggregations are posited as either undergoing formation and leaderless or as established and led by authorized or self-appointed spokespersons who seek to mobilize the parts or otherwise articulate and advance their interests.

Although the ensuing analysis treats aggregation at a very high level of abstraction and as a series of never-ending processes, I do not claim that it is sufficient as a building block for a new paradigm. Such a conclusion requires a much more extended inquiry than is set forth here, not to mention the identification of the other building blocks out of which a viable conceptual structure can be fashioned. But at least this formulation is suggestive of what may be involved if we opt for modeling rather than muddling or meddling.

The concept of aggregation

As indicated, an aggregation is conceived to be a whole (or macro unit) composed of parts (or micro units) whose actions are sufficiently similar to be summable into the whole and an aggregative process refers to the interactions whereby such transformations occur. The smallest micro unit in world politics is the individual, but all aggregations of individuals from two-person groups to nation-states to international organizations can also be viewed as micro units if they are treated as parts of more encompassing wholes. Aggregations can also be treated as macro units if there are no reasons to focus on how their actions are transformed into larger wholes. For example, bureaucratic agencies are macro units embracing individuals as micro units, whereas from a broader perspective the agencies are micro units embedded in such macro units as governments, large corporations, or international organizations.

The key to making a full break with the differentiated state paradigm and constructing new ones to replace it lies in the readiness to treat all collectivities as susceptible either to aggregative processes that transform them into larger wholes or to disaggregative processes that transform them from wholes into parts.[11] These processes are nothing less than the causal flows in international relations, the dynamics through which action is initiated, sustained, redirected, or terminated on the world stage. Thus, whether one is concerned with a state's foreign policy, the population explosion, a balance of power, an arms race, the Third World's demands for greater equity, or a resource scarcity, its place in the larger scheme of world politics becomes more elaborately and more incisively manifest when it is viewed as the product of, or a contributor to, any or all of several aggregative processes.

Three aggregative processes strike me as especially fundamental. One results in unintended aggregations, another in articulated aggregations and the third in mobilized aggregations. These three types are distinguished by the ways in which their micro parts come together into macro wholes.

In the unintended process the micro parts are aggregated whenever the similarity of their parts is recognized, but not acted upon (e.g. migrations), whereas in the other two processes recognition is accompanied by action on the part of spokes-persons (e.g. immigration regulations). Leadership activities do not accompany unintended aggregations because the similar actions of their micro parts may stem from a variety of sources. Indeed, their similar actions may be undertaken for very different, perhaps even conflicting, private purposes. Yet, being the same, they can be summed. These unintended sums may be recognized by journalists, scholars, and/or other observers who have occasion to take note of the separate but similar actions that comprise the aggregation in the course of performing their responsibilities. For reasons suggested below, however, the unintended aggregation is not the basis of action on the part of those who sum its parts through recognition. It is simply a structural feature of the world scene that may play a crucial, if passive, role in the course of events. A resource scarcity typifies an unintended aggregation. It results from individuals or groups consuming the resource for their own private reasons and, in so doing, creating a scarcity. None of the micro units intended the shortage, but their separate actions aggregated to such an outcome.

Frequently, of course, the actions of micro units are undertaken for similar purposes. If so, obviously they will also be similar in content and recognized as aggregating to a larger whole. Less obvious is the similarity of the purposes of the micro units that leads them to permit or select spokespersons to act on behalf of their summed actions. That is, the micro units intend – or at least allow – their aggregation and they intend it to be recognized and organized in such a way that action can be continuously taken on behalf of their collective interests. It is this process that I refer to as an articulated aggregation. It is exemplified by the activities of multinational corporations, rebel movements, trade unions, profes-sional societies, or international organizations, all of whose spokespersons seek to promote and preserve the concerns of their stockholders, members, followers, and any other micro units of which they may be composed. Most notably perhaps, an articulated aggregation is illustrated by the foreign policies of a state, which are framed and advanced by its spokespersons on the basis of the prior and continu-ing actions of its citizens that permit their aggregation into the state. The spokes-persons and those towards whom their policies are directed presume that through aggregation they enjoy sufficient support of the citizenry-micro units to articulate its interests. To be sure, on rare occasions the actions of foreign policy officials are lacking a support base and thus do not represent accurate summations of the micro units. But these exceptions also reveal the nature of articulated aggrega-tions, since they normally result in the ouster of the officials (as when Anthony Eden launched an English invasion of the Suez Canal in 1956 or when Lyndon Johnson escalated US involvement in Vietnam).

The third basic type of aggregative process occurs when the similar actions of micro parts are stimulated by spokespersons who seek to sum them into a particu-lar whole for a particular purpose. Normally an articulated aggregation is the focus of such efforts (as when states go to war or when some leaders of the Third World generate support among their colleagues in the Group of 77 to reinforce demands for a New Economic Order); but sometimes an unintended aggregation is the target of the stimuli (as when spokespersons for governments try to get people to conserve energy or when aspiring politicians attempt to seize leadership of a grass-roots revolt against high taxes). Whichever may be the target of the efforts, it is the result of this process that I call a mobilized aggregation.

It is important to stress that the summing of the micro units of an aggregation into a macro whole is a process undertaken and sustained, not by the micro units themselves, but by observers and/or leaders (i.e. spokespersons) who recognize, articulate, and/or mobilize them. The collective consequences of individual actions, in other words, only become aggregations when they are identified as cumulative sums. And they only become politically relevant aggregations when their sums are both identified and used by spokespersons to advance, resist, or otherwise contest claims vis-à-vis the community.

Individuals might band together to press a claim, but even their concerted actions do not become those of an aggregation until their summed demands are articulated by their leaders and acknowledged by those of whom the demands are made. Spontaneous street mobs, organized protest marches, impulsive buyer resistances, or planned consumer boycotts, for example, do not become summed aggregations until the summing is experienced and reacted to as a collective action.

It follows that the relationship between the micro units of an aggregation and its macro spokespersons can vary greatly, from a tight, one-to-one relationship in which the latter do not act without the consent of the former to a loose, tenuous relationship in which the spokespersons need not be particularly concerned about the accuracy of their sums. Most aggregations are of the loose, tenuous type (thereby giving rise to the need for creative and effective leadership). Of course, in the long run spokespersons have much to gain through maximizing the accuracy of their aggregated sums, as the more accurate they are, the closer they are in touch with their support base and thus the more effectively can they cite evidence to support their claims.

Whatever the accuracy with which the parts are summed, there is one sense in which inaccuracy is bound to occur: the aggregated whole is bound to be larger than the sum of its parts whenever the similar actions that comprise an aggregation are articulated or mobilized by its spokespersons and their assertions and activities thereby become the basis of issues in the political arena. At such points the needs and wants of the aggregation acquire an existence apart from its micro units. The aggregation becomes an entity unto itself, capable of pressing, resisting, bargaining, and accommodating demands, and in so acting its spokespersons render it into a whole that exceeds the sum of its parts.

Uses of the concept

Crude as it may be, this initial formulation of the several types of aggregation can serve the paradigm-building task in a number of ways. One is that it lends itself to close empirical examination. Although the interactions of masses of people can be extremely circuitous, complex, and subtle, in this formulation the ways in which micro units cumulate into macro units are concrete and identifiable; aggregation occurs when similar actions are recognized, summed, and articulated. Recognition and summation are manifest in birth rates, agricultural outputs, industrial production figures, election outcomes, trade patterns, and a host of other indicators that are regularly published or readily compiled. Similarly, articulation is empirically manifest in the activities of spokespersons who continuously recognize and sum the aggregations for which they act.

Second, by conceiving of the collectivities that sustain world politics as aggregative processes rather than structural parameters, we allow for the dynamics of change at all levels of analysis and under all possible circumstances. Viewed as aggregations whose formation depends on the convergence of similar behavior, collectivities appear less as enduring constants and more as being in continuous flux. If we can discipline ourselves to see the world, not as a cluster of nations, alignments, or publics, but as a cluster of ever-changing aggregative processes – of parts forming wholes, coming apart, re-forming and doing so in such a way that the wholes are sometimes roughly equal to the sums of their parts and sometimes greater than the sums – then we ought to be better able to pick up and rearrange the components of the paradigms that collapsed under the weight of pervasive change.

The capacity of the aggregation concept to render us more sensitive to the dynamics of change is especially relevant to the long-standing practice of viewing certain circumstances as the "realities" of world politics – as those deeper structures comprising long-standing habits, cultural tendencies, economic imperatives, and sociological necessities entrenched in the environment that are beyond manipulation and yet profoundly condition what people do and how communities function. As considered here, however, all such "realities" are unintended aggregations that, being composed of recognizable parts, may be susceptible to manipulation (i.e. to transformation into articulated or mobilized aggregations). The energy problem, for example, is often posited as consisting of realities embedded in the interaction between the world's oil reserves and the consumption patterns of an industrial civilization. Recent efforts in the West to get people to change their energy-utilization habits constitute an attempt to render an unintentional aggregation into a mobilized one and, notwithstanding the apparent failure of such efforts, it suggests the emergence of a readiness on the part of spokespersons to undertake manipulation of what not long ago had been regarded as unmanipulable. Much the same can be said about ocean problems, food shortages, currency fluctuations, and the population explosion.

Fourth, by treating aggregative processes as parameters of world politics, we put the individual person more centrally on to the global stage. Aggregations begin with and build upon concrete and identifiable individuals who, through recognized and articulated similar behavior, become groups, communities, governments, nations, international balances and the like. Putting the person on to the global stage is important because the decentralization of authority, the fragmentation of societies, and the emergence of interdependence issues bring the origins and dynamics of politics into the homes and jobs where individuals make choices and undertake actions. The population explosion is perhaps the clearest example of how aggregative processes can be traced back to the individual level, but the relevance of the motorist, the banker, the farmer, the fisherman, and the terrorist to, respectively, the energy crunch, monetary instability, food shortages, ocean problems, and political upheaval is indicative of the large degree to which the structures of world politics have become ever more solidly rooted in the soil of individual orientations and behavior. Indeed, the declining competence of governments can be traced partly, if not primarily, to mounting distrust of public institutions on the part of citizens.

A fifth advantage of this formulation is that it can hasten our break with any paradigm that relies on states as the prime sources of causation. By focusing on aggregations and their spokespersons, we allow ourselves to analyze varied behavior on the global stage without having to presume the importance of states or implicitly rank them as more significant than other types of actors. Indeed, this formulation enables us to get away not only from states as abstract actors but also from the very notion of action being the product of any abstraction. As conceived here, action is located where it originates empirically and is maintained, that is, in and by individuals. For the only actors in this formulation are the individuals who comprise aggregations and those who serve as spokespersons for them.

Sixth, the notion of spokespersons offers the potential of a fresh approach to analyzing the policy-making process. Instead of being forced to treat such processes as bounded by the political and legal constraints of states, we can focus on the dynamics whereby the spokespersons experience, sum, assess, and articulate the interests of their aggregations and then interact with other spokespersons of other aggregations. Sometimes these interactions occur within governments (thus resulting in what are now called policy decisions), sometimes in bargaining between governments (thus giving rise to policy outcomes) and sometimes in the non-governmental arena, where political parties, interest groups, professional associations, and other groups compete for the support of citizens and the attention of officials. But mostly aggregations extend across the boundaries that separate agencies within governments, that divide governments from each other and that differentiate governments from the private sector. Thus the consequences of mounting interdependence and fragmented authority are likely to be built into any analysis of what happens when spokespersons articulate and mobilize their aggregations.

A seventh reason why the concept can serve as a useful building block for a more appropriate paradigm is that its several types provide a uniform basis for analyzing any of the diverse issues that may be on the world's agenda at any moment in time. Any issue can be viewed as a problem posed by an unintended aggregation or as arising out of a competition among articulated or mobilized aggregations. Whatever its aggregative foundations, the issue can be dissected and probed by examining the dynamics, the motivations, presumptions, and/or habits whereby the actions of individuals allow for and lead to their aggregation and the articulation of their collective needs and wants. Thus, despite the diversity of their contents, the structures, overlaps, and consequences of the prevailing issues can be contrasted and compared. Hopefully, such comparative analyses can lead to a more precise specification of a parsimonious typology of aggregative processes which, in turn, can facilitate the derivation of a few basic causal principles around which the beginnings of a paradigm can be organized.

It follows that the distinctions among the several types of aggregation should also better enable us to discern the similarities between the newer socio-economic issues spawned by mounting interdependence and the older military-diplomatic issues that continue to occupy prominent places on the global agenda. Presumably any new paradigm that evolves will have to surmount the inclination to treat the socio-economic issues as interlopers, as unconventional aspects of world politics that require special treatment. These new issues are likely to endure and we have to begin to treat them as integral parts of world politics. To be sure, since most socio-economic issues derive from the habits and patterns of millions of persons, they evolve in different ways and at different rates than do most military-diplomatic issues. Hence the former are much less subject to articulated aggregation than are the latter and they are also less susceptible to mobilization.[12] Nevertheless, viewing both types of issues as aggregative processes at least renders them comparable and enables us to contrast them in meaningful ways.

A final advantage inherent in the concept of aggregation is that it provides a means of observing how the global agenda is formed, with issues rising and falling, some crowding their way to the top of the agenda, some lingering on its periphery and others never making it at all. By tracing how unintended aggregations are transformed into those that are articulated or mobilized, we can begin to see how activities at various levels of organization do or do not become linked to each other and, as a result, how the linked actions can culminate in a place on the global agenda.

The conversion of an aggregation into a public issue occurs when its recognition is followed by spokespersons for macro units who have reasons for calling attention to the similar actions of the micro units highlighting the need to respond to their collective implications (say, the importance of the patterns formed by the purchases of citizens or the significance of the policy patterns formed by the decisions of officials). The spokespersons can speak on behalf of the aggregation or they can speak about it, contending that it enhances or threatens certain values. In either case, once an aggregative process thus enters the articulation stage, it can become controversial if spokespersons for different aggregations contest the claims made on its behalf. When enough spokespersons become involved, the aggregation becomes the basis of an issue competing for a place on the agenda of a political system. Stated somewhat differently, the articulation of an aggregation links it to actions at more encompassing levels of organization. Whether this occurs through the parts being mobilized to form a whole or simply through articulation of the interests recognized as the sum of the parts, the result is the same: the spokespersons precipitate processes of aggregation that can move through more and more encompassing levels until they pass beyond national boundaries and culminate in transnational and international activities.

Thus, for example, do votes become electoral mandates and thus do the decisions of officials become the policies of governments. And so, too, do electoral mandates become societal demands and so do governmental policies become international conflicts. As the processes of aggregation move on from level to level, at some point their dynamics either wane or gather more force, with the result that the aggregation either fails to push its way as an issue on to the agenda of political systems or its urgency becomes unavoidable and it becomes an issue with which systems must cope. Having long been ignored by the spokespersons of most aggregations, discrimination against minorities in the United States followed such a pattern and eventually acquired status as a civil rights issue on the national agenda. And this particular aggregative process has continued to unfold to the point where it has now been pushed ever more securely on to the global agenda.

From building blocks to theory building

Whatever its many potential virtues, of course, the concept of aggregation is not in itself a sufficient foundation for a new paradigm. As formulated, it is just a building block, subject to any of a number of possible uses. Other concepts are needed and so is the inspired creativity that can weave them together into a theoretical cloth. Among others, the concepts of role, authority, and legitimacy ought to be considered in this regard. The first can be viewed as the source of the similar behavior out of which aggregations are formed and the last two can serve as the stitching, so to speak, that links the micro parts of aggregations once they have been recognized and their interests articulated.[13] Developing these concepts for this purpose, however, will take some work. This is especially so in the case of authority. Although there is a vast and rich literature on the concept that should be consulted, it needs to be supplemented and enlarged with fresh thought. Virtually all the existing literature treats authority in a legal context, whereas the goal of the modeling approach is to free us of state-centric paradigms by allowing for aggregative processes that do not necessarily sum to relevant collectivities based on formal legal structures.[14]

As for the inspired creativity that can cement the building blocks into a coherent and parsimonious model, here one can only reiterate that modeling is preferable to muddling or meddling and urge that recourse to creativity be an endless commitment. The various types of aggregation need to be played with in our minds, imagined as responses to different conditions, fostering different outcomes, and governed by different, lawful properties. And perhaps we should explore the possibility of treating the global agenda as an overarching structure that imposes coherence on diverse issues without presuming the orderliness of a society. A playful mind may not be enough to capture and discipline all the changes that are transforming world politics, but it surely is a necessary prerequisite to paradigmatic progress.

15 Territorial affiliations and emergent roles

The shifting nature of identity in a globalizing world[1]

A small agency responsible for marking and maintaining the expansive border between the United States and Canada has fallen so far behind it may never catch up . . . The agency, the International Boundary Commission, has warned that the border markers are deteriorating and parts of the border are becoming overgrown by trees and brush to the point that the border's location could be lost in some areas.

(news item[2])

If globalization is best defined in terms of boundary-spanning activities, as I have argued elsewhere that it is,[3] it involves among other things the potential for radically new orientations toward territory in the minds of elites and ordinary citizens as well. The attachment to land as a place where one grew up and lives has long been inviolate, beyond questioning as the basis for loyalties and commitments. However, with the advent of the boundary-spanning activities that sustain globalization and have made the world a much smaller place, the meaning of territory may be undergoing profound changes that are altering the nature of economies, polities, and societies. The ever-expanding spate of literatures on global governance, transnational civil societies, and cosmopolitan citizenship are but one indicator that territory is undergoing transformation as an organizing concept in the lives of people.[4]

Needless to say, the redefining of the meaning of territory is not a rapid process. Rather, it occurs slowly, unevenly, and incrementally and has yet to acquire a relentless momentum. The attachments to territory are deep-seated and of long and historic standing. They are attachments that are not easily abandoned and in most cases their diminution occurs unbeknownst to those who subscribe to them verbally. Indeed, when challenged many people will proclaim their continuing love for their piece of the homeland even as their conduct suggests the emergence of new attachments that override, or at least supplement, the salience of territory. For large numbers of people around the world, moreover, the subtle shift away from deep commitments to territoriality may have yet to begin or is only just beginning to unfold. Only in the long run, for reasons outlined below, is such a shift likely to occur and new terminal entities emerge as the focus of deep commitments that edge out the local territory as the highest loyalty.

The local–global nexus

Numerous reasons explain why territorial affiliations are now in flux. Due to new technologies – perhaps especially the jet aircraft, the cell phone, and the Internet – time and distance have taken on new meanings whereby the isolation of people in their local circumstances has diminished. What is global today is also local, and vice versa; or to use phrasing I prefer, what is distant is also proximate and vice versa.[5] Hence it seems probable that the more the distant impinges on the proximate, the more is it likely that people will experience confusion as to where the sources of their identity lie. This likelihood may, to repeat, take a long time, even generations, before the confusion is sufficient to frame doubts about the nature of "home" and the meaning of territory.

Stated differently, for a preponderance of people in all parts of the world the site of their birth and upbringing will never be forgotten,[6] but in the long run – i.e. when they move into careers and become involved in a multiplicity of activities – the salience of these sites is likely to diminish as the distant impinges ever more on the proximate. Childhood memories fade if they no longer reside in the communities of their upbringing, and as they do, so do their sense of territoriality. But, it might well be argued, the linking of territory to childhood and adolescence gets replaced by links to countries as territories, to being an American, a German, or a Thai; or if geographic regions and institutions eventually become increasingly salient, to being a North American, a European, or a Southeast Asian. Under these circumstances, in other words, nationalism or regionalism replace childhood attachments as the basis for contextualizing territory.

One can hardly quarrel with this line of reasoning. Nationalism, or at least attachment to country, is certainly a pervasive phenomenon that highlights the likelihood of territoriality continuing to be a central consideration in the daily lives of people. Nevertheless, as the distant encroaches ever more fully on the proximate, even this more encompassing dimension of territoriality seems likely to be minimized. For at the core of territoriality as it is experienced by individuals is identity – that sense of being part of a larger aggregation, of being progressively, say, an uptowner, a Philadelphian, a Pennsylvanian, an American. In other words, territorial identities are collective. They connote groups of people with similar ties, attachments, and heritages. However, territory is only one basis for collective identities. There are innumerable others, many of which are likely to supercede the territorial as salient features of our lives. There is the occupational (lawyers, farmers, professors), the political (conservatives, liberals, radicals), the religious (Protestants, Jews, Muslims), the gender (feminists, lesbians, gays, straights), the economic (wealthy, middle class, poor), the racial and ethnic (blacks, Hispanics, Asians), the marginalized (handicapped, obese, prisoners), the artistic (painters, musicians, dramatists), the traveler (tourists, guides, nomads), the healers (doctors, therapists, dentists), and so on across an ever-increasing number of collective identities. Increasingly, in other words, these nonterritorial collective identities seem likely to supplement, if not to replace, those linked to geographic places as people age and boundaries get increasingly spanned and become increasingly irrelevant.

Another way to conceive of identities is as social roles in social systems. Every identity is a role to which expectations are attached by their occupants and by others. Much of the behavior of individuals is a response to role expectations; and as collective roles and identities proliferate, so do the conflicts among them. In the most extreme cases the conflicts give rise to an "identity crisis," but more often than not such crises are of short duration as most people become increasingly adept at managing the multiplicity of roles they occupy and the overlaps and conflicts among them. Both the overlaps and the conflicts become less and less paralyzing for individuals as they become accustomed to living in a world where the local–global nexus is the predominant feature of daily life. Indeed, it can readily be argued that the skills developed to cope with the multiplicity of role expectations inherent in the distant becoming proximate serve to minimize and routinize acceptance of the diminishing sense of territoriality.

The self

Apart from, and perhaps preceding, collective identities are individual identities: those qualities, orientations, fears, hopes, and values that individuals perceive as uniquely their own, as their "self." The notion of the self as differentiated from all of one's collective identities is a major feature of modernity, of conditions in which identities are not ascribed by any kind of religious or secular authority. The self has become our authority. It enables us to stand apart and ask,

> Who am I? But this can't necessarily be answered by giving name and genealogy. What does answer this question for us is an understanding of what is of crucial importance to us. To know who I am is a species of knowing where I stand. My identity is defined by the commitments and identifications which provide the frame or horizon with which I can try to determine from case to case what is good, or valuable, or what ought to be done, or what I endorse or oppose. In other words, it is the horizon within which I am capable of taking a stand.[7]

Put differently, it is the self to which those who would mobilize our support must appeal, hoping that the appeal is consistent not only with the collective identity we share with the mobilizer, but also with our individual tastes and values.

The question immediately arises of how to analyze the self in a complex world that is less and less territorial. It is not enough to assert that one or more of the multiplicity of social roles that people occupy can serve to explain how they conduct themselves in response to the local–global nexus. That nexus offers such endless possibilities for choice that people cannot rely on their collective identities as guides to their action or inaction. More often than not they have to fall back on their individual identities – their selves – to assess how to cope with the challenges that arise when the distant impinges on the proximate. Collective identities and individual orientations may converge, but the local–global nexus poses a host of situations wherein such a convergence provides little or no guidance to action. None of the collective identities listed above indicate how one should respond when the distant becomes proximate: does one cling to the proximate, resist the distant, or treat the nexus as a synthesis to which one adapts? Can a framework be designed to meaningfully investigate and generalize about characteristic responses to the local–global nexus?

Twelve analytic worlds

Obviously, different "selves" respond to these questions in a variety of ways. Elsewhere I have developed one such framework for probing how individuals respond to the local–global nexus,[8] an abbreviated version of which is presented here. At the core of the framework is the notion that orientations toward territory are undergoing, for most people, a shift toward any of the twelve "worlds," of which only one is territorial. More accurately, with one exception, persons in all the worlds are at different points on a learning curve that involves absorbing the idea that the local–global nexus is tearing away at their conceptions of territory. Some may have a keen sense of locality, but the sense of home as a geographic place is giving way to conceptions of it as defined by the dynamics of globalization – by the flow of ideas, practices, money, pollution, trade, jobs, drugs, terrorism, and crime across the boundaries that used to protect them from foreign influences.

Four of the twelve worlds are global, four are local, and four are private. People in the four global worlds are Affirmative Globals, Resistant Globals, Specialized Globals, or Territorial Globals. All of them share tendencies to think and act on a scale that exceeds a local context even as they are differentiated by the way in which large scale is conceived and differentiated. The Affirmative Global world is populated by people, ordinary people as well as activists and elites, who share positive orientations toward the processes of globalization, viewing them as moving humankind toward greater prosperity and integration. While the Resistant Globals are no less worldwide in the scale of their orientations, they regard one or more of the prevailing processes that sustain globalization as detrimental to the well-being of peoples. Similarly, the Specialized Globals are persons whose territorial orientations are not locally bounded but who are oriented toward only limited issues on the global agenda. The scale of thought and action of the Territorial Globals, on the other hand, is large but territorially bounded. Foreign policy officials are quintessential (though not the only) examples of Territorial Globals inasmuch as they are concerned about problems that arise anywhere abroad even as their concerns are framed in terms of their country's interests and are thus necessarily territorially specific.

Residents of the four local worlds – the Affirmative Locals, Resistant Locals, Exclusionary Locals, and Insular Locals – are all low on the learning curve traced by the local–global nexus. Their horizons all tend to be proximate even though, with one possible exception, they may well be aware of remote events and situations that can have consequences for them. Nevertheless, they interpret distant proximities through local lenses, as readily absorbable into their long-standing practices and worldviews. The one possible exception is the Insular Locals, who are conceived to be exclusively concerned with spatial proximities, with the geographically near-at-hand, with circumstances that can be directly encountered. They have yet to start up the learning curve and are thus the last to experience the proximity of the distant. For a host of reasons (including global television, the cell phone, and other technological innovations), however, there are good reasons to anticipate a continuing diminution of the Insular Locals around the world.

In contrast to the Insular Locals, on the other hand, the Resistant Locals and the Exclusionary Locals contextualize proximity and allow for the spatially remote to be near-at-hand, but the Resistant Locals perceive the geographically remote as so threateningly close as to necessitate opposition, whereas the Exclusionary Locals are inclined to avoid the distant proximities they view as becoming too close. Finally, the Affirmative Locals are individuals who are neither isolated nor inclined to retreat in the face of globalizing dynamics. They are capable of absorbing external encroachments on their own terms without fearing their local world will lose its integrity. In sum, the Insular Locals tend to live in closed communities; the Resistant Locals tend to live in political arenas; the Exclusionary Locals tend to live in enclaves; and the Affirmative Locals tend to live in open communities.

If residents of the local worlds are low on the learning local–global curve, those in the four private worlds are either unaware there is such a curve or they have rejected its validity. The former consists of the Tuned-out Passives and the Circumstantial Passives, while those in the latter are either the Alienated Cynics or the Alienated Illegals. All four of these worlds are populated by people who, for different reasons, lack or have lost a sense of connection to the local–global nexus. In the case of the two passive worlds, the Tuned-out Passives may be fully aware of their apathy toward any local or global connection but do not avail themselves of ample opportunities afforded by time, energy, and resources to forge such connections. The Circumstantial Passives, on the other hand, are those persons whose daily conditions are such as to leave them no time, energy, or resources to care about anything beyond their daily efforts to maintain their subsistence. Their life situations are marked by a lack of education and a hand-to-mouth existence that compels them to focus so intensely on the daily needs of food, clothing, and shelter that no larger community is of relevance.

The distinction between the two alienated worlds derives from the degree of alienation their populaces have experienced. The Alienated Cynics are those who refrain from engagement with any political world. They do not vote, join organizations, or otherwise participate in political processes. In contrast, the Alienated Illegals are politically active, but they are so self-conscious about their own alienation that they resort to illegal, even violent, behavior to express their contempt for the political mainstreams that sustain the local–global nexus.

Of course, the populations in none of the twelve worlds are constant. They fluctuate as varying situations stimulate people to migrate from one world to another, as conditions improve for some who are Circumstantial Passives, as some in any of the local or global worlds are so depressed by the decline in the respect for politicians, governments, the media, and other public institutions that they adopt the orientations of the Alienated Cynics – to mention but a few of the dynamics that can lead to movement among the worlds. Yet, despite the fluctuating populations of the twelve worlds, it is important to stress that the people in all of them are seen, analytically, as being essentially rooted into habit, as having to contest the inclination to stay put in their worlds when new horizons or commitment tempt them to revise their orientations. The long-run trend is probably in the direction of people increasingly shifting toward global orientations and diminished attachment to territory, but such tendencies may not easily prevail in the face of life-long habits and incentives that reinforce the attitudes that moved them into the local or private worlds to which they were originally attracted.[9]

Conclusions

It should be noted that the foregoing formulation excludes any place for the nation-state. More accurately, it is considered local as the distant becomes ever more proximate. As such, it may be a possible focus of concern on the part of the Affirmative, Resistant, or Exclusionary Locals, many of whom may view national governments as promoting or inhibiting their local preoccupations.

Additionally, it is important to emphasize that the twelve worlds are analytic and not empirical. They are individual orientations and not collective identities. Most people are doubtless unaware of the orientations ascribed to them by this framework, and they certainly do not organize themselves along such lines. Nevertheless, it seems clear that the local–global nexus is fostering the emergence of new roles in which territoriality is essentially irrelevant. In this sense the epigraph describing the unknown location of parts of the Canadian–American border is a metaphor for the slow erosion of the meaning and centrality of geographic space.

Let me set forth my overall perspective on territorial affiliations by concluding with a poem. It is an adaptation of an old nursery rhyme that I used to relate to my then young daughter. It reads like this:

> For years, with considerable care
> I traced a boundary that wasn't there
> It wasn't there every day
> Gee, I wanted it to go away

> At last, I am ready to declare
> That the boundary was never there
> And no matter what you say
> It wasn't there again today

And so now it seems clear
We must let the boundary disappear
Let it yield pride of place
To a new and wide political space

A space that is so manifestly near
As to be a broad and porous frontier
Where new and old actors vie
Seeking to shape pieces of the pie

16 Capabilities and control in an interdependent world[1]

In pondering the changing nature of "national power," two recent but contradictory examples come to mind as indicative of profound changes occurring in the nature and dynamics of whatever it is we mean when we refer to the "power" of nations. One example is the "failure" of American "power" in Vietnam. The other is the "success" of Arab "power" in the 1973–4 oil embargo. What kind of changes these examples indicate, however, is obscure. Do they suggest that military "power" has diminished (hence the Vietnam failure) and that economic "power" has become more effective (hence the oil embargo success)? Do they point up the increasing variability of "power" considerations? Do they suggest that generalized characterizations of national "power" are no longer reasonable? Or do they highlight the limitations of the "power" concept, suggesting that it is a concept without meaningful content and with misleading connotations?

If the last question is addressed first and the parameters of the concept precisely delineated, all four of these questions can be answered in the affirmative. Such is the thrust of the ensuing pages. The ambiguous and misleading uses of the "power" concept are set forth at the outset and an alternative formulation outlined. The latter is then applied to the changing nature of world politics, to the evolution of economic and other new, nonmilitary types of issues, and to the implications of these issues for the nature of national "power."

The "power" concept and its limitations

To stress that conventional usage of the "power" concept results in misleading ambiguities is not in any way to deny that profound changes have occurred in world politics and that these have greatly altered the dynamics whereby nations employ their "power" to pursue and achieve their foreign policy goals. The changes are independent of the way in which the concept is formulated. Appreciation of their scope and direction, however, becomes difficult if they are traced with imprecise and obfuscating conceptual equipment. Vietnam and the oil embargo can thus be seen as illustrative of both substantive change and conceptual disarray.

Stated differently, the surprises that attended the inability of the "mighty" United States to prevail in Vietnam and the ability of the "weak" Arab states to induce altered postures in the industrial world regarding their conflict with Israel are but the most recent and dramatic examples supporting a long-standing conviction that the concept of national "power" confounds and undermines sound analysis.[2] Little is accomplished by explaining the surprising quality of these events in terms of the changing nature of "power." Such an explanation merely asserts that surprising events occurred because unrecognized changes had transpired in whatever may have been the sources of the events. Likewise, to stress that military "power" has given way to economic "power" is not to enlarge comprehension of why American policies in Vietnam and the Arab oil embargo had such contradictory outcomes. Had the conventional usage of the concept of "power" been more precise, with its empirical referents more accurately identified, there would have been no surprise with respect to Vietnam and the embargo. Indeed, conceivably neither the war in the former nor the crisis surrounding the latter would have occurred if officials had more clearly grasped the "power" concept and disaggregated it into its component parts at the time policies toward these situations were evolving.

The two examples clearly highlight the central problem with the concept because they both suggest that the success or failure of foreign policy efforts is dependent on the possession of appropriate resources in sufficient abundance to prevail in conflict situations. So viewed, the United States "failed" in Vietnam because it lacked the requisite military resources and Middle East countries "succeeded" because they had sufficient economic resources. Nothing could be more misleading. Such an interpretation overlooks the equally crucial facts that the North Vietnamese were not overly impressed by American military resources and the Western industrial nations were impressed by the oil which Middle East states could or could not make available.

Possessed resources, in other words, are only one aspect of "power"; actions and reactions through which actors relate to each other are another aspect; and neither aspect is alone sufficient. Put even more pointedly, whatever else it may connote, national "power" involves relational phenomena. Whether it is considered in the bipolar period when military considerations predominated, or whether it is assessed in the present era when economic and transnational factors are more salient, national "power" can only be understood in the context of how the actors involved relate to and perceive each other. The resources each "possesses" may well be relevant to the way in which they perceive each other, but the outcome of the way in which they exercise "power" toward each other is primarily a consequence of how they assess, accept, resist, or modify each other's efforts.

Stated in still another way, the "power" of a nation exists and is subject to meaningful assessment only insofar as it is directed at and responded to by other actors. All the possessed dimensions of "power" imaginable will not have the anticipated and seemingly logical outcomes if those toward whom they are directed perceive the possessions otherwise and thereby withhold the expected compliance. This is perhaps the prime lesson of both the Vietnam War and the oil embargo, the lesson that renders the two seemingly diverse situations highly comparable.

Unfortunately, for reasons having to do with the structure of language, the concept of "power" does not lend itself to comprehension in relational terms. Without undue violation of language, the word "power" cannot be used as a verb.[3] It is rather a noun, highlighting "things" possessed instead of processes of interaction. Nations influence each other; they exercise control over each other; they alter, maintain, subvert, enhance, deter, or otherwise affect each other, but they do not "powerize" each other. Hence, no matter how sensitive analysts may be to the question of how the resources used by one actor serve to modify or preserve the behavior of another, once they cast their assessment in terms of the "power" employed they are led – if not inevitably, then almost invariably – to focus on the resources themselves rather than on the relationship they may or may not underlie.[4]

The tendency of the concept of "power" to focus attention on possessed qualities is clearly illustrated by the pervasive inclination to rank states in terms of their "power" as defined by these attributes. Indeed, analyzing the attributes and resources of states in such a way as to classify some as superpowers, some as great powers, others as regional or middle powers, and still others as small powers is the standard approach to the concept. Nor have changes on the world scene altered this conventional treatment of the concept. Most analysts tend to account for the changes by assessing how they affect the mix of attributes and resources states possess and then derive conclusions as to whether, say, the United States is still number one, whether China has moved ahead of Western Europe and Japan as number three, and whether all of these plus the Soviet Union form a world of five superpowers that has come to replace the bipolar world of the postwar era.[5]

There is a remarkable paradox in the compulsion to analyze world affairs in terms of rankings of relative strengths and weaknesses. As students of international politics we are primarily interested in what states do or do not get each other to do, and yet we are diverted from concentrating on such relational phenomena by our reliance on a concept that focuses on the secondary question of their attributes and resources.

This is not to say, of course, that the attributes and resources that states bring to bear in their foreign relations are irrelevant. The "power" they possess underlies their officials' estimates of what can and cannot be accomplished abroad, just as the estimates made by those toward whom their actions are directed depend on calculations of the attributes and resources that may be operative. Furthermore, no matter how the possessed or deficient resources may be perceived and assessed, they are likely to shape what happens when states interact with each other. The more a state possesses the attributes and resources appropriate to its goals in a situation, the more its actions are likely to move it toward the objectives sought. So "national power" can have some predictive and analytic value if it is estimated in the context of its appropriateness to situations – but to add this condition is to highlight again the significance of relational phenomena. For estimates of how one or another "power" factor may be appropriate to a given situation requires attention to the resources, expectations, and likely responses of other parties to the situation.

How, then, to focus on both the possession and interaction dimensions of "power" without being driven by the structure of language to an overriding preoccupation with the former dimension? My answer to this question is simple, though its simplicity should not be allowed to obscure the degree to which it reduces ambiguity and allows us to concentrate on the prime questions that concern us. For years I have solved this conceptual problem by dropping the word "power" from my analytic vocabulary (thus the use here of quotation marks), replacing it with the concept of capabilities whenever reference is made to attributes or resources possessed and with verbs such as control or influence whenever the relational dimension of "power" is subjected to analysis.[6]

This disaggregation of the "power" concept virtually compels analysts to keep their eyes on the interaction phenomena primarily of interest to them because any assessments they may make of existing or potential resources and attributes are bound to be manifestly incomplete and insufficient. Their conceptual equipment will necessitate that they inquire into how the assessed resources and attributes may or may not contribute to the control of desired outcomes or otherwise influence the attitudes and behaviors of other actors. Stated differently, modifying or preserving situations and trends abroad – i.e. controlling them – depends on a wide range of variables, only some of which involve the resources and attributes of the parties to the control relationship; disaggregation of the "power" concept facilitates consideration of the full range of these variables.

Another important virtue of this disaggregated approach is that it facilitates concentration on the capabilities of governments to engage in cooperative action abroad. For historical reasons stemming from the independence of states in the international system, the "power" concept has come to have conflictual connotations. "Power" is ordinarily conceived to be applied against potential adversaries or any obstacles that block the path to goal achievement. It is not normally viewed as embracing resources and attributes that are employed for the realization of objectives through concerting efforts with other states. Consequently, analysts have long had the tendency to conceive of "power" in military terms, military action being the last resort through which states seek to maintain their independence. Yet, as elaborated below, world politics is increasingly marked by interdependence, by new issues that cannot be addressed or resolved through the threat or use of military capabilities and that instead require cooperation among states if obstacles to goals are to be diminished or eliminated. In addition to the maintenance of physical security and territorial integrity, national "power" today must be exercised with respect to the problems of oceans, exchange rates, pollution, agricultural production, population size, energy allocation, and the many other issues fostered by mounting interdependence. The distinction between capabilities and control, being free of long-standing conflictual connotations, should facilitate more cogent analysis of the role states play in resolving (or sustaining) these issues. At least the distinction should allow for a fuller treatment of those organizational skills and knowledge bases from which spring the dynamics of these newer issues than would be the case if analysts relied on the undifferentiated "power" concept.

To be sure, many of those who are accustomed to the "power" concept stress that they have in mind a broad range of factors that extend well beyond military capabilities. And, indeed, frequently the concept is formulated in ways to include national morale, societal cohesion, leadership development, and many of the other intangible attributes and resources that underlie the foreign policy efforts of states. Even the more sophisticated formulations, however, frequently succumb to the historical tendency associated with' the "power" concept and analyze non-military capabilities as if they were designed only to serve conflictual purposes. It is no accident, for example, that the problems of monetary stability, devaluations, and exchange rates are frequently cast as problems of "economic warfare." And surely it is a measure of the extent to which the "power" concept habitually provokes military and conflictual connotations that when the problem of agricultural production and distribution is treated in the context of national "power," it is typically conceived as a "food-as-a-weapon" issue.

The narrowing scope of military capabilities

None of the foregoing is to say that military capabilities are no longer available to statesmen or that they have become unwilling to use force as a means of controlling circumstances abroad. To stress mounting interdependence and the emergence of new issues is not to deny that arms races mark the world scene, that weapons production and sales is a global industry, that threats by states to use force are an almost daily occurrence, or that all too frequently states seek to control outcomes by resorting to their military capabilities. Rather, it is to say that for a variety of reasons, all of which sum to greater complexity within states and greater interdependence among them, the range through which military capabilities can achieve effective control has narrowed substantially in recent decades and that, consequently, a host of new types of abilities have become increasingly relevant if states are to maintain any control over their environments. Stated in conventional terms, "national power" is today far more multifaceted than ever before.

It is important to appreciate that the narrowing scope of military capabilities is not simply a function of the advent of nuclear weapons and the deterrence systems they have spawned. The ever-present possibility of a nuclear holocaust has made officials more cautious in their readiness to resort to military instruments of statecraft. The advent of the nuclear age, however, is only one reason why military capabilities have declined in relative importance. A seemingly much more crucial reason derives from the many ways in which an ever more dynamic technology and ever growing demands on the world's resources have shrunk the geographic, social, economic, and political distances that separate states and vastly multiplied the points at which their needs, interests, ideas, products, organizations, and publics overlap. Quite aside from the activities of governments, what happens within states would appear to have wider ramifications across their boundaries and these proliferating ramifications have created, in turn, an ever widening set of external control (i.e. foreign policy) problems for governments.

The more societies, cultures, economies, and, polities become interdependent, the less do the resulting conflicts lend themselves to resolution through military threats and actions. The threat and use of force is maximally effective, to the extent it is effective at all, when control over territory or compliance with the exercise of authority is at stake. But, new problems of interdependence involve attitudinal and behavioral patterns that have few, if any, territorial or legitimacy dimensions.

To modify or preserve these patterns governments must rely on much more variable and subtle means of control – means which are as complex and technical as the social, cultural, scientific, and economic dimensions out of which the patterns emerged and through which they are sustained. Military forms of control are most applicable in situations where issues cannot be split, refined, or redefined – where compliance gets cast in either/or terms – whereas the newer issues of interdependence are pervaded with so many nuances and subparts that control can be exercised only with respect to limited areas of behavior and can result in compliance that is not likely to be more than partial and incremental.

The narrowing scope of military capabilities can be readily illustrated by some hypothetical situations that once might have seemed logical but that appear patently absurd today. Imagine, for example, one state threatening a resort to force if another did not comply with its demand for currency devaluation. Or consider the likelihood of two neighboring states going to war over a question of pollutants that flow downstream or downwind across their common borders. Compliance with demands in such situations is likely to result from complex bargaining and the very absurdity of seeking to control them through the use or threat of force is a measure of the degree to which interdependence has fragmented the issues that comprise world politics today. Indeed, one does not have to resort to hypothetical situations to make this point. It will be recalled that during the height of the dislocation that accompanied the Arab oil embargo several analysts proposed that the West threaten, and possibly even undertake, military action in order to sustain the flow of oil from the region if a lifting of the embargo failed to occur.[7] This proposal involved control efforts so manifestly inappropriate to the situation that it failed to generate much support in or out of governmental circles.

Since it also bears on the problem of employing capabilities relevant to maximizing control over the newer issues generated by mounting interdependence, one other reason why military capabilities have become more narrowly circumscribed needs to be noted. It involves the greater self-consciousness of ethnic, racial, linguistic, and other subgroups within nation-states, a sense of identity that has led such groups to become increasingly coherent, articulate, and demanding. Few states are so homogeneous as to have avoided the contention and fragmentation inherent in the worldwide process through which subnational loyalties have come to rival, if not to replace, those directed toward national states. While it may well be that these disintegrative tendencies are both a source and a consequence of interdependence – in the sense that the proliferation of transnational relationships both stems from and contributes to heightened subgroup consciousness –

one clearly discernible result of the dispersal of loyalties is that national governments are no longer as capable as they once were of mobilizing the kind of unquestioning support that is necessary for effective military operations. The American effort to effect control in Vietnam, resisted by subnational groups within the United States, not to mention the enormous mobilization problems encountered by the South Vietnamese in Vietnam, is an example of how the disenchantment of subgroups and their ties abroad have reduced the scope of military instruments available to most states.

Indeed, the declining capacity of national governments to govern is not confined to foreign military undertakings. For most, if not all, governments the decline spans an entire range of issue-areas, both domestic and foreign. The greater internal division, the persistence of severe economic dislocations, the continued depletion of resources, the emergence of interdependence issues that cannot be resolved through unilateral action, the increased competence of transnational actors – these are but a few of the many developments that have resulted in governmental performances that fall short of aspirations and that further diminish the public support most governments once enjoyed. As will be seen, this generalized diminution of the capacity to mobilize domestic support is no less central to the handling of the newer nonmilitary problems of interdependence than to the traditional issues of national security.

The structure of interdependence issues

If, as indicated earlier, the newer issues of world politics are unlike those involving military security and do not consist primarily of territorial and legitimacy dimensions, what are their main characteristics? In the answer to this question lies the basis for assessing the changing nature of "national power." Four characteristics seem salient as central features of all the diverse issues of interdependence, from those involving monetary stability to those associated with food–population ratios, from the uses of the ocean to the abuses of the atmosphere, from the discovery and distribution of new energy sources to the redirection of trade and the reallocation of wealth. Perhaps the most persuasive characteristic of all such issues is the large degree to which they encompass highly complex and technical phenomena. To grasp how food production can be increased, ocean bottoms utilized, pollutants eliminated, and solar energy exploited is to acquire mastery over physical and biological processes that involve an extraordinary range of subprocesses, the interaction of which is not easily understood, much less easily controlled. To grasp how monetary stability can be maintained, population growth reduced, and wealth reallocated is to achieve comprehension of social, cultural, and economic processes that are equally complex and no less difficult to control. Most of these issues of interdependence and moreover, overlap so thoroughly that proposed solutions to any one of them have important ramifications for the others, thereby further complicating their highly technical character.

Quite aside from the politics of coping with these new kinds of issues, their structures and contents require new kinds of advanced scientific and social scientific knowledge if efforts to control them are to be undertaken and minimally successful. It is hardly an exaggeration to assert that what weapons and troops are to the traditional problems of national security, so are scientific knowledge and technological sophistication to the newer dimensions of security.

A second major characteristic of interdependence issues is the large degree to which many of them encompass a great number of nongovernmental actors whose actions are relevant to issue management. This decentralized character of most interdependence issues is in sharp contrast to the conventional foreign policy situation – such as a treaty negotiation or a severance of diplomatic relations – in which the course of events is shaped largely by choices that government officials make. Indeed, virtually by definition an interdependence issue involves the overlap of many lives, so much so that the unfolding of the issue depends on decisions (or lack of decisions) made by countless individuals, none of whom is necessarily aware of what others have decided (or not decided). The actions of innumerable farmers, for example, are central to the problem of increased food production, just as many pollution issues depend on choices made by vast numbers of producers, energy conservation on millions of consumers, and population growth on tens of millions of potential parents. To be sure, governmental choices and actions can influence whether the decisions made by the multitude of persons encompassed by such issues are consistent and appropriate – which is precisely why the mobilization of domestic support has become increasingly relevant to foreign affairs. But the very fact of such decentralization renders the handling of interdependence issues very different from the standard means of framing and implementing foreign policy.[8]

A third major feature of interdependence issues arises out of the combination of their decentralized structure and the technical knowledge on which they rest. These two variables interact in such a way as to fragment the governmental decision-making process through which such issues are considered. More precisely, in the United States and other industrial societies with large public bureaucracies the link between most such issues and particular clienteles among the citizenry endows the governmental agencies and subagencies responsible for tending to the welfare of the relevant clientele with unusual degrees of authority and political clout. And this clout is further augmented by the fact that such agencies tend to acquire a governmental monopoly of the technical expertise needed to cope with the issues in their jurisdiction. Hence in the American case, for example, units of the Treasury Department tend to carry the day on monetary issues and bureaus within the Agriculture Department tend to monopolize decision-making on questions pertaining to the production and distribution of various foodstuffs. Whenever an issue draws on several expertises, of course, the fragmented authority that has evolved with respect to it leads to especially intense bureaucratic wrangling, or at least to the need for elaborate interdepartmental committees to handle it.

In either event, whether an issue is processed by a single bureaucratic unit or by several subunits, a main consequence of the dispersed expertise is to diminish the capacity of top officials to maintain control over it. Whereas the traditional issues of foreign and military policy are founded on nationwide constituencies and can be managed by heads of state and prime ministers through their foreign offices and military establishments, interdependence issues render the politically responsible leadership much more subject to the advice, direction, contradictions, and compromises that emanate from a fragmented bureaucratic structure. They normally do not have the time or expertise to master the knowledge necessary to grasp fully such issues and ordinarily they lack the political fortitude to resist, much less reject, the pressures from the special clienteles that seek to be served by the issues. The role of expertise, of whether the expert is on tap or on top, has long been a problem in the military area,[9] but this problem is miniscule in comparison to the place which scientists, engineers, agricultural economists, demographers, biologists, and many other types of experts have come to assume in the newer issues of interdependence.[10]

Allusion has already been made to a fourth structural characteristic of all interdependence issues that appears to have major consequences for the changing nature of capabilities and control, namely, the large extent to which the management and amelioration, if not the resolution, of such issues requires multilateral cooperation among governments. Any issue is, by definition, founded on conflict, but issues can differ considerably in the degree to which the conflicts that sustain them can be isolated, contained, or otherwise managed unilaterally by governments. The conventional diplomatic and strategic issues of foreign policy, springing as they do from conflicts over territory and legitimate authority, can often be pressed, resisted, or ignored by a government without concurrence by other governments. Hard bargaining and negotiating concessions may follow from the positions which a government adopts on such matters, but these can be broken off, suspended, or otherwise limited – and the issues thereby left unmanaged – if the government finds it expedient to do so. The newer issues of interdependence, on the other hand, do not lend themselves so readily to unilateral action. Many of them spring from conflicts over the uses and abuses of the natural environment – the air (e.g. pollution), the land (e.g. food productivity), the water (e.g. ocean resources) – which do not conform to political boundaries and which most governments can thus neither dismiss nor handle on their own. Instead agreements among governments must be developed even as each presses positions that best serve its own interests. Such is the nature of interdependence issues, be they conflicts over the natural or the socio-economic environment. Defiance, avoidance, rejection, and other forms of conflict behavior can be temporarily employed for tactical advantage, but the interdependence will not disappear nor will the issues it spawns be contained. Eventually knowledge has to be exchanged and some form of agreement achieved among those states interdependently linked by their shared reliance on the same environment.

The international monetary policy of the United States during John Connally's term as Secretary of the Treasury from 1970 to 1972 illustrates the limits of such strategy. It will be recalled that Connally took a defiant and uncompromising stance toward other states in order to win concessions in the restructuring of the international economic system. The instability of the existing economic order, however, persisted and the United States soon felt compelled to turn to a more accommodative posture. Perhaps an even better example of the way in which interdependence issues tip the balance in the direction of cooperative behavior is provided by the Organization of Petroleum Exporting Countries (OPEC). The members of that organization may have many differences over oil-pricing policies, but they must – and do – bury some of these in order to render OPEC more effective and thereby achieve their individual goals through collective action.

Capabilities and control in an interdependent world

Given the narrowed scope of military capabilities, the declining capacity of governments to mobilize domestic support, and the technical, decentralized, fragmented, and accommodative structure of interdependence issues, it is not difficult to trace substantial changes in the capabilities that states bring to world politics and the extent and manner of the control they can exercise over events and trends abroad. An almost infinite number of changes can be identified, thus confining the ensuing discussion to only those changes that seem most profound and enduring.

Turning first to the transformations that are likely to occur (and may have already begun) in the control dimension of national "power," several nonmilitary techniques are available for foreign policy officials to use in their efforts to modify or preserve the patterns that comprise the newer issues of world politics. Bargaining over differences, trading issues off against each other, promises of future support, threats of future opposition, persuasion through appeals to common values, persuasion through the presentation of scientific proof – these are the prime control techniques through which the problems of interdependence must be addressed. They are, of course, as old as diplomacy itself, but they have taken on new meaning in the light of the decline of force as a viable technique and in view of the complex nature of the interdependence issues. In particular, the last two of these nonmilitary techniques seem destined to become ever more salient as instruments of statecraft. The inclination to rely on appeals to common values, with a corresponding diminution in the tendency to threaten reprisals, appears especially likely to emerge as central to the conduct of foreign affairs. The fact that interdependence issues cannot be handled unilaterally, that foreign policy officials must engage in a modicum of cooperation with counterparts abroad in order to ameliorate the situations on which such issues thrive, means that the rhetoric, as well as the substance, of control techniques must shift toward highlighting the common values that are at stake.

Nor is this rhetorical shift likely to be confined to the bargaining that occurs behind closed doors. The decline of a sense of national identity and the emergence of more pronounced subnational loyalties seem likely to impel foreign policy officials to refer more frequently to shared international values in their public pronouncements as well as their private negotiations. That is, appeals to national interest and loyalties seem likely to become less compelling as means of mobilizing domestic support, so that positions on interdependence issues will have to be sold internally in terms of their consistency with the aspirations of external parties to situations.

Resort to scientific proof is a second control technique that seems headed for much greater use in the years ahead. The complex and technical nature of most interdependence issues seems likely to lead officials to place heavy reliance on the data and knowledge they have gathered as they seek to persuade counterparts abroad of the soundness of their positions. To be sure, there has always been a knowledge component of sound diplomacy. Statesmen have long preferred to seek desired modifications of behavior abroad through rational argument before turning to coercive techniques of control. If persuading others of their inherent logic and validity can advance goals, the costs of success are much less than is the case when the threat or use of force produces movement toward goals. Historically, however, the technical dimension of issues has not been as pervasive as it is in this era of interdependence, with the result that appeals founded on scientific proof were rarely controlling. Thus, despite their preferences, the practice of statesmen across centuries has been largely one of nonrational argumentation. But today's issues cannot be readily separated from their knowledge bases. To take positions on interdependence issues that ignore their technical and scientific underpinnings is to risk pursuit of counterproductive policies. Hence it seems highly probable that foreign policy officials will become increasingly inclined to achieve and maintain control through efforts to "prove" to adversaries and friends alike the validity of their positions.

This is not to say, of course, that the inherent logic and validity of data bearing on interdependence issues will necessarily, or even frequently, be persuasive and yield the desired modifications of behavior. Such issues are not free of values. They do not rest on an objective reality that speaks with a single and coherent voice to statesmen of all countries. One need only recall the persistent differences between industrial states and those in the Third World over the sources and dynamics of economic progress and dislocation to appreciate that the knowledge bases of even the most complex interdependence issues are subject to varying interpretations, depending on the perspectives and goals of policy makers. Yet, although future statesmen may thus be prone to bring their knowledge bases into line with their policies rather than vice versa, and even though they are therefore likely to resist and counter "proofs" advanced by adversaries, these tendencies will probably become less and less pronounced as technical knowledge becomes ever more central to the conduct of foreign affairs. The inclination to proceed from and cling to scientific proof as a basis for negotiation would thus seem to be headed for much greater priority in the array of control techniques on which officials depend. And who knows, in more than a few instances perhaps the proofs will seem compelling and serve to modify attitudes and behavior that in the past could have been expected to remain unaffected by this form of control.

It must be stressed that these anticipated changes in the exercise of control are not posited as replacing the conventional practices of statecraft. To highlight tendencies toward greater appeals to shared values and greater reliance on scientific proof is not to herald the dawn of a new era in which rational discourse and harmony mark world affairs. The old issues of territorial jurisdiction and the scope of legitimate authority are not about to pass quickly from the scene and the conflicts and hard bargaining which they generate are not about to disappear suddenly as interdependence mounts. Rather, the anticipated changes are seen as extensions of the art of statecraft, as broadening the mix through which officials seek to adapt to their external environments. Whether the long-run alterations in this mix will be sufficient to foster steady progress toward a more rational and orderly world can hardly be estimated at this time. The possibility of such progress is clearly inherent in the changing nature of control and the shifting capabilities of states (outlined below), but one ought not be so naive as to overlook the many variables that can perpetuate or deepen the differences among states and that can even encourage resort to nonrational techniques of control.

The advent and structure of interdependence issues also point to several important changes in the capabilities dimension of rational "power." Again these changes are best viewed in the context of a new mix, of long-standing aspects of capabilities continuing to be crucial to the conduct of foreign affairs even as mounting interdependence has made other, previously peripheral aspects relatively more significant. The fertility of the soil, the minerals and other resources possessed, the configurations of geography, the size and skills of populations, the breadth and equipment of the military establishment – these are but a few of the attributes that continue to differentiate the strong from the weak and to shape the extent and direction of the control that states can exercise abroad. Growing interdependence has not diminished the role of such attributes – in some cases (e.g. oil reserves) it has even increased their role – but rather it has enlarged the composite of possessed qualities from which effective control derives.

The capacity to develop and apply scientific and technical knowledge is perhaps the attribute that has undergone the greatest transformation. The complexity of interdependence issues and their close link to the natural environment means that states are likely to be better able to cope with and procure benefits from their external settings the more they possess the ability to comprehend the dynamics whereby land, air, and water resources can be used and abused. The depth, breadth, flexibility, and commitment of a state's scientific establishment have thus come to rival its military establishment as a national resource. And, in turn, this attribute highlights the centrality of a state's educational system and its ability to produce a continuous flow of analytic, wide-ranging, and technically competent citizens. The considerable stress states in the developing world place on establishing technological institutes and sending students abroad for advanced training is but one of the more obvious measures of the degree to which the capacity to generate and utilize knowledge has entered the ranks of prime national attributes.

Societal cohesion is another capability that has acquired prime importance. The decentralized nature of interdependence issues and the widening consequences of the attitudes and decisions of subnational groups has made external control efforts ever more dependent on the degree to which these subgroups perceive their interests as shared and served by the policies of their national governments. The greater the cohesiveness in this regard, the more does it seem likely that foreign policy officials will be able to pursue successfully those courses of action they deem essential to the management of interdependence issues. The readiness of American farmers, for example, to harmonize their production schedules with the requirements of proposed international agreements on the distribution and storage of foodstuffs constitutes a critical element in the United States government's ability to undertake successful negotiations on such matters. Of course, the degree of societal cohesion – and the mobilization potential thereby created – has always been a critical factor in the military area, but its centrality to other areas of foreign policy has not been so extensive. The emergence of interdependence issues has changed all this and, combined with the shifting loyalties of subnational groups, has rendered the cohesion attribute a major component of national capabilities.[11]

The capacity of public bureaucracies to overcome – or at least compensate for – the fragmentation inherent in interdependence issues is still another attribute that has become increasingly important in recent years. The readiness of one subagency to inform other relevant subagencies of its activities is not a predisposition that comes easily to units of a bureaucracy. On the contrary, rivalry is probably more securely embedded in bureaucratic structures than coordination, and these structural tendencies seem likely to be exacerbated by the fragmentation, decentralization, and specialization that accompanies interdependence. It follows that states that can continuously adapt their decision-making structure to mounting interdependence – that can train and utilize the relevant expertise, that can sensitize officials to the implications of their choices for other governmental units working on other problems of interdependence, that can find techniques for generating innovative proposals and for transforming destructive rivalries into creative tensions, that can develop scientific proofs which support appeals to transnational values – will bring to the conference tables of the world considerable advantages not accruing to those that conduct bureaucratic politics and diplomacy as usual. The capacity to render large-scale governmental organizations relevant to existing problems has always been an important component of national "power," but its role would appear to be even more central as world affairs become ever more complex.[12]

Closely related to the increasing importance of decision-making variables is the capacity of officials to frame and pursue policies designed either to build new international institutions or to give new directions to long-established patterns. As previously noted, by their very nature interdependence issues tend to require multilateral cooperation among governments for their amelioration. The ability to contribute to the evolution of such institutions and patterns can vary considerably, depending on the readiness of societies, their publics, and their governments to acknowledge that their futures are interdependently linked and to adapt to the changing circumstances which may thereby arise. The adaptation of national societies can take several forms,[13] including maladaptive assessments of the way in which domestic life is interwoven into foreign affairs. Adaptation and maladaptation involve nothing less than the images which citizens and officials hold of themselves in relation to their external environments. If these images are unrealistic and fail to account for the need to sustain cooperative foreign policies, then burdens rather than benefits are bound to mount with interdependence. Inasmuch as the images underlying the adaptive capacities of states derive from the functioning of their communication systems, the viability of their value frameworks, the flexibility of their political ideologies, and the dynamics of their educational systems, as well as the structure of their public bureaucracies, it seems quite evident that the capability for multilateral cooperation will not come readily to governments. Equally obvious is the fact that governments that can enlarge this capability will achieve greater measures of national security than will those that do not.

If the foregoing analysis of the changing mix of capabilities that accompany mounting interdependence is accurate, it seems reasonable to generalize that "national power" is on the decline, that the capacity of individual states to control developments abroad is diminishing and will continue to diminish. Some will remain relatively "strong" and others relatively "weak," and some may become relatively stronger and others relatively weaker, but in absolute terms all seem likely to become less able single-handedly to modify or preserve patterns in their external environments. Why? Because it seems unlikely that any state, even the most industrially advanced, can develop a scientific community with sufficient breadth and depth to cope with all the diverse issues of interdependence; because everywhere societies seem destined to become less cohesive and the mobilizing capacities of their governments less effective; and because everywhere bureaucracies seem likely to become more fragmented. Whether the decline in overall capabilities to enhance national security will result in a corresponding diminution of international security, however, is less clear. As interdependence impinges ever more tightly, so may the adaptive capacities of states allow them to evolve a greater readiness for multilateral cooperation.[14] The years ahead may thus be witness to a profound paradox in which the decline of national "power" is matched, and perhaps even exceeded, by the rise of international "power."

17 The skill revolution as a dynamic process[1]

I am not educated, but I can think.

(Meisie Ndlovu[2])

The tin line had been done two weeks now. Mr. James [the manager] did not fill out the forms properly for to get the foreign exchange to buy the material. It comes from Canada. The IMF man control the thing now, you know, so things have to be just so. And we workers suffer 'cause production shut down 'cause we need those things. And Mr. James, he's a fool to play with it. We ask him where the material, and he say it's coming. We know he mess it up. Jamaica doesn't have the money no more. Each factory must wait a turn to get the money. I hear the tin is on the dock in Toronto, waiting to be shipped here.

(Unnamed Jamaican woman[3])

These epigraphs highlight the central themes of the ensuing pages. They tell a story of growth, of people evolving capacities that are more refined and incisive than ever before. They speak to the human condition at the outset of a new century. They tell us not to underestimate what people can do.

There are numerous reasons why the skills of people are expanding in every realm of activity, at every level of community, and in every part of the world. Elsewhere I have suggested that the pattern is so pervasive that it can justly be called the "skill revolution."[4] One prime source of the revolution is the fact that throughout the world, in every country, men, women, and children are getting more and more education.[5] Another is global television, which is introducing people in heretofore remote parts of the world to ideas, places, cultures, and skills that they have not previously encountered. Still another source is the vast movement of people – everyone from the business executive to the immigrant, from the tourist to the terrorist – around the world that also serves to acquaint people with new ideas, places, and cultures, thereby freeing up imaginations and enlarging skills.[6] A fourth source involves the ever-growing complexity of the world and its ever-larger cities, processes that confront people with new challenges that require new skills to meet. Finally, and hardly less important, new technologies, especially the

Internet and e-mail, are serving to enlarge the capacity to frame new ideas and search for obscure information, skills for which history has no prior counterpart.

Nor do these several sources unfold in isolation. They are, rather, profoundly interactive, with each impacting on and reacting to the others, thereby hastening the pace at which the skill revolution accelerates. The ensuing discussion undertakes to highlight the interactive processes that render the skill revolution increasingly dynamic. It argues that the revolution is bound to continue with the passage of time and the advent of new, more educated generations who travel more widely and who have been reared on the latest technological innovations.

Empowerment

A central theme of the literature devoted to the impact of the Internet on the skills of people focuses on the large extent to which they have been empowered by the new technology.[7] Although the processes whereby empowerment occurs are rarely explicated, the implicit understanding appears to involve an expanding grasp of where, when, and how to engage in collective action. The seeming plethora of large numbers of diverse citizens protesting in various streets throughout the world is considered to be the result of people and organizations communicating with each other and spreading information by e-mail, fax, cell phones, and teleconferencing as to the purposes, locales, and timing of the protest marches. The size and frequency of such protests are regarded as located on a rising curve that derives its strength and growth from the empowerment of the participants, from their growing knowledge that micro people can have macro consequences if they act in concert. And indeed, there is anecdotal evidence that the targets of the protests are mindful of the policies the marching protesters seeks to alter: there are good indications, for example, that this form of empowerment has been institutionalized, that crowds invariably gather to protest whenever the boards of the IMF, the World Bank, and the WTO hold their annual meetings at accessible locations. The recent pattern wherein the boards are convened at remote and inaccessible locations is surely an indication of a sensitivity of the boards to the collective actions of empowered citizens.

Some contend that the empowerment argument is misleading. People may be empowered by the new technologies, it is conceded, but what counts is the power wielded by elites and the deafness of their ears when it comes to acting on the messages articulated by the protest marches, letter-writing campaigns, and other forms of collective action. We live in a messy, complex, and nonlinear world, it is further asserted, and the ordinary person simply cannot keep up with either the pace or content of the rapid transformations underway throughout the world. Thus, despite the efforts of activists who have mastered the art of mobilizing large crowds, ordinary folk are unable to carry through when dusk falls and the marchers disband. In effect, the argument concludes, social movements are transitory and unable to sustain the momentum necessary to impact meaningfully on the elites in a position to effect change.

Skill expansion as a process

To probe these competing perspectives it is useful to conceive of the skill revolution as an evolving process, as consisting of a set of dynamic variables (rather than constants) that may prove to be a powerful mechanism for change. At the core of the process is the interplay between technologies, education, and experience. All three of these dynamics elevate people everywhere onto a growth curve that incrementally – and sometimes swiftly – enables them to arrest the attention of elites in positions of power.

For those in the industrial world the process begins with formal education early in life, while children in the developing world start with experience, with the hard realities that attend getting from one day to the next. In both cases what is learned is not so much a storehouse of information but a bundle of working knowledge, of premises and understanding of how things work, of when and how to apply the skills that the working knowledge facilitates. In both worlds the sequence of skill expansion has quickened in recent years with the advent of the new microelectronic technologies. For many children throughout the world today using the Internet is as commonplace as skipping rope or playing in a sandbox. To be sure, what they learn at an early age involves games rather than surfing the Web or reading about other cultures. But to manipulate games on the Internet is to add to a working knowledge that can serve as a skill base for more sophisticated activities as maturation unfolds.

In short, the skill revolution is founded on an interactive sequence that lasts a lifetime, with each increment of experience, education, and technological know-how building on the previous increments and resulting in more talented people. More than that, the widespread use of cell phones and the Internet have accelerated the sequence at a stunningly exponential rate and there is every reason to believe they will continue to do so.

Of course, the acceleration of the skill revolution does not necessarily mean that people are experiencing a comparable growth in their readiness to engage in collective action. To have more refined skills at one's disposal does not assure that one will use the expanded skills effectively. For those who are criminals, terrorists, or drug dealers, the acceleration of their skills will not moderate their evil ways; rather, it will enhance their capacities to exercise their form of evil. On balance, however, there are reasons to welcome the continued acceleration of the skill revolution inasmuch as a preponderance of the world's people do not intend to visit harm on others and, equally important, as generational change seems destined to further quicken the acceleration of each component that sustains the sequence of the skill revolution.

Wisdom

There is a pronounced tendency on the part of many who stress the power of elites to downplay the capacities of ordinary people, to cite polls indicating ignorance of places and events, to downplay the skill revolution on the grounds that it only encompasses those with a university education, to dismiss as misguided the self-assessments of people like Meisie Ndlovu cited in the first epigraph. But as previously implied, wisdom is not confined to the educated elite and, indeed, it often does not characterize their words and conduct. Experience can be a great teacher, perhaps especially for those who have no other way of comprehending how the world works. Whether it is the Vermont farmer, the urban homeless, the Chinese peasant, or the dockworker in Jamaica, a grasp of how the world works to foster their plight is acquired and transformed into working knowledge. And that transformation may well stimulate the skill sequence such that it leads to a commitment to more education, as was the case with Meisie Ndlovu, who spent three months hitch-hiking weekly to study construction management and subsequently built her own three-bedroom home and a successful construction company.

To be sure, in most cases expanded wisdom may not lead to intensified political action. A host of factors, many beyond the control of even the wisest people, can intervene to prevent their participation in protest marches. But it does allow for the other components of the skill revolution to unfold, a process that surely widens the pool of people upon whom the mobilizing elite can draw to apply their skills.

Generational change

As mentioned earlier, the skill revolution is likely to accelerate with the passage of time and the advent of generations reared on the computer. Moreover, the impact of generational change will not be confined to societies in the developed world. Data presented in the next chapter point clearly to a similar impact in the developing world. These data seem to insure that the sequences of the skill revolution will accelerate as the next generations replace those with vast numbers of computer illiterate people.

Conclusions

It is not easy to contemplate how the world will be different when it is composed of populations increasingly familiar with the complexities of urban life, with the hardware and software of computers, with capacities to generate, use, and exchange information and ideas that their parents and grandparents did not have. And if this pattern is supplemented by the trend toward more and more people acquiring more and more education, it seems likely that the skill revolution will become ever more explosive.

Some might contend that any of the sequences of the skill revolution could be disrupted, even reversed, by authoritarian governments. And it is surely the case that governments can prevent people from leaving or entering their country, just as they have developed means for exercising some control over the flow of information and ideas through the Internet. Such reasoning, however, underestimates the power of the skill revolution, sustained as it is by the expanding curiosity and tenacity of people everywhere and in every age group. Perhaps more than any other kind of revolution, past or present, the skill revolution seems likely to change the nature of societies and alter the course of history.

18 Generational change and Internet literacy[1]

I really want to move to Antarctica. I'd want my cat and Internet access, and I'd be happy.

(A sixteen-year-old boy in Pittsburgh[2])

The ensuing analysis probes whether the generations now in their early thirties or younger are likely to differ from their predecessors by virtue of being the first to be fully comfortable and literate with information technologies – the computer and its Internet, e-mail, and search capacities – when they come to occupy positions of power and prestige in the decades ahead. Will their decision-making skills be more incisive, their grasp of complexity more substantial, their dexterity in framing and implementing policies more proficient, their respect for knowledge and expertise more secure and temperate, their talent for forming consensuses and reaching compromises more extensive, their attitudes more subtle and nuanced, their organizations more effective? In short, in what ways might it matter that children today have been found to be "much heavier users of the Internet and all its services than were their parents"?[3]

It would be premature to offer definitive answers to such questions. Only time will tell whether generational changes will stem from much greater Internet literacy. At this point in time, with many in the older generation relatively illiterate in comparison to their offspring, we can only speculate about the consequences that might flow from an age group that can fully exploit all the resources offered by computers.

While one analyst argues that, "in some ways, global satellite TV and Internet access have actually made the world a less understanding, less tolerant place,"[4] here a less precise, more open-ended response is developed: even though it is much too early to assess the full consequences of the Internet for individuals and societies because an Internet-literate generation has yet to fully replace its predecessors, it seems likely that when the replacement occurs and the present young generation enters the ranks of elites, activists, and thoughtful citizens throughout the world the nature of politics and economics within and between countries will be, for better or worse, profoundly different than is the case today. To be sure, generational change has always been a primary dynamic in the life of societies, but the changes that lie ahead flowing from the combination of more extensive satellite television and ever greater Internet literacy may be as profound as (if not more than) any that have previously marked the modern era. Anticipating whether the result will be diminished or enlarged understanding and tolerance on a worldwide scale, below I argue that information technologies are morally neutral and that therefore the generational changes that accompany the growth of the Internet are more likely to affect the skills with which the technologies are employed than the degree of understanding and tolerance they engender. But this point is best explored after elaborating on how the extensive Internet literacy among those in today's younger generation sets it apart from their elders.

Actually, usage of both the Internet and satellite dishes has undergone rapid growth in recent years, with each medium having contributed substantially to the spread of ideas, pictures, and information to every corner of the earth. But while the spread via television may be approaching a point of saturation, the same cannot be said of the Internet, partly because large numbers of people still do not have access to computers and partly because the skills required to use the Internet vary from rudimentary to sophisticated while the use of television involves little more than turning on the set. Thus, as more and more people acquire access to the Internet and replace their rudimentary skills with a greater capacity to exploit its many facets, so will the relationship between generational change and information technologies come into focus. Among other things, for example, satellite television is a one-to-many medium that can facilitate the spread of ideas, pictures, and information and thereby expand or diminish understanding and tolerance, but the Internet is a many-to-many medium that can also serve as a means for mobilizing people and translating their levels of understanding and tolerance into action.[5] The more the Internet skills of individuals are refined, in other words, the greater is their involvement in political processes likely to be.

The resistance of older generations

Based on considerable anecdotal evidence as well as systematic findings, it is reasonable to conclude that today's older generations have been largely perplexed and intimidated by the Internet and its potential uses, so much so that many of their members assume that their learning curve does not allow for keeping up with and using the access to the knowledge and communications afforded by the Internet. More than a few of us in the older generations have not only experienced pride in the computer skills of our children and their children, but our pride is usually accompanied by the assumption that there is no way in which we can match the successor generations in this respect. Indeed, some of us happily acknowledge we are Neanderthals when it comes to taking advantage of the computer and surfing the Web, contending that after all we have gotten along fine without such skills and thus have no need to acquire them at this late date.

I wrote the previous sentence while looking at my e-mail in the office of a small hotel on the Greek island of Hydra. When I asked the owner if he used the computer, his answer in broken English was unqualified: "No, I have no idea how it works. I got it for my daughters when they visit." And he is not alone. I have encountered a number of persons and intellectuals of my generation in the United States whose Neanderthal attitudes are more elaborate but no less clear-cut, often indicating they have no idea whatever of the potential ways in which the Internet may be of assistance to them.

Others of us sense the potential utility of the Internet and the computer, and we have even mastered some of their rudimentary uses such as e-mail and easily accessible data bases, but we remain humble and perplexed when faced with more sophisticated tasks.[6] Partly the perplexity stems from an inability to grasp the underlying processes on which the Internet and its numerous dimensions are founded; partly it derives from a resistance to evolving the habits necessary to employing the various routines and alternative mechanisms through which the Internet may serve diverse and complex needs; partly it is linked to a sense of inundation over the vast amounts of knowledge that have suddenly become available;[7] and partly it may be rooted in a conviction that our capacity for remembering detail has waned and is thus not up to mastering all the wrinkles of which the Internet consists. Stated differently, our perplexity originates with long-standing immersion in empirical and visible phenomena and, consequently, a difficulty in envisioning cyberspace as a place that confounds "the wider array of familiar distinctions – e.g. presence/absence, body/persona, offline/online – through which we have tended to understand what we see and what we do not see, who we are, where we are, and the communities to which we belong."[8] While younger generations are quite content to have cyberspace liberate them from "the confines of apartment walls, office cubicles, and state borders precisely by presenting users with a seeming boundless frontier space, enabling the freedom of movement to travel, within seconds, to sites across the country or, for that matter, across the world,"[9] older persons tend to be set in their ways and thus not ready for liberation on this scale. It is not that they resist liberation; it is simply that they do not comprehend its availability. Unlike their juniors, they do not have the immediate impulse to turn to the Internet for any problem that may arise – from simple questions like the weather or the automobile route for a trip, to the complex issue of Internet usage in diverse foreign countries.

I include myself among this perplexed generation. While I am in awe of the fact that I can communicate with my office easily, quickly, and cheaply from an island in the Aegean, and while I am invariably stunned whenever I find and access obscure articles in obscure journals, age has filled my memory bank and I am endlessly turning to others for help in using the Internet effectively – and even then the help I receive seems more a form of magic than a logical exploitation of available equipment. Admittedly this may be a personal failing, but I suspect it is more an instance of the old adage about the limits of teaching old dogs new tricks. The contrast between my computer skills and those of my students is too sharp to dismiss the discrepancy as simply one older person's quirks.

The competence of younger generations

Elsewhere I have argued that people everywhere in the world have undergone a skill revolution, a three-part upheaval consisting of an expansion of analytic, emotional, and imaginative competencies.[10] The Internet, global satellite television, and the computer are not the only sources of this upheaval – more education, more travel, and coping with the challenges of complex urban communities are among the other major sources – but the newer communications technologies are certainly one of the prime factors that underlie the relatively greater competence of younger generations. One national survey, for example, found that American children ages two to five averaged 27 minutes a day at the computer, while the figures for children six to 11 and 12 to 17 averaged 49 and 63 minutes a day respectively.[11] In short, for many young people taking full advantage of the diverse uses of the Internet has become second nature, a set of talents and proclivities they do not even know they possess unless they encounter the Internet illiteracy of their seniors.[12]

Perhaps the best, though hardly the only, example of this second nature is to be found among techies and hackers, most of whom entered the computer world before they turned twenty years old and virtually all of whom are still under thirty years old. Unable to resist the challenge of solving difficult computer problems, and knowing that the problems are capable of solution if worked at hard and long enough, techies and hackers can spend hours in front of their monitors, depriving themselves of sleep and having junk food at their side in order not to waste time in finding the solutions. Where older persons tend to become sufficiently frustrated to abandon quickly a task when the Internet fails to yield the desired solution in a reasonable time, techies and hackers are driven by the knowledge that a solution exists and do not quit until it is found. Thus did their all-consuming fascination with the virtual world opened up by cyberspace contribute substantially to its expansion and growth. While some hackers have an unforgiving contempt for those they view as novices in their usage of the Internet – as "clueless newbies" – techies tend to be very helpful to those who seek assistance, thereby serving to empower individuals and advance the skill revolution.[13]

Of course, hackers often do not always use their competence on behalf of such worthy purposes.[14] Many are loners who, like vandals, simply try to cause damage for its own sake. Yet, the fact that virtually all of the known less high-minded hackers in recent years have been young poses interesting questions about the ways in which the older and younger generations may differ in their values as well as their skills and whether such differences portend more contentious eras in the future. It is accepted wisdom that people and generations tend to become more conservative as they age, but have the Internet and other information technologies altered the scope and depth of these tendencies? Could it be that the hackers are an expression of a readiness on the part of younger generations to challenge authority and thus contribute to what elsewhere I have referred to as pervasive crises of authority that plague governments and nongovernmental institutions throughout the world?[15] And if so, will significant changes unfold as the hacker generation becomes middle-aged and then elderly? The answers are as elusive as they are provocative and must be posed as highly tentative.

On the other hand, this is not to imply that hackers are likely to dominate younger generations. Rather, it is to illustrate an extreme version of a culture in which older generations do not readily participate. Most persons in the younger generations will lead more "normal" lives and will be comfortable in cyberspace, knowing that the Internet is a valuable tool they can use efficiently and effectively when situations warrant it. Indeed, as they mature and take on leadership responsibilities they may well be required to contest egregious hackers who invade privacy and pose other threats to the wellbeing of their organizations.

Nor should the foregoing finding that young Americans are heavier users of the Internet than their parents be interpreted as confined to the United States. The generational differences in Internet literacy are worldwide in scope, and the difference between younger professionals in Asia, Africa, and Latin America and their elders is probably even greater than in the United States, where experience with technological innovations has long been a part of daily routines. Indeed, while the proportion of persons in the developing world who have access to the Internet is substantially less than is the case for the United States and Europe, the concentration of users among young people in Asia, Africa, and Latin America is probably greater than elsewhere in the world. A random sample of patterns for the last two years in these regions illustrates this probability: in India, "75% of all adults who access the Internet are in the age group of 15–34 years";[16] in Thailand, "Most Thai users are in the age group of 20–29 years";[17] in Malaysia, "it can be stated that the number of middle-aged and older persons surfing the Net will be far smaller than the number of youths . . . It has been estimated that more than 90 percent of Malaysian users are young people below 30 years, and the majority are school children or college students";[18] in China, "New survey results show that younger people, and people with less education than previously are getting online . . . [Their] average age. . . is 28";[19] in twelve Arab countries 79 percent of those with Internet access are under 35 years of age;[20] in the Philippines, 81 percent of Internet users are under 30 years old, "Because they are not intimidated by technology and it has become a part of their lives";[21] in Lithuania, "61 percent of all computer users are under 30 years old," with "the higher the age group, the lower the incidence of computer use";[22] in South Africa, "The average age of web users is 35, but with the biggest age group being those between 20 and 30";[23] and in Malta, "the main users were registered amongst the 16–24 bracket [and] the use of Internet decreased proportionally with the rise in the age groups, fading away to practically nil for the over 65 years age group."[24]

It bears repeating that these data represent only the small proportion of persons in these countries who have Internet access. Their ranks are growing rapidly, but their numbers still remain far short of those in the developed world, thus contributing to what is known as the digital divide that separates the relative access of the rich and poor within and between countries. While interesting programs are designed to narrow the divide among youth in developed countries,[25] many of the younger people in the developing world who do have access acquire it by visiting the numerous Internet cafés that are opening throughout the cities and towns of the developing world.[26] As the newer technologies become increasingly available in the offices, homes, and cafés of the developing world and thus increasingly integral to its daily routines, presumably Internet literacy will spread rapidly through upcoming generations.

Speculative conclusions

Assuming, then, that younger generations are more Internet literate than their seniors, let us return to the questions raised at the outset, to speculating about the ways in which politics might change when societies come to consist of elites, activists, and thoughtful citizens who are fully at home with computers and their diverse uses. Needless to say, the task is to trace just noticeable differences (JNDs) rather than wholesale changes.[27] But small as they may be, tracing just noticeable differences is not a trivial exercise. If statisticians are correct in hypothesizing that normally everything, people included, regresses to the mean, then identifying possible ways in which the computer-literate generation might be different from their predecessors by one or more JND is a challenging undertaking. At the very least such an effort may spur further research into what could prove to be important political phenomena.

My inclination is to answer the original questions in the affirmative. It is plausible that the decision-making skills of computer-literate generations – those in the private sector as well as public officials – will be more refined than their predecessors. Having become sensitive to, and adept at exploiting, the vast array of knowledge offered by the Internet, they will have a more acute respect for knowledge and its complexity and, accordingly, a greater inclination to offset their temperamental impulses and a lesser readiness to fall back on their intuitive, undocumented feelings about situations. When one is fully familiar with the depth and breadth of information available on the Internet, it becomes difficult, if not impossible, simply to dismiss the need to check out, confirm, modify, or reject what seems at first glance to be self-evident. In addition, knowing the huge range of available information and insights available on the world wide web is likely to enable people to give more license to their imaginations, to ponder alternatives that earlier generations might have considered unexplorable and thus absurd and not worth an investiture of time. More than that, familiarity with extraordinary resources of the World Wide Web may heighten inclinations to acknowledge that innumerable grays exist between blacks and whites. To be sure, those with high responsibilities may not have enough time to thoroughly surf the web for clarity on the problems they face, but they are likely to be less quick to rush to judgment and they can also assign the surfing tasks to subordinates. This greater appreciation of complexity and nuance may, in turn, facilitate greater proficiency in framing and implementing policies as well as helping to develop consensuses and achieving compromises in contentious organizational meetings. To repeat, such changes may involve no more than one JND. People will continue to have their failings, prejudices, and bureaucratic loyalties, and thus they will surely continue to sift information that affirms their prejudices; nevertheless, such weaknesses are more likely to be contested the more they are conversant with what the Internet offers.

At the societal level several changes seem likely. First, the capacity to mobilize like-minded others may lead to one or more JND differences between Internet-literate generations and their predecessors. The former now form "smart mobs," a label for "groups of people equipped with high-tech communications devices that allow them to act in concert – whether they know each other or not."[28] While collective actions are marked by a long history, today smart mobs form among the young who are adept at using the new electronic equipment, with one observer arguing that the "convergence of wireless communications tech-nologies and widely distributed networks allow swarming on a scale that has never existed before[, a shift] along the lines of those that began to occur when people first settled into villages and formed nation-states." Indeed, as a result of this shift, "we are on the verge of a major series of social changes that are closely tied to emerging technologies."[29] Put in more political terms, as whole generations posses the new equipment and acquire the habit of using it unthink-ingly, street clashes seem likely to become more frequent and widespread, with larger numbers of protesters on both sides of any issue, than has previously been the case.

Even if it is less conspicuous, another generation induced societal change may be no less significant. It concerns the circulation of ideas and opinions relevant to public affairs. Thoughtful citizens in today's younger generations are accustomed to surfing the Internet for news on, say, CNN or MSNBC – even to assuring that they receive the news they want, as such sources allow site visitors to request e-mail on issues of interest to them – whereas their elder counterparts wait until they get home to catch the evening news. The technology of the Internet thus empowers individuals to receive the content that is important to them at times that are convenient, while those who rely on television wait until the end of their work day before focusing on the events elsewhere in the world. Accordingly, it can be argued that as the younger generations age, they will be more consequential than the present older generations in the sense that they will initiate the cascades of information that frame public opinion earlier in the day. By the time the evening news comes on the air, much of the public may already have formed its opinions. The Drudge Report's role in the Clinton–Lewinsky affair is illustrative in this regard. Once the Internet publication reported the existence of a stained dress, public opinion cascaded so quickly that the evening newscasts had little role in that political situation. One could probably cite numerous such cases that mark the Israeli–Palestinian conflict, not to mention the increasing frequency of steep intra-day climbs and falls in stock markets.

Still another societal change involves notions of privacy. It too appears to be "undergoing a generational shift." Only newly aware that extensive information about them has made its way into data bases on the Internet, "those in their late 20s and 30s are going to feel the brunt of the transition" to a world in which there are fewer and fewer secrets. In effect, the transition is difficult because they "grew up with more traditional concepts of privacy even as the details of their lives were being captured electronically."[30]

Conversely, some changes seem unlikely to become pervasive. The aforementioned reasoning that "in some ways, global satellite TV and Internet access have actually made the world a less understanding and tolerant place" is a misleading statement. If information technology is essentially neutral in the sense that it can be used to promote both good and bad outcomes, depending on a host of other circumstances,[31] there is no reason to presume that the understanding and tolerance of younger generations is likely to be altered as a consequence of being more adept at using the Internet than their elders. Shifting degrees of understanding and tolerance, or misunderstanding and intolerance, stem from circumstances other than the technologies that purvey them. To be sure, frequent scenes of young people protesting in the streets of Palestine and elsewhere in the Middle East suggest that satellite broadcasting and the Internet have lately fostered increasing levels of anger and misunderstanding. As one observer put it,

> At its best, the Internet can educate more people faster than any media tool we've ever had. At its worst, it can make people dumber faster than any media tool we've ever had. The lie that 4,000 Jews were warned not to go into the World Trade Center on Sept. 11 was spread entirely over the Internet and is now thoroughly believed in the Muslim world. Because the Internet has an aura of "technology" surrounding it, the uneducated believe information from it even more. They don't realize that the Internet, at its ugliest, is just an open sewer, an electronic conduit for untreated, unfiltered information. Worse, just when you might have thought you were all alone with your extreme views, the Internet puts you together with a community of people from around the world who hate all the things and people you do.[32]

Be that as it may, to conclude there is less understanding and tolerance in the Muslim world since September 11th and the onset of hostilities between Israelis and Palestinians is neither to describe the direction of change in other regions nor is it to allow for Muslims who are not taken in by untreated and unfiltered information.[33] More than that, such an observation ignores the skill revolution and the ways in which increasing Internet literacy have facilitated more penetrating analysis on the part of more and more people. For every person made dumber by the new technologies, there may well be one or more persons whose horizons have been pushed back and whose levels of understanding and tolerance have been elevated. Certainly there are hundreds of millions of people in various parts of the world other than the Middle East who accept that the victims of the terrorist attacks were people from all walks of life and religions, that none were warned to stay away from their jobs on that day. The outcome of the worldwide competition between understanding and misunderstanding and between tolerance and intolerance is far from certain and will depend on much more than information technologies.

In short, generational change and Internet literacy do appear to be causally linked at this time. But the links can be overstated, especially as Internet Neander-thals will no longer constitute the older generation in another couple of decades. There will doubtless be new information technologies, but it is hard to imagine them making generational differences of the kind that presently prevail.

Part V

The analysis of foreign policy

19 Pre-theories and theories of foreign policy[1]

Two basic shortcomings, one philosophical and the other conceptual, would appear to be holding back the development of foreign policy theory.[2] Let us look first at the philosophical shortcoming. If theoretical development in a field is to flourish, empirical materials that have been similarly processed must be available. It is no more possible to construct models of human behavior out of raw data than it is to erect a building out of fallen trees and unbaked clay. The trees must be sawed and the clay must be baked, and the resulting lumber and bricks must be the same size, shape, and color if a sturdy and coherent building is to be erected. Note that the design and function of the structure are not determined by the fact that the materials comprising it have been similarly processed. The same bricks and lumber can be used to build houses or factories, large structures or small ones, modern buildings or traditional ones. So it is with the construction and use of social theories. There must be, as it were, a pre-theory that renders the raw materials comparable and ready for theorizing. The materials may serve as the basis for all kinds of theories – abstract or empirical, single- or multi-country, pure or applied – but until they have been similarly processed, theorizing is not likely to occur, or, if it does, the results are not likely to be very useful.

Unlike economics, sociology, and other areas of political science, the field of foreign policy research has not subjected its materials to this preliminary processing. Instead, as noted above, each country and each international situation in which it participates is normally treated as unique and nonrecurrent, with the result that most available studies do not treat foreign policy phenomena in a comparable way. Thus it is that the same data pertaining to the external behavior of the Soviet Union are interpreted by one observer as illustrative of Khrushchev's flexibility, by another as reflective of pent-up consumer demands, and by still another as indicative of the Sino–Soviet conflict. To recur to the analogy of physical materials, it is as if one person cut up the fallen trees for firewood, another used them as the subject of a painting, and still another had them sawed for use in the building of a frame house.

It must be emphasized that the preliminary processing of foreign policy materials involves considerably more than methodological tidiness. We are not referring here to techniques of gathering and handling data, albeit there is much that could be said about the need for standardization in this respect. Nor do we have in mind the desirability of orienting foreign policy research toward the use of quantified materials and operationalized concepts, albeit again good arguments could be advanced on behalf of such procedures. Rather, the preliminary processing to which foreign policy materials must be subjected is of a much more basic order. It involves the need to develop an explicit conception of where causation is located in international affairs. Should foreign policy researchers proceed on the assumption that identifiable human beings are the causative agents? Or should they treat political roles, governmental structures, societal processes, or international systems as the source of external behavior? And if they presume that causation is located in all these sources, to what extent and under what circumstances is each source more or less causal than the others? Few researchers in the field process their materials in terms of some kind of explicit answer to these questions. Most of them, in other words, are not aware of the philosophy of foreign policy analysis they employ, or, more broadly, they are unaware of their pre-theories of foreign policy.[3]

To be sure, foreign policy researchers are not so unsophisticated as to fail to recognize that causation can be attributed to a variety of actors and entities. For years now it has been commonplace to avoid single-cause deterministic explanations and to assert the legitimacy of explaining the same event in a variety of ways. Rather than serving to discipline research, however, this greater sophistication has in some ways supplied a license for undisciplined inquiry. Now it is equally commonplace to assume that one's obligations as a researcher are discharged by articulating the premise that external behavior results from a combination of many factors, both external and internal, *without* indicating how the various factors combine under different circumstances. Having rejected single-cause explanations, in other words, most foreign policy researchers seem to feel they are free *not* to be consistent in their manner of ascribing causation.

Perhaps the best way to indicate exactly what a pre-theory of foreign policy involves is by outlining the main ingredients of any pre-theory and then indicating how the author has integrated these ingredients into his own particular pre-theory. Although the statement is subject to modification and elaboration, it seems reasonable to assert that all pre-theories of foreign policy consist of either five sets of variables or are translatable into five sets. Listed in order of increasing temporal and spatial distance from the external behaviors, for which they serve as sources, the five sets are what we shall call the individual, role, governmental, societal, and systemic variables.

The first set encompasses the characteristics unique to the decision-makers that determine and implement the foreign policies of a nation. Individual variables include all those aspects of a decision-maker – his values, talents, and prior experiences – that distinguish his foreign policy choices or behavior from those of every other decision-maker. John Foster Dulles' religious values, De Gaulle's vision of a glorious France, and Khrushchev's political skills are frequently mentioned examples of individual variables. The second set of variables pertains to the external behavior of officials that is generated by the roles they occupy and that would be likely to occur irrespective of the individual characteristics of the role occupants. Regardless of who he is, for example, the US ambassador to the United Nations is likely to defend American positions in the Security Council and General Assembly. Governmental variables refer to those aspects of a government's structure that limit or enhance the foreign policy choices made by decision-makers. The impact of executive–legislative relations on American foreign policy exemplifies the operation of governmental variables. The fourth cluster of variables consists of those nongovernmental aspects of a society that influence its external behavior. The major value orientations of a society, its degree of national unity, and the extent of its industrialization are but a few of the societal variables which can contribute to the contents of a nation's external aspirations and policies. As for systemic variables, these include any nonhuman aspects of a society's external environment or any actions occurring abroad that condition or otherwise influence the choices made by its officials. Geographical "realities" and ideological challenges from potential aggressors are obvious examples of systemic variables that can shape the decisions and actions of foreign policy officials.

But these are only the ingredients of a pre-theory of foreign policy. To formulate the pre-theory itself one has to assess their *relative potencies*. That is, one has to decide which set of variables contributes most to external behavior, which ranks next in influence, and so on through all the sets. There is no need to specify exactly how large a slice of the pie is accounted for by each set of variables. Such precise specifications are characteristics of theories and not of the general framework within which data are organized. At this pre-theoretical level it is sufficient merely to have an idea of the relative potencies of the main sources of external behavior.

Note that constructing a pre-theory of foreign policy is not a matter of choosing to employ only one set of variables. We are not talking about levels of analysis but about philosophies of analysis with respect to one particular level,[4] that of national societies. We assume that at this level behavior is shaped by individual, role, governmental, societal, and systemic factors and that the task is thus one of choosing how to treat each set of variables relative to the others. Many choices are possible. Hundreds of pre-theories can be constructed out of the possible ways in which the five sets of variables can be ranked. Some analysts may prefer to use one or another of the rankings to analyze the external behavior of all societies at all times. Others may work out more complex pre-theories in which various rankings are applied to different societies under different circumstances.[5] Whatever the degree of complexity, however, the analyst employs a pre-theory of foreign policy when he attaches relative potencies to the main sources of external behavior.

Attaching causal priorities to the various sets of variables is extremely difficult. Most of us would rather treat causation as idiographic than work out a consistent pre-theory to account for the relative strength of each variable under different types of conditions. One way to overcome this tendency and compel oneself to differentiate the variables is that of engaging in the exercise of mentally manipulating the variables in actual situations. Consider, for example, the US-sponsored invasion of Cuba's Bay of Pigs in April 1961. To what extent was that external behavior a function of the individual characteristics of John F. Kennedy (to cite, for purposes of simplicity, only one of the actors who made the invasion decision)? Were his youth, his commitments to action, his affiliations with the Democratic party, his self-confidence, his close election victory – and so on through an endless list – relevant to the launching of the invasion and, if so, to what extent? Would any president have undertaken to oust the Castro regime upon assuming office in 1961? If so, how much potency should be attributed to such role-derived variables? Suppose everything else about the circumstances of April 1961 were unchanged except that Warren Harding or Richard Nixon occupied the White House; would the invasion have occurred? Or hold everything constant but the form of government. Stretch the imagination and conceive of the US as having a cabinet system of government with Kennedy as prime minister; would the action toward Cuba have been any different? Did legislative pressure derived from a decentralized policy-making system generate an impulse to "do something" about Castro, and, if so, to what extent did these governmental variables contribute to the external behavior? Similarly, in order to pre-theorize about the potency of the societal variables, assume once more a presidential form of government, place Kennedy in office a few months after a narrow election victory, and imagine the Cuban situation as arising in 1921, 1931, or 1951; would the America of the roaring twenties, the depression, or the McCarthy era have "permitted," "encouraged," or otherwise become involved in a refugee-mounted invasion? If the United States were a closed, authoritarian society rather than an open, democratic one, to what extent would the action toward Cuba have been different? Lastly, hold the individual, role, governmental, and societal variables constant in the imagination, and posit Cuba as 9,000 rather than 90 miles off the Florida coast; would the invasion have nevertheless been launched? If it is estimated that no effort would have been made to span such a distance, does this mean that systemic variables should always be treated as overriding, or is their potency diminished under certain conditions?

The formulation of a pre-theory of foreign policy can be further stimulated by expanding this mental exercise to include other countries and other situations. Instead of Kennedy, the presidency, and the US of 1961 undertaking action toward Cuba, engage in a similar process of holding variables constant with respect to the actions taken by Khrushchev, the monolithic Russian decision-making structure, and the USSR of 1956 toward the uprising in Hungary. Or apply the exercise to the actions directed at the Suez Canal by Eden, the cabinet system, and the England of 1956. Or take still another situation, that of the attack on Goa carried out by the charismatic Nehru and the modernizing India of 1961. In all four cases a more powerful nation initiated military action against a less powerful neighbor that had come to represent values antagonistic to the interests of the attacker. Are we therefore to conclude that the external behavior of the US, Russia, England, and India stemmed from the same combination of external and internal sources? Should the fact that the attacked society was geographically near the attacking society in all four instances be interpreted as indicating that systemic variables are always relatively more potent than any other type? Or is it reasonable to attribute greater causation to individual factors in one instance and to societal factors in another? If so, what is the rationale for subjecting these seemingly similar situations to different kinds of analysis?

Reflection about questions similar to those raised in the two previous paragraphs has led this observer to a crude pre-theory of foreign policy in which the relative potencies of the five sets of variables are assessed in terms of distinctions between large and small countries, between developed and underdeveloped economies, and between open and closed political systems. As can be seen in Table 19.1, these three continua give rise to eight types of countries and eight different rankings of relative potency. There is no need here to elaborate at length on the reasoning underlying each ranking.[6] The point is not to demonstrate the validity of the rankings but rather to indicate what the construction of a pre-theory of foreign policy involves and why it is a necessary prerequisite to the development of theory. Indeed, given the present undeveloped state of the field, the rankings can be neither proved nor disproved. They reflect the author's way of organizing materials for close inspection and not the inspections themselves. To be theoretical in nature, the rankings would have to specify *how much* more potent each set of variables is than those below it on each scale, and the variables themselves would have to be causally linked to specific forms of external behavior.

To be sure, as in all things, it is possible to have poor and unsound pre-theories of foreign policy as well as wise and insightful ones. The author's pre-theory may well exaggerate the potency of some variables and underrate others, in which case the theories which his pre-theory generates or supports will in the long run be less productive and enlightening than those based on pre-theories which more closely approximate empirical reality. Yet, to repeat, this pre-theory is not much more than an orientation and is not at present subject to verification.

While it is impossible to avoid possession of a pre-theory of foreign policy, it is quite easy to avoid awareness of it and to proceed as if one started over with each situation. Explicating one's conception of the order that underlies the external behavior of societies can be an excruciating process. As in psychoanalysis, bringing heretofore implicit and unexamined assumptions into focus may compel one to face considerations that one has long sought to ignore. Some of the assumptions may seem utterly ridiculous when exposed to explicit and careful perusal. Others may seem unworkable in the light of new knowledge. Still others may involve mutually exclusive premises, so that to recognize them would be to undermine one's previous work and to obscure one's present line of inquiry.

And even as one comes to live with the results of explication, there remains the intellectually taxing task of identifying the variables which one regards as major sources of external behavior and of then coming to some conclusion about their relative potencies under varying circumstances. Such a task can be very difficult indeed. Long-standing habits of thought are involved, and analysts may have become so habituated that for them the habits are part of ongoing reality and not of their way of perceiving reality. In addition, if these habits provide no experience in pre-theorizing about the processes of causation, it will not be easy to tease out variables and assess their potencies. For example, while it is relatively simple to

Table 19.1 An abbreviated presentation of the author's pre-theory of foreign policy, in which five sets of variables underlying the external behavior of societies are ranked according to their relative potencies in eight types of societies

Geography and physical resources	Large Country				Small Country			
State of the economy	Developed		Underdeveloped		Developed		Underdeveloped	
State of the polity	Open	Closed	Open	Closed	Open	Closed	Open	Closed
Rankings of the variables	Role Societal Govern- mental Systemic Individual	Role Individual Govern- mental Systemic Societal	Individual Role Societal Systemic Governmental	Individual Role Govern- mental Systemic Societal	Role Systemic Societal Govern- mental Individual	Role Systemic Individual Governmental Societal	Individual Systemic Role Societal Governmental	Individual Systemic Role Govern- mental Societal
Illustrative examples	US	USSR	India	Red China	Holland	Czechoslovakia	Kenya	Ghana

observe that a De Gaulle is less restrained in foreign policy than a Khrushchev, many analysts – especially those who insist that every situation is unique and that therefore they do not possess a pre-theory – would have a hard time discerning that the observation stems from their pre-theoretical premise that individual variables have greater potency in France than in the Soviet Union.

Great as the obstacles to explication may be, however, they are not insurmountable. Patience and continual introspection can eventually bring implicit and unexamined premises to the surface. The first efforts may result in crude formulations, but the more one explicates, the more elaborate does one's pre-theory become.

But, it may be asked, if the purpose of all this soul-searching is that of facilitating the development of general theory, how will the self-conscious employment of pre-theories of foreign policy allow the field to move beyond its present position? As previously implied, the answer lies in the assumption that the widespread use of explicit pre-theories will result in the accumulation of materials that are sufficiently processed to provide a basis for comparing the external behavior of societies. If most researchers were to gather and present their data in the context of their views about the extent to which individuals, roles, governments, societies, and international systems serve as causal agents in foreign affairs, then even though these views might represent a variety of pre-theories, it should be possible to discern patterns and draw contrasts among diverse types of policies and situations. Theoretical development is not in any way dependent on the emergence of a consensus with respect to the most desirable pre-theory of foreign policy. Comparison and theorizing can ensue as long as researchers make clear what variables they consider central to causation and the relative potencies they ascribe to them. For even if one analyst ascribe the greatest potency to individual variables, while another views them as having relatively little potency and still another regards them as impotent, they will have all provided data justifying their respective assumptions, and in so doing they will have given theoreticians the materials they need to fashion if-then propositions and to move to ever higher levels of generalization.

Penetrated political systems

But all will not be solved simply by the explication of pre-theories. This is a necessary condition of progress toward general theory, but it is not a sufficient one. Research in the foreign policy field would appear to be hindered by conceptual as well as philosophical shortcomings, and we will not be able to move forward until these more specific obstacles are also surmounted. Not only must similarly processed materials be available if general theory is to flourish, but researchers must also possess appropriate concepts for compiling them into meaningful patterns. Although rendered similar through the explication of pre-theories, the materials do not fall in place by themselves. Concepts are necessary to give them structure and thereby facilitate the formulation of if-then propositions.

The need to supplement processed materials with appropriate concepts is clarified by our earlier architectural analogy. One cannot erect a building merely by acquiring lumber and bricks. It is also necessary to be cognizant of engineering principles – that certain pieces of lumber should be placed upright, that others should be laid crosswise, and that the bricks should be laid on top of each other rather than interspersed among the lumber. Note again that the design and function of the building are not dependent upon these initial uses of the processed materials. To know which pieces of lumber are uprights and which are to be laid crosswise is not to determine how they are to be placed in relation to each other. So long as it is not done counter to the laws of gravity, the uprights and the crosspieces can be juxtaposed in all kinds of ways to form all kinds of buildings for all kinds of purposes. So it is with theories. An almost unlimited number can be fashioned out of similarly processed data so long as the initial organization of the data is consistent with the subject the theories are designed to elucidate. Regardless of the nature of a theory, however, if it is constructed out of inappropriate concepts, it is no more likely to endure than buildings erected in defiance of sound engineering principles or the laws of gravity.

Two interrelated conceptual problems seem to be holding back the development of general theories of external behavior. One concerns the tendency of researchers to maintain a rigid distinction between national and international political systems in the face of mounting evidence that the distinction is breaking down. The second difficulty involves an inclination to ignore the implications of equally clear-cut indications that the functioning of political systems can vary significantly from one type of issue to another. Anticipating much of the ensuing discussion, the interrelationship of the two problems is such that a new kind of political system, the penetrated system, is needed to comprehend the fusion of national and international systems in certain kinds of issue-areas.

Myriad are the data that could be cited to illustrate the increasing obscuration of the boundaries between national political systems and their international environments. These boundaries may consist of activities that result in "the authoritative allocation of values for a society,"[7] or of interacting roles that sustain a society "by means of the employment, or threat of employment, of more or less legitimate physical compulsion,"[8] or of processes in a society that "mobilize its resources in the interest of [positively sanctioned] goals,"[9] or "of the more inclusive structures in a society that have recognized responsibility for performing, at a minimum, the function of goal-attainment by means of legitimate decisions."[10] But however such boundaries may be drawn, ever since World War II they have been constantly transgressed by non-societal actors. The manner of transgression, moreover, has been quite varied. As these recent interaction sequences illustrate, even the last stronghold of sovereignty – the power to decide the personnel, practices, and policies of government – has become subject to internationalization:

- When asked how he managed to continue in office despite a major shift in the control of the national government, the mayor of a city in Colombia replied, "The American Ambassador arranged it."[11]

- "Ordinarily the [US] aid missions have stayed aloof from local administrative differences, but there have been instances like that in Thailand where the mission served as a liaison unit among several departments of a ministry, enabling them to carry out important tasks that never would have been done otherwise."[12]
- President Urho K. Kekkonen [of Finland] suggested tonight that opposition leaders who had incurred the hatred of the Soviet Union should withdraw into private life for the good of Finland. Dr. Kekkonen made his suggestion in a radio and television report to the nation on his talks with Premier Khrushchev of the Soviet Union. The Finnish President spoke less than three hours after having returned from Novosibirsk in Siberia, where Mr. Khrushchev had agreed to postpone the joint defense negotiations demanded by Moscow on October 30. If the politicians to whom the Soviet Union objects should retire, Dr. Kekkonen said, there would not be "the slightest doubt" that Finland could continue neutral in "all situations."[13]

Presumably the foregoing are common occurrences, and not isolated incidents, in the postwar era. As one observer notes with respect to underdeveloped societies, "What happens in India or Iran is no longer intelligible in terms of parochial Indian or Iranian events and forces, but must be seen as part of a world transformation in which these particular pockets of semi-autonomy are working out their distinctive yet somehow parallel destinies."[14] Nor are developed nations so self-sufficient as to be immune from internationalization. The evidence is extensive that foreign elements have become central to certain aspects of the decision-making process of the United States.[15] Even our major political institution, the presidency, has been internationalized. According to the prevailing conceptualization of the office, the president is necessarily responsive to demands from five constituencies, "from Executive officialdom, from Congress, from his partisans, from citizens at large, and from abroad."[16]

In short, "the difference between 'national' and 'international' now exists only in the minds of those who use the words."[17] Unfortunately most political scientists are among those who still use the words. Notwithstanding widespread recognition that the postwar "revolution in expectations" in the non-industrial parts of the world, the reliance of developing societies on foreign aid, the competition among industrial powers to provide aid, and the ever-quickening pace of technological change have greatly intensified the interdependence of nations and beclouded the line that divides them from their environments, most analysts have not made corresponding adjustments in their conceptual frameworks and have instead clung rigidly, and often awkwardly, to the national–international distinction. To be sure, there is widespread recognition that the boundaries separating national and international systems are becoming increasingly ambiguous,[18] but it is equally true that this recognition still awaits expression in conceptual and theoretical terms. The Sprouts, for example, concede that rigorous adherence "to the distinction between intra-national (or domestic) and extra-national (external) factors leaves certain highly important factors out of the picture," but they are nevertheless prepared to accept these omissions on the grounds that "the distinction has value for certain purposes."[19]

Nor do students of international and comparative politics differ in this respect. The concern of the former with international systems and of the latter with national systems remains undiluted by the postwar fusion of the two types. While those who specialize in international systems acknowledge that such systems are largely subsystem dominant (i.e. their stability, goals, and processes are primarily the result of actions undertaken by the national systems of which they are comprised), one is hard pressed to cite any models of regional or global international systems that allow for differential subsystem impacts. Instead, the builders of international models tend to proceed on the assumption that the acknowledgment of subsystem dominance is the equivalent of explicit conceptualization. Likewise, students of national systems acknowledge that international events can significantly condition, even profoundly alter, the structure and dynamics of internal political processes, but they nevertheless treat the national system as a self-contained unit and no room is made in their models for the impact and operation of external variables. At most, such variables are handled by a notation that national systems have to develop and maintain foreign policies that facilitate adaptation to the international environment. The purpose of such a notation, however, is less that of attaining comprehension of how international systems penetrate national systems and more that of isolating those factors which would otherwise confound the conceptualization of national systems. In effect, by viewing foreign policy as taking care of events abroad, students of comparative politics free themselves of the responsibility of accounting for the penetration by international systems and enable themselves to focus on the internal processes that "normally" comprise national systems.

The rigidity of the national–international distinction is further illustrated by the wide gulf that separates students of comparative and international politics. It is the author's experience that each group is essentially uninterested in the work of the other. In one sense, of course, this is as it should be. We specialize in some fields because they arouse our interests, and we avoid others because they do not. But it is regrettable that when a specialist in comparative politics and a specialist in international politics get together, they tend to talk past each other. On two occasions of lengthy professional interaction between two such specialists, they were observed to have been first perplexed, then dismayed, and finally wearied by each other's commentary.[20] The student of national systems is interested in what large groups of people (the citizenry) do either to each other or to the few (officialdom), whereas the student of international systems concentrates on what the few (nations) do either to each other or to the many (foreign publics). In addition, the actors who comprise national systems compete much more extensively for each other's clientele than do those in international systems. Given these differences in the number of actors and the goals of their interaction, students of international politics accord a much more prominent place to strategy and rationality in their thinking than do students of national politics, who are preoccupied with gross behavior that is often nonrational.

As a consequence of these divergent interests, researchers in the one field tend not to be motivated to keep abreast of developments in the other. Students of international politics have little familiarity with the writings of their comparative politics colleagues and thus they are usually bewildered when their colleagues talk about political functions, goal attainment, and political culture. Contrariwise, rare are students of comparative politics who have read major works on international politics and thus rarely can they participate meaningfully in discussions of deterrence theory, foreign policy decision-making, and the balance of power.

Deeply entrenched habits of thought also sustain the rigidity of the national–international distinction. Most analysts are trained to emphasize the differences rather than the similarities between national and international politics. Rare is the graduate program that provides systematic training in the comparison of national and international systems. Hardly less rare are the programs that equip students with a capacity to compare international systems. Rather, "comparison" has a very strict meaning in political science today; one learns only to compare practices and policies at subnational or national levels. It is not surprising, therefore, that graduate programs list comparative and international politics as two separate fields to be offered for the Ph.D. To offer a field of study in international politics is to be conversant with political activities undertaken in the absence of "a structure of authoritative decision-making," whereas to offer a field in comparative or national politics requires familiarity with the ways in which the presence of legitimacy and a legitimizing agency (government) enhance, limit, or otherwise condition the conduct of politics.[21] Indeed, students of comparative politics become so accustomed to casting their analyses in terms of the structure of authority that they even tend to lose interest in national systems when the structure breaks down and chaos and violence prevail.[22]

Of all the habits that reinforce the reluctance of political scientists to modify the national–international distinction in the light of changing empirical patterns, none is more damaging than the tendency to posit political systems as functioning "in a society" or in some other unit equivalent to a nation. This unnecessary and essentially arbitrary limitation of the scope of the processes defined as political will be found in every major conceptualization that has been advanced in recent years. As indicated above, Easton identifies the authoritative allocation of values as the core of political activity, but immediately restricts his conception by adding that the values must be authoritatively allocated "in a society." Such an addition seems more gratuitous than logical. Certainly it is not necessary to his formulation. What about the elders of a village who reapportion the land, the representatives on a city council who decide on slum clearance and provide for urban renewal, or the members of the Council of Ministers of the European Economic Community who increase the tariff on chicken imported from the United States? Surely such activities constitute the allocation of values. Surely, too, they are authoritative for persons residing in the units affected by each allocation. And surely, therefore, Easton would be inclined to investigate them, even though his focus would be a village, city, or region rather than a society.

Obviously the tendency to house polities in societies would not serve to reinforce the national–international distinction if it were accompanied by an inclination to apply the concept of society to any social unit with shared norms and interdependent institutions. However, although lip service is often paid to such an inclination, it does not in fact prevail. Most – and possibly all – analysts have in mind national units and not villages, cities, or supranational communities when they refer to societies. The reasons for this convergence at the national level can be readily discerned. Analysts are interested in theorizing about greater and not lesser loyalties, about ultimate and not immediate authority, about the making and not the initiating of decisions; and for decades all these processes have tended to culminate at the national level. Conflicts between national societies and lesser units (such as villages or cities), for example, have traditionally been resolved in favor of the nation. So have clashes between national societies and supranational units. Legally, militarily, and politically, in other words, the actions of national officials have prevailed over those of village elders, city counselors, or supra-national ministers. Faced with a choice, people have attached greater loyalty to national than to subnational or supranational units. As a result, the decision-making mechanisms of national societies have long enjoyed a legitimacy, an authoritativeness, and an inclusiveness that no other unit could match.

To restate our central point, however, major alterations in this pattern occurred in the middle of the twentieth century. As has already been indicated, the national society is now so penetrated by the external world that it is no longer the only source of legitimacy or even of the employment of coercive techniques. The probability that most social processes will culminate at the national level has diminished, and instead the "most inclusive" structures through which groups strive to attain goals are increasingly a composite of subnational, national, and supranational elements.

It must be emphasized that these changes involve considerably more than a significant increase in the influence wielded by nonmembers of national societies. We are not simply asserting the proposition that the external world impinges ever more pervasively on the life of national societies, albeit such a proposition can hardly be denied. Nor are we talking merely about the growing interdependence of national political systems. Our contention is rather that in certain issue-areas (see below) national political systems now permeate, as well as depend on, each other and that their functioning now embraces actors who are not formally members of the system. These nonmembers not only exert influence upon national systems but also actually participate in the processes through which such systems allocate values, coordinate goal-directed efforts, and legitimately employ coercion. They not only engage in bargaining with the system, but they actually bargain within the system, taking positions on behalf of one or another of its components. Most important, the participation of nonmembers of the society in value-allocative and goal-attainment processes is accepted by both its officialdom and its citizenry, so that the decisions to which nonmembers contribute are no less authoritative and legitimate than are those in which they do not participate. Such external penetration may not always be gladly accepted by the officials and citizens of a society, but what renders decisions legitimate and authoritative is that they are felt to be binding, irrespective of whether they are accepted regretfully or willingly.[23] No doubt both the Finnish president and people were less than delighted by the aforementioned participation of Soviet officials in their electoral processes, but the decisions that resulted from such participation do not appear to have been more widely challenged in Finland than are other decisions made exclusively by members of the society.

One could, of course, reject this line of reasoning on narrow legal grounds. From the perspective of the law, the participation of nonmembers in a society's deliberations can never be regarded as more than the exercise of external influence. Strictly speaking, Soviet officials have no "right" to participate directly in Finnish affairs. They cannot vote in Finnish elections, and they are not entitled to nominate candidates for office. They are *non*members, not members, of Finnish society, and thus their actions in Finland can never be viewed as legitimate or authoritative from a strict juridical standpoint. To repeat, however, the functioning of national political systems contrasts so sharply with this narrow legal construction that the latter is hardly adequate as a basis of political conceptualization. Activities and processes – and not legalities – define the boundaries of political systems. Our interest is in political science and not in legal science, albeit the two need not be as discrepant as the situations discussed here.

The foregoing considerations not only lead to the conclusion that cogent political analysis requires a readiness to treat the functioning of national systems as increasingly dependent on external events and trends, but they also suggest the need to identify a new type of political system that will account for phenomena which not even a less rigid use of the national–international distinction renders comprehensible. Such a system might be called the *penetrated political system*,[24] and its essential characteristics might be defined as follows: a penetrated political system is one in which *nonmembers of a national society participate directly and authoritatively, through actions taken jointly with the society's members, in either the allocation of its values or the mobilization of support on behalf of its goals.*[25] The political processes of a penetrated system are conceived to be structurally different from both those of an international political system and those of a national political system. In the former, nonmembers indirectly and non-authoritatively influence the allocation of a society's values and the mobilization of support for its goals through autonomous rather than through joint action. In the latter, nonmembers of a society do not direct action toward it and thus do not contribute in any way to the allocation of its values or the attainment of its goals.

Obviously operationalization of these distinctions will prove difficult. When does an interaction between two actors consist of autonomous acts, and when does it amount to joint action? When are nonmembers of a society participants in its politics, and when are they just influential non-participants? Furthermore, how extensive must the participation by nonmembers be in order that a penetrated political system may come into existence?

In a sense, of course, operational answers to these questions must necessarily be arbitrary. What one observer treats as direct participation another may regard as indirect influence. Further clarification of the distinguishing features of penetrated systems, however, can be accomplished by citing some concrete examples of them. Vietnam and the Congo are two obvious ones. The US's role in the former and the UN's role in the latter clearly involve thoroughgoing participation in the allocation of Vietnamese and Congolese values and in efforts to mobilize popular support for the selected values. No less thoroughgoing as penetrated systems were Japan and Germany from the end of World War II to the end of their occupation by the Allies.[26] The satellite arrangements between the Soviet Union and the countries of Eastern Europe since World War II or between the Soviet Union and Cuba since 1961 also illustrate thoroughgoing penetrated systems. So does mainland China during the period between the advent of the Sino–Soviet bloc in 1949 and the latter's deterioration after the withdrawal of Soviet technicians from China in 1960. Less thoroughgoing but nonetheless significant examples of penetration are the role of American citizens, companies, and officials in Cuba prior to 1958; the participation of US officials in India's defense planning subsequent to the Chinese attack of 1962; the activities of the British armed forces in post-independence Kenya; the US's abandonment of Skybolt as a weapon for the British defense system; the aforementioned behavior of American aid officials in Thailand; and indeed the operation of any foreign aid program in which the aiding society maintains some control over the purposes and distribution of the aid in the recipient society. Equally indicative of the emergence of a penetrated system is the acceptance of a growing number of non-diplomatic foreign agents in the United States.[27]

As these examples indicate, penetrated systems, like international and national ones, are not static. They come into being, develop, or disappear as capabilities, attitudes, or circumstances change. Mainland China was a penetrated system during the 1950s, but emerged as a national system during the 1960s. Contrariwise, for centuries British defenses were national in character, but now they seem destined to be sustained through penetrative processes. Cuba represents the change, rather than the emergence or disappearance, of a penetrated system; for decades its politics was penetrated by the United States, but in recent years the latter has been replaced by the Soviet Union as the penetrator.

At the same time the examples suggest that it is false to assume that penetrated systems merely represent stages in the evolution or deterioration of national systems. As indicated by the Cuban example, and even more by that of East Germany, penetrated systems can be relatively permanent forms of political organization. Recognition of the relative permanence of certain types of penetrated systems will prove especially difficult for those who cling to the national–international distinction. Such an outlook fosters the view that the integrative or disintegrative processes prevalent in a region must inevitably culminate in its consolidation into a single national system or its fragmentation into two or more national systems. Yet there is no inherent reason why the processes which lead to the solidification of national systems should not also operate in penetrated systems. Given a Cold War context, what has happened in East Germany may well be prototypical rather than exceptional in the case of newly established penetrated systems.

Another characteristic of penetrated systems suggested by the foregoing examples is that national societies (as defined, say, by actual or proposed membership in the United Nations) always serve as the site for penetrated systems. Unlike an international system, which encompasses interaction patterns that occur between societies, the processes of a penetrated system unfold only in the penetrated society. In no way is such a system conceived to embrace the value allocations that occur in the societies to which the nonmembers belong and which account for their participation in the politics of the penetrated society. An inquiry into China as a penetrated system in the 1950s, for example, would not require investigation of value allocations that were made in Moscow, albeit a full analysis of the Sino–Soviet bloc during that decade would involve an examination of China as a penetrated system, the Soviet Union as a national system, and the two together as an international system.

Still another characteristic of a penetrated system is indicated by the examples of the Congo and Cuba – namely, that the nonmembers of such a system can belong either to an international organization or to another society and that in the latter case they can either hold official positions or be merely private citizens. The existence of a penetrated system is determined by the presence of nonmembers who participate directly in a society's politics and not by their affiliations and responsibilities.

More significantly, all but the last of the examples listed earlier indicate that penetrated systems are characterized by a shortage of capabilities on the part of the penetrated society and that an effort to compensate for, or take advantage of, this shortage underlies the participation of nonmembers in its politics. The shortage may be of an economic kind (as in the case of recipients of foreign aid); it may involve military weaknesses as in Vietnam or Finland; it may stem from a lack of social cohesion (as in the Congo); or it may consist of an overall strategic vulnerability (as in Cuba). Whatever the nature of the shortage, however, it is sufficiently recognized and accepted by the members of a penetrated society to permit legitimacy to become attached to the direct participation of the nonmembers in the allocation of its values.[28] Hence it follows that penetrated systems are likely to be as permanent as the capability shortages which foster and sustain them.

But the last listed example, that of increasing numbers of non-diplomatic foreign agents registered in the United States, cannot be dismissed merely as an exception. Capability shortages may underlie most penetrated systems, but obviously penetration of the United States did not occur for this reason. Yet because of the nature of the penetration the US example is not as contradictory as it might seem at first glance. For again a capability imbalance would appear to have encouraged the growth of penetrative processes, the difference being that the United States possesses a relative abundance rather than a relative shortage of capabilities. Just as a society's shortages lead nonmembers to participate in its politics, so does the existence of plenitude serve to attract participation by nonmembers who wish to obtain either financial aid or political support.[29] Thus it is reasonable to speculate that as long as richly endowed societies maintain institutions that permit access to their resources, they are bound to become penetrated in certain respects.[30]

All the cited examples also reveal that for a penetrated system to function, there must be intensive face-to-face interaction between members and nonmembers of a society. Values cannot be authoritatively allocated, or goal-attaining activities authoritatively mobilized, from afar. Nonmembers of a society must come into contact with its officials and/or its citizenry in order to acquire sufficient information about the society's needs and wants to participate in its value-allocative processes in ways that are sufficiently acceptable to be authoritative. Moreover, even if the nonmembers could obtain appropriate information about the society without interacting with its members, their efforts to contribute to the allocation of its values would still be lacking in authority. While authority is often attached to mystical and distant entities, to be effectively sustained it requires some visible and human embodiment. The members of a society are not likely to regard the demands or suggestions of nonmembers as binding (that is, as authoritative) unless they have had some firsthand acquaintance with them.

This is not to say, of course, that intensive face-to-face interaction between members and nonmembers of a society occurs only in a penetrated system. Nor is it to imply that nonmembers of a society can contribute to the allocation of its values only through intensive face-to-face interaction with its members. It is quite commonplace for the political processes of international systems to underlie the reallocation of values in societies and to do so either with or without face-to-face interaction. Prolonged negotiations over a treaty which reallocates the values of all the signatories to it are illustrative of the former process, and an extreme example of the latter is provided by two societies that sever all contacts and then reallocate their values in response to the subsequent threats each makes toward the other. Although in both cases nonmembers contribute to the allocation of a society's values, both examples would nonetheless be regarded as reflecting international and not penetrative processes because in neither illustration do nonmembers participate directly in the allocation of a society's values. This is self-evident in the case of the two societies that sever relations, but it is no less true in the treaty example. For while the signatories to a treaty join together in face-to-face interaction in order to conclude it, each representative makes a commitment only with respect to his own society, and thus his actions at the negotiating table do not involve participation in the allocative processes of other societies.[31] In other words, treaties are best viewed as the sum of autonomous acts rather than as the result of joint action.

One final point with respect to penetrated systems needs to be made. As it stands at present, our formulation suffers from a lack of differentiation. Obviously there is a vast difference between the penetrated systems that have developed in Vietnam and the Congo and those that have evolved with respect to British or Indian defenses. In the former cases penetration is thoroughgoing, whereas in the latter it is limited to the allocation of a highly restricted set of values. Nonmembers may participate directly in the determination and attainment of Indian military goals, but clearly they are not a party to the processes whereby India's linguistic problems are handled. In Vietnam, on the other hand, nonmembers have been centrally involved in efforts to mobilize support for certain religious values as well as for a military campaign. Accordingly, so as to differentiate degrees of penetration as well as the structural differences to which they give rise, it seems appropriate to distinguish between multi-issue and single-issue penetrated systems, the distinction being based on whether nonmembers participate in the allocation of a variety of values or of only a selected set of values.

The issue-area concept

The conclusion that national societies can be organized as penetrated political systems with respect to some types of issues – or issue-areas – and as national political systems with respect to others is consistent with mounting evidence that the functioning of any type of political system can vary significantly from one issue-area to another. Data descriptive of local, party, legislative, national, and international systems are converging around the finding that different types of issue-areas elicit different sets of motives on the part of different actors in a political system, that different system members are thus activated in different issue-areas, and that the different interaction patterns which result from these variations produce different degrees of stability and coherence for each of the issue-areas in which systemic processes are operative.

Perhaps the most impressive data along these lines are to be found in Dahl's inquiry into the politics of New Haven.[32] Using systematic survey techniques, Dahl examined the processes of governmental and non-governmental leadership activated by situations in three issue-areas – urban redevelopment, education, and nominations. His finding is stunning: the "overlap among leaders and subleaders" in the three areas involved only 3 percent of his sample, and only 1.5 percent were leaders in all three areas.[33] In effect, there are at least three New Haven political systems, and to know how values are allocated and how support is mobilized in any one area is not to be knowledgeable about the operation of these processes in the other areas.[34]

Similar findings on legislative and national systems are reported by Miller and Stokes, who employed survey data to correlate the attitudes of congressmen, the attitudes of their constituencies, and the congressmen's perceptions of their constituencies' attitudes in three major issue-areas–social welfare, foreign involvement, and civil rights.[35] Again the results compel reflection: the differences between the operation of the processes of representation in the civil rights area, on the one hand, and in the social welfare and foreign involvement areas, on the other, proved to be highly significant statistically, constituting "one of the most striking findings of this analysis."[36] Given such variability at the center of the political process, again it seems reasonable to assert that there are at least two American national systems, and to comprehend the dynamics of one is not necessarily to understand the functioning of the other.

Still another indication of the importance of issue-areas has been uncovered in studies of the processes through which political parties mobilize support. For example, using interview data, Chalmers probed decision making within the Social Democratic Party of West Germany and was led to conclude that, in effect, the party consists of two independent organizational mechanisms.[37] He found that different party leaders and different party followers engaged in different modes of deciding upon ideological matters on the one hand and campaign issues on the other, the differences again being such that knowledge of the party's functioning in one area did not ensure comprehension of its dynamics in the other. Nor do international systems appear to be different in this respect. Although here the data are more impressionistic than systematic, it does seem clear that the structure and functioning of international systems can vary significantly from one issue-area to another. Consider the Communist international system; plainly it operates differently in the admit-China-to-the-UN area than it does in the area bounded by disarmament questions. Or take NATO: it has been a vastly different system with respect to Berlin than with respect to independence movements in Africa. Likewise, to cite an equally clear-cut dyadic example, the functioning of the US–USSR international system in the Berlin issue-area bears little resemblance to the processes through which it allocates values and mobilizes support for the attainment of its goals in the disarmament or wheat-production areas.

Whether they are impressionistic or systematic, in short, the data on issue-areas are too impressive to ignore. Conceptual allowance must be made for them if theorizing in the foreign policy field is to flourish. Indeed, the emergence of issue-areas is as pronounced and significant as the breakdown of the national–international distinction. Taken together, the two trends point to the radical conclusion that the boundaries of political systems ought to be drawn vertically in terms of issue-areas as well as horizontally in terms of geographic areas.[38] Stated in the context of the present world scene, the data compel us to cast our analyses as much in terms of, say, civil rights political systems, economic-development political systems, and health-and-welfare political systems as we do in terms of local, national, and international systems.

However, as in the case of the national–international distinction (and in part because of it), political scientists have not been inclined to make the conceptual adjustments which the data on issue-areas would seem to warrant. Certainly the more theoretically oriented analysts, with one notable exception, have not proceeded from the assumption that issues generate structurally and functionally significant differences.[39] Even Dahl ignores the relevance of issue-areas in a subsequent conceptualization of politics and polities.[40] Similarly, and again with one important exception, empirical-minded researchers have not followed up the implications of the findings cited above. One is hard pressed to find empirical analyses of particular systems that explicitly explore the relevancy, strength, and boundaries of different kinds of issue-areas.[41] Instead most researchers continue to treat cities, parties, legislatures, and nations as if their processes of allocating values and mobilizing support for goals were constants rather than variables.[42] To be sure, fine distinctions between cities or parties or legislatures or nations are recognized and closely analyzed, but the same sensitivities are not trained on the variability within a given horizontal system.[43]

The neglect of issue-areas in systematic inquiry is all the more perplexing because there is one respect in which intuitively, and often unknowingly, political scientists do employ the concept: although reasons are rarely given for the distinction, one is usually made between foreign and domestic policy. Throughout the discipline it is assumed that national political systems function differently in formulating and administering foreign policies than they do in domestic areas; most universities, for example, offer both undergraduate and graduate courses in "The Formulation of American Foreign Policy," a subject presumably sufficiently unlike "The Formulation of American Domestic Policy" to warrant separate presentation. However, since the reasoning underlying the distinction is never made explicit, its implications have not been recognized, and the idea of categorizing phenomena according to issue-areas has not been applied elsewhere in the discipline. Sociologists have developed subfields in industrial sociology, the sociology of law, the sociology of education, the sociology of religion, the sociology of art, the sociology of science, the sociology of medicine, the sociology of demographic behavior, the sociology of crime, and the sociology of mental illness, as well as in the sociology of the family, urban sociology, rural sociology, political sociology, and the sociology of particular societies.[44] Yet political scientists do not offer courses in, say, the politics of employment, the politics of transportation, the politics of conservation, the politics of foreign aid, the politics of civil liberties, the politics of agriculture, the politics of defense strategy, the politics of health, the politics of commerce, the politics of education, and so on.[45]

The conceptual and empirical neglect of issue-areas would appear to stem from several sources. One is the sheer force of habit. Most analysts have become accustomed to perceiving and structuring political phenomena in terms of horizontal systems. Hence, confronted with findings like Dahl's, most researchers would be inclined to treat them merely as interesting characteristics of local communities rather than as pervasive phenomena that necessitate reconsideration of one's approach to the discipline.

The habit of horizontal analysis is reinforced by the tendency of some, and perhaps even many, researchers to view horizontal political systems as dominated by a "power elite" who perform the function of allocating all the system's values. A legislature has its "inner club," a party its "bosses," an executive his "kitchen cabinet," a community its "influentials," and an international organization its "powerful" – all of whom are believed to interact in the same way whenever they make decisions for, or mobilize support in, their respective systems. Such an approach is obviously incompatible with a recognition of issue-areas as a meaningful concept. Notwithstanding the findings uncovered by Dahl and others, however, power-elite theories still abound, and the strength of the habit of horizontal analysis remains undiminished.

Neglect of issue-areas would also seem to stem from a view that the issues which preoccupy horizontal systems are unique rather than recurrent and that therefore any model which posits them as variables encourages the writing of case histories rather than the testing of hypotheses and the construction of theories. Issues are temporary and situational, the reasoning seems to be, and to see horizontal systems functioning in terms of them is thus to reduce actors and action to a level of specificity that inhibits the discernment of patterns and regularities. Unlike the power theorists, in other words, some analysts appear to accept the validity of the issue-area data even as they discount them on the grounds that such data reflect historical rather than political processes. The difficulty with this line of reasoning is that it is based on an excessively narrow conception of the nature of an issue-area. Both vertical systems and the issue-areas in which they function are best conceived in terms of broad types of values and the recurring need to allocate them. Hence, although issues may be temporary and situational, issue-areas are persistent and general. Each area must be conceptualized at a high enough level of abstraction to encompass a variety of vertical systems, and each of the latter must in turn be conceived as based on a continual processing of the values that its structure is designed to allocate. This is why Dahl, for example, constructed his three issue-areas out of data for fifty-seven, eight, and ten occasions when questions pertaining, respectively, to urban redevelopment, education, and political nominations were at issue during periods of nine, seven, and twenty years.

The boundaries of issue-areas and of the vertical systems within them would seem to be the focus of another more sophisticated line of reasoning that neglects both the concept and the evidence of its importance. The reasoning is that a system consists of "a boundary-maintaining set of interdependent particles"[46] and that while issue-areas and vertical systems certainly contain interdependent parts, their boundaries are not self-maintaining. Why? Because the processes of allocating values and mobilizing support within an issue-area are too vulnerable to continuous and significant external interference to justify treating their interdependent parts as political systems. And why should the boundaries of issue-areas be so vulnerable? Because bargaining among issue-areas is a major characteristic of geographic and other types of horizontal systems. Indeed, the stability of such systems is considered to be crucially dependent on their ability to resolve conflicts in one area by compromising in other areas. Hence, the argument concludes, the essential characteristic of boundary-maintenance – that the components of a system be so related as to divide the system from its environment – will at best be obscure and at worst non-existent in vertical systems.

There can hardly be any dissent from much of this reasoning. It is certainly true that the outcome of interaction patterns within an issue-area can be greatly influenced by external variables. The strong pull which national security considerations can exert in the area of civil liberties provides an obvious example. And surely it is also incontestable that bargaining among issue-areas can frequently occur in horizontal systems. Indeed, this is virtually a defining characteristic of logrolling in legislatures.

The recognition of these points, however, does not diminish the potential relevance of the issue-area data. For the fact is that no political system has unmistakable and impermeable boundaries. Legislatures are penetrated by executives and parties; executives penetrate legislatures and parties; and parties in turn are penetrated by executives and legislatures. Local communities are penetrated by regional ones, and regional units are penetrated by national systems; and, as we have seen, it is increasingly difficult to distinguish national systems from their international environments. In short, the boundaries of horizontal systems are also far from invulnerable, perhaps no less so than those of vertical systems.[47] Certainly bargaining among horizontal systems can be just as consequential for the participating units as that which occurs among vertical systems. Executive–legislative relations and inter-nation relations provide obvious examples. Consider the former: plainly the extent of the impact which executives and legislatures can have on each other is no less than the pull which issues can have on each other within even the most logrolling type of legislature.

In fact, one can think of some horizontal systems that are *less* boundary-maintaining than some vertical systems. To take an extreme example, compare the horizontal system known as Vietnam and the vertical one known as disarmament, as they appear to be functioning at the present time. The boundaries of the former are so obscure that classifying it as a penetrated system is the only way in which its processes of allocating values and mobilizing support become comprehensible. On the other hand, it is not nearly so difficult to discern the line dividing the disarmament area from its environment. Governments take positions, seek support from other governments, send representatives to Geneva, and then attempt to allocate values with a minimum of penetration from other issue-areas. To be sure, in the end values are rarely allocated and deadlock usually results, but this outcome is due less to the intrusion of other issues than it is to the rigidity of the positions which actors bring to disarmament negotiations.

In other words, the argument that vertical systems are vulnerable because of the stability requirements of horizontal systems may not be as valid as it appears at first glance. Precisely opposite considerations may prevail in some instances. To maintain stability, horizontal systems may have to insulate certain issue-areas and prevent bargaining across their boundaries. Such a process of insulation may occur under two considerations: first, it may be precipitated whenever the actors of a horizontal system have common goals in one area but their lack of agreement on other matters results in the recognition that progress toward the attainment of the common goals can only be achieved through insulating the issue-area. The disarmament area within the US–USSR system would seem to be illustrative in this regard. Second, the process of insulation may be initiated whenever the actors of a horizontal system lack agreement in one area but their concurrence in other areas leads them to agree to contain the conflict in order to prevent it from destabilizing the other areas or the entire system. For many years the handling of civil rights issues in the United States corresponded to this pattern.

In short, further elaboration, rather than continued neglect, of the issue-area concept would seem to be in order. None of the arguments against the construction of vertical political systems out of identifiable issue-areas fully offset the compelling evidence that horizontal systems function differently in different areas. Let us turn, therefore, to the task of specifying more precisely the nature of issue-areas and the location of vertical systems within them.

Stated formally, an issue-area is conceived to consist of *(1) a cluster of values, the allocation or potential allocation of which leads (2) the affected or potentially affected actors to differ so greatly over (a) the way in which the values should be allocated or (b) the horizontal levels at which the allocations should be authorized that (3) they engage in distinctive behavior designed to mobilize support for the attainment of their particular values.* If a cluster of values does not lead to differences among those affected by it, then the issue-area is not considered to exist for that group of actors, and their relationships with respect to the values are not considered to form a vertical system. If a cluster of values does divide the actors affected by it, but if their differences are not so great as to induce support-building behavior, then the issue-area, and its vertical systems, is considered to be dormant until such time as one of the actors activates it by pressing for a reallocation of the value cluster. If a cluster of values induces support building on the part of the affected actors, but if their behavior is not distinctive from that induced by another cluster of values, then the issue-area is considered to encompass both clusters, and both are also regarded as being processed by the same vertical system.

It will be noted that the boundaries of vertical systems are delineated not by the common membership of the actors who sustain them (as horizontal systems are), but rather by the distinctiveness of the values and the behavior they encompass. The actors determine the state of a vertical system – whether it is active, dormant, or nonexistent – but the boundaries of the system are independent of the identity of the actors who are active within it. In fact, the horizontal affiliations of its actors may be quite varied. Some might be members of local systems. Others might belong to national systems. Still others might be participants in penetrated or international systems. The cluster of values associated with economic development provides an example of an issue-area that encompasses actors at every horizontal level.

This is not to imply, of course, that either the actors, the values, or the behaviors that form the parameters of a vertical system are simple to identify. A number of operational problems will have to be resolved before empirical research on vertical phenomena yield worthwhile results. In particular, answers to three questions must be developed: how are the values over which people differ to be clustered together into issue-areas? At what level of abstraction should they be clustered? What characteristics render the behavior evoked by one cluster of values distinctive from that stimulated by other clusters?

The general line of response to the first two questions seems reasonably clear. A typology of issue-areas ought to be something more than a mere cataloguing of the matters over which people are divided at any moment in time. For vertical systems to be of analytic utility, they must persist beyond the life of particular actors. As has already been implied, not much would be accomplished if "issue-area" meant nothing more than the conventional usage, in which an "issue" is equated with any and every concrete historical conflict that ensues between identifiable individuals or groups. Thus a typology of issue-areas must be cast in sufficiently abstract terms to encompass past and future clusters of values as well as present ones. Obviously, too, the level of abstraction must be high enough to allow for clusters of values that evoke behavior within all types of horizontal systems, from local communities to the global community. At the same time the typology cannot be so generalized as to erase the distinctiveness of the behavior which characterizes the vertical systems in each of its areas.

For the present, of course, any typology must be largely arbitrary. Until systematic and extensive data on the distinctive nature of certain issue-areas are accumulated, the lines dividing them cannot be drawn with much certainty. In order to suggest further dimensions of the concept, however, let us adopt a simple typology that seems to meet the above criteria. Let us conceive of all behavior designed to bring about the authoritative allocation of values as occurring in any one of four issue-areas: the *territorial, status, human resources*, and *nonhuman resources areas*, each of which encompasses the distinctive motives, actions, and interactions evoked by the clusters of values that are linked to, respectively, the allocation of territorial jurisdiction, the allocation of status within horizontal political systems or within nonpolitical systems, the development and allocation of human resources, and the development and allocation of nonhuman resources. Examples of vertical systems located in the territorial area are the persistent conflict over Berlin, the continuing Arizona–California controversy over rights to the Colorado River, and the recurring efforts to effect a merger of the Township and Borough of Princeton, New Jersey. Status-area systems are exemplified by the long-standing problem of whether mainland China should be admitted to the United Nations, the unending racial conflict in South Africa, and the perennial question of higher pay for police officers faced by every American town. Enduring efforts to provide medical care for the aged, unceasing problems of population control, and periodic disputes over the training of teachers are illustrative of vertical systems that fall in the human resources area. Certain foreign aid programs, most housing and highway programs, and many agricultural policies illustrate the kinds of vertical systems that are classified in the nonhuman resources area.

In other words, each of the four issue-areas is conceived to embrace a number of vertical political systems, and the boundaries of each vertical system are in turn conceived to be determined by the scope of the interaction that occurs within it. Thus, as implied above, some vertical systems may function exclusively at local horizontal levels; others may be national in scope; still others may be confined to interaction at the international level. Given the interdependence of life in the nuclear age, however, empirical inquiry would probably find that an overwhelming preponderance of the world's vertical systems range upward and downward across several horizontal levels. Table 19.2, by using brief identifying labels for currently existing vertical systems in all four issue-areas, is designed to provide an even more concrete set of examples of the pervasive extent to which vertical systems extend across horizontal levels. Each system is entered in the table at the approximate horizontal level at which it came into existence, but crudely scaled arrows have been attached in order to suggest the subsequent extension of its scope. The scarcity of systems without arrows is intentional and designed to represent the small degree to which life in the nuclear age can be confined to a single horizontal level.

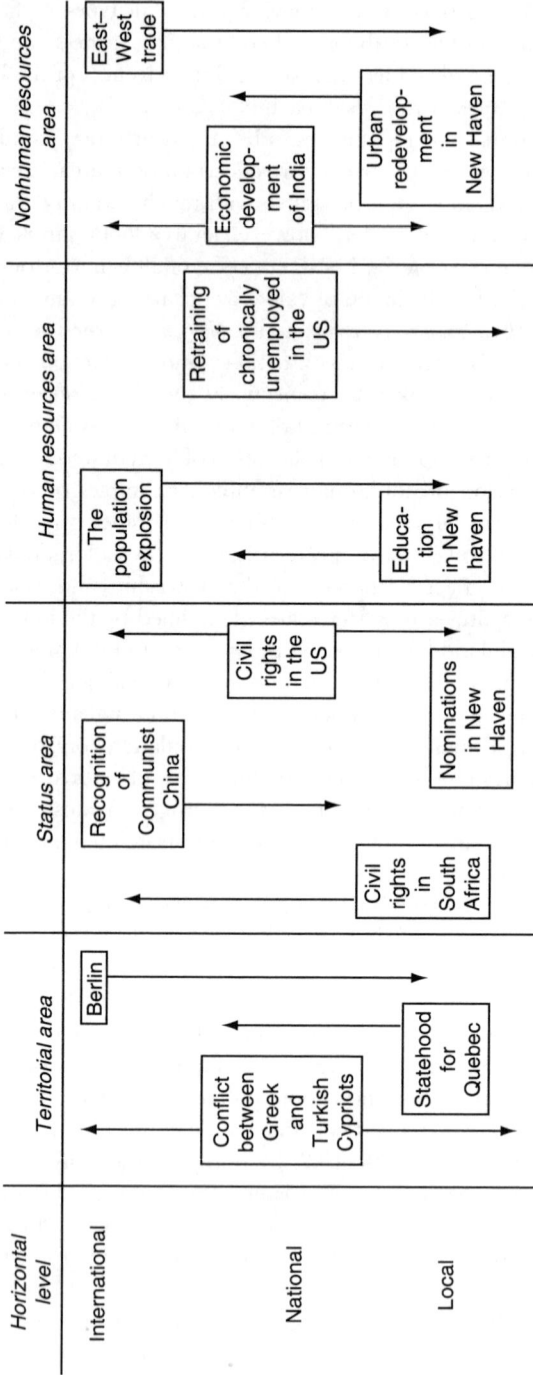

Table 19.2 Examples of vertical systems in each of the four issue-areas

Arrows suggest the degree to which the scope of each system was extended across horizontal levels subsequent to its activation

But how, it may well be asked, does this particular typology meet the criterion that the value clusters in each area must evoke distinctive motives, actions, and interactions on the part of the affected actors? Granted that the values themselves differ, why should it be presumed that these differences are sufficient to produce differentiation in the functioning of the systems that allocate the values in each issue-area? As previously indicated, the answers to these questions must of necessity be somewhat vague. Since the issue-area concept has not been the focus of systematic inquiry, data which would allow for comparisons of the functioning of vertical systems are not available, and any typology has perforce to be constructed out of crude impressions about the reasons for the findings uncovered by Dahl and others. In the case of the foregoing typology the four issue-areas were derived from an impression that the motives, actions, and interactions of political actors are crucially related to the degree of tangibility of both the values which have to be allocated and the means which have to be employed to effect allocation.[48] With respect to motives and actions, it was reasoned that the affected actors would be more strongly motivated and more persistently active the *greater* the tangibility of the *means* (since the rewards and costs to the actor of allocating a particular cluster of values are likely to be clearer the more easily comprehensible are the means necessary to realize the values); and that the more actors affected and active, the *lesser* the tangibility of the ends (since tangibility involves specificity, and thus the aspirations of a greater number of actors are likely to be encompassed by issues in which intangible goals are at stake). With respect to interaction, the presumption was made that the greater the tangibility of both the *ends* and *means* involved in an allocative process, the more the tendency to bargain among the affected actors would increase. In short, among the distinctive characteristics of an issue-area is the number of affected actors, the intensity of their motivations to act, the frequency with which they act, and the extent of their readiness to bargain with each other.

That four main issue-areas derive from the foregoing is readily apparent. The processes of allocating tangible values through the use of tangible means will differ significantly from those in which intangible ends and means are involved; both of these will in turn be distinguished from the processes whereby tangible values are allocated through the utilization of intangible means; and still a fourth pattern of distinctive motives, actions, and interactions will occur whenever tangible means are employed to achieve intangible ends. In short, we have fashioned a 2 × 2 matrix (Table 19.3), each cell of which corresponds more or less closely to one of the four kinds of values that are presumed to sustain political behavior.

Table 19.3 Matrix of means and ends

		MEANS	
		Intangible	*Tangible*
	Intangible	*Status area*	*Human resources area*
ENDS			
	Tangible	*Territorial area*	*Nonhuman resources area*

Although crude and impressionistic, this derivation of the distinctiveness of the issue-areas does seem to hold up when one engages in the exercise of locating empirical findings in the matrix. Let us take Dahl's data as an example, and assume for purposes of illustration that the tangible–intangible scale of ends is operationalized in terms of whether the values involved can be photographed with a camera and that the tangibility of means is measured by the extent to which money must be expended in order to acquire the values. The values represented by education cannot be photographed, albeit money is necessary to build the schools and pay the teachers – prerequisites to the realization of educational values. Hence vertical systems designed to process educational issues fall in the human resources area of the matrix. Similarly, nominations in New Haven are not photographable, and, unlike the building and maintenance of a school system, money is not needed to have them allocated in a desired fashion. Thus they would be classified in the status area. Likewise, urban redevelopment in New Haven – or the need for it – is readily photographable, and great quantities of money must be committed to its realization, thereby locating it in the nonhuman resources area. Since Dahl offers no data for the territorial area, let us conclude this exercise with the example of Berlin as a vertical political system. In this case, the erection of the wall in August 1961 testifies poignantly to the photographability of the values involved. Yet diplomatic persuasion, rather than money and the military capabilities it buys, must obviously serve as the means through which a Berlin settlement will ultimately be accomplished.[49]

The impression that the fit between this formulation and empirical phenomena is sufficient to warrant further development of the typology is reinforced by one other consideration. The assumption that the tangibility of ends and means determines the number of affected actors and the extent of their readiness to bargain with each other permits specific conclusions about distinctive characteristics of at least two of the issue-areas. On the one hand, the status area, being composed of both intangible ends and means, is likely to evoke more uncompromising political behavior on the part of more actors than any of the other three; on the other hand, the nonhuman resources area, being composed of both tangible ends and means, is likely to evoke more bargaining on the part of fewer actors than any of the other areas. That these two conclusions correspond to the differences between concrete vertical systems in each area can be readily demonstrated. Compare, for instance, the processes whereby values pertaining to civil rights are allocated with those that mark the allocation of values in the field of transportation (e.g., the development of rivers, harbors, and roads). Clearly, more persons are aroused by the former cluster than by the latter, and plainly, too, uncompromising positions are as characteristic of civil rights issues as horse-trading is of rivers and harbors allocations.

Indeed, it is noteworthy that these characteristics of the status area would seem to be so powerful as to create still another distinctive characteristic of that area: the boundaries of vertical systems in the status area would appear to be more capable of expansion than are systems in any other area. Because they arouse a greater number of actors and a more uncompromising set of orientations, status issues can quickly move upward, downward, and sideward, once they are activated. The demand for civil rights in Angola, the attempt of James Meredith to enter the University of Mississippi, and the recognition of Communist China are illustrative of the vertical dynamism of status issues. Their horizontal dynamism – their capacity for intruding upon other issue-areas – is exemplified by recent civil rights debates in the United States. It was equally apparent in November 1963, when the arrest of a Yale professor in Moscow proved to be far more unsettling to the US–USSR system (as it was then being sustained in wheat and disarmament negotiations) than a concurrent flare-up of the Berlin crisis.

Conclusion

The implications of the foregoing conceptual adjustments for the construction of foreign policy theory are clear.[50] If the above formulation has any validity, the external behavior of horizontal systems at the national level is likely to vary so greatly in scope, intensity, and flexibility in each of the four issue-areas that any theory of foreign policy will have to include if-then propositions which reflect these variations. Similarly, theoretical account will have to be taken of the external behavior of penetrated systems. Their relations with the rest of the world will obviously be partly a function of differences in the degree and nature of the penetration they experience. Moreover, since the extent and manner of penetration are likely to vary from one issue-area to the next, any theory will have to encompass these additional differences.

Indeed, the penetrated and vertical systems concepts would seem to be sufficiently important to warrant revision at the pre-theoretical level. It seems reasonable to presume, for instance, that the relative potency of systemic variables would be greater in penetrated systems than in those that are strictly of a national kind. Thus the pre-theory summarized in Table 19.1 could fruitfully be doubled in scope by subdividing each of the eight columns into "penetrated" and "nonpenetrated" categories and introducing eight new rankings which elevate the systemic variables, say, one notch in each of the eight penetrated systems. Likewise, if the distinctive characteristics of the status and nonhuman resources areas have been correctly estimated, it is easy to envision still another expansion of the pre-theory – a twofold expansion in which societal variables are elevated one position in the rankings for status areas (because more members of the system are likely to be aroused to make more uncompromising demands) and lowered one rank in those for nonhuman resources areas (because fewer system members are likely to make less stringent demands). Table 19.4 presents these possible expansions of the pre-theory that the penetrated and vertical systems concepts facilitate.

While these concepts greatly complicate the task of theory building, they do not dictate or limit the kind of theory that can be constructed. As emphasized throughout, all we have done in this chapter is to identify and amplify the

Table 19.4 A further elaboration of the author's pre-theory of foreign policy, in which five sets of variables underlying the external behavior of societies are ranked according to their relative potencies in sixteen types of societies and three types of issue-areas

Country	Economy	Polity	Penetration	Status area	Nonhuman resource area	Other areas
Large Country	Developed Economy	Open Polity	Penetrated	so r r sy sy	r sy so g g	g g sy so i
			Non-penetrated	so r r so i	r g so sy g	g so g sy i
		Closed Polity	Penetrated	r r r sy g	i i i r g	g g g so sy · so sy
			Non-penetrated	r r r g g	i i i g so	g g sy so sy
	Underdeveloped Economy	Open Polity	Penetrated	i i i r so	i i i r sy	so g g sy g
			Non-penetrated	i i i so r	i i i r sy	r so sy g g
		Closed Polity	Penetrated	i i i r sy	i i i sy g	r r g so g
			Non-penetrated	i i i r r	i i i r g	g g so so sy
Small Country	Developed Economy	Open Polity	Penetrated	sy sy sy so r	so r r g so	r g so g i
			Non-penetrated	r r r so sy	r r r sy g	so g g i i
		Closed Polity	Penetrated	sy sy sy r r	i i i so g	g so g i
			Non-penetrated	r r r sy sy	i i i g so	g g so so
	Underdeveloped Economy	Open Polity	Penetrated	sy sy sy i i	i i i so r	r g so g g
			Non-penetrated	i i i sy sy	sy sy sy so r	r g so g g
		Closed Polity	Penetrated	sy sy sy i i	i i i r r	r r g so so
			Non-penetrated	i i i sy sy	sy sy sy r r	r r g so so

i = individual variables r = role variables g = governmental variables so = societal variables sy = systemic variables materials out of which any theory of foreign policy must be fashioned. A wide range of theories can be built out of these materials, and nothing inherent in the latter determines the design, elegance, and utility of the former. The analyst must supply these qualities, which is what makes the task of theory building awesome and challenging.

20 Pre-theorizing about foreign policy in a globalized world[1]

Nearly four decades ago I developed a pre-theory of foreign policy organized around five clusters of variables at five levels of analysis – the individual, role, governmental, societal, and systemic levels. The essential thrust of the pre-theory involved estimating the relative "potency" of the different types of variables for any country and then assessing how a particular country might conduct itself abroad in response to diverse situations.[2]

While the world has changed enormously in the intervening years, so have my concerns as a student of world affairs. The changes in world politics are rooted in the acceleration of the processes of globalization that began late in the twentieth century, changes that were central to my moving away from foreign policy analysis and toward a more holistic approach to the course of events.[3] Yet, I still find the pre-theory formulation compelling. Indeed, it now seems more relevant than ever and, happily, it readily accommodates the transformations that have altered the relative potency of each variable cluster. The ensuing pages will explore these changes and how they have affected the conduct of foreign policy in the present period.

The dynamics of globalization

A perspective on the underpinnings of globalizing processes presently underway in the world is, obviously, a prerequisite to analyzing how a pre-theoretical approach to foreign policy may be useful in the present period. Stated succinctly, eight dynamics that drive globalization serve to summarize the transformations at work in every issue area at every level of community.[4] The eight dynamics are so interrelated and interactive, so inextricably linked to each other, that none can be treated as primary. All of them have considerable causal potency and thus the brief discussion of them that follows should not be interpreted as an implicit ranking of their relevance.

One involves what I call a "skill revolution" – the notion that everywhere, in the developed as well as the developing world, the skills of individuals have changed such that their capacity for analytically, emotionally, and imaginatively comprehending distant events have enlarged.[5] This transformation at the micro level of social and political life has significant consequences inasmuch as it underlies the empowerment of people and thus the potency of both variables in both the individual and societal clusters. Individuals are not conceived to be converging around similar values or becoming equally competent. Rather, the skill revolution is posited as enlarging the capacity of people in the context of their own circumstances and cultures.

A second dynamic consists of what I call an "organizational explosion" – the processes by which new associations are rapidly, perhaps even exponentially, forming and proliferating. Partly driven by the growing preoccupation with environmental and human rights issues, partly a consequence of the skill revolution, partly stimulated by the complexities of an ever more globalized world, and greatly facilitated by the Internet and other recent microelectronic technologies, people everywhere are reaching out to each other in order to concert their interests and serve their goals. And they are doing so horizontally through networking as well as in hierarchical structures. The data descriptive of the organizational explosion are so staggering[6] that it can readily be concluded the world stage has become increasingly crowded and dense with collective actors.

A third dynamic involves a mushrooming of authority crises in innumerable communities and countries throughout the world. In some conspicuous instances such crises take the form of prolonged violence, but even more pervasive are authority crises not marked by violence but by communities, societies, states, and international institutions being so paralyzed and entrenched in stalemate that they are unable to frame and move toward their goals. To some extent these authority crises are the consequence of the rapidity of the transformations that sustain globalizing processes, and in part they are also intensified by the skill revolution and the organizational explosion even as they also reinforce the pace and depth of these other two dynamics.

A fourth dynamic concerns what I call a "mobility upheaval" – the processes by which people are on the move from every part of the world to many other parts of the world. Some of them move permanently, some do so only temporarily, but taken together they amount to an endless and vast flow, everyone from the tourist to the terrorist, from the migrant to the businessman and woman, from the professional to the entertainer. It is a flow that adds to skill levels, that facilitates organizational proliferation and coherence, and that contributes to authority crises.

A fifth dynamic focuses on the numerous technological innovations that have so rapidly and so recently evolved in many fields, from communications to transportation, from biotechnology to agriculture, from miniaturization to medicine, to mention only the more conspicuous domains wherein technology contributes greatly to the transformations sustained by globalization. It would be erroneous to conceive of any of the technologies in deterministic contexts,[7] but there is little question that they have contributed substantially to the interdependence of groups and societies, to what has aptly been called the death of time and distance.

A sixth dynamic involves the many processes through which states, territory, and sovereignty have taken on new meanings – processes that, in effect, have lessened the capacities of states, altered the meaning of territoriality, and diminished the scope of sovereignty. States are still key actors on the global stage, but the skill revolution, the organizational explosion, the mobility upheaval, the technological innovations, and the authority crises have increasingly rendered them less able to control the flow of goods, money, people, ideas, drugs, pollution, and crime in and out of their jurisdictions. As a consequence their territorial boundaries are more permeable and their sovereignty is less comprehensive.

Seventh, overall global structures have undergone bifurcation. A multi-centric world now functions – sometimes cooperatively, sometimes conflictually, and at all times interactively – alongside the traditional and long-standing state-centric world. The multi-centric world is composed of diverse nongovernmental actors, from advocacy groups to issue networks, from professional societies to trans-national corporations, from truth commissions to business alliances, and a host of others that, taken together, are loosely connected through their status as nongovernmental actors even as they often differ among themselves. Stated differently, the multi-centric world represents the large extent to which the other dynamics noted above have led to a highly disaggregated world.

Lastly, but by no means least, the globalization of national economies is a powerful dynamic of change, with corporations seeking to increase their market shares by moving their production facilities to sites where labor costs are cheaper and by adjusting the marketing strategies to local cultures and practices. The advent of neoliberal economic policies in many countries that used to oppose free enterprise mechanisms has substantially contributed to the vitality of the mobility upheaval, the skill revolution, and the organization explosion, not to mention the weakening of states and the solidifying of bifurcated global structures.

Foreign policy in a globalizing world

All eight of the foregoing dynamics have had substantial consequences for the relative potency of the variables that shape the content of foreign policy. Most notably perhaps, they have reduced the relevance of foreign policy as an aspect of world politics. More accurately, they have served to constrain the freedom of decision and action that marked the foreign conduct of countries prior to the acceleration of globalization. Like states, foreign policies are still important in a variety of circumstances, but their importance has been greatly reduced in many situations. Put in still another way, much about the way the world works can be explained without resort to foreign policy explanations and, indeed, a preponderance of the interesting questions about world affairs often seem irrelevant to the deliberations of public officials. When their actions are relevant, they are, so to speak, the last steps in processes that have their roots in the economies, societies, and cultures of a shrinking world. An examination of how each of the eight globalizing dynamics has impacted upon the five variable clusters of the pre-theory clarifies this overall conclusion.

Individual variables

Whereas the application of the pre-theory in the 1960s accorded little potency to this cluster in large, developed, and open societies, it seems clear that this potency has swollen considerably in response to the dynamics of globalization. Not only are individuals and publics more skillful in recognizing and articulating their interests, but also they have a greater capacity to know when, where, and how to engage in collective action. While many persons may remain passive and uninvolved in foreign affairs in all parts of the world, their numbers are shrinking everywhere as a consequence of their electronic links to networks, their exposure to global television, their increased readiness to become affiliated with – and even join – organizations that advance their interests, and their enhanced skills at tracing and judging the course of events. Increasingly, in short, publics and those who comprise them can no longer be taken for granted by either foreign policy officials or leaders in the multi-centric world. It could even be said that the Battle of Seattle and the subsequent anti-globalization protests marked, for better or worse, the maturation of individual variables into a major force on the global stage.

Role variables

This cluster was conceived to refer to the expectations that foreign policy makers experience as they conduct and conclude their deliberations – expectations held by their superiors, bureaucracies, domestic publics, and foreign adversaries and allies. Given the complexities and cross-currents that sustain globalizing processes, it is reasonable to presume that variables in this cluster are not nearly so powerful as was the case in the more "simple" days of the Cold War. At that time the expectations were comparatively clear, or at least comparatively easy to calculate, because the demands from both at home and abroad were cast mostly in us–them terms. Today, however, the complexities of our time have resulted in a multiplicity of consequences seeming plausible for any decision alternative that may be pondered, thus making it increasingly difficult for decision makers to know what is expected of them. Indeed, the expectations themselves are likely to be ever more contradictory as globalizing dynamics render the distant ever more proximate and outcomes ever more problematic. It could be argued that the complexities and contradictions accorded policy makers a free hand in the past to pursue goals of their own choosing, but all the evidence negates such reasoning. Rather, the leeway afforded leaders to act independently appears greatly reduced by the expansion and contradictions of the role expectations to which they are exposed from both within their societies and from counterparts abroad.[8]

Governmental variables

Given a declining relevance of states, territory, and sovereignty in an era of globalization, it follows that the potency of governmental variables has also declined. To invoke the authority of governmental policies no longer carries the weight it once did. The greater potency of individual, societal, and systemic variables (see below) has limited, in some cases severely, what governments can accomplish either on the world stage or in their efforts to mobilize domestic publics. Furthermore, the complexities of situations today are mirrored in policy-making bureaucracies, thereby further limiting their capacity to speak and act unequivocally and in a single voice. In an importance sense, therefore, governments have become followers rather than leaders of the course of events. Their deliberations may still matter, and internal bureaucratic squabbles can still have consequence, but such variables appear far less potent than they did in earlier eras.

Societal variables

In the case of this cluster, on the other hand, it seems self-evident that their potency has increased substantially. With individuals more skillful, with organizations more coherent, plentiful, and active, with communication channels more open and numerous as well as more filled with an ever-increasing flow of messages, the relevance of societies – their fears, tensions, and aspirations – appears much greater than ever in the past. Or, if societies are less rather than more coherent than ever, more divided by issues that once were settled, the potency of societal variables remains high as the internal conflicts make it that much more difficult for foreign policy officials to mobilize adequate support for their policies.

Systemic variables

This is perhaps the cluster that has undergone the most transformation. The bifurcation of global structures, the increasing density of actors on the global stage, the transnationalization of advocacy groups, the weakening of states and the ease with which flows of ideas, money, people, goods, pollution, drugs, and crime can cross their borders, and the repercussions of global financial crises are but a few of the dynamics that have substantially increased the potency of systemic variables and thereby added to the constraints with which foreign policy officials must contend.

Conclusions

In sum, it is hardly surprising that the excitement and challenge posed by comparative foreign policy analysis has, for me, dwindled. The key phrase in this sentence is "for me." I am not arguing that comparing foreign policies and assessing what countries are likely to do under varying circumstances is essentially dull and an enterprise that others should abandon. That would be an arrogance to which I do not subscribe. I readily envision the analytic tasks that focus on what states do abroad serving to motivate others in sustained and creative endeavors. And I still believe it is possible to develop viable theories of foreign policy through the use of comparative methods. Yet, to repeat, my present orientations are toward treating foreign policies as end products of complex and fascinating processes to which the dynamics of globalization in our time have given rise.

21 China in a bifurcated world

Competing theoretical perspectives[1]

> We playwrights, who have to cram a whole human life or an entire historical era into a two-hour play, can scarcely understand this rapidity [of change] ourselves. And if it gives us trouble, think of the trouble it must give political scientists, who have less experience with the realm of the improbable.
>
> (Vaclav Havel[2])

Some might argue that exploring international relations (IR) theory for an understanding of Chinese foreign policy is wasted effort, that China's unique 3,000-year history of essential isolation locates it outside the purview of any general theory that might be applicable to other states. While such reasoning may seem especially specious in this period of turbulent change, its soundness has never been compelling and its applicability to other periods has always been questionable at best. For all its uniqueness, China has long been an actor in the international system and has thus been subject to the same dynamics and controls that are inherent in the system and that condition all states. Furthermore, even if one fully rejects the applicability of general theory, one would have to have a general theory from which the rejection is derived. To see China as different, as acting out of unique historical, strategic, and cultural circumstances, is to have a theory of the established and recurrent patterns from which China deviates. Inescapably, in other words, observers must fall back on some form of theory, crude and implicit as it may be, in order to identify those features of a country's resources, processes, and dynamics that are judged to be relevant to its conduct on the world stage. Given the inexhaustible detail that might be relevant, the whole story of a country's foreign policy cannot be told. Inevitably observers have to select some dimensions of the story as important and dismiss others as trivial, and to undertake this necessary task they have to fall back on some theoretical notions, irrespective of whether they know they are doing so.

The controversy over US responses to the Chinese crackdown in Tiananmen Square offers a good illustration of the inescapable relevance of theory. Both those who supported the Bush administration's cautious responses – the sending of high-level officials to Beijing, its lifting of some sanctions, and its renewal of most-favored-nation procedures – and those who argued for more punitive measures proceeded from theoretical premises. Both anticipated outcomes on the basis of scenarios they constructed about how the Chinese leadership and economy would react to varying degrees and forms of external pressure. The Administration hypothesized that harsh policies would further isolate China and inhibit economic expansion, whereas their critics contended that tougher policies would force the Chinese to relax their controls and soften their handling of domestic dissent. Such expected outcomes, for both the advocates and the critics of the policies, may have seemed like self-evident empirical realities, but in fact they were only expectations, implicit hypotheses derived from theoretical notions of how either (for the advocates) Chinese society and its leaders or (for the critics) all societies and officials cope with external pressures.

We have no choice, in short, but to place China in a larger theoretical context. Even as those analysts who condemn theorizing proudly claim they only "tell it as it is," so do they implicitly engage in the essential theoretical tasks of tracing causation and assessing how diverse factors contribute to the events and trends of interest. Their long years as specialists may give them a "feel" for China, but it hardly frees them from the intellectual processes whereby propositions are asserted, behavior and institutions examined, patterns identified, inferences drawn, and conclusions advanced. Indeed, the very experience that accords them status as respectable "old China hands" may even be counter-productive in the sense that it can build confidence in their long-acquired wisdom and thereby reinforce their conviction that theorizing is a time-wasting, irrelevant enterprise.

Theory as a sustainer of inquiry

This is not to imply that the application of IR theory to Chinese circumstances is easily accomplished. Vaclav Havel's foregoing observation is well taken. To probe the sources of any country's foreign policies is surely to take on "trouble," and to probe what moves the Chinese in world affairs is even more surely to venture into "the realm of the improbable." Indeed, the theorizing task can be as confounding as it is clarifying and the results can be frustratingly ambiguous, encouraging one to wonder whether it was worth the effort. In the first place, the dynamics and controls that are inherent in the system and condition the foreign policies of all states do not remain constant. They can shift as the structures and processes of the international system respond to the winds of change. This means that the demands on China from abroad will vary from era to era, forcing the theorist to theorize anew as each systemic transformation presents states with fresh adaptive challenges to which they must respond.

Moreover, the application of theory is difficult, even in a period of relative constancy, because several theoretical formulations are available for interpreting both the systemic pressures on states and their responses to them. Each formulation posits any state both as confronted by a different set of external challenges and as drawing upon a different set of motives and dynamics in responding to the demands from abroad. And, given the welter of data that can be mustered to analyze the behavior of any state, each theoretical formulation can generate impressive empirical evidence in support of its propositions about how that state frames and conducts the policies through which it is linked to the world. In short, there can be as many Chinas in world politics as there are theories of China and theories of world politics.

To confound matters further, even as each theory posits international structures over which states have little or no control and to which they must conform, so does it encompass other dimensions of the world scene that are theorized to vary within a wide range and that thus allow room for states to maneuver and adjust their policies to varying internal needs and aspirations. Accordingly, to probe any IR theory for an understanding of where China may fit in the course of events is, initially, to examine those aspects of global structure that are presumed to lock China into the international system, and then to explore those aspects that the theory treats as subject to at least a modicum of Chinese control. We shall have occasion to take note of China's adaptive circumstances in the context of alternative conceptions of the constraints imposed by global structures (see Figure 21.2).

Additional confusion can arise from epistemological differences in which the theory concept can easily get mired. For some analysts theorizing is a rigorous enterprise that involves the framing of interrelated propositions that purport to identify and explain why events unfold as they do. In this more stringent conception of theories propositions are so fully interrelated that in testing them the confirmation of one has specified outcomes for the others. A looser notion of theory employed by other analysts also posits a general conception of how and why world politics unfold as they do, but at the same time such theories do not consist of interrelated hypotheses that anticipate precise developments under specified conditions. Consequently, the less rigorous view of theories is not overly concerned with testing propositions or refining them to achieve greater precision. Rather, such frameworks tend to be used as if their core premises are essentially accurate, thus allowing for analytic attention to focus on the empirical insights that flow from their application to particular situations. In the ensuing discussion both rigorous and looser forms of theory will be considered.

Notwithstanding the foregoing difficulties that haunt the theoretical enterprise, we have no choice but to undertake it. To repeat, we cannot avoid selecting certain dimensions of China's role in the world as important and dismissing others as trivial; and being bound in this way, we can only gain by being explicit about how we differentiate among the important and the trivial aspects of the subject. Explicitness allows us to see where we went astray in the event our theories prove unfounded. In so doing, explication serves as the prime mechanism for making the corrections that are necessary to get our probes more securely back on track. Perhaps no less valuable, explication can also serve as a stimulus to further research, thereby intensifying – or at least sustaining – our collective efforts to clarify the dynamics of world politics. In this sense, even those explicit theories that prove to be egregiously erroneous can advance understanding by virtue of having identified premises and interpretations to be eschewed. Indeed, if the egregiously erroneous theory provokes analyses that seek to demonstrate how and why it went off course, it will have accomplished a great deal simply by having initiated a dialogue. One could well argue that egregiously erroneous theory, which stimulates further research, is preferable to narrow and cautious theory that proves accurate but does not generate further enquiry.

Clarifying the theoretical task

To generate the clarity and precision that a theoretical perspective offers, we need to be clear and precise at the outset about what the task of probing the links between IR theory and China entails. Perhaps the most important task involves a readiness to acknowledge that no single perspective has cornered the truth on China, that several theoretical perspectives are available for sorting out its enormous complexities, and that thus identifying the most appropriate of the competing theories is energy well spent. Presumably, for example, such a theory would have to treat Chinese foreign policy as the product of both internal and external pressures and to view those who make and conduct the foreign policy of China as located astride the crucial points wherein the dynamics of international and domestic politics converge and either remain in tension or are synthesized into coherent and enduring behavior.

Hardly less important, the theoretical task requires acknowledging uncertainty as to how these internal and external dynamics interact. If the processes whereby China participates in world politics were self-evident, there would be no need to explore competing theoretical perspectives. To be theoretical is to avoid taking the fundamentals of IR or foreign policy for granted; instead the word "theory" orients us to treat the fundamentals as subject to variation and thus as open to diverse interpretations. Put differently, to be theoretical is to be tasked with puzzles, with probing how diverse sources of behavior might give rise to diverse outcomes.

Among other things, in short, "theory" is a code word for gaps in our understanding. It signifies that our comprehension of the complexity of political processes and international dynamics is elusive and variable. If our understanding of actors, relationships, and systems was thoroughgoing, we could readily describe and explain why and how they do what they do. But, for all kinds of reasons, our grasp in the realm of foreign policy is limited and we are compelled to fill the gaps by falling back on indirect but systematic deductive and/or inductive reasoning – theory rather than direct empirical observation. A great deal is known about China, its history, resources, and culture, and much is also grasped about the dynamics of IR, but how the two go together, how they account for the collective role played in global life by a quarter of the world's population, is far from clear. Only through a resort to theorizing can we begin to sort out the competing dynamics that differentiate the important from the trivial dimensions of China's role and thereby clarify the interplay of the sources which underlie its conduct.

This explicit acknowledgement of puzzlement and the need for theory is all the more imperative because of the extraordinary transformations that are at present under way in world politics. With the end of the Cold War, the collapse of Communist ideology, the restructuring of Europe, the wave of democratic movements, the changes in South Africa, the decline of hegemons, and a host of other developments that seemed so unlikely only a short time ago, both the policy-making and IR communities have been stunned rather than affirmed by the scale and direction of the alterations in global affairs. National leaders, editorial writers, professional social scientists, along with the many other specialists who should have anticipated the end of an era, have given voice to an endless series of bewildered exclamations over how rapidly the basic foundations of world politics have eroded. Few among us were able to escape the premises of the Cold War sufficiently to envision its collapse. For all our accomplishments in the study of international relations, and for all the intelligence available to the world's bureau-cracies, very few reached the level of analytic freedom that would have enabled them to assert, "But of course, the Cold War was an anachronism that could not last and we discerned its deterioration as long ago as, say, the advent of Solidarity in 1980!"

So, if there ever was a time when the theoretical enterprise is imperative, it is now! Here in the early years of the 1990s, as evidenced by the end of the post-war era and the first crisis of the post-Cold War period in the Persian Gulf, the underpinnings of a newly emergent global structure are (at best) obscure, a cir-cumstance that cries out for theorizing afresh, for returning to the drawing board to ascertain why our long-standing theoretical perspectives failed to anticipate the changes. The widely shared surprise over the course of events in 1989–91 is a measure of theoretical vacuity, and recognition of the breadth of this vacuum is a necessary first step toward new formulations that account for the abrupt cessation of old patterns and the surfacing of new ones.

To be sure, the rapidity of profound change can also tempt one to fall back on the certainties of prior understandings. One need only resort to the convenient assertion, "Just wait, the old patterns will reassert themselves," to dismiss the transformations as transitory and thereby preserve long-standing assumptions. But, as noted, there are good reasons not to be so overwhelmed by the unfolding dynamics of change as to succumb to simplistic temptations. To recognize alter-native theoretical perspectives is to highlight the intellectual opportunities that lie in the transforming dynamics. By being ready to analyze several variants of theory, we give ourselves license to yield to our puzzlement.

But how to exercise this license? How to sort out the global from the regional, the international from the national, the general from the particular, the universal from the unique? What intellectual operations does the application of IR theory to Chinese foreign policy require? Is the task one of hypothesizing about how the established practices and the extraordinary transformations constrain, facilitate, stimulate, or otherwise condition the conduct of all states and their foreign policy-making processes – a methodological holism which presumes that China's con-duct can be fully explained by the interests and structures of the international system? Or does it involve focusing specifically on China and how its conduct is shaped by its unique history, culture, institutions, and economy – a method-ological reductionism which assumes that global politics is to be explained solely by the behavior of its parts and Chinese conduct solely by its constituent elements? Or is a combination of the two required, a synthesis of theories of world politics and theories of China which posits external and internal dynamics as interactive? Is the distinction between the two types of theory grounded in such substantively different foci as to militate against synthesis, or does it point to a perspective which is neither holistic nor reductionist and yet employs elements of both methodologies in a way that holds the potential for creative syntheses?

While much that follows presumes the desirability and possibility of creative syntheses – if not at the hands of a single theorist, then through collaborative inquiry – sorting out answers to these questions is not a simple matter. Faced with so much change both within and among societies, not to mention the continuing obfuscation of the distinction between foreign and domestic policy as the world becomes ever more interdependent, it is all too easy to confound international and national dynamics and, in so doing, to exceed one's expertise. Consider, for example, a central Chinese issue on today's global agenda, that of whether – and to what extent – controls over the movement, organization, and speech of citizens will be relaxed and the fundamental prerequisites of democratic expression allowed to flourish. What kind of issue is this? Viewed in conventional terms, it is clearly a domestic issue, a matter for the Chinese polity to address and resolve through its own decision-making procedures. From this perspective, it is an issue that is best probed by specialists in Chinese history, politics, and society, analysts who can bring to bear an expertise informed by years of study organized around the nature of China. However, with the shrinkage of social and geographical distances and the emergence of global norms which place high value on human rights, the Chinese regime's treatment of its people is no longer just a domestic matter. The Chinese may protest that the world is illegally intruding upon its internal affairs, but such protests are unlikely to be heeded by a world that no longer accepts a country's sovereign privilege to exceed due processes of law by incarceration, torture, or otherwise assaulting the essential liberty and dignity of its citizens. Thus human rights in China today are thoroughly an international rather than a domestic issue and, as such, the functioning of its polity also has to be probed by those whose expertise encompasses the nature of international institutions, the role of transnational organizations, and the structures through which global regimes exercise influence and contest violations of their principles.

Indeed, paradoxical as it may seem, how China treats its own citizens is, in large measure, perhaps its most important foreign policy problem. All of the action in the human-rights arena taken or avoided by Chinese officials may occur on Chinese soil, but the implications of these actions are so worldwide in scope that the Chinese leadership has to derive them from the same kind of foreign policy calculations which underlie their treaty negotiations or their search for trading partners abroad. Viewed in this way, the future of human rights in China taps into the expertise of foreign policy specialists who focus on the ways in which national leaders seek to achieve a balance between the internal and external demands to which they are subjected.[3]

Nor is human rights the only issue-area that transcends the conventional foreign–domestic boundary. Hardly less obfuscating are all the concerns that focus on the question of how – and to what extent – national economies should be centrally controlled or organized around the play of markets. It used to be that such issues were strictly domestic matters that fell in the domain of students of comparative politics. But with the advent of a global economy and the dependence of national economies on the international flow of credit, currency, information, and goods, domestic economic policies and the commitment of polities to capitalism have been relocated from the internal to the external arena and become no less central to the expertise of international political economists than they are to comparative specialists. Viewed in this way, it is noteworthy that the US's prime reason for not coming down more severely on China for its human rights record was precisely that of wanting to promote capitalist tendencies within China.

In short, to undertake the intellectual operations required to probe deeply into the dynamics of a country's foreign policy, all of us need to expand our expertises, or at least our analytic sensitivities, beyond their narrow disciplinary confines.[4] In the case of the People's Republic of China, IR theorists need to tool up in the details of Chinese culture and politics, just as China specialists need to enlarge their horizons to incorporate the processes that sustain world politics. And as we proceed to expand our competencies in these ways, all of us need to be alert to the need to identify means for synthesizing our diverse perspectives, concepts, and findings. The ultimate theoretical task is to trace how the external and the internal are interactive, how international dynamics impact upon and shape Chinese conduct at home and abroad and, conversely, how these domestic dynamics impact upon and shape international structures and the actions that other countries direct toward China.[5] Such theoretical syntheses, it should be quickly noted, will not consist of hypotheses that specify the interaction of independent and dependent variables; rather they will be comprised of propositions that delineate the feedback loops wherein the dependent variables become independent variables in the next stage of the ongoing processes through which China and its external worlds react to each other.

As will be seen (below and Table 21.3), a useful mechanism for highlighting the ways in which synthesizing theory can be most fruitfully developed is that of identifying alternative (but plausible) conceptions of both Chinese and global politics that might evolve in the future and then exploring what the available IR theories have to say about the range of choices and/or constraints that each form of global politics opens up or closes off for each of the Chinas. In order to move toward such a synthesis, however, it is first necessary to differentiate among the IR theories that lend themselves to the application of this mechanism.

Available IR theories

IR theory has never enjoyed a period when its practitioners converged around a single paradigm. Instead, the field has long been marked by a competition among theories that are, for the most part, founded on mutually exclusive premises about the identity and motives of salient actors, the configuration of macro-structures, the wellsprings of causal dynamics, the prospects for systemic transformation, and the centrality of conflict and cooperation as political processes. At least four broad theoretical perspectives – some quite rigorous, others much less so – command the attention of analysts.

Before delineating some of the differences among these perspectives, however, it is useful to note a few underlying assumptions that are widely shared by theorists of all persuasions. Most agree that world politics is sustained by a set of structural arrangements which foster recurrent patterns and infuse coherence into the course of events. All concerned thus see developments in world politics as springing from an underlying order, from causes that render IR phenomena susceptible to meaningful theorizing. No extant perspective argues that the course of events derives from random or haphazard factors that would make the theoretical task impossible.

Furthermore, the various theories that clamor for adherents share an understanding that the underlying order includes nation-states as collective actors whose conduct is central to the nature of global structures and whose interactions contribute to the shaping of a hierarchical international system. They do not agree on the centrality of the role played by nation-states, but no extant perspective depicts a world in which such actors are conspicuously absent.

Most (though not all) analysts seem to share the recognition that the currents of change have been running deep during the last years of the twentieth century, that a business-as-usual orientation no longer pervades the halls of government, the squares where people gather, the boardrooms of corporations, or the cable traffic of diplomats. Equally important, the diverse theories share a conception of the change dynamics as being global in scope, as rendering the world so much more interdependent as to make even its most remote communities subject to the repercussions of events that originated in distant lands. They may differ on the degree to which systemic change is feasible, but no extant perspective contends that regional or local dynamics are so powerful as to locate the key causal dynamics beyond the grasp of a theory of the global system.

Once one's analytic eye moves beyond these basic commonalities, however, the differences among the various theories begin to matter. Depending on which theory one employs, the nature of systemic structures, the degree of hierarchy, the role of states, the salience of other actors, and the pace and direction of change all take on a different coloration. Table 21.1 offers the essential elements of the four prime models of the international system that presently command the most attention. A number of other models could be included in Table 21.1 (as could variants of each of those listed), but here it is sufficient to take note of these four generic types. By reading down the columns one can discern the internal coherence of each model and by comparing across the rows one can readily trace some of the major ways in which they are differentiated. Rather than separately assessing the current relevance of each model, it suffices for present purposes to note how all of them seem inappropriate as instruments for probing the new structures and dynamics of global politics that have become increasingly manifest in recent years and that seem destined to mark world affairs well into the next century. Such

Table 21.1 Four models of the international system

	Realism	Neo-realism	Pluralism	Marxism/globalism
Type of model	Descriptive and normative	Deductive	Descriptive and normative	Descriptive and normative
Central problems	Causes of war. Conditions of peace	Co-operation as well as conflict	Broad agenda of social, economic, and environmental issues arising from gap between demand and resources	Inequality and exploitation.
Concept of the current international system	Structural anarchy	States form international regimes in an anarchic structure	Global society. Complex interdependence (structure varies by issue area)	Uneven development World capitalist system
Key actors	Geographically based units (tribes, city-states, nation-states, etc.)	States, regimes	Highly permeable nation-states plus a broad range of non-state actors, including IGOs, IOs, NGOs, and individuals	Class interests
Loyalties to	Geographically-based groups	States	Declining loyalty to nation-states; to emerging global values and institutions that transcend those of the nation-state and/or to subnational groups	To class values and interests that transcend those of the nation-state

Central processes	Search for security and survival	Search for economic and physical security through cooperation and regimes	Aggregate effects of decisions by national and non-national actors. How units (not limited to nation-states) cope with growing agenda of threats and opportunities arising from human wants	Modes of production and exchange. International division of labor in a world capitalist system
Likelihood of system transformation	Low (basic structures of system have revealed ability to persist despite many other kinds of changes)	Low except when hegemons decline or are replaced	High in the direction of the model (owing to the rapid pace of technological change, etc.)	High in the direction of the model (owing to inherent contradictions within the world capitalist system)
Sources of theory, insights, and evidence	Politics, history	Micro-economics as well as politics and history	Broad range of social sciences. Natural and technological sciences	Marxist-Leninist theory (several variants)

Sources: Except for the addition of the second column and the substitution of different headings for the third and fourth columns, the table is from Ole R. Holsti, "Models of International Relations and Foreign Policy," *Diplomatic History*, 13 (Winter 1989), pp. 24–25. A similar formulation (which uses the headings for the third and fourth columns) can be found in Paul R. Viotti and Mark V. Kauppi (eds.), *International Relations Theory: Realism, Pluralism, Globalism* (New York: Macmillan, 1987), p. 11. For still another comparable formulation, see James N. Rosenau, "Order and Disorder in the Study of World Politics," in Ray Maghroori and Bennett Ramberg (eds.), *Globalism versus Realism: International Relations' Third Debate* (Boulder, Co: Westview, 1982), p. 3.

an analysis also leads naturally to a discussion of how a fifth model, what I call the "bifurcation model," more closely approximates the emergent structures and dynamics of global politics with which China, like all states, must contend today.

Since they are the least amenable to change, the realist and neo-realist paradigms are perhaps the most out of phase with the emergent structures and dynamics of world affairs. The world is becoming increasingly complex, inter-dependent, and decentralized, and as a consequence states and their governments are becoming increasingly ineffective. They may still be able to resort to force to control opposition among their citizenries (as China and Burma did in 1989), but they are much less able (as the Russian state so clearly illustrated in 1990–1) to solve the economic and social challenges posed by resource scarcities, population pressures, subgroup restlessness, and a post-industrial world which is transforming the nature of loyalties, work, commerce, and many other dimensions of daily life. Yet both the realist and neo-realist paradigms are conceptually ill equipped to cope with these changes. Both are founded on the assumption of an underlying constancy in world affairs. And thus both continue to presume that states are the pre-eminent actors on the world stage and to make no allowance for the dimin-ution of their authority. While governments founder and alternative groups, social movements, and transnational organizations become increasingly central, realists and neo-realists continue to focus on states as rational actors that calculate their interests in terms of their relative power and as ever capable of resorting to force in the event their interests are thereby served.[6] To be sure, there remain issue arenas wherein states still retain their predominance and where their conduct remains consistent with the core premises of realism. But the boundaries of these arenas are increasingly narrowed by the dynamics of global change, and realists have yet to adjust their paradigms to account for these changes and the widening realms in which states are less authoritative. Indeed, realists are not averse to defending the absence of change mechanisms in their paradigm by pointing to the longevity of the interstate system and stressing that it would not have lasted nearly four centuries if it had been vulnerable to the transformational dynamics that seemed so salient at particular times.

Some modification of this view of realism needs to be made with respect to neo-realists. While hard-core realists focus on the likelihood of conflict and war, neo-realists are more ready to acknowledge that states can define their interests in terms of economic as well as physical security, thereby enabling them to under-take cooperative policies and participate in the formation of international regimes devoted to maintaining order and stable arrangements in particular issue areas.[7] The neo-realist paradigm does not systematically posit transformational dynamics that impel states to cooperate, but it does allow for change of this kind and, in so doing, it parts company with its realist predecessor. At the same time changes of this sort are seen by neo-realists as occurring within the context of an unchanging state system dominated by self-interested states. Neo-realists are no more ready than realists to make conceptual allowances for the erosion and dispersion of state authority and the increasing relevance of other actors.[8]

Nor are the Marxist and globalist paradigms suited to tracing and explaining the transformations presently under way in world politics. They both stress the dominant role played by the capitalist world economy and the ways in which states and other actors have to conform their policies to the premises and demands of a single globalized economy, but any other kinds of change are not anticipated by their perspective.[9] Most notably, neither Marxism nor globalism allows for the ways in which the postindustrial shift away from manufacturing and toward information as the key processes of economic activity has eroded class lines and diminished the likelihood of class conflict. The collapse of Communist ideologies and command economies in Eastern Europe and Russia has revealed the insufficiencies of these paradigms as a means of understanding the underlying shifts in global structures. Marxists and globalists might contend that the changes in Eastern Europe and Russia are indicative of the power of the world capitalist system, but such reasoning falters when democratic movements rather than class conflicts are acknowledged as prime sources of the shifts away from command economies.

Pluralist perspectives, being explicitly geared to a broad issue agenda and the processes of complex interdependence, correspond more closely to the new dynamics of world politics than any of the others listed in Table 21.1. Pluralism does recognize the permeability of states and the advent of subnational and supranational actors as the foci of activity and loyalty. This flexibility enables pluralists to accord greater weight to the dynamics of change than to those of constancy and, as such, they can more nearly approximate the world in and to which China must respond as the future unfolds than can those who employ the other three paradigms. The difficulty here, however, is that no pluralist perspective offers a conception of overall structures. To specify that states are permeable and that international political processes vary from issue to issue is not to indicate the nature of new global structures or how they manage the varying issue dynamics. Like the other approaches, pluralism presumes that world politics is founded on an underlying order, that developments do not unfold at random, and that thus all is not sheer chaos. Nevertheless, it does not even hint at what the pillars of the underlying order may be. Presumably, for example, the permeability of states varies from issue to issue, but pluralists do not address the conditions that prevail when permeability is relatively high and those that are operative when it is relatively low. In short, pluralists do not employ rigorous IR theories; theirs are more in the nature of open-ended frameworks that can offer insights into any developments that may occur.[10] Unlike the other approaches, pluralism is incapable of yielding egregiously erroneous predictions.

Confronted with cogent reasons for doubting the utility of the four major paradigms that mark IR theory today, I have undertaken a wholesale reconceptualization of world politics with a view to accounting for the dynamics of recent transformations while at the same time not being so open-ended as to lack the basic requisites of theory. I call it a "bifurcationist" paradigm because, unlike the realist models, it postulates a considerable diminution in the relevance of states, but, unlike the Marxist, globalist, and pluralist models, it does not posit states as essentially of secondary importance. Instead, the world is seen as having evolved an underlying bifurcated structure consisting of two major components, the state-centric system and the multi-centric system. These two worlds of world politics are conceived as independent of each other and yet as also interactive, sometimes competitively and sometimes cooperatively. In the state-centric world, states continue as prominent actors and they manage those aspects of world politics that focus on the formal ties of societies and the boundary, military, diplomatic, and security arrangements through which global order is maintained. In the multi-centric world, a wide range of other types of collectivities are the central figures and their concerns are largely the economic, social, and cultural aspects of world politics that link societies to each other. Actors from both worlds are active in the other – pressing, protesting, negotiating, yielding, resisting – but each world has its own goals, rules, and processes that sustain their separate structures and absorb the continuing acceleration of global interdependence.[11]

The bifurcationist paradigm focuses on two prime sets of tensions deemed to be unfolding in world politics during the present era: one highlights the tensions between change and continuity and the other involves the tensions that flow from the clash of centralizing and decentralizing dynamics which shape the changes and sustain the continuities. The paradigm posits the unfolding of these tensions in world politics as bounded by three prime parameters that normally serve as limits constraining the day-to-day fluctuations of its variables.[12] Each of these parameters is conceived to be at present under such stress that, together, they have cumulatively fostered a profound transformation of the global system, what I regard as the first genuine turbulence in 300 years.[13]

Five prime systemic tendencies are viewed as interactively having brought on the turbulent transformation. One involves the shift from an industrial to a post-industrial order and focuses on the dynamics of technology, particularly on those technologies associated with the microelectronic revolution that have made social, economic, and political distances so much shorter, the movement of ideas, pictures, currencies, and information so much faster, and thus the interdependence of people and events so much greater. A second is the emergence of issues – such as atmospheric pollution, terrorism, the drug trade, currency crises, and AIDS – that are the direct products of new technologies or the world's greater interdependence and are distinguished from traditional political issues by virtue of being transnational rather than national or local in scope. A third dynamic is the authority crises that stem from the reduced capacity of states and governments to provide satisfactory solutions to the major issues on their political agendas, partly because the new issues are not wholly within their jurisdiction, partly because the old issues are also increasingly intertwined with significant international components (e.g. agricultural markets and labor productivity), and partly because the compliance of their citizenries can no longer be taken for granted. Fourth, with the weakening of whole systems such as states, subsystems have acquired a correspondingly greater coherence and effectiveness, thereby reinforcing tendencies toward decentralization (what I call "subgroupism") at all organizational levels that are in stark contrast to the centralizing tendencies (such as nationalism) of earlier decades and that are in deep tension with the centralizing tendencies (transnationalism) of the present fostered by the new interdependence issues and the globalization of national economies.

Finally, there is the feedback of the consequences of all the foregoing for the skills and orientations of the world's adults who comprise the groups, states, and other collectivities that have had to cope with the new issues of interdependence and adjust to the new technologies of the postindustrial order: with their analytic skills enlarged and their orientations toward authority more self-conscious, today's persons-in-the-street are no longer as uninvolved, ignorant, and manipulable with respect to world affairs as were their forebears. Most importantly for present purposes, the refined skills of citizens have diminished their habitual patterns of compliance and heightened their sensitivities to the diverse aggregative processes whereby micro-actions are converted into macro-outcomes. As indicated by the numerous street rallies that toppled regimes in Eastern Europe and Russia (and failed to do so in China and Burma), people are now more confident that what they do matters, that the large macro-processes of communities, societies, and international systems are not so remote as to be impervious to their inputs.[14]

The interactive impact of these five dynamics as sources of the bifurcation of global politics is summarized in Figure 21.1. Here it is implied that none of the dynamics is in itself sufficient to have brought about a global transformation, but that their convergence in recent years has had a substantial impact on the overall structures of world politics and the way in which issues on the global agenda get processed.

China in a bifurcated world

If this bifurcationist assessment of global politics is essentially sound, the implications for China are considerable. Most notably, with greater autonomy accruing to diverse actors in the multi-centric world who are not bound by the legalities and constraints of adhering to the precepts of sovereignty, Chinese authorities will find it increasingly difficult to remain aloof from world politics. They may repeatedly affirm that their domestic politics, their handling of dissent, and their economic policy-making processes are internal matters with respect to which the world has no right to intercede, but the most they can hope to accomplish along these lines is a restraint within the state-centric world and a readiness of its states to seek a modicum of control over actors in the multi-centric world intent upon stirring up discontent or altering trade-investment arrangements within China. And even these restraints are unlikely to be extensive if China does not make some concessions to the outside world and adapt its domestic practices to global norms. As is stressed below, the way in which the world responds to China is crucially dependent on the way in which China responds to the world.

A measure of the tensions involved in China's adaptation to a bifurcated, dynamically changing world is presented in Figure 21.2. Depicted there is the convergence of some of the internal and external demands with which Chinese authorities have to cope. The juxtaposition of these conflicting pressures, many of which border on being mutually exclusive, highlights the likelihood that China's

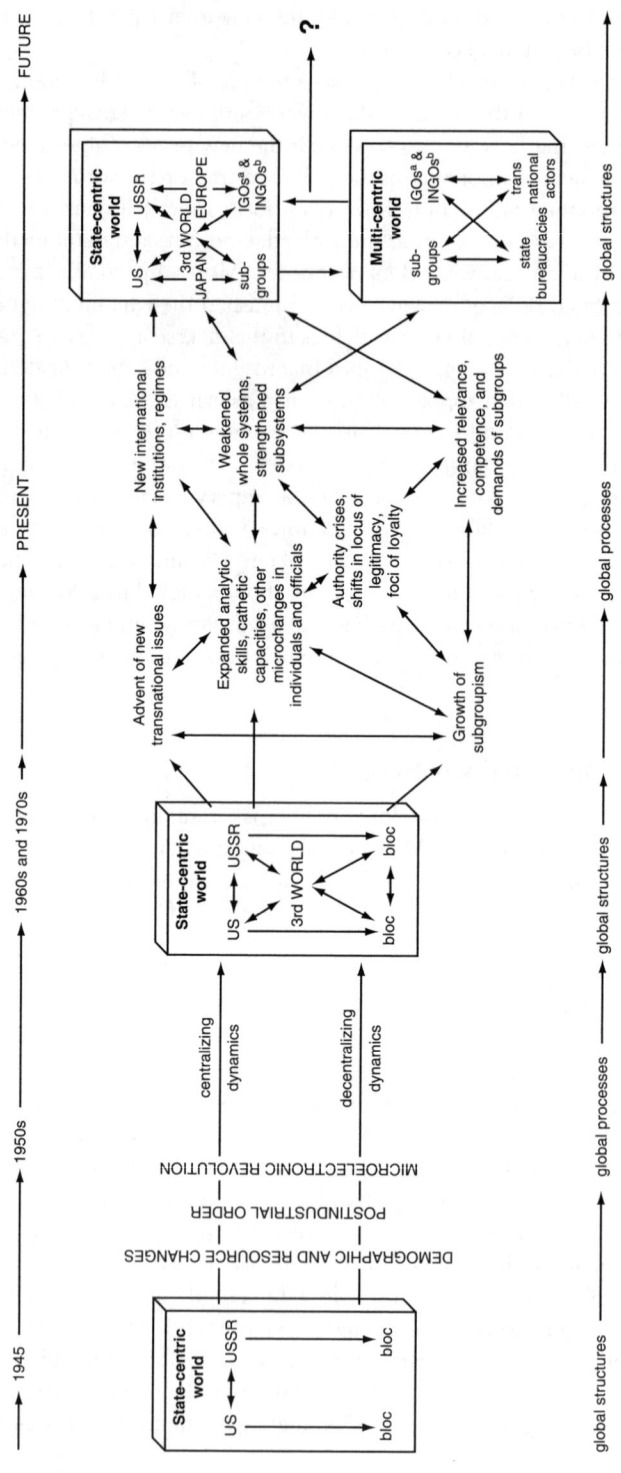

Figure 21.1 The two worlds of world politics

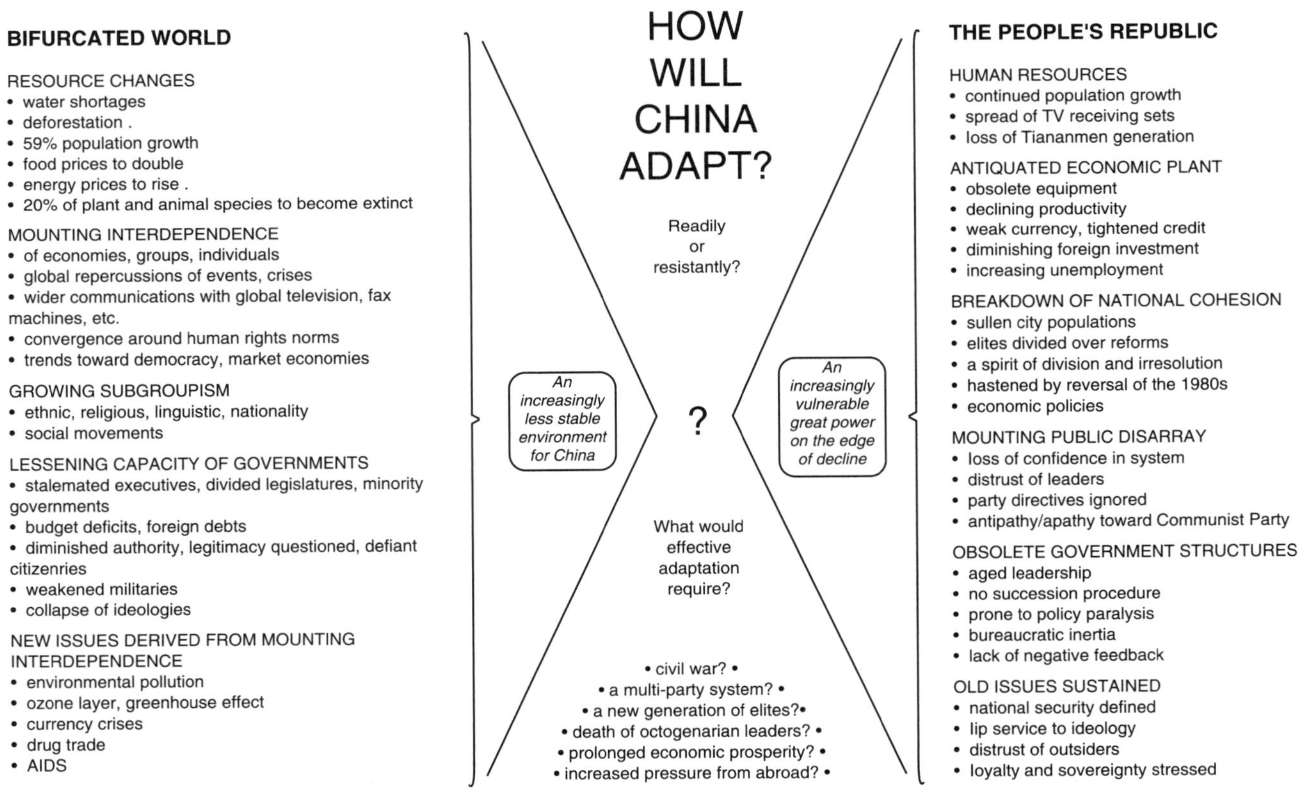

THE PEOPLE'S REPUBLIC

HUMAN RESOURCES
- continued population growth
- spread of TV receiving sets
- loss of Tiananmen generation

ANTIQUATED ECONOMIC PLANT
- obsolete equipment
- declining productivity
- weak currency, tightened credit
- diminishing foreign investment
- increasing unemployment

BREAKDOWN OF NATIONAL COHESION
- sullen city populations
- elites divided over reforms
- a spirit of division and irresolution
- hastened by reversal of the 1980s
- economic policies

MOUNTING PUBLIC DISARRAY
- loss of confidence in system
- distrust of leaders
- party directives ignored
- antipathy/apathy toward Communist Party

OBSOLETE GOVERNMENT STRUCTURES
- aged leadership
- no succession procedure
- prone to policy paralysis
- bureaucratic inertia
- lack of negative feedback

OLD ISSUES SUSTAINED
- national security defined
- lip service to ideology
- distrust of outsiders
- loyalty and sovereignty stressed

HOW
WILL
CHINA
ADAPT?

Readily
or
resistantly?

An increasingly vulnerable great power on the edge of decline

?

An increasingly less stable environment for China

What would
effective
adaptation
require?

- civil war?
- a multi-party system?
- a new generation of elites?
- death of octogenarian leaders?
- prolonged economic prosperity?
- increased pressure from abroad?

BIFURCATED WORLD

RESOURCE CHANGES
- water shortages
- deforestation .
- 59% population growth
- food prices to double
- energy prices to rise .
- 20% of plant and animal species to become extinct

MOUNTING INTERDEPENDENCE
- of economies, groups, individuals
- global repercussions of events, crises
- wider communications with global television, fax machines, etc.
- convergence around human rights norms
- trends toward democracy, market economies

GROWING SUBGROUPISM
- ethnic, religious, linguistic, nationality
- social movements

LESSENING CAPACITY OF GOVERNMENTS
- stalemated executives, divided legislatures, minority governments
- budget deficits, foreign debts
- diminished authority, legitimacy questioned, defiant citizenries
- weakened militaries
- collapse of ideologies

NEW ISSUES DERIVED FROM MOUNTING INTERDEPENDENCE
- environmental pollution
- ozone layer, greenhouse effect
- currency crises
- drug trade
- AIDS

Figure 21.2 China in a bifurcated world

future in a bifurcated world will be troubled and marked by continuing uncertainty and upheaval.[15]

How well – and whether – the Chinese manage to adapt to the challenges depicted in Figure 21.2 takes the analyst into another realm of theory, that of foreign policy decision making. Since the application of alternative models of decision making is heavily dependent on the specifics of Chinese history, culture, and politics, an assessment of the relevance of these models is not appropriate to the tasks undertaken here. It is useful, however, to note the existence of three such models by way of further emphasizing the close links between IR theory and the foreign policies of particular countries. These are summarized in Table 21.2. A comparative first glance at them suggests that each is descriptive of one or another aspect of Chinese policy-making processes; but even though they are not mutually exclusive models, they may serve Chinese specialists well as a guide to the dimensions of China on which to focus for an understanding of its capacity for effectively adapting to the dynamics presently shaping and sustaining global politics.[16]

Toward synthesis: available IR theories and alternative Chinas

But is the bifurcation of global politics an enduring or a transitory arrangement? Can China hope for a return to a predominant state-centric world that is more respectful of its sovereignty? An answer to these questions is facilitated by exploring the further question of whether the bifurcationist conception is theoretically grounded or, like pluralism, simply another broad framework. If it is theoretically grounded, then it becomes possible to assess its potential longevity as a basis for global structures. And the test of its "theoreticalness" is a relatively easy one: is the bifurcation model susceptible to negation? Could the course of future events prove it to be egregiously erroneous? An affirmative score on this test is clearly warranted. The proposition that world politics has undergone a fundamental bifurcation is a theory and not merely a framework because at least three different long-run developments could negate this core concept: (1) the balance between the centralizing and decentralizing tendencies in world politics could tip modestly in favor of the former and restore the authority and effectiveness of states and their interstate system sufficiently to peripheralize the multi-centric world and its diverse actors; (2) the balance between the centralizing and decentralizing tendencies in world politics could tip fully in the former direction and give rise to a world society and/or a global economy with their own governance mechanisms, thus peripheralizing both the state-centric and multi-centric worlds; and (3) the balance between the centralizing and decentralizing tendencies in world politics could tip fully in the latter direction and result in a neo-medieval world of such extensive pluralism as to peripheralize the state-centric world.[17]

Conceivably, in other words, the structures sustaining the bifurcated two worlds of world politics are only transitory and are destined to give way to further transformation in conformity with one of these three scenarios. Only if the

Table 21.2 Three models of decision-making

	Bureaucratic politics	Group dynamics	Individual decision-making
Conceptualization of decision-making	Decision-making as the result of bargaining within bureaucratic organizations.	Decision-making as the product of group interaction.	Decision-making as the result of individual choice.
Premises	Central organizational values are imperfectly internalized. Organizational behavior is political behavior. Structure and standard operating procedures affect substance and quality of decisions.	Most decisions are made by small elite groups. Group is different from the sum of its members. Group dynamics affect substance and quality of decisions.	Importance of subjective appraisal (definition of the situation) and cognitive processes (information processing, etc.).
Constraints on rational decision-making	Imperfect information, resulting from: centralization, hierarchy, and specialization. Organizational inertia. Conflict between individual and organizational utilities. Bureaucratic politics and bargaining dominate decision-making and implementation of decisions.	Groups may be more effective for some tasks, less for others. Pressures for conformity. Risk-taking propensity of groups (controversial). Quality of leadership. "Groupthink".	Cognitive limits on rationality. Information-processing distorted by cognitive consistency dynamics (unmotivated biases). Systematic and motivated biases in causal analysis. Individual differences in abilities relating to decision-making (e.g. problem-solving ability, tolerance of ambiguity, defensiveness and anxiety, information-seeking, etc.).
Sources of theory, insights, evidence	Organization theory. Sociology of bureaucracy. Bureaucratic politics.	Social psychology. Sociology of small groups.	Cognitive dissonance. Cognitive psychology. Dynamic psychology.

Source: Ole R. Holsti, "Models of International Relations and Foreign Policy," Diplomatic History, Vol. 13 (Winter 1989), p. 31.

present balance between centralizing and decentralizing tendencies does not fluctuate substantially will the bifurcationist model be affirmed. Elsewhere I argue that there are good reasons to anticipate that this enduring bifurcation scenario is likely to persist as far as one can see into the future,[18] but the point here is that the possibility of it not enduring highlights its susceptibility to egregious error and, thus, its theoretical underpinnings.

Indeed, not only do these four global scenarios allow for the negation of the bifurcationist model, they also allow for the affirmation of the other IR theories. It will be recognized that an unfolding of the restored-state system scenario would vindicate any variant of realism, that the evolution of the world-society scenario would support variants of globalism, and that the advent of the neo-medieval scenario would sustain variants of pluralism.

From this differentiation among alternative IR theories, it should be clear that any country's foreign policy will be vitally affected by the structures of world politics that prevail in any era. In terms of the range of choices and/or constraints opened up or closed off for any country, it matters whether the realists, pluralists, globalists, or bifurcationists are right about the nature of world politics that is emerging out of the ruins of the Cold War. More specifically, it matters for China whether international politics is dominated by states, by a multiplicity of diverse actors, by a single, integrated global system, or by a bifurcated two worlds of world politics. Each of these is likely to create a different milieu wherein Chinese foreign policy must be conducted. Each will offer a different degree of responsiveness to Chinese initiatives and demands, just as each will exert different degrees of pressure upon China for change. But, obviously, the degree of responsiveness and pressure emanating from the different global milieus will vary depending on the basic nature and policies of China in any era. In terms of the world's reactions, for example, it matters whether China is seeking to preserve a command economy or aspires to developing a market economy. And, plainly, it can matter whether China is on an authoritarian or democratic course in the relations between its leadership and its citizenry.

It is here, in the convergence of three reasonable scenarios of the Chinese future (one that is unchanging and marked by an authoritarian regime that maintains rigid political and economic controls, another that undergoes relatively slow change as the regime maintains its political controls but relaxes them over the economy, and a third that undergoes relatively dynamic change as the regime exercises only a minimum of political and economic control) and four plausible forms of global politics (one a centralized world dominated by states and their governments, a second which is decentralized and chaotic as the authority of states becomes increasingly ineffective, a third which is centralized and orderly as global institutions and norms become increasingly predominant, and a fourth in which both centralizing and decentralizing dynamics lead to bifurcated arrangements that foster, in effect, two worlds of world politics), that the foundations of theoretical syntheses can be laid. Table 21.3 summarizes the estimated degrees of global responsiveness and pressure likely to mark the fifteen circumstances created by the interaction of the three Chinese and five global scenarios. Here it can be

Table 21.3 The responsiveness of five global structures to three different Chinas

GLOBAL STRUCTURES	Most relevant IR model	An unchanging China with an authoritarian regime that maintains rigid political controls and a command economy	A slowly changing China with an authoritarian regime that maintains rigid political controls but allows for market economies	A dynamically changing China with a regime that maintains only a minimum of political and economic control
A world of restored state authority	Realism	Reluctant acceptance.	Acceptance, plus enthusiasm for changes.	Wary but accepting of intensified pluralism.
	Neo-realism	Efforts to induce change through economic incentives.	Efforts to sustain economic changes through further incentives.	Welcomes relaxed controls, but concern expressed over paralyzing dissent.
A chaotic world as breakdown of state authority continues and global norms do not evolve	Pluralism	No clear pattern; some actors ready to deal unqualifiedly with China; others resist doing so.	Changes are applauded even as actors press for further relaxation of political and economic controls.	China's official and unofficial ties to world proliferate and foster uncertainties that are distressful for Chinese officials.
Increasingly integrated world society or capitalist world economy	Globalism, Marxism	Pressure for change fostered by greater interdependence or international capitalism.	Change welcomed; pressures for more maintained.	Perplexed by changes toward decentralization and exerts pressure for reversal of course.
Co-equal and autonomous state-centric and multi-centric worlds	Bifurcationism	States reluctantly accept China's authoritarian controls; most other actors do not.	All actors accept economic changes but some press for political liberalization.	All actors welcome changes and seek strengthened relationships with counterparts in China.

seen that, indeed, these differences can be considerable, with the degree of external pressure tending to diminish, and the extent of responsiveness abroad tending to increase, the more China changes in the case of the pluralist and bifurcation models even as somewhat different or contrary patterns are anticipated in the case of the realist and Marxist-globalist models.

Consider, for example, the differences between the international milieu with which the alternative Chinas will have to interact if world politics evolves toward the restored-state-system scenario on the one hand or the bifurcation scenario on the other. The former milieu, consisting predominantly of other states that are respectful of each other's sovereignty and that value each other's capacity to make decisive commitments on behalf of their self-interests, is likely to be essentially responsive to Chinese initiatives, irrespective of China's internal structures and practices. The more dynamic and far-flung the change at work in China, the greater will be the concern abroad about the Chinese regime's stability and its capacity to maintain its commitments and, thus, the greater will be the wariness of other states; but such caution is unlikely to be so great as to alter the essential external acceptance of China's initiatives. In a restored state system of effective and authoritative actors, states have good reasons to calculate that, other things being equal, the most they can hope to obtain from their counterparts abroad is reciprocity, a readiness to accord trade concessions, diplomatic cooperation, and military gestures on the basis of how they respond to others. Reciprocal action, sometimes characterized as a tit-for-tat strategy, is thus characteristic of the cooperative interaction of states in a world where their authority remains intact.[19] Furthermore, with their sovereignty viewed as inviolate, they will not be subjected to extensive pressures for change from abroad on the grounds of distress over their domestic affairs. Other states, aware that interfering in the domestic affairs of another opens up their internal affairs to outside interference, will normally prefer to adhere to the non-interventionary rules of the system rather than risk rendering their institutions vulnerable to outside meddling. Accordingly, it is hardly surprising that strong evidence has been uncovered which demonstrates that in the world of superpower politics – a world that perhaps comes closest today to the premises of realists' models – China has enjoyed reciprocity in its interactions with the United States and the former Soviet Union.[20] Nor is it surprising from a state-centric perspective that the Bush administration has adhered to the rules of the state-centric world by not harping on the Tiananmen Square massacre and by renewing supportive policies consistent with China's requests.

In coping with the milieu of a bifurcated world, on the other hand, China is likely to encounter less responsive and more aggressive orientations abroad. If it continues to have an authoritarian regime that exerts rigid political controls and retains a command economy, both business corporations and human rights groups in the multi-centric world are likely to press for a relaxation of economic and political controls, a pressure which China will experience both directly from diverse sovereignty-free actors and indirectly from governments subjected to domestic pressures to break with the practices of non-intervention and reciprocity in so far as China is concerned. If moderate change allowing for movement toward a market economy occurs in China, the international milieu will become more responsive and some of the external pressure will ameliorate as other states and multinational corporations seek to explore the potentials of China's market. If the pace of internal change is extended to include a relaxation of political controls, the pressure from abroad will be greatly reduced and the responsiveness of sovereignty-free actors will be greatly increased, even as the ensuing uncertainties encourage caution on the part of actors in the state-centric world.

An insight into the complex mix of support and caution, of responsiveness from actors in the state-centric world and aggressive hostility from their counterparts in the multi-centric world, confronting China during this period of structural bifurcation in global politics is provided by the saga of a French journal, *Actuel*, which launched a crusade to support the Chinese democratic movement after the massacre in Tiananmen Square in June 1989. In subsequent months *Actuel* recruited fifteen other magazines in Europe and South America to join with it in a fax blitz of China. A mock issue of the *People's Daily* was printed featuring news of the exiled liberation movement, eye-witness accounts of the massacre, and other stories noxious to the Chinese regime. A list of "nearly every fax number" for the more than 6,000 fax machines in China was also published along with a page of transmission instructions. "Within days, fax machines all over China were jammed with the mock edition of the newspaper transmitted not only by the several magazines, but also by their readers. It was estimated that at one point nearly 200 faxes an hour were being sent from France alone, with French celebrities and politicians joining schools and businesses in the effort. Although on a smaller, more personal scale, the 'fax-in' continues today."[21]

If these actions emanating from the multi-centric world are a poignant demonstration of the present-day impossibility of any state remaining isolated from the rest of the world, so does *Actuel*'s second undertaking reveal that the state-centric world is still very much a part of the processes of global politics. *Actuel* raised enough money by the spring of 1990 to buy and equip a ship – named the Goddess of Democracy in memory of the statue erected in Tiananmen Square prior to the massacre – as a pirate radio station designed to anchor off the Chinese mainland and to beam round-the-clock news and other programs toward it, thereby making the ship into "a floating tribune to human rights."[22] The Chinese government, however, warned other governments against assisting the project and ultimately it had to be abandoned because several governments in the Far East heeded the warning and refused to let the Goddess of Democracy enter their ports and take aboard the necessary transmitting equipment.[23] In this case, in other words, China's external milieu favored the posture of actors in the state-centric world over that of their multi-centric counterparts, but the more general point illustrated by this example is the mix of supportive and aggressive elements that comprise the external stimuli to which countries are subjected under the bifurcated structures of the present global system.

This is, of course, not the place to elaborate at length on the potential for theoretical synthesis implied in Table 21.3. Obviously, the scheme needs to be refined by China hands that can enrich the context and expand the number of alternative Chinas that comprise the columns of Table 21.3 and by specialists on Chinese foreign policy who can replace the entries in the cells of the matrix with estimates of how the various Chinas might respond to the different global structures derived from the several IR theories. Efforts along these lines, I would argue, would allow for theorists and policy analysts to come together in fruitful collaboration on the question of how this complex and important country's relations with its neighbors and the world at large are likely to evolve in the years ahead.

22 Toward single-country theories of foreign policy

The case of the USSR[1]

The study of foreign policy cries out for developmental theory, for formulations that anticipate how the major determinants of a country's external behavior interact across time. In recent decades sociologists have evolved a subfield of life-cycle sociology, psychologists have accorded subfield status to developmental psychology, economists have done the same for developmental economics, and political scientists have used various labels to identify a subfield of political development. Comparable tendencies in the foreign policy field, however, have yet to stir. Indeed, for very different reasons, both area specialists and comparative foreign policy analysts tend to reject the very idea of a developmental subfield that is committed to scientific methods and that aspires to building viable and testable theory. Committed to accounting for the unique details and cultural nuances that differentiate their region or country of concern, area specialists tend not see themselves as engaged in a scientific enterprise. For them, historical narrative and idiographic inquiry are the preferred modes of analysis and any attempt to frame testable theory about their region or country tends to be viewed as a violation of the very diversity that renders it distinctive. Comparativists, on the other hand, resist the idea of a developmental subfield because they do regard their endeavors as scientific and fear that a focus on development across time will confine them, perforce, to a single case and accounting for the impact of specific events, foci they see as the very antithesis of science with its stress on identifying and explaining central tendencies among many cases.

To be sure, comparativists occasionally pay lip service to the legitimacy of using the premises of science to compare a single country's policies across different time periods. But the prime thrust of their theoretical efforts has been to compare different actors at the same time or under similar circumstances. To my knowledge, in fact, no comparativist honors the idea of single-country theory in practice; or at least one is hard pressed to identify a theory of any country's foreign policy that is grounded in the epistemology and methods of science. Single-country theories do exist in abundance – those of the Soviet Union are perhaps especially numerous – but they are the products of either diplomatic historians or area specialists who rely on historical examples to demonstrate how the pieces fit together and, in so doing, conspicuously avoid explicit hypotheses as to how specified variables will interact under specified conditions.

This gap in the comparative literature is all the more glaring when viewed in the context of current affairs. Perhaps a preponderance of the problems that arise in world politics involve the behavior of a single country. What will the Soviets do in Afghanistan? Is Peru able to follow a new course in handling its international debts? How will the United States respond to terrorism? These are examples of the myriad single-country problems that are presently on the world's agenda. But somehow students of comparative foreign policy have yet to develop a systematic approach to such questions. The commitment to comparative analysis has focused attention so thoroughly on types of actors – such as bureaucracies, developed countries, or African states – that can be contrasted as to obscure the need to be similarly systematic about the single actor. Also, since the analysis of a single actor is bound to require accounting for its unique history and culture, the idea of using scientific methods to probe its conduct is likely to seem impossible to those who conceive of science as suited only to the investigation of generic types.

Assuming the core of scientific theory involves expectations as to what happens when specified variables interact under specified circumstances, the ensuing discussion suggests that it may be possible to construct developmental or single-country theories of foreign policy without forgoing the basic commitments of science. Indeed, I would argue that efforts along this line are mandatory if the comparative study of foreign policy is to evolve a full storehouse of equipment for exploring the wide range of phenomena encompassed by the field. Furthermore, single-country theories may also prove valuable as components of broader formulations about the interactions of two or more states. Conceivably they may even facilitate the construction of more general models about the class of actors in which the country subjected to this form of theorizing is located.

In short, broad theoretical development and the analysis of specific foreign policy problems are not incompatible enterprises. To argue for single-country theory is neither to reject a nomothetic orientation nor to abandon the search for generalizable knowledge that spans a single sequence of events. The commitment to "anti-case study" approaches is not diminished,[2] or in any way undermined, by focusing on the foreign policy processes and actions of a single country. As a number of scholars have noted,[3] the specific case can be used for theory development if care is exercised in the identification of its wider relevance and the specification of its key variables.

The Soviet Union as a theoretical case

In order to explore the potentials of single-country theory, the analysis that follows focuses on the USSR as a concrete example. The Soviet Union is especially challenging in this regard not only because of its importance on the world scene, but also because information about its policy-making processes is relatively scarce. If viable single-country theory about the Soviet system can be developed, it ought to be possible to do at least as well in theorizing about any country.

In a sense political scientists are fortunate that information about Soviet policy-making processes is scarce and access to its officials minimal, that – as Churchill once commented – the USSR is a riddle wrapped in a mystery inside an enigma. Under these conditions we need not fear being overwhelmed by data, relying too heavily on skewed samples, or succumbing to the fallacy of letting the facts speak for themselves: nor need we feel inundated by the extensive information that can flow from press conferences, legislative hearings, interagency rivalries, or any of the other channels through which important voices are sorted out from a multiplicity of sources. Stated differently, in seeking to comprehend the USSR we have the advantage of not being able to peek into the black box and thus are free to be imaginative about the ways in which the inputs from abroad and the domestic scene get converted into policies and actions.

Put in another way, we can luxuriate in being forced to theorize. The scarcity of facts, samples, and data leaves us no choice but to conceptualize the dynamics operative upon and within the black box that has long enveloped the Soviet policy-making organization. And having been compelled to explicate our expectations as to how these dynamics function, we are then in the happy position of needing to look only at outcomes to test our theorizing. Just as the experimental psychologist can test hypotheses about learning by varying rewards and punishments to observe the effects on behavior rather than by exploring the workings of the psyche, so can we extend our knowledge of the Soviets by assessing the fit between stimuli and responses without having to trace or measure any intervening effects.

To some extent, of course, this euphoria over the prospects of solving Soviet riddles is forced. A plenitude of information, facts, and data is, plainly, preferable to a scarcity. The capacity to interview officials and ponder hearing transcripts is preferable to not being able to do so. On the other hand, the riddle-mystery-enigma conception of the USSR has hindered scholarship by providing a rationale to cling to, rather than test, preconceptions about its dynamics. Instead of aggressively framing testable hypotheses about how Soviet behavior may vary in response to different stimuli, the dominant tendency is to be intimidated by the paucity and unavailability of information and thus either to refrain from theorizing explicitly or to be so inhibited in developing rigorous propositions as to settle for untestable speculation that is bound to confine and curb inquiry. These inclinations can be overcome, however, if the scarcity of data is treated as opportunity rather than obstacle.

And, outrageous as it may seem, there are good reasons to reverse our perspective in this way. Parading methodological horribles and empirical obstacles offers no route to creative theory and sound knowledge. Einstein did not shrink from theorizing about the physical universe because the capacity to observe and measure it from deep in space did not exist. Rather he played the game of "as if," proceeding as if the capacity to test his theories was, or would eventually become, available. Equally important, the propounding of his relativity theory was an incentive to the development of the methodology and technology necessary to test it. Much the same can be said about the Soviet universe. If we play down the closedness of the Soviet system and proceed as if it was open to observation, we are likely to be more incisive and creative in our theorizing about it and, subsequently, more innovative in the development of techniques for generating relevant data with which to test and perfect our understanding.[4]

A second reason not to be overly sensitive to the closedness of the Soviet system is the ever-present possibility of new openings, or at least new peepholes, in the black box. In the 1950s, for example, no one foresaw that Stalin's daughter would flee to the West and write about her father,[5] that Khrushchev's memoirs would be published,[6] or that the highest ranking Soviet official in the United Nations would defect and publish an account of how foreign policy is formulated in the USSR.[7] Just as science fiction thrived by highlighting the theoretical possibility of deep probes in outer space, in other words, so must we allow for the theoretically possible advent of changes in the Soviet system that permit more direct observation of its policy-making processes. Indeed, even in the absence of such changes, the passage of time is bound to reveal more and more about these processes as their outcomes cumulate across decades. The recent spate of leadership successions is a case in point. The enlargement of these outcomes from three to six since 1980 has greatly facilitated comprehension of institutionalization in the Soviet system and how its structures handle the recruitment and consolidation of top officials.

Besides, we are not averse to asserting conclusions about what occurs in the black box. Rare is the student of the Soviet Union who does not have a position on its foreign policy goals, its openness to long-term change and influence, its capacity for policy reversals, or the relative importance of its internal and external commitments. Many analysts, to be sure, are quick to note the limits of their informational base, but these limits are no bar to the holding of perspectives which posit the Soviets as aggressive, or cautious, or pragmatic in world affairs and rigid, or inefficient, or innovative in the domestic arena. Indeed, the informational limits often seem to relieve analysts of a felt need to be skeptical about their interpretations and to permit them to adhere to uncomplicated and unqualified, if not ideological and polemical, conceptions of Soviet motives and actions. More importantly for present purposes, the sturdiness of the black box encourages the conviction that the only way to know anything about the Soviets is through a familiarity with Russian history and culture – that is, area studies – that can at least yield projections of past patterns. Scientific theorizing, many Russian specialists seem to say, is fruitless in such a research setting, albeit they do not shrink from using historical experience to justify assertions, perspectives, and positions on what the USSR is up to at any moment in time.

In short, the paucity of information does not prevent theorizing about Soviet dynamics; it only inhibits thorough, rigorous, and systematic theorizing. Persuaded that they are dealing with riddles, mysteries and enigmas, many analysts tend to downplay the utility of established standards of social scientific inquiry, tending instead to interpret whatever happens in the Soviet Union as reaffirming their notions of what drives that system. The first law of social dynamics – that we see what we want to see – thus rarely gets subjected to thorough, rigorous and systematic challenges in the field of Soviet studies. The idea of manipulating variables, holding some constant and treating others as interactive, appears to be viewed as hopeless, given the lack of access to data, and this sense of futility in turn fosters a resistance to framing theory and hypotheses that can be tested and falsified.[8] It is as if analysts believe that falsifiable theory should be developed only if the capacity to falsify it is immediately available. The possibility that such theory might be clarifying even in the absence of a falsification capacity, or that it might fruitfully be explored through synthetic, less comprehensive research methodologies, is apparently overlooked in the face of seemingly insurmountable obstacles to direct observation.[9]

An instructive example of these atheoretical tendencies to cling to preconceptions and not to frame propositions that can be systematically tested is provided by the many analysts who, perhaps unknowingly, posit the Soviet system as impervious to change. One could cite, for instance, a number of studies in which the Russians are seen as never wavering in their foreign policy goals.[10] Undoubtedly the continuities of Soviet life are more powerful than the impulses to innovate and change, but it violates everything we know about social systems to presume that they can adhere to a never-ending constancy in foreign affairs, that goals and priorities are not altered across generations, and that the emergence of new technologies, institutions, leaders, and social structures have no consequences for the values that underlie policy making. Or at least we know enough along these lines to warrant pausing frequently to assess the presumption of constancy. Unfortunately, however, all too often such pauses are conspicuous by their absence. All too often analysts seem to treat the Kremlin as so capable of converting every dynamic of change into yet another instance of prior practice that they – the analysts – do not question the possible rigidities of their own premises.

In sum, in trying to fathom modern-day Russia, analysts need to come to terms with an overriding question: namely, how willing are they to treat the Soviet Union as a case among many and to what extent are they inclined, on the other hand, to treat it as a unique polity, with a unique history, culture, and circumstances? Virtually all of the literature on the USSR is crucially shaped by the answer to this question. And since it involves the proper route to understanding, it is a question that divides analysts, leading often to fruitless disputes that intensify the divisiveness without clarifying the question. My own view, as will be seen, is that both the single- and multiple-case perspectives can be creatively employed in theorizing about Soviet politics and that the theory-building enterprise is set back by the tendency not to be explicit as to the relative strength one attributes to dynamics derived from unique circumstances and those derived from more encompassing factors. Moreover, as will also be noted, the assertion that both the idiographic and nomothetic approaches are relevant stems from substantive premises and not from a wishy-washy impulse to find a middle ground between two extremes. Nor is the stress on synthesis a way of avoiding hard analytic choices. Rather, it is rooted in the assumption that any country is a composite of both unique and general factors, that there are dimensions of Soviet experience common to all industrialized and industrializing societies even as there are dimensions rooted in Russian history.[11] The task is to recognize these disparate elements and then synthesize them into coherent theory. A large step in the direction of such theory is acknowledging that such a synthesis is both viable and legitimate.[12]

There is a powerful urgency in the need to develop synthesized theories of the Soviet Union. Life-and-death questions are being decided by top officials in the West on the basis of crude and impressionistic expectations that are neither systematic nor testable, but that are nonetheless presumed to have empirical validity. Recently, for example, supporters of tests of anti-satellite weapons in space argued for the testing program on the grounds that it "would create pressure on the Soviet Union to negotiate more seriously at arms control talks in Geneva."[13] Whatever their truth or falsity, theoretical conclusions of this order are too crucial to be left to epistemologically naive politicians and bureaucrats. They need to be made aware of themselves as participants in the theoretical enterprise, and such a sensitivity is going to develop only if scholars lead the way by demonstrating through their competing constructs both the dangers and rewards of explicit theorizing.

The nature of single-country theory

Given a euphoric orientation that stresses the fertility rather than the futility of the USSR as a research focus, how does one proceed? How to develop thorough, rigorous, and systematic theory about the Soviet Union that identifies key variables and specifies how they can be expected to vary under different conditions? The answer lies, first, in acquiring the confidence that such theory can be framed and, second, achieving syntheses between specific knowledge of Russian culture and history and general knowledge of the dynamics of industrialized and multi-ethnic societies with vast resources and longstanding international commitments. Such syntheses amount to what might be called single-country theory, a form of theorizing that appears to involve a contradiction in terms and thus may seem flawed to both the area specialist and the empirical comparativist. To overcome skepticism about the viability of such theory, and to build confidence in its feasibility, an explanation of its nature and construction is in order.

The objections of area specialists to single-country theory are likely to focus on the idea of deriving propositions about the Soviet Union from generalized models and findings relevant to how politics and economics unfold in certain classes of countries or under certain kinds of conditions. Such propositions are bound to be too broad, they argue, to allow for the historical experiences and cultural premises that are unique to the Soviets: yes, the USSR is industrialized and, yes, it is a superpower; but any propositions derived from these realities have only the most general relevance to the Soviet Union, its location in both Europe and Asia, its longstanding patterns of authoritarian rule, its Communist revolution, its unending aspirations to a warm-water port, its suffering in World War II, and all the other characteristics which set it apart from other countries, even those that have also undergone industrialization and achieved great-power status. Only through intensive probing of its distinguishing characteristics, the area specialists conclude, can a grasp of the Soviet system be developed. And even then, what is grasped is not so much theoretical as it is sound understanding, since the personality of leaders and situational dynamics can vary so much as to nullify any theory.

Comparativists, on the other hand, are likely to doubt the utility of single-country theory on the grounds that knowledge is developed only by comparing across units and not by allowing for the operation of unique cultural and historical circumstances in a single unit. For them, sound theory that is explanatory and predictive can never be rooted in the particularistic dimensions of a system. It must involve generalizations that apply to more than one case and, accordingly, that ignore the specific characteristics that differentiate one country from another. Yes, the USSR is uniquely astride Eurasia and, yes, it has never had adequate access to a warm-water port or been free of authoritarian regimes; but such realities of its history and culture only have theoretical import if they are cast, interactively, in a larger context. To know that tsarist and Communist leaders alike aspired to a warm-water port, for example, is not to anticipate how Soviet officials are likely to respond today to a confrontation with the United States over Turkey, Iran, or Iraq. Only propositions derived from, say, deterrence theory or findings relevant to how countries react in crisis situations, the comparativists conclude, can be of use in this regard.

In short, the comparativists contend that the area specialists lack a more encompassing, nomothetic context, and the latter see the former as woefully inattentive to idiographic detail. And this gap often seems so wide that rarely do either the generalists or the specialists attempt to bridge it, much less incorporate each other's findings and insights into their own formulations.[14] Yet, despite their differences, achieving theoretical synthesis between the two perspectives is not nearly as difficult as it may seem. All that is required is a concession on the part of the generalists that comparing shifts in the key variables that sustain the same system across time is as much a form of scientific inquiry as comparing their operation across different systems, while all the specialists need to concede is that the functioning of any system at a moment in time can derive from generalized dynamics that condition many systems as well as from its unique cultural and historical experiences. Making these concessions may not be easy for an analyst unaccustomed to reasoning otherwise, but their logic strikes me as impeccable.

Consider the case for within-system, across-time comparisons. Scientific inquiry involves the anticipation, identification, measurement and interpretation of patterns embedded in a number of data points. The investigator compares the patterns in different units as they might vary in response to specified stimuli or the emergence of different conditions. What renders these procedures scientific is not the nature of the units, but the availability of enough data points to form patterns and enough evidence of stimuli and/or conditions that are sufficiently different to justify before-and-after comparisons. If the data are sufficient and the breakpoints separating the before-and-after patterns clear-cut,[15] therefore, it does not matter whether the comparisons are made across several units or within one. The latter offers a laboratory for scientific inquiry in the sense that its structures, processes and policy outcomes at different moments in time constitute different system states and outcomes – and thus different data points – that can be analyzed for patterns and fitted (or not) to theory. If the unit is the Soviet Union, the patterns are those of a single country and an explanation of them can thus be viewed as a single-country theory.

Viewed in this way, generalists need not fear compromising a core value. Their commitment to uncovering recurring patterns would not be jeopardized because a single country need not be construed as a case history. They would be treating the Soviet Union not as a single data point, but as a series of cases no less subject to comparative analysis than any sample drawn from a larger population. Indeed, it can be readily argued that such comparisons have considerable advantages over those made in a multi-unit format inasmuch as the continuities and differences across time all occur within the same unit, thus enabling single-country compara-tivists to hold a great many more variables – such as those linked to culture and history – constant than can their across-country counterparts.

An obvious example of how within-unit comparison can underlie theorizing about the USSR is the extensive hypothesizing in which analysts engage when successions bring a new leader to the very top. Will Gorbachev prove to be a self-serving party bureaucrat like Brezhnev? Or a maverick like Khrushchev? Will Gorbachev's generation, which did not fight in World War II, prove to be more pragmatic and less ideological than its predecessors?[16] Such questions involve different values for key variables at different time points and, as such, they compel comparative analysis. For Khrushchev, Brezhnev, and Gorbachev are differenti-ated not only by their personalities; each is also expressive of what the Soviet system did and did not permit in their era – through, say, the values underlying the party's recruitment and advancement policies as well as the prevailing state of the Soviet economy – and thus juxtaposing them analytically need not be cast simply in historical and chronological terms. An interrupted time series design can also be employed by treating the regimes of successive leaders as separate data points susceptible to disaggregation into variables and constants, with the end of each regime being regarded as a breakpoint and the interactive outcomes among the variables then contrasted for continuities and changes.[17]

This is not to imply, however, that breakpoints in Soviet history only occur when new leaders come to power or that the advent of new leaders necessarily constitute breakpoints. Such may not be the case if one's theory highlights vari-ables other than those associated with leadership changes. The acquisition of nuclear capabilities, a major defection in Eastern Europe, or a decision to pro-mote the use of personal computers are illustrative of developments that might also be worthy of delineating as breakpoints for analytic purposes. Whether indi-vidual leaders or macro dynamics are delineated, however, the point is that diverse breakpoints can be identified and that therefore single-country theory does not necessarily amount to single-case analysis. It can be comparative analysis if it involves contrasting outcomes.

The concession required of area specialists may also loom as hazardous and compromising. Acknowledging the relevance of generalized dynamics runs exactly counter to their premise that understanding is to be found in the particular and the unique, in those qualities and experiences that set the Soviets apart from any other people or country. Furthermore, it follows from such an acknowledge-ment that area specialists can no longer confine their attention to the USSR. They must, in addition, branch out to grasp the underpinnings of processes such as industrialization, bureaucratization, socialization, legitimization, foreign policy formulation, and the many other general dynamics that sustain human collect-ivities in the post-industrial era. Hence reluctant to divert their energy away from their prime concerns in order to develop a broader but questionable theor-etical perspective and perhaps for other reasons as well, many area specialists are blinded by the idea of uniqueness; and the more they insist that the Soviet Union is unique under all circumstances, the more do they deprive themselves of access to rich theory about processes that are surely, in some respects, operative in the USSR.

It is as if area specialists often fear conceding that the operation of common stimuli across systems can result in comparable outcomes on the grounds that doing so is to deny that any cultural and historical factors are relevant and influen-tial. Such, of course, is not the case; in fact, often the specialists themselves rely on comparative insights in the course of focusing on the particulars of Soviet experi-ence. Ponder, for example, how most specialists shared in the expectation held by generalists that the Soviets would eventually return to the arms control bargaining table even though they adamantly insisted when they left in December, 1983, that they would resume negotiations only if the newly deployed US missiles in Western Europe were withdrawn. How did the specialists derive this expectation? Through an extrapolation from past practices in Soviet diplomacy or an understanding of how unique features of the Russian character lead to temporary face-saving rituals prior to the acceptance of political setbacks? Probably not. The greater likelihood is that they expected the Soviets to reverse the refusal because of a generalized dynamic operative upon and in any nation-state, namely, that it does not refrain from abandoning prior pledges when the external environment becomes increasingly threatening to its physical security. And this is especially true of superpowers with nuclear capabilities, irrespective of historical and cultural factors that may lead in a contrary direction. There are, in short, certain con-straints and/or requirements of economic, political and social life to which the leadership of any polity is compelled to be sensitive, and acknowledging as much in no way negates the relevance of the constraints and requirements embedded in the unique circumstances of every polity.

Herein, of course, lies the core of single-country theory. The conclusion that leaders and publics in any society at any moment in time are responsive to both their own pasts and the dynamics of prevailing domestic and international struc-tures can serve as the basis for deriving explicit, elaborate, integrated, and testable hypotheses which, when measured and assessed on either side of diverse historical junctures, will constitute a synthesis that meets all the standards of viable scientific theory while not ignoring the relevance of idiographic detail. More importantly in the case of the Soviet Union, such theory can enjoy the confidence of both specialists and generalists and thus facilitate their cooperation in confronting the challenges and opportunities posed by all those riddles wrapped in all those mysteries inside all those enigmas.

Let us be more specific. A theory of a single country is founded on the premise that at any moment in time that country's behavior is a product of two convergent sets of dynamics. One is all the distinctive features of its political structure, economic organization, and cultural history. The second embraces all those processes that are common to countries with the same characteristics. Indeed, viewed as social processes, these two sets of dynamics are not so much independent of each other as they are interactive and locked into reinforcing tensions: "As techniques of communication and physical mobility develop, it is becoming more difficult to conceive of uniquely distinctive or autonomous societies ... Yet divergent lines of historical development and the effects of different physical environments do not vanish in a few decades, however rapidly contemporary technology is diffused and however extensive the network of communications."[18]

In other words, any country is both different from all others and similar to some of them, the differences stemming from its unique circumstances and the similarities being the result either of structural requirements inherent in polities, economies, and societies at comparable stages of development or of forces at work on a transnational scale in a particular era. Hence any single-country theory must synthesize idiographic and nomothetic knowledge, that is, the most salient aspects of a country's uniqueness as well as the dynamics it shares with other countries. Enough is known about the processes of industrialization, for example, to expect them to foster the evolution of large-scale organizations in any society which industrializes and, in so doing, to give rise to processes of bureaucratic politics even as the bureaucratic politics of any one country are shaped by its particular cultural norms. Bureaucratic politics in the Soviet Union and the United States, to carry the example one step further, are thus presumed to have in common those qualities – such as the tendency of subordinates to report what they think their superiors want to hear – which attach to any large-scale organization, but at the same time to differ to the extent that the norms that Americans and Russians bring to organizational life differ.

Possible approaches to single-country theory

There are a number of precedents to which one could turn for guidance in blending the work of area specialists and comparative generalists. In medicine, for example, such a blend amounts to routine practice. Consider the response to a diseased kidney. On any patient the doctor focuses a broad understanding of how kidneys function and how they interact differently with different blood pressures and heart problems on the one hand, and what is known about the patient's medical history on the other. Hence the diagnosis is, in effect, a single-person theory of the kidney, blending both general and particular knowledge. Many of the same blending procedures are used with respect to comprehending political parties and the dissident wing, legislatures and the legislator, terrorism and the terrorist, crowds and the agitator, traffic jams and the motorist, markets and the consumer, and, indeed, any situation where the focus of inquiry embraces both macro and micro dynamics.

But how to proceed in foreign affairs? How to combine the unique and the general with respect to international systems and the nation state? Around what issues, or through what procedures, should the foundations of a single-country theory be organized and the cooperation of area specialists and empirical comparativists facilitated. Several sets of issues and procedures come to mind here. One involves focusing the dialogue between generalists and specialists on those questions about Soviet dynamics where their respective forms of inquiry lead them to discrepant and conflicting interpretations. To concentrate on those dynamics where both converge around the same understanding is not to subject the methods and findings of either to a test, but confronting each with contrary findings about the same dynamics is to compel both to reconsider the premises, conceptual equipment, and observations on which their analyses rest and, no less important, to face directly alternative lines of reasoning. It would be instructive, for example, if specialists who explained Russian actions in Afghanistan in terms of a longstanding aspiration to surround the USSR with supportive buffer zones could enter into a challenging dialogue with generalists who discerned an alternative interpretation of the same behavior in bureaucratic rivalries. At the very least such dialogue would force both groups to acknowledge those aspects of Soviet life they hold constant and those for which they allow variance in the process of articulating their perspectives, an acknowledgement which will surely serve as a useful and vivid reminder of how the perspectives on the Soviet Union are rooted in their intellectual processes rather than in those of reality.

More often than not, admittedly, such confrontations may affirm for each group the soundness of the procedures they employ, but at the same time there may be crucial ways in which the process of confrontation leads to revisions in which some of the assumptions and methods of the other are seen to be useful and adaptable. And the more generalists and specialists engage in such dialogues and thus begin to accommodate each other's perspectives and materials, the more will the resulting incremental syntheses contribute to the development of a single-country theory of the USSR.

Instead of breaking off their dialogue when they come upon disagreements, in other words, it is precisely at those points where generalists and specialists get agitated over each other's statements about the Soviet Union that their dialogue should begin. An air of harmony and accomplishment may not follow, but at least both will have confronted the toughest theoretical question of all: under what circumstances, and to what extent, do unique aspects of Soviet life modify and/or override the dynamics inherent in economic development and superpower responsibilities, and vice versa? Given a clash between the specific and the general, which prevails and which yields? The traditional work ethic or the industrial requirement? The expansionist impulse or the nuclear restraint? The power of the party or the potential of home computers? The controls of the apparatus or the extension of global interdependence? The fading memories of World War II or the emergent challenges of a microelectronic revolution? The ideological commitment or the need to adapt? Or, put in terms of a research agenda, when, where, and to what extent does one look to Russian culture and history for guidance and when does one rely on models of societal, economic, and international systems?

One basis for answering this last question is provided in Table 22.1, the two

Table 22.1 Factors central to a theory of the USSR

Idiographic factors	Nomothetic factors
• History of political stability (156) • A nationality problem: domestic pressures for rectification of national grievances (149) • Soviet citizens expect to be governed, not left free to pursue any path; hence publics tend to be "undemanding" (167) and docile (156, 162) • Food prices kept artificially low to minimize discontent (162) • Inefficient agriculture (262) • Bureaucratic habit of intruding intermediaries into economic relationships (261) • Traditional Russian-Soviet nationalism is both defensive and aggressive (5, 16) • Sense of encirclement by adversaries and intense memories of suffering in World War II (4) • Satisfaction over increased power and status since World War II (24) • An explicit but flexible ideology that allows for sectarian, activist, and reformative interpretations (41, 77) • Common experiences and career patterns among leaders (76) • Serious energy crunch pending for a variety of reasons (238–9) • Tensions in relations with Eastern Europe (247 ff.) • Supportive communist parties throughout the world (433) • Traditional Soviet fear of being used by its clients (e.g. Cuba) (337–8) • Longstanding left–right cleavage within the leadership (344) • Memories of Stalin's excesses (89) • Foreign policy successes are principal means whereby elites legitimate their policy system; hence diminished "free hand" in foreign affairs (13) • A one-party dictatorship (363) • Relative weight of individual at apex of the political structure remains far greater in the USSR than in the USA (381)	• Reliance of rulers on large national armed forces and the production of large range of goods to keep population satisfied (155) • Industrialization renders domestic conditions more relevant to foreign policy (155) and fosters less compartmentalization of foreign and domestic issues (109, 414) • Growing access to the decision-making process in foreign policy • Increased social mobility and an occupational structure shifting toward more prestigious jobs, thus resulting in more people with some stake in the system (163–4) • Increased intelligentsia, diminished peasantry (165) • A wiser, more alert public in foreign affairs (353) • A fluctuating economy, with periods of slowdown reducing the regime's maneuverability and making military preparedness more costly (413) • Complexity fostering a "need-to-know" explosion, an erosion of autocratic rule, and a politics of argumentation rather than of "label-sticking" (104) • Profound demographic changes involving reduced fertility, severe labor shortages, pending crisis of productivity, and marked slowdown in economic growth (203–25, 246) • Dependence on external resources (grain, technology, etc.) unless growth in consumption severely cut (168) • Dynamics of collective decision-making (363, 366) generating a more structured policy-making process based on compromise (110) • "Rallying around the flag" consensus readily occurs in international crises (49) • Internationalization of nationality problem (148) • Hard-currency problems in managing trade with the West (193, 301, 413) • Inexorable process of functional differentiation since Stalin (349) • Relative weight of traditional political culture diminishing (356) • Learning process that emancipates top elites from doctrinal stereotypes (359)

Source: The parenthetic numbers after each entry refer to the pages in S. Bialer (ed.), *The Domestic Context of Soviet Foreign Policy* (Boulder, CO: Westview Press, 1981), from which the entries were obtained.

columns of which list, respectively, some of the idiographic and nomothetic factors that are cited in the literature on the Soviet Union as central to its development and conduct. Although the literature search used to compile Table 22.1 was limited in scope,[19] the results seem sufficient to highlight the tasks involved in constructing a single-country theory. Presumably a thoroughgoing theory of the USSR would at least have to consider, if not to synthesize, all or most of the dynamics set forth in both columns of the table. Another basis for integrating the specific and general-ized aspects of Soviet experience is suggested below in the context of my theory of national adaptation. Whatever means are used to achieve a confrontation between idiographic and nomothetic factors, however, the point here is that theoretical progress is bound to ensue if the clash between the two can be kept as the focus of any dialogue between empirical theorists and Soviet specialists.

Perhaps it is useful to note that in some respects such dialogues occur frequently in Western policy-making organizations. Whenever, say, responses to Soviet actions in Afghanistan need to be framed, doubtless advocates of various alterna-tives clash over Moscow's goal in the situation. These dialogues, however, are much briefer and less far ranging than those suggested here. Transcripts of them might be of benefit to the scholar, but their purpose is to make sound policy and thus the implications of the various interpretations are pursued only to the point where consensus around a policy choice is achieved. The dialogues designed to develop single-country theory, on the other hand, cannot be so attenuated. To evolve a blend of the general and the particular they cannot rely simply on verbal interchange and compelling argumentation. Rather the challenges must take the form of demonstration through empirical proof, of assessing the fit of data to hypotheses through rigorous standards of acceptable evidence.

A second procedure for building a synthesized theory of the USSR would be that of focusing the dialogues of generalists and specialists on the values and decision rules at work when the Soviets engage in those behaviors that are most discrepant with Western orientations. We have become so accustomed to these discrepancies that they no longer seem baffling and, instead, we take them for granted, as if their sources are self-evident and immune to change. And, in so doing, we tend to cloak them in simplistic labels and categorize them in descrip-tive rather than explanatory terms, thus closing off what may be obscure but valuable openings in the black box.

Consider, for example, Soviet reactions to the shooting down of the Korean airliner or to the charge that they have cheated on prior arms control agreements. Their denials and countercharges often seem so contrived that scholars as well as journalists and politicians in the West readily dismiss them as "propaganda" and unrelated to whatever may empirically be the case. Our own perception of such events is rooted in such different values – that under no circumstances is the murder of innocent travelers justifiable or the violation of authoritative diplomatic agreements warranted – that we are inclined, at best, to forgo our usual research impulses to frame alternative explanations and probe for the dynamics underlying the denials and countercharges. At worst, it is all too easy to treat such unfathom-able reactions to evidence, proof, and assertions as founded on "warped" decision rules. In either event, the result is that we retain our unquestioning assumptions and bypass the important question of what constitutes the decision rules on which the Soviet "propagandistic" denials and countercharges are grounded.[20]

Precisely because such behaviors provoke us to resort quickly and unthinkingly to ready-made interpretations, they can usefully serve as a spur to our theory-building efforts. We could, for instance, try to imagine the offices in which the Soviet propagandists work and to which word first comes of the downing of the Korean airliner or charges of cheating on arms control agreements. If our imagination then attempts to reconstruct what the relevant officials do with the information – who they consult, what kind of deliberations they engage in, what values they fall back on to give meaning to the information – the pictures that come to mind are likely to be far more complex than is implied by the notion of mere "propaganda"[21] To presume that the reactions of such officials are only propaganda is, usually, to assume that decisions are made by rote, without hesitation, as if the calculation of ploys was simple. And in so doing we may easily overlook a very complex process that rests on a series of decision rules pertaining to when the officials treat the information as accurate, when Western claims about it are accepted, when they are accepted but seen as too damaging to acknowledge, when the claims give enough pause to check out the information through the intelligence system, when the feedback from the intelligence system is murky and therefore a clear-cut propaganda line is not evident, and when a whole range of other possible responses might be undertaken by those who, at each stage, are responsible for framing and issuing the "propaganda."

In other words, it seems inconceivable, if our understanding of human behavior is in any way reliable, that Soviet reactions spring exclusively from a rote set of decision rules which say, in effect, "deny everything." Presumably the decision rules and processes for those situations in which the USA and USSR assert discrepant perceptions, evaluations, and interpretations are elaborate and not removed from the information reported by the Soviet intelligence network. Soviet interpretations may be far removed from American "truths," but they do have their own system of "truths" that is embedded in the value and decisional framework through which their reactions are processed. It is a framework, moreover, that is embedded in the orientations of those who gather intelligence, in the minds of Soviet foreign service officers who interpret it, in the perceptual screens of top officials, and in the conventions of committee procedures and interagency rivalries.

> "Propaganda" reactions, in short, spring from larger contexts, and it is a focus on these contexts that might serve the task of theory building. If we can avoid taking them for granted and instead recognize them as complex as well as discrepant from our own value systems, such decision rules can provoke us to search ever more deeply for the systems of values that sustain the Soviet policy-making organization.[22]

A third procedure for fashioning a viable model of the Soviets involves seizing upon traces of change in their behavior and reconstructing alternative scenarios as to what promoted the occurrence of change and what constraints may lie in any precedents it may set. Involved here are less changes of policy content and more changes of procedure. The former may be merely tactical and situational, but the latter could reflect the beginning of enduring responses to altered balances and/or new perceptions of needs and challenges. It seems a minor matter, for example, but there may be theoretical mileage in seizing on the recent tendency of top Soviet officials to hold open press conferences. Marshal Ogarkov did this after the shooting down of the Korean airliner and so did Foreign Secretary Gromyko several months later after the resumption of arms control talks. These are, indeed, the slimmest of traces, mere hints at the surface of underlying change. And they may also be expressive of the most superficial kinds of change, momentary adjustments to a public relations problem. On the other hand, being close together in time, the two press conferences suggest an emergent pattern which, given an aggressive theoretical impulse, at least ought to trigger the imagination and lead to posing and probing a series of questions: what transformations are occurring in the world that lead the Soviet policy-making organization to break with a long-standing policy of merely proclaiming reactions rather than exposing top officials to the hazards of press conferences? Is the emergent pattern reflective of what one observer perceives as the emergence of "a sense of quasi-accountability" to domestic elites by the makers of Soviet foreign policy?[23] What kind of exchange might have occurred among the Soviet policy makers who decided upon this new procedure for coping with potential setbacks? Did they view the idea of an open press conference as shocking at first or was it widely perceived as a useful innovation? Did their deliberations include recognition that in initiating the new procedure they might foster expectations in future situations that could constrain and limit their options? Did they discuss with Ogarkov or Gromyko how he should respond to certain questions, warn him against pitfalls, discuss his goals, and suggest a casual style? Or was there no prior briefing? Did Ogarkov and Gromyko simply decide on their own that the situation called for a Western-style press conference?

Such questions may seem trivial in some respects. But one never knows where they might lead and the builder of single-country theory cannot afford to ignore any signs of structures undergoing change. And especially where the black box is so heavily guarded, such signs must be seized upon and fully mined for their theoretical ore.[24]

A fourth focus for single-country theory is that realm of politics wherein domestic and foreign dynamics converge. As technology renders the world smaller and increasingly interdependent, this convergence becomes ever more salient to the welfare, integrity, and survival of nation-states. Indeed, if states are to adapt to a fast-changing world, increasingly they will have to devote resources and energies to balancing the complex external and internal demands to which growing interdependence has given rise. This adaptive problem has become universal, and in its universality lies the core around which single-country theory can be constructed. That is, being a crucial and all-encompassing problem faced by all countries, both the area specialist and the comparative generalist can usefully focus upon it and thereby synthesize their respective skills and epistemologies. The specialist has a contribution to make to the theory because the leadership of any country derives its orientations toward the domestic–foreign convergence partly from the country's particular historical, cultural, and geographic experiences. At the same time the comparativist has a lot to contribute theoretically because, even as they draw on their unique circumstances, the leaders of all countries must confront a number of general dynamics inherent in the requirements of industrialization, the state of the world economy, and the structure of world politics as they seek to cope with the convergence. Stated differently, any leadership is faced with the necessity of evolving priorities in the relative importance it attaches to internal and external demands. Leaderships may differ greatly in the priorities they maintain, but maintaining some kind of balance between coping with problems at home and meeting challenges from abroad is a necessity. Why? Because, to repeat, not to maintain an effective internal–external balance is to run the risk of failing to adapt to a world that is undergoing rapid transformation.

Elsewhere I have developed a theoretical perspective which, whatever its shortcomings, does focus on the processes through which countries do or do not cope with the convergence of challenges from at home and abroad. I call it a theory of the adaptation of whole systems – either national societies[25] or national states[26] – and at first glance it would seem especially easy to theorize about the Soviet Union as an adaptive system.[27] The USSR is, after all, a superpower deeply involved in a nuclear arms race during a period of mushrooming economic constraints, circumstances that thrust guns-or-butter issues to the fore and highlight the tensions between internal needs and external requirements, between stimulating the domestic economy and contesting foreign adversaries. Indeed, precisely because their commitments are global in scope, superpowers today are compelled to monitor their self-environment orientations continuously. Each proposed new weapons system points to the possibility of a comparable diminution in consumer goods, just as every proposal for new investments at home hints at the likelihood of a corresponding contraction abroad. There is, of course, more to national adaptation than coping with guns-or-butter conflicts, but for analytic purposes they can usefully serve to illustrate how a theory of the USSR might be developed.

Conclusion

Doubtless there are many more strategies that could be employed to evolve a single-country theory of the Soviet Union or, indeed, of any system. The point here has not been to indicate a preferred strategy, but rather to stress that such theory can be constructed in the context of a commitment to comparative inquiry.

Whatever strategy may be employed, moreover, it should be clear from the foregoing suggestions for probing the riddles, mysteries and enigmas of the USSR that the goal of single-country theory is not that of anticipating or explaining a specific action or event. No scientific theory aspires to such precision and it would be erroneous to conceive of single-country theory as an exception in this regard. To extrapolate from the idea of a single-country theory to a single-event prediction would be to misunderstand and exaggerate the kind of specialist–generalist synthesis being advocated. The goal is, rather, to develop a theory of the Soviet Union that explains the likely developments and/or choices at crucial junctures, at those moments in the life of the USSR when emergent structures clash with persistent patterns, when continuities may seem increasingly counter-productive relative to the possibilities of change, when domestic needs and foreign challenges are in conflict. The persistence of crop failures, the recurrent under-production of a stagnant economy, the currency crisis or oil embargo abroad, the guns-or-butter problem posed by new rounds in the arms race – these are the kind of critical turning points in which the making of choices seems inescapable and to which a single-country theory can be meaningfully addressed. As a life-course sociologist might put it, single-country theory focuses on the conjunction of economic time, political time, and social time on the one hand, and historical time and cultural time on the other, during those eras when the dynamism of new technologies and the renewal of collective aspirations are stirring upheaval in the course of world affairs.

23 National interest[1]

The concept of the national interest is used in both political analysis and political action. As an analytic tool, it is employed to describe, explain, or evaluate the sources or the adequacy of a nation's foreign policy. As an instrument of political action, it serves as a means of justifying, denouncing, or proposing policies. Both usages, in other words, refer to what is best for a national society. They also share a tendency to confine the intended meaning to what is best for a nation in foreign affairs.

Beyond these general considerations, however, the two uses of the concept have little in common. In its action usage the concept lacks structure and content but, nevertheless, serves its users, political actors, well. As an analytic tool the concept is more precise and elaborate but, nevertheless, confounds the efforts of its users, political analysts. These differences arise out of the fact that the national interest is rooted in values ("what is best"). While analysts have discovered that the value-laden character of the concept makes it difficult to employ as a tool of rigorous investigation, actors have found that this very same characteristic renders the concept useful both as a way of thinking about their goals and as a means of mobilizing support for them. That is, not only do political actors tend to perceive and discuss their goals in terms of the national interest, but they are also inclined to claim that their goals *are* the national interest, a claim that often arouses the support necessary to move toward a realization of the goals. Consequently, even though it has lost some of its early appeal as an analytic tool, the national interest enjoys considerable favor as a basis for action and has won a prominent place in the dialogue of public affairs.

History of the concept

The national interest has a much longer history as an instrument of action than as a tool of analysis. According to a historian [Charles A. Beard] who traced past uses of the term, political actors made claims on behalf of the national interest as early as the sixteenth century in Italy and the seventeenth century in England.[2] At that time claims made in the name of "the will of the prince," "dynastic interests," *raison* d'etat, and other older catchwords began to lose their effectiveness as a new form of political organization, the nation-state, came into being and served as the political unit to which men owed their allegiance. Thus, the old terms were gradually replaced by new ones that reflected the new loyalties. The national interest was one of these, as was "national honor," "the public interest," and "the general will." Beard also found that "the term, national interest, has been extensively employed by American statesmen since the establishment of the Constitution."[3]

Many decades elapsed, however, before the national interest attracted attention as a tool of analysis. Not until the twentieth century, when two world wars made it clear that mass publics had both a vital stake in foreign affairs and played a vital role in them, did analysts focus on the national interest as a concept which could be used to describe, explain, and assess the foreign policies of nations. Beard was himself one of the first to develop the concept for this purpose and to distinguish it from the "public interest," which through convention has come to be used in reference to the domestic policies of nations.

Initially, the national interest appealed to analysts whose main concern was to evaluate the foreign policies which led to World War II. Impressed with the thought that the global conflict might have been avoided if the British and the French had not acquiesced to Hitler at Munich in 1938 and if the United States had not adopted isolationist policies throughout the 1930s, a number of analysts turned to the national interest as a way of determining the adequacy and effectiveness of past, present, or future policies. They reasoned in retrospect that the advent of World War II made it clear that the prewar policies of the three nations were ill-advised and that the policies proved to be contrary to the best interests of England, France, and the United States. To these analysts it thus seemed obvious that the best interest of a nation is a matter of objective reality and that by describing this reality one is able to use the concept of the national interest as a basis for evaluating the appropriateness of the policies which a nation pursues. Because of their underlying assumption that the national interest can be objectively determined, we shall call these analysts "objectivists."

It should be noted that most objectivists do not have an explicit and elaborate rationale for their approach to the national interest. Interested primarily in analyzing the contents of foreign policy, the objectivists are not particularly concerned about the methodological and philosophical foundations of their inquiries. They make no special effort to explain how and why their descriptions of the national interest are in accord with reality because, for them, the correspondence between their descriptions and the objective situation is self-evident. Objectivists thus leave to their readers the task of inferring their conceptualization of the national interest from substantive observations which are as variable as the situations which they describe.

It is possible, however, to derive some insight into the underlying rationale of the objectivists from the writings of one analyst who did undertake to develop an explicit framework for explaining why his substantive interpretations of the national interest reflect objective reality. The analyst is Hans Morgenthau, whose works advance "a realist theory of international politics" founded on the concept of national interest. "Interest is the perennial standard by which political action must be judged and directed," Morgenthau wrote,[4] emphasizing that, therefore, the "objectives of a foreign policy must be defined in terms of the national interest."[5] And exactly what constitutes the interest of a nation? Morgenthau recognized that "the kind of interest determining political action in a particular period of history depends upon the political and cultural context within which foreign policy is formulated,"[6] but he envisioned accounting for these contextual factors by defining interest in terms of power.[7] For Morgenthau the power at a nation's command relative to that of other nations is, at any moment in time, an objective reality for that nation and thus serves to determine what its true interest is and should be. As will be seen, however, the difficulty with Morgenthau's formulation is the lack of a method for determining what a nation's relative power is. That is, he does not indicate how use of the criterion of power will enable nations to "follow . . . but one guiding star, one standard for thought, one rule for action: *the national interest.*"[8]

As the discipline of political science gave increasing emphasis to scientific explanation, another group of analysts joined the objectivists in converging upon the national interest as an analytic concept. Concerned less with evaluating the worth of foreign policies and more with explaining why nations do what they do when they engage in international action, this group found the national interest attractive as a possible means of probing the sources of foreign policy. They reasoned that nations do what they do in order to satisfy their best interests and that by describing these needs and wants the analyst would be in a position to use the concept of the national interest as a tool for explanation, These analysts, in other words, deny the existence of an objective reality which is discoverable through systematic inquiry. For them the national interest is not a singular objective truth that prevails whether or not it is perceived by the members of a nation, but it is, rather, a pluralistic set of subjective preferences that change whenever the requirements and aspirations of the nation's members change. For want of a better term, hereafter we shall call those who approach the national interest in this way the "subjectivists."

The advent of the decision-making approach to international politics[9] provided the subjectivists with an additional rationale for their approach to the national interest. Partly as a reaction to the objectivists and partly out of a concern to render concepts usable by linking them to observable behavior, students of decision making contend that the national interest, being composed of values (what people want), is not susceptible of objective measurement even if defined in terms of power and that, accordingly, the only way to uncover what people need and want is to assume that their requirements and aspirations are reflected in the actions of a nation's policy makers. For these analysts, in other words, the national interest is whatever the officials of a nation seek to preserve and enhance. As two leading spokesmen for this approach put it, "The national interest is what the nation, i.e., the decision-maker, decides it is."[10]

It is worthy of emphasis that although the objectivists and subjectivists differed profoundly in their premises and conclusions, both came to accept the appropriateness of analyzing foreign policy and international politics in terms of the national interest. To be sure, the two groups focused on different phenomena when they investigated the national interest, but they both emphasized that its relevance to the external actions of nations was considerable.

Limitations of the concept

Despite the claims made for the concept and notwithstanding its apparent utility, the national interest has never fulfilled its early promise as an analytic tool. Attempts by both objectivists and subjectivists to use and apply it have proven fruitless or misleading, with the result that, while textbooks on international politics continue to assert that nations act to protect and realize their national interests, the research literature of the field has not been increased and enriched by monographs which give central prominence to the concept.

The reasons for this failure of the concept as an analytic tool are numerous. One is the ambiguous nature of the nation and the difficulty of specifying whose interests it encompasses. A second is the elusiveness of criteria for determining the existence of interests and for tracing their presence in substantive policies. Still another confounding factor is the absence of procedures for cumulating the interests once they have been identified. This is in turn complicated by uncertainty as to whether the national interest has been fully identified once all the specific interests have been cumulated or whether there are not other, more generalized values which render the national interest greater than the sum of its parts.

These limitations are readily discernible in the premises and writings of the objectivists. What is best for a nation in foreign affairs is never self-evident. More important, it is not even potentially knowable as a singular objective truth. Men are bound to differ on what constitute the most appropriate goals for a nation. For, to repeat, goals and interests are value-laden. They involve subjective preferences, and thus the cumulation of national interests into a single complex of values is bound to be as variable as the number of observers who use different value frameworks. Yet the objectivists proceed on the assumption that some values are preferable to others (for example, that it is better for the nation to survive than not to survive) and that therefore it is possible to discover, cumulate, and objectify a single national interest. Consequently, the objectivists find it possible to characterize every foreign policy as either reflecting or opposing the national interest. Indeed, it was precisely this line of reasoning that enabled them to posit an objective reality about the conditions of prewar Europe and to conclude that Great Britain and France did not follow their national interests when they ignored this reality and acquiesced to Hitler at Munich.

However, such reasoning breaks down as soon as it is recalled that the national interest is rooted in values. If every member of a nation wishes to have it go out of existence by joining a larger world federation, who is to say that the goal or act of federation is contrary to that nation's interest? If the British and the French believed they were satisfying their wants and needs when they compromised at Munich, who is to say they were wrong and acted in violation of their national interests? The analyst who does make such an observation is merely enjoying the benefits of hindsight to justify the superiority of his own values over those of the British and French policy makers who decided to acquiesce to Hitler (obviously, the policy makers would have acted differently if they could have foreseen the consequences of acquiescence). Since values are not susceptible of scientific proof, the objectivists have never been able to demonstrate the validity of their assessments of the extent to which foreign-policy actions reflect a nation's interest. To explain that a certain policy is in the national interest, or to criticize it for being contrary to the national interest, is to give an imposing label to one's own conception of what is a desirable or undesirable course of action.

The objectivists do not consider that their own values serve as criteria for determining the substantive content of the national interest. Rather, as has been noted, they conceive of a nation's power as the source of what is best for it and as the basis for ranking some values as preferable to others. From their point of view, a nation's power has an objective existence and thus values need not enter into a determination of its national interest. The objectivists concede that the national interest may be defended, criticized, or explained in value, rather than power, terms. Such formulations, however, are regarded as merely ideological justifications and rationalizations which conceal the true nature of the policy under consideration. Policy makers may claim that moral principles serve as the basis for their actions, but the objectivists assume that in fact "statesmen think and act in terms of interest defined as power."[11]

This reasoning of the objectivists is essentially erroneous. The dictates of power are never clearly manifest. Power is as elusive and ambiguous a concept as is interest. Its components are a matter of dispute. Furthermore, many power components consist of intangibles, such as morale, which are difficult to measure. Even more difficult, if not impossible, is the task of cumulating the tangible and intangible components into a single entity called "the power of a nation." For not only does the cumulation of unlike factors constitute a difficult problem in itself, but it also necessitates the introduction of values. To cumulate the components of power one must assess the relative importance of each component, and such an assessment can only be made by referring to the goals which the power is designed to serve. Hence, whether he wishes to or not, the analyst must inevitably fall back on a value framework – the one from which goals are derived – if he is to define the national interest in terms of power. It follows that there is no reason to assume that different analysts will necessarily arrive at similar, much less identical, interpretations of what a nation's power dictates its national interest to be.

In short, there may be an "objective reality" about the situations in which nations find themselves at various periods of history, but neither predictively nor retrospectively can its contents be clearly demonstrated. A description of the national interest can never be more than a set of conclusions derived from the analytic and evaluative framework of the describer. The objectivists unknowingly concede this point whenever they criticize foreign policies for not being in a nation's interest. For such a criticism contradicts their view that the national interest determines the contents of what nations do abroad. For example, Morgenthau goes to great lengths in his writings to show how "a foreign policy guided by moral abstractions, without consideration of the national interest, is bound to fail,"[12] an observation which undermines his assumption that policy makers always think and act in terms of interest defined as power.

Nor have the various subjectivist approaches to the national interest been conspicuously successful. Although subjectivists carefully and explicitly avoid the premise that the national interest can be objectified, their formulations and uses of the concept are far from free of its inherent limitations. The recognition that many groups in a nation have different and often conflicting concepts of what external actions and policies are best for it – and that consequently the national interest is a reflection of these preferences rather than of objective circumstances – gives rise to as many conceptual and methodological difficulties as it avoids. First there is the problem of which groups constitute a nation. Should the boundaries of a nation be equated with those of national societies or does a nation consist of persons with a common background who speak the same language? If the latter, more traditional formulation is used, then analysis is complicated by the fact that some nations exist within or extend beyond the boundaries of national societies. Such nations may have neither governments nor foreign policies, so that inquiries into their interests would be far removed from the concerns which attract attention to the concept of national interest. For this reason most subjectivists equate nations with national societies and employ the terms interchangeably. In other words, the national interest usually means the societal interest.

Defining the nation in this way, however, is a relatively minor problem and only proves troublesome for the terminological purist. Much more difficult is the problem which follows immediately from the assumption that nations are heterogeneous units encompassing a multitude of ethnic, cultural, social, and other types of groups, namely, the problem of identifying and classifying all the diverse and conflicting interests which clamor for satisfaction in a national society. Stated simply, how does the observer determine which groups have an interest in a particular foreign policy and how does he specify what the substantive contents of the interests of each group are? The subjectivist's obvious reply is that interests are equivalent to the demands and recommendations which group spokesmen in the society articulate and press. But this answer is of little help to the researcher. The groups with specialized interests in modern industrial societies are so numerous, and the types of policies in which they have a stake are so varied, that the quantitative dimensions of such a procedure render it virtually unusable. Furthermore, even if this quantitative problem could be overcome, there would remain the qualitative task of accounting for the groups whose interests lack a spokesman (for example, future generations, consumers, and repressed minorities). Presumably this can only be accomplished through estimates of what is best for such groups, a procedure which brings the subjectivist perilously close to the objectivist's practice of ascribing his own values to others.

Nor does the subjectivist's dilemma end here. Assuming that he is somehow able to identify all the expressed and unexpressed interests of a society, he must then combine the multiplicity of values into a meaningful whole. Not to do so would be to treat the national interest as a mass of contradictory needs and wants, a procedure which is hardly suitable to the description, explanation, and evaluation of foreign-policy goals. But in order to aggregate many contradictory values into an over-all formulation of the national interest, one must face the probability that some of the specific interests carry greater weight than others, and it is this probability that perpetuates the dilemma. For it raises the question of how the relative weight of the conflicting interests is to be determined. The most tempting solution is to attach weights on the basis of one's own assessments, but this procedure would again lead the subjectivist down the misleading path followed by the objectivist.

Most subjectivists avoid these complex, seemingly insurmountable problems by relying on a procedural rather than a substantive definition of the national interest. Rather than attempt to sum the values that prevail in a society, they rely on the society's political processes to do it for them. That is, they fall back on a decision-making conception in which the foreign-policy goals that a society sets for itself are considered to result from bargaining among the various groups claiming satisfaction of their needs and wants. If some interests carry greater weight than others, it is assumed that the differences will be recognized and accounted for in the policy-making process. In other words, regardless of whether democratic or authoritarian procedures are employed, the needs and wants of groups within national societies are assumed to constitute demands that policy makers must sort out and obey, an assumption which relieves the observer from having to resort to his own values to determine which interests are weightier. Operationally, the substantive content of the national interest thus becomes whatever a society's officials decide it to be, and the main determinant of content is the procedure by which such decisions are made.

This approach also allows for the operation of generalized values which render the national interest greater than the sum of its parts. If the over-all perspective of their high offices leads policy makers to conclude that the demands made upon them are, taken together, insufficient to serve the welfare of the nation, and if they therefore superimpose their own values on the decision-making process, then clearly the analyst can treat the national interest as more than the cumulated total of subnational interests without falling back on his own view of what is best for the society he is examining.

Yet the decision-making approach to the national interest also suffers from limitations. The main weakness is that it is not always possible to ascertain when a policy has been officially decided upon, since most policies undergo a continuous process of evolution and revision as external conditions change and internal demands shift. This difficulty cannot be circumvented by focusing on the values which officials espouse at any point in the decision-making process. For the various officials of a society often hold and assert different conceptions of what the goals of foreign policy ought to be. Under these circumstances, which usually prevail in open democratic societies, the analyst gets little guidance from the formulation that the national interest of a society is what its duly constituted policy makers claim it to be. The United States offers a good example of this dilemma. Not infrequently does it happen that the president, members of his cabinet, other executive branch officials, and the leaders, committees, and individual members of Congress pursue values and policy goals which are in direct conflict and which they all contend are best for the nation. Who is correct? Operationally, they all are, as they all have some official responsibility for formulating and executing foreign policy. What, then, is the national interest? The question seems unanswerable unless the analyst is willing to fall back on his own values to decide which officials express the soundest and most representative views.

A second difficulty with the decision-making approach concerns closed authoritarian societies. Many groups in such societies have no opportunity to articulate their needs and wants, thereby undermining the assumption that the various interests of a society are sorted and summed in its political processes. It hardly seems plausible, for example, to equate the national interest of Germany during the Nazi period with the actions, pronouncements, and aspirations of Hitler. Such a formulation runs counter to the concerns which make the national interest attractive as an analytic concept. Yet, under the decision-making approach the analyst has no choice but to view Hitler's purging of the Jews and his launching of World War II as in the German national interest. To do otherwise is either to fall back on an objectivist view that there is a "true" national interest of Germany which Hitler violated or to be confronted with the insuperable problem of identifying and aggregating the unarticulated interests of the various groups then existent in Germany.

Future of the concept

There can be little wonder, then, that the national interest has not sparked research or otherwise lived up to its early promise as an analytic tool. All the approaches to it suffer from difficulties which defy resolution and which confound rather than clarify analysis. As political inquiry becomes more systematic and explicit, the concept is therefore likely to be used less and less. Serious doubts about its analytic utility have already been expressed,[13] and it seems probable that objectivists and subjectivists alike will find that they can evaluate and explain foreign-policy phenomena adequately without having to resort to the national interest as an over-all explanation or characterization.

The trend toward more systematic inquiry is not the only reason why the abandonment of the concept is likely to be hastened in the future. The ever greater interdependence of nations and the emergence of increasing numbers of supranational actors is also bound to diminish reliance on the concept. Increasingly, decision makers act on behalf of clusters of nations as well as their own. They identify their own interests as inextricably tied to the welfare of their region, their continent, or their way of life. Many US officials, for example, now argue that the public must make sacrifices for Latin America because a higher standard of living throughout the Western Hemisphere is in the best interests of the United States. Similarly, other statesmen make decisions with a view to enhancing unformalized supranational communities, such as "the West," "the Arab world," and "the Communist bloc," or formalized economic and political unions, such as the Common Market, Malaysia, and the West Indies Federation. Clearly such global tendencies further reduce the utility of an attempt to explain international behavior in terms of the national interest.

Yet, the national interest cannot be entirely abandoned. Even though the nation is declining in its importance as a political unit to which allegiances are attached, the process of decline is many decades – perhaps even centuries – away from an end. Political actors will no doubt continue to make extensive use of the national interest in their thinking about foreign-policy goals and in their efforts to mobilize support for them. And, to the extent that they do, political observers must take cognizance of the national interest. In other words, while the national interest has little future as an analytic concept, its use in politics will long continue to be a datum requiring analysis.

Notes

1 Introduction

1 *Turbulence in World Politics: A Theory of Change and Continuity* (Princeton, NJ: Princeton University Press, 1990); *Along the Domestic–Foreign Frontier: Exploring Governance in a Turbulent World* (Cambridge: Cambridge University Press, 1997); and *Distant Proximities: Dynamics Beyond Globalization* (Princeton, NJ: Princeton University Press, 2003). A full listing of all the papers and books serves as an appendix to Volume II.

2 Included here are both the first (Chapter 7) and most recent papers (Chapter 9) that have been published, one on entering the academic profession and the other reflecting years later on what such a career entails.

3 The most extensive autobiographical essay can be found in James N. Rosenau, *Distant Proximities: Dynamics Beyond Globalization* (Princeton, NJ: Princeton University Press, 2003), Chap. 19. Less extensive but similar essays include "Confessions of a Pre-Postmodernist: Or Can an Old-Timer Change Course?" in Neil L. Waters (ed.), *Beyond the Area Studies War: Toward a New International Studies* (Hanover, NH: University Press of New England, 2000), pp. 181–89; "R.I.S. Interview with Jim Rosenau," *Review of International Studies*, Vol. 26 (2000), pp. 465–75; "A Transformed Observer in a Transforming World," *Studia Diplomatica*, Vol. LII, No. 1–2 (1999), pp. 5–14; "The Scholar as an Adaptive System," in J. Kruzel and J. N. Rosenau (eds.), *Journeys Through World Politics: Autobiographic Reflections of Thirty-Four Academic Travelers* (Lexington, MA: Lexington Books, 1989), pp. 53–68.

4 For some recent efforts to tackle the change problem, see the citations in footnote 4, p. 20, of Rosenau, *Distant Proximities*.

2 The future of politics

1 This chapter was excerpted and reprinted from *Futures*, Vol. 31 J. N. Rosenau, "The Future of Politics," pp. 1005–16, Copyright 1999, with permission from Elsevier.

2 Roland Robertson, "Social Theory, Cultural Relativity and the Problem of Globality," in Anthony D. King (ed.), *Culture, Globalization and the World-System* (Minnesota, MN: University of Minnesota Press, 1991) pp. 79, 80 (italics in the original).

3 For a disquieting assessment of this trend, see Nicholas Lemann, "The New American Consensus: Government of, by, and For the Comfortable," *New York Times Magazine*, November 1, 1998, pp. 37–43, 68–72.

3 Building blocks of a new paradigm for studying world politics

1 This chapter was originally written for the International Symposium on Non-State Actors and New International Realities, Pantelon University, Athens, Greece, January 30, 2004.

2 For a full discussion of the imprisoning nature of conceptual jails, see James N. Rosenau, *Turbulence in World Politics: A Theory of Change and Continuity* (Princeton, NJ: Princeton University Press, 1990), Chap. 2.

3 Rosenau, *Turbulence in World Politics*.

4 For a full discussion of the skill revolution, see James N. Rosenau, *Distant Proximities: Dynamics Beyond Globalization* (Princeton, NJ: Princeton University Press, 2003), Chap. 10.

5 Ulrich Neisser (ed.), *The Rising Curve: Long Term Gains in IQ and Related Measures* (Washington, DC: American Psychological Association, 1998).

6 James N. Rosenau and W. Michael Fagen, "Increasingly Skillful Citizens: A New Dynamism in World Politics?" *International Studies Quarterly*, Vol. 41 (December 1997), pp. 655–86.

7 For example, see David Bornstein, "A Force in the World, Citizens Flex Social Muscle," *New York Times*, July 10, 1999, p. B7; "Sins of the Secular Missionaries," *The Economist*, January 29, 2000; and Norimitsu Onishi, "Nongovernmental Organizations Show Their Growing Power," *New York Times*, March 22, 2001, p. A10.

8 See Robert D. Putnam, *Bowling Alone: The Collapse and Revival of American Community* (New York: Simon & Schuster, 2000).

9 Rosenau, *Turbulence in World Politics*, Chap. 10

10 See, for example, Ronnie D. Lipschutz, "Reconstructing World Politics: The Emergence of Global Civil Society," in Rick Fawn and Jeremy Larkins (eds.), *International Society After the Cold War: Anarchy and Order Reconsidered* (New York: St. Martin's Press, 1996), pp. 101–31.

11 My preferred labels are "sovereignty-bound actors" for states and "sovereignty-free actors" for what most analysts call non-state actors. See Rosenau, *Turbulence in World Politics*, p. 36.

12 Greg Myre, "Israel Warns Powell on Peace Team; He Rejects Criticism," *New York Times*, December 3, 2003, p. A3.

13 While these two umbrella organizations do not convene in the same locales, they now meet at the same time, as if to compete for headlines. See, for example, Saritha Rai, "The Loud Answer to Davos, in Bombay This Year, Is Antiwar," *New York Times*, January 22, 2004, p. A8, and Mark Landler, "Iran's Leader Mixes Hope with Defiance in Davos Talk," *New York Times*, January 22, 2004, p. A9.

14 For a detailed account of how this procedure led to the turbulence model, see Rosenau, *Distant Proximities*, Chap. 19.

15 See Webster Stone, "Moscow's Still Holding: Twenty-five Years on the Hot Line," *New York Times Magazine*, September 18, 1988, pp. 60, 67.

16 These differences are highlighted in Richard Price, "Review Article: Transnational Civil Society and Advocacy in World Politics," *World Politics*, Vol. 55 (July 2003), pp. 579–606, and Jan Aart Scholte, *Democratizing the Global Economy: The Role of Civil Society* (Coventry: Centre for the Study of Globalization and Regionalization, University of Warwick, 2003).

17 A similar formulation can be found in Daphné Josselin and William Wallace, "Non-State Actors in World Politics: A Framework," in Daphné Josselin and William Wallace (eds.), *Non-State actors in World Politics* (New York: Palgrave, 2001), pp. 2–4.

18 In this connection see Georg Sorensen, *The Transformation of the State: Beyond the Myth of Retreat* (New York: Palgrave Macmillan, 2004).

19 For a lengthy discussion of the nature and potential of SOAs, see Rosenau, *Distant Proximities*, Chaps. 12 and 13.

20 John Boli and George M. Thomas (eds.), *Constructing World Culture: International Nongovernmental Organizations Since 1875* (Stanford, CA: Stanford University Press, 1990).

21 Kevin Maguire, "How British Charity Was Silenced on Iraq," *The Guardian*, November 28, 2003.

22 See Jon Christensen, "Asking the Do-Gooders to Prove They Do Good," *New York Times*, January 3, 2004, p. A15.

4 Rigid boundaries: states, societies, and international relations

1 This chapter combines parts of two prior essays. One is excerpted from "Unfulfilled Potential: Sociology and International Relations," a contribution to a symposium published in the *International Review of Sociology*, Vol. 12, No. 3 (November 2002), pp. 543–47 (http://www.tandf.co.uk/journals). The other is a paper presented at the Annual Meeting of the International Studies Association, New Orleans, March 26, 2002, devoted to an evaluation of the *Handbook of International Relations*, edited by Walter Carlsnaes, Thomas Risse, and Beth Simmons (Thousand Oaks, CA: Sage, 2002).

2 If the umbrella is operationalized in terms of membership in the International Studies Association (ISA) – surely a good operational definition now that the ISA has grown to more than 3,000 members – the preponderance of political scientists in the field is especially conspicuous. Despite continuous efforts to expand the disciplinary scope of its members, the ranks of ISA include few sociologists, historians, anthropologists, economists, and even fewer who are not social scientists.

3 The ASA does have three sections that logically come under the IR umbrella – Peace, War and Social Conflict, International Migration, and Political Economy of the World Systems – but members of only the last of these organize panels at meetings of the International Studies Association or have writings that are conspicuously cited in the IR literature.

4 Some outstanding exceptions include the work of John Boli, Anthony Giddens, Michael Mann, John Meyer, Martin Shaw, and Immanuel Wallerstein.

5 Walter Carlsnaes, "The Agency-Structure Problem in Foreign Policy Analysis," *International Studies Quarterly*, Vol. 36 (September 1992), pp. 245–70, and Alexander Wendt, "The Agency-Structure Problems in International Relations," *International Organization*, Vol. 41 (Spring 1987), pp. 335–70.

6 See, for example, Michael Buraway *et al.*, *Global Ethnography: Forces, Connections, and Imaginations in a Postmodern World* (Berkeley, CA: University of California Press, 2000); Joan Huber (ed.), *Macro–Micro Linkages in Sociology* (Newbury Park, CA: Sage, 1991); Thomas J. Scheff, *Microsociology: Discourse, Emotion, and Social Structure* (Chicago, IL: University of Chicago Press, 1990); J. C. Alexander *et al.* (eds.), *The Micro–Macro Link* (Berkeley, CA: University of California Press, 1987); H. J. Helle and S. N. Eisenstadt (eds.), *Micro-Sociological Theory* (Beverly Hills, CA: Sage, 1985); K. D. Knorr-Cetina and A. V. Cicourel (eds.), *Advances in Social Theory and Methodology: Toward an Integration of Micro- and Macro-Sociologies* (Boston, MA: Routledge & Kegan Paul, 1981); and Randall Collins, "On the Microfoundations of Macrosociology," *American Journal of Sociology*, Vol. 86 (March 1981), pp. 984–1014.

7 With only a modicum of success, I have recently undertaken to solve the problem. See James N. Rosenau, *Distant Proximities: Dynamics Beyond Globalization* (Princeton, NJ: Princeton University Press, 2003).

8 It should be noted, however, that at least briefly Talcott Parsons did move into the IR field. See his "Order and Community in the International Social System," in James N. Rosenau (ed.), *International Politics and Foreign Policy: A Reader in Research and Theory* (New York: Free Press of Glencoe, Inc., 1961), pp. 120–9.

9 *Handbook*, pp. 168–70.

5 Powerful tendencies, startling discrepancies, and elusive dynamics: the challenge of studying world politics in a turbulent era

1 This chapter was originally published in the *Australian Journal of International Affairs*, Vol.

50 (April 1996), and is reprinted here by permission of Taylor & Francis (www.tandf.co.uk/journals).

2 James N. Rosenau, "Patterned Chaos in Global Life: Structure and Process in the Two Worlds of World Politics," *International Political Science Review*, Vol. 9 (October 1988), pp. 357–94.

3 James N. Rosenau, "Distant Proximities: The Dynamics and Dialectics of Globalization," a paper presented as the Morgan Lecture, Dickinson College, Carlyle, PA, October 27, 1993. A substantial elaboration of the concept can be found in James N. Rosenau, *Distant Proximities: Dynamics Beyond Globalization* (Princeton, NJ: Princeton University Press, 2003).

4 James N. Rosenau, *Turbulence in World Politics. A Theory of Change and Continuity* (Princeton, NJ: Princeton University Press, 1990).

5 For a succinct version of this formulation, see Mary Durfee and James N. Rosenau, *Thinking Theory Thoroughly: Coherent Approaches to an Incoherent World* (Boulder, CO: Westview Press, 2000), Chap. 3. In addition to *Turbulence in World Politics*, the trilogy includes *Along the Domestic–Foreign Frontier: Exploring Governance in a Turbulent World* (Cambridge: Cambridge University Press, 1997), and *Distant Proximities: Dynamics Beyond Globalization*.

6 For written expressions of this ambivalent perspective, see Robert Gilpin, *War and Change in World Politics* (New York: Cambridge University Press, 1981), p. 7; Alan James and Robert H. Jackson, "The Character of Independent Statehood," in A. James and R. H. Jackson (eds.), *States in a Changing World: A Contemporary Analysis* (Oxford: Clarendon Press, 1993), pp. 5–8; Stephen D. Krasner, "Sovereignty: An Institutional Perspective," in James A. Caporaso (ed.), *The Elusive State: International and Comparative Perspectives* (Newbury Park, CA: Sage, 1989), Chap. 4; Eugene B. Skolnikoff, *The Elusive Transformation: Science, Technology, and the Evolution of International Politics* (Princeton, NJ: Princeton University Press, 1993), p. 7; and Kenneth N. Waltz, *Theory of International Politics* (Reading, MA: Addison-Wesley, 1979), p. 94.

7 For an extensive elaboration of this thesis, see Saskia Sassen, *The Global City: New York, London, Tokyo* (Princeton, NJ: Princeton University Press, 1991).

8 These are expounded in Charles Tilly, *Big Structures, Large Processes, Huge Comparisons* (New York: Russell Sage Foundation, 1984).

6 Political science and political processes: narrowing the gap?

1 Originally delivered at a Conference on the Social Sciences in the 21st Century, sponsored by the Hong Kong Baptist University, Hong Kong, June 20, 2000; this chapter was subsequently published in Frank H. Fu (ed.), *The Development of Social Sciences in the 21st Century* (Hong Kong: Faculty of Social Sciences, Hong Kong Baptist University, 2001), pp. 32–47, and is reprinted here by permission.

2 For an effort to demonstrate the ways in which different cultural premises give rise to varying forms of political inquiry, see James N. Rosenau (ed.), *Global Voices* (Boulder, CO: Westview Press, 1993).

3 While there are many such debates in the professional journals, the controversy has spilled over into the popular media. For an example as well as a succinct summary of the deep divisions that revolve around rational-choice approaches, see the opposing articles in "Political Scientists Debate Theory of 'Rational Choice,'" *New York Times*, February 26, 2000, one by Morris P. Firorina entitled, "When Stakes Are High, Rationality Kicks In," and the other by Ian Shapiro entitled, "A Model That Pretends to Explain Everything."

4 See, for example, Peter B. Evans, Harold Jacobson, and Robert Putnam (eds.), *Double-edged Diplomacy: International Bargaining and Domestic Politics* (Berkeley, CA: University of California Press, 1993); Geoffrey Garrett, "Global Markets and National Politics: Collision Course or Virtuous Circles?" *International Organization*, Vol. 52 (1998),

pp. 787–824; Robert O. Keohane and Elinor Ostrom (eds.), *Local Commons and Global Interdependence: Heterogeneity and Cooperation in Two Domains* (London: Sage, 1995); Helen V. Milner, *Interests, Institutions and Information: Domestic Politics and International Relations* (Princeton, NJ: Princeton University Press, 1997); and Ronald Rogowski, *Commerce and Coalitions* (Princeton, NJ: Princeton University Press, 1989).

5 A good example of the strength of subfield boundaries is the pervasive resistance to treating the United States as one country among many and thus as falling within the comparative politics subfield. In every department with which I am familiar American politics and government is defined as a separate subfield. In my experience the logic that analyses of the US ought to be located in a comparative context and sub-jected to the premises and procedures of that subfield is invariably and vigorously rejected.

6 James N. Rosenau, "In Search of Institutional Contexts," a paper presented at the Conference on International Institutions: Global Processes-Domestic Consequences, Duke University, April 9–11, 1999.

7 For an extended analysis of this boundary and its porosity, see James N. Rosenau, *Along the Domestic–Foreign Frontier: Exploring Governance in a Turbulent World* (Cambridge: Cambridge University Press, 1997).

8 Among the exceptions in the international relations field are Barry Buzan and R. J. Barry Jones (eds.), *Change and the Study of International Relations: The Evaded Dimension* (London: Pinter, 1981); K. R. Dark, *The Waves of Time: Long-Term Change and International Relations* (London: Pinter, 1998); Joshua Goldstein, *Long Cycles: Prosperity and War in the Modern Age* (New Haven, CT: Yale University Press, 1988); K. J. Holsti, *Change in the International System: Essays on the Theory and Practice of International Relations* (Brookfield, VT: Edward Elgar, 1991); and George Modelski, *Long Cycles in World Politics* (Basing-stoke: Macmillan, 1987).

9 For a cogent analysis that explores the failure of observers to anticipate the momentous events of 1989–1991, see John Lewis Gaddis, "International Relations Theory and the End of the Cold War," *International Security*, Vol. 17 (Winter 1992–3), pp. 3–58.

10 The fragmegration concept was first developed in James N. Rosenau, " 'Fragmegrative' Challenges to National Security," in Terry Heyns (ed.), *Understanding US Strategy: A Reader* (Washington, DC: National Defense University, 1983), pp. 65–82. For a sub-sequent and more elaborate formulation, see James N. Rosenau, *Along the Domestic–Foreign Frontier: Exploring Governance in a Turbulent World* (Cambridge: Cambridge University Press, 1997), Chap. 6.

11 See, for example, Stuart Hall, "Old and New Identities, Old and New Ethnicities," in Anthony D. King (ed.), *Culture, Globalization and the World-System: Contemporary Conditions for the Representation of Identity* (Minneapolis, MN: University of Minnesota Press, 1997); Ulf Hannerz, *Transnational Connections: Culture, People, Places* (London: Routledge, 1996); Arjun Appadurai, *Modernity at Large: Cultural Dimensions of Globalization* (Minneapolis, MN: University of Minnesota Press, 1996); and Kevin R. Cox (ed.), *Spaces of Globaliza-tion: Reasserting the Power of the Local* (New York: Guilford Press, 1997). For fragmegrative analyses by business executives and journalists, see Dee Hock, *Birth of the Chaordic Age* (San Francisco, CA: Berrett-Koehler Publishers, 1999), and Thomas L. Friedman, *The Lexus and the Olive Tree* (New York: Farrar, Straus and Giroux, 1999).

12 Among the single-word labels designed to suggest the contradictory tensions that pull systems toward both coherence and collapse are "chaord," a label that juxtaposes the dynamics of chaos and order, "glocalization," which points to the simultaneity of globalizing and localizing dynamics, and "regcal," a term designed to focus attention on the links between regional and local phenomena. The chaord designation is pro-posed in Hock, *Birth of the Chaordic Age*; the glocalization concept is elaborately developed in Roland Robertson, "Glocalization: Time-Space and Homogeneity-Heterogeneity," in Mike Featherstone, Scott Lash, and Roland Robertson (eds.), *Global Modernities* (Thousand Oaks, CA: Sage, 1995), pp. 25–44; and the regcal formulation

can be found in Susan H. C. Tai and Y. H. Wong, "Advertising Decision Making in Asia: 'Glocal' versus 'Regcal' Approach," *Journal of Managerial Issues*, Vol. 10 (Fall 1998), pp. 318–39. I prefer the term "fragmegration" because it does not imply a territorial scale and broadens the focus to include tensions at work in organizations as well as those that pervade communities.

13 For a full discussion of the skill revolution as a micro dynamic, see James N. Rosenau, *Turbulence in World Politics: A Theory of Change and Continuity* (Princeton, NJ: Princeton University Press, 1990), *passim*. For a test of the skill revolution as an empirical hypothesis, see James N. Rosenau and W. Michael Fagen, "Increasingly Skillful Citizens: A New Dynamism in World Politics?" *International Studies Quarterly*, Vol. 41 (December 1997), pp. 655–86.

14 These "scapes" are discussed in Arjun Appadurai, *Modernity at Large: Cultural Dimensions of Globalization* (Minneapolis, MN: University of Minnesota Press, 1996), pp. 33–37.

15 For an elaboration of the eight sources of fragmegration, see James N. Rosenau, *Distant Proximities: Dynamics Beyond Globalization* (Princeton, NJ: Princeton University Press, 2003), Chap. 3.

16 J. David Singer, "The Levels-of-Analysis Problem in International Relations," *World Politics*, Vol. XIV (October 1961), pp. 77–92.

17 See, for example, J. C. Alexander *et al.* (eds.), *The Micro–Macro Link* (Berkeley, CA: University of California Press, 1987), and K. D. Knorr-Cetina and A. V. Cicourel (eds.), *Advances in Social Theory and Methodology: Toward an Integration of Micro- and Macro-Sociologies* (Boston, MA: Routledge & Kegan Paul, 1981).

18 In my *Distant Proximities: Dynamics Beyond Globalization* I confronted the micro–macro puzzle directly and may have even made some progress in resolving it, but there remains a long way to go before clarity is achieved.

19 Jan Art Scholte, *Globalization: A Critical Introduction* (New York: St. Martin's Press, 2000), pp. 66–67.

20 Wolfgang H. Reinicke, "The Other World Wide Web: Global Public Policy Networks," *Foreign Policy* (Winter 1999–2000), p. 45.

21 Scholte, *Globalization*, p. 86.

22 *ITU Internet Reports 2004: The Portable Internet*. Geneva; ITU, 2004 (http://www.itu.int/osg/spu/publications/portableinternet/ExecSummFinal2.pdf).

23 John Markoff, "Tiniest Circuits Hold Prospect of Explosive Computer Speeds," *New York Times*, July 16, 1999, p. A1.

24 Torch Books (Simon & Schuster), 1992.

7 The birth of a political scientist

1 Originally published in *PROD*, Vol. 3 (January 1960), pp. 19–21. That journal was later renamed *American Behavioral Scientist*, and the article is reprinted here with permission from Sage Publications.

8 Intellectual identity and the study of international relations, or coming to terms with mathematics as a tool of inquiry

1 This chapter was originally published in *Mathematical Models in International Relations*, Dina A. Zinnes and John V. Gillespie (eds.), pp. 3–9, Copyright © 1976 by Praeger Publishers, Inc. Reproduced by permission of Greenwood Publishing Group, Inc., Westport, CT.

9 Courage versus caution: a dialogue on entering and prospering in IR

1 This chapter, co-authored with Ersel Aydinli, was originally published in the *International Studies Review*, Vol. 6 (2004), pp. 511–26 and is reprinted here with permission from Blackwell Publishing.

2 *Distant Proximities: Dynamics Beyond Globalization* (Princeton, NJ: Princeton University Press, 2003).

3 Graham T. Allison, *Essence of Decision: Explaining the Cuban Missile Crisis* (Boston, MA: Little, Brown, 1971).

4 James N. Rosenau, *Turbulence in World Politics: A Theory of Change and Continuity* (Princeton, NJ: Princeton University Press, 1990).

5 James N. Rosenau, "Pre-Theories and Theories of Foreign Policy," in R. Barry Farrell (ed.), *Approaches to Comparative and International Politics* (Evanston, IL: Northwestern University Press, 1966), pp. 27–92.

6 James N. Rosenau, *Along the Domestic–Foreign Frontier: Exploring Governance in a Turbulent World* (Cambridge: Cambridge University Press, 1997).

7 Ersel Aydinli and J. Mathews, "Are the Core and Periphery Irreconcilable? The Curious World of Publishing in Contemporary International Relations," *International Studies Perspectives*, Vol. 1, pp. 289–303.

8 James N. Rosenau (ed.), *International Politics and Foreign Policy: A Reader in Research and Theory* (New York: Free Press, 1961; revised edition, 1969).

9 Rosenau, *Distant Proximities*, p. 420.

10 *Ibid.*, p. 407.

11 *Ibid.*, p. 418.

12 James N. Rosenau (ed.), *Linkage Politics: Essays on the Convergence of National and International Systems* (New York: Free Press, 1969).

13 M. Mitchell Waldrop, *Complexity: The Emerging Science at the Edge of Order and Chaos* (New York: Simon and Schuster, 1993).

14 Rosenau, *Distant Proximities*, p. 413.

15 James N. Rosenau, "The Adaptation of the United Nations in a Turbulent World," in Ramesh Thakur (ed.), *The United Nations at Fifty: Retrospect and Prospect* (Dunedin: University of Otago Press, 1996) pp. 229–40.

16 Heidi Hobbs (ed.), *Pondering Postinternationalism* (Albany, NY: State University of New York Press, 2000).

17 James N. Rosenau, David A. Earnest, Yale W. Ferguson, and Ole R. Holsti, *On the Cutting Edge of Globalization: An Inquiry into American Elites* (Boulder, CO: Rowman & Littlefield, 2005).

10 Comparison is a state of mind

1 This chapter was originally published in *Studies in Comparative Communism* (now called *Communist and Post-Communist Studies*), Vol. III (Spring/Summer 1975), pp. 57–61, and is reprinted here by permission.

2 I edited both books, which together contain 32 papers by ICFP members written expressly for meetings of the ICFP. The two books are *Comparing Foreign Policies: Theories, Findings and Methods* (New York: Wiley, 1974) and *In Search of Global Patterns* (New York: Free Press, 1976).

3 Patrick J. McGowan (ed.), *Sage Yearbook of Foreign Policy Studies* (Beverly Hills, CA: Sage, Vol. I, 1973; Vol. II, 1974).

4 James N. Rosenau, Philip M. Burgess, and Charles F. Hermann, "The Adaptation of Foreign Policy Research: A Case Study of an Anti-Case Study Project," *International Studies Quarterly*, Vol. 17 (March 1973), pp. 119–144.

11 CFP and IPE: the anomaly of mutual boredom

1 This chapter was originally published as "CFP and IPE: The Anomaly of Mutual Boredom," Copyright 1988 from *International Interactions*, Vol. 14, No. 1. Reproduced by permission of Taylor and Francis, Inc., http://www.tandf.co.uk/journals

2 For an exception here, see Harvey Starr, "Rosenau, Pre-Theories and the Evolution of the Comparative Study of Foreign Policy," a paper presented at the Annual Meeting of the International Studies Association, Anaheim, 1986.

3 For an insight into how far the CFP field has progressed in these respects, see Charles F. Hermann, Charles W. Kegley, Jr., and James N. Rosenau (eds.), *New Directions in the Study of Foreign Policy* (Boston, MA: Allen & Unwin, 1987).

4 For one effort along this line, see Bahgat Korany, "The Take-Off of Third World Studies? The Case of Foreign Policy," *World Politics*, Vol. XXVI (1983), pp. 465–87.

5 A discussion of this problem can be found in James N. Rosenau, "Authority Structures in North–South Relations: A Search for Conceptual Uniformity," a paper presented at the Annual Meeting of the American Political Science Association, New Orleans, 1985.

6 Maurice A. East, Stephen A. Salmore, and Charles F. Hermann, (eds.), *Why Nations Act: Theoretical Perspectives for Comparative Foreign Policy Studies* (Beverly Hills, CA: Sage, 1978).

7 See, for example, Richard C. Snyder, Henry Bruck, and Burton M. Sapin, *Decision-Making as an Approach to the Study of International Politics* (Princeton, NJ: Organizational Behavior Section, Princeton University, 1954).

8 I. M. Destler, *Making Foreign Economic Policy* (Washington, DC: The Brookings Institution, 1980).

9 See, for example, Charles W. Kegley and Eugene Wittkopf, *American Foreign Policy: Pattern and Process*, 2nd ed. (New York: St. Martin's Press, 1982).

10 Starr, "Rosenau, Pre-Theories and the Evolution of the Comparative Study of Foreign Policy."

11 Reproduced here as Chapter 21.

12 Starr, "Rosenau, Pre-Theories and the Evolution of the Comparative Study of Foreign Policy," p. 10.

13 Exceptions can be found in Bruce Moon, "Political Economy Approaches to Comparative Foreign Policy," a paper presented at the Conference on New Directions in the Comparative Study of Foreign Policy, Columbus, OH., 1985, and John S. Odell, *US International Monetary Policy: Markets, Power, and Ideas as Sources of Change* (Princeton, NJ: Princeton University Press, 1982).

14 Odell, *US International Monetary Policy*, pp. 39–75.

15 *Ibid.*, p. 44, italics added.

16 *Ibid.*, p. 348.

17 My rule-of-thumb for distinguishing between macro and micro phenomena is founded on the dichotomization of human interaction into that which is essentially of a face-to-face kind (micro) and that which is not (macro).

18 Again Odell is an exception here inasmuch as he explores and identifies "the circulation of policy ideas" in decision-making circles as a powerful source of change (*US International Monetary Policy*, pp. 39–75).

19 Indeed, the diversity of perspectives here includes some observers who argue that "the political science *profession* offers little more than mainstream economics to understanding international political economy." W. Ladd Hollist and James A. Caporaso, "International Political Economy Research: What Is It and Where Do We Turn For Concepts and Theory?" in W. L. Hollist and L. Tullis (eds.), *An International Political Economy* (Boulder, CO: Westview Press, 1985), p. 39 (italics in the original).

20 Robert A. Dahl, and Charles E. Lindblom, *Politics, Economics, and Welfare* (New York: Harper & Brothers, 1953).

21 Susan Strange, "What About International Relations?" in S. Strange (ed.), *Paths to International Political Economy* (London: George Allen & Unwin, 1984), pp. 183–97.
22 Harold and Margaret Sprout, *Environmental Factors in the Study of International Politics* (Princeton, NJ: Center of International Studies, Princeton University, 1956).
23 Kenneth N. Waltz, *Theory of International Politics* (Menlo Park, CA: Addison-Wesley Publishing Co., 1979).
24 Talcott Parsons, *Structure and Process in Modern Societies* (New York: Free Press, 1960).
25 See, for example, Roger Benjamin and Stephen L. Elkin (eds.), *The Democratic State* (Lawrence, KS: University Press of Kansas, 1985); W. Ladd Hollist and LaMond Tullis (eds.), *An International Political Economy* (Boulder, CO: Westview Press, 1985); Martin Staniland, *What Is Political Economy?* (New Haven, CT: Yale University, 1985); and Susan Strange (ed.), *Paths to International Political Economy*.

12 The theoretical imperative: unavoidable explication

1 This chapter was originally published in the *Asian Journal of Political Science*, Vol. 11 (December 2003), pp. 7–20, and is reprinted here by permission.
2 See, for example, John Urry, *Global Complexity* (Cambridge: Polity Press, 2003), and David S. Alberts and Thomas J. Czerwinski (eds.), *Complexity, Global Politics, and National Security* (Washington, DC: National Defense University, 1997). See also the next chapter in this volume.
3 James N. Rosenau, *Along the Domestic–Foreign Frontier: Exploring Governance in a Turbulent World* (Cambridge: Cambridge University Press, 1997), *passim*.
4 James N. Rosenau, *Distant Proximities: Dynamics Beyond Globalization* (Princeton, NJ: Princeton University Press, 2003), *passim*.
5 Rosenau, *Distant Proximities*, Chap. 13.
6 Serge Schmemann, "A Growing List of Foes Now Suddenly Friends," *New York Times*, October 5, 2001, p. B3.
7 Yale H. Ferguson and James N. Rosenau, "Superpowerdom Before and After September 11, 2001: A Postinternational Perspective," a paper prepared for presentation at the Annual Meeting of the International Studies Association, Portland, Oregon, February 26–March 1, 2003, p. 1. This paper was subsequently translated into French and published in *Études Internationales*, Vol. XXXV (December 2004), pp. 623–39.
8 See, for example, Alexander Wendt, *Social Theory of International Politics* (Cambridge: Cambridge University Press, 1999).
9 J. David Singer, "The Levels-of-Analysis Problem in International Relations," *World Politics*, Vol. XIV (October 1961), pp. 77–92.
10 Rosenau, *Distant Proximities*, *passim*.
11 Rosenau, *Distant Proximities*, Chap. 3.
12 I am indebted to David Earnest for the calculations that resulted in this total.
13 For an exploration of this presumption, see James N. Rosenau, "Many Globalizations, One International Relations," *Globalizations*, Vol. 1, No. 1 (September 2004), pp. 1–8, reproduced here as Chapter 6 of Volume II.

13 Many damn things simultaneously – at least for a while: complexity theory and world affairs

1 This chapter was originally published in *Theoria: A Journal of Social and Political Theory*, No. 93 (December 1999). Copyright Faculty of Human and Management Sciences, University of KwaZulu-Natal, Pietermaritzburg.
2 For the most recent and extended formulations of the concept, see my *Along the Domestic–Foreign Frontier: Exploring Governance in a Turbulent World* (Cambridge: Cambridge University Press, 1997), Chap. 6, and *Distant Proximities: Dynamics Beyond Globalization* (Princeton, NJ: Princeton University Press, 2003), *passim*.

3 "Ontologies are not arbitrary constructions; they are the specification of the common sense of an epoch." Robert W. Cox, "Critical Political Economy," in Bjorn Hettne (ed.), *International Political Economy: Understanding Global Disorder* (London: Zed Books, 1995), p. 34.

4 For a discussion of the nature of these diverse "scapes," see Arjun Appadurai, "Disjuncture and Difference in the Global Cultural Economy," *Public Culture*, Vol. 2 (1990), pp. 1–23.

5 See, for example, John L. Gaddis, "International Relations Theory and the End of the Cold War," *International Security*, Vol. 17 (Winter 1992–3), pp. 5–58.

6 Cf. Roger Lewin, *Complexity: Life at the Edge of Chaos* (New York: Macmillan Publishing Co., 1992), and M. Mitchell Waldrop, *Complexity: The Emerging Science at the Edge of Order and Chaos* (New York: Simon and Schuster, 1992).

7 John H. Holland, *Hidden Order: How Adaptation Builds Complexity* (Reading, MA: Addison-Wesley, 1995).

8 Stuart Kauffman, *At Home in the Universe: The Search for Laws of Self-Organization and Complexity* (New York: Oxford University Press, 1995).

9 For a title pointing in the opposite direction, see Kevin Kelly, *Out of Control: The New Biology of Machines, Social Systems, and the Economic World* (New York: Addison-Wesley, 1994).

10 Jessica Lipnack and Jeffrey Stamps, *The Age of the Network: Organizing Principles for the 21st Century* (New York: Wiley, 1994), p. 48.

11 James N. Rosenau, *Turbulence in World Politics: A Theory of Change and Continuity* (Princeton, NJ: Princeton University Press, 1990).

12 High complexity and high dynamism in a system's prime parameters is the condition that defines when the system enters a period of turbulence. Cf. Rosenau, *Turbulence in World Politics*, p. 78.

13 Other single-word labels designed to suggest the contradictory tensions that pull systems toward coherence and collapse are "chaord," a label that juxtaposes the dynamics of chaos and order, and "glocalization," which points to the simultaneity of globalizing and localizing dynamics. The former designation is proposed in Dee W. Hock, "Institutions in the Age of Mindcrafting," a paper presented at the Bionomics Annual conference, San Francisco, CAI, photocopy, October 22, 1994, pp. 1–2, while the latter term is elaborately developed in Roland Robertson, "Glocalization: Time-Space and Homogeneity-Heterogeneity," in Mike Featherstone, Scott Lash, and Roland Robertson (eds.), *Global Modernities* (Thousand Oaks, CA: Sage, 1995), pp. 25–44. I prefer the term "fragmegration" because it does not imply a territorial scale and broadens the focus to include tensions at work in organizations as well as those that pervade communities.

14 As one complexity theorist put it, referring to self-organization as a natural property of complex genetic systems, "There is 'order for free' out there." Stuart Kauffman, quoted in Lewin, *Complexity*, p. 25. For a cogent and extensive analysis of the concept, see Louise K. Comfort, "Self-Organization in complex Systems," *Journal of Public Administration Research and Theory*, Vol. 4 (July 1994), pp. 393–410.

15 Lewin, *Complexity*, p. 192.

16 Holland, *Hidden Order*, p. 93.

17 The notion of physiological constraints setting adaptive limits is developed in W. Ross Ashby, *Design for a Brain*, 2nd ed. (New York: Wiley, 1960), p. 58, whereas the substitution of acceptable limits in the case of human systems is developed in James N. Rosenau, *The Study of Political Adaptation* (London: Frances Pinter Publishers, 1981), pp. 31–40.

18 For a full elaboration of this conception of adaptation, see Rosenau, *The Study of Political Adaptation*, Chap. 4.

19 Lewin, *Complexity*, p. 19.

20 For an extensive account that traces the end of apartheid back to Mandela's links to

South African President F. W. de Klerk while he was still in prison, see Allister Sparks, "The Secret Revolution," *The New Yorker*, April 11, 1994, pp. 56–78.

21 R. David Smith, "The Inapplicability Principle: What Chaos Means for Social Science," *Behavioral Science*, Vol. 40 (1995), p. 22.

22 Holland, *Hidden Order*, p. 98.

23 For the use of this phrase, see Smith, "The Inapplicability Principle," p. 30.

24 Cf. Murray Gell-Mann, *The Quark and the Jaguar* (New York: W. H. Freeman, 1994), p. 345.

25 James N. Gardner, "Mastering Chaos at History's Frontier: The Geopolitics of Complexity," *Complexity*, Vol. 3, No. 2, p. 31 (italics in the original).

26 Holland, *Hidden Order*, p. 15.

27 Stephen Guastello, *Chaos, Catastrophe, and Human Affairs: Application of Nonlinear Dynamics to Work, Organizations, and Social Evolution* (Mahwah, NJ: Lawrence Erlbaum Associates, 1995), p. 1.

28 Holland, *Hidden Order*, p. 168.

29 For an eye-opening sense of how rapidly the social sciences have advanced in recent years, consider that it was only several decades ago that, for the first time, a gifted analyst arrested systematic attention to the dynamics of informal patterns of organizations, an insight that is today taken for granted. Cf. Herbert A. Simon, *Administrative Behavior: A Study of Decision-Making Behavior in Administrative Organization* (New York: The Macmillan Co., 1945).

30 Michael Shermer, "The Crooked Timber of History," *Complexity*, Vol. 2, No. 6 (1997), pp. 23–9.

31 I owe the notion of "staggered" sequences to a paper by Heather Freeman in a graduate seminar at the George Washington University.

14 Muddling, meddling, and modeling: alternative approaches to the study of world politics in an era of rapid change

1 *Millennium: Journal of International Studies*. Sections of this chapter first appeared in *Millenium*, Vol. 8, No. 2 (1979), pp. 499–523, and are reproduced here with substantial alterations with the permission of the publisher.

2 For a succinct review of a variety of efforts to employ the meddling approach, see Kal J. Holsti, "A New International Politics? Diplomacy in Complex Interdependence," *International Organization*, Vol. 32 (Spring 1978), pp. 513–30.

3 For example, see J. R. Handelman, J. A. Vasquez, M. K. O'Leary, and W. D. Coplin, "Color It Morgenthau: A Data-Based Assessment of Quantitative International Relations Research," a paper presented to the Annual Meeting of the International Studies Association (Syracuse, NJ: Syracuse University Press, 1973).

4 Examples here are John W. Burton, *World Society* (London: Cambridge University Press, 1972), and Richard A. Falk, *A Study of Future Worlds* (New York: Free Press, 1975).

5 For a useful discussion of this point, see Jeffrey Harrod, "International Relations, Perceptions and Neo-Realism," *The Year Book of World Affairs*, Vol. 31 (1977), pp. 289–305.

6 For an analysis that emphasizes such a bias and argues that the changes are superficial in comparison to the continuities of world politics, see F. S. Northedge, "Transnationalism: The American Illusion," *Millennium*, Vol. 5 (Spring 1976), pp. 21–7.

7 For some systematic attempts to assess the degree of structural change in the global system, see P. J. Katzenstein, "International Interdependence: Some Long-Term Trends and Recent Changes," *International Organization*, Vol. 29 (Autumn 1975), pp. 1020–34; R. R. Kaufman, H. I. Chernotsky, and D. S. Geller, "A Preliminary Test of the Theory of Dependency," *Comparative Politics*, Vol. 7 (April 1975), pp. 303–31; and R. Rosecrance, A. Alexandroff, W. Koehler, J. Kroll, S. Laqueur, and J. Stocker, "Whither Independence?" *International Organization*, Vol. 31 (Summer 1975), pp. 425–72.

8 Two observers, for example, note that the study of "international relations is an American invention dating from the time after World War I when the American intellectual community discovered the world. Like most American essays in regard to the world, it has been enthusiastic, well-financed, faddist, nationally-oriented, and creating more problems than it solves." Fred Warner Neal and Bruce D. Hamlett, "The Never-Never Land of International Relations," *International Studies Quarterly*, Vol. 13 (September 1969), p. 283.

9 Robert L. Heilbronner, "Inescapable Marx," *The New York Review of Books*, Vol. XXV (June 29, 1978), p. 34.

10 *Ibid.*, p. 35.

11 That the ensuing analysis deals only with aggregative processes is not meant to imply that there need be no concern about the causal flows from macro to micro units. On the contrary, as noted elsewhere, the processes of disaggregation are also central to any paradigm-building effort. Aggregative and disaggregative processes, however, differ in certain key respects and I focus only on the former. For an initial consideration of the latter, see James N. Rosenau, "The Tourist and the Terrorist: Two Extremes on a Transnational Continuum," a paper presented at the Workshop on Transnational and Transgovernmental Relations and International Outcomes, European Consortium for Political Research, Grenoble, France, April 8, 1978, and subsequently translated into French and published in *Etudes Internationales*, Vol. X (June 1979), pp. 219–52.

12 For a useful elaboration of this point, see R. L. Paarlberg, "Domesticating Global Management," *Foreign Affairs*, Vol. 54 (April 1976), pp. 563–77.

13 For an initial effort to probe how the concept of authority might be used as a building block for a new paradigm, see James N. Rosenau, "International Studies in a Transnational World," *Millennium*, Vol. 5 (Spring 1976), pp. 1–20. An initial formulation of the role concept in this context can be found in my "The Tourist and the Terrorist" paper (see Note 11).

14 For a cogent analysis that notes the difficulties inherent in applying the concept of authority to the non-legal structures that sustain international phenomena, see Harry Eckstein, "Authority Patterns: A Structural Basis for Political Inquiry," *American Political Science Review*, Vol. 67 (December 1973), pp. 1142–61.

15 Territorial affiliations and emergent roles: the shifting nature of identity in a globalizing world

1 This chapter was originally presented at the 5th Pan-European International Relations Conference, The Hague, September 11, 2004.

2 "Parts of US–Canadian Border Disappear in Brush as Maintenance Money Is Tight," *New York Times*, April 4, 2004, p. 21.

3 James N. Rosenau, "The Complexities and Contradictions of Globalization," *Current History* (November 1997), pp. 360–64.

4 This is a recurrent theme in James N. Rosenau, *Distant Proximities: Dynamics Beyond Globalization* (Princeton, NJ: Princeton University Press, 2003).

5 Rosenau, *Distant Proximities*, Chap. 1.

6 Exceptions here are those persons whose families were always on the move from the time of birth, such as children of the military or diplomats. For these people territoriality in the sense of birth and childhood have no meaning at all.

7 Charles Taylor, *Sources of the Self: The Making of the Modern Identity* (Cambridge, MA: Harvard University Press, 1989), p. 27.

8 Rosenau, *Distant Proximities*, Chaps. 4–8.

9 For a discussion of movement among the worlds, see Rosenau, *Distant Proximities*, Chap. 8.

16 Capabilities and control in an interdependent world

1 This chapter was originally published in *International Security*, 1:2 (Fall, 1976), pp. 32–49. © 1976 by the President and Fellows of Harvard College and the Massachusetts Institute of Technology. Reprinted here by permission.

2 My convictions in this regard were first developed in my essay, *Calculated Control as a Unifying Concept in the Study of International Politics and Foreign Policy* (Princeton, NJ: Center of International Studies, Princeton University, 1963).

3 I understand this is the case in all languages.

4 For example, see James W. Howe, "Power in the Third World," *Journal of International Affairs*, Vol. 29 (Fall 1975), pp. 113–28; and Susan Strange, "What Is Economic Power, and Who Has It?" *International Journal*, Vol. 30 (Spring 1975), pp. 207–24.

5 For sophisticated analyses of recent changes on the world scene that nevertheless fail to break away from the tendency to rank possessed attributes and resources, see Seyom Brown, "The Changing Essence of Power," *Foreign Affairs*, Vol. 51 (January 1973), pp. 286–99; and Stanley Hoffmann, "Notes on the Elusiveness of Modern Power," *International Journal*, Vol. 30 (Spring 1975), pp. 183–206. A somewhat more successful effort to probe systematically the relational consequences of relative changes in the possessed qualities of states can be found in Klaus Knorr, *The Power of Nations: The Political Economy of International Relations* (New York: Basic Books, 1975).

6 For elaboration of this breakdown, see James N. Rosenau, *The Scientific Study of Foreign Policy* (New York: Free Press, 1971), pp. 231–36.

7 This line of reasoning was later developed more elaborately in Edward Friedland, Paul Seaburg, and Aaron Wildavsky, *The Great Détente Disaster: Oil and the Decline of American Foreign Policy* (New York: Basic Books, 1975), and Robert W. Tucker, "Oil: The Issue of American Intervention," *Commentary*, Vol. 57 (January 1975), pp. 21–31.

8 For a cogent discussion of this point, see Robert L. Paarlberg, "Domesticating Global Management," *Foreign Affairs*, Vol. 54 (April 1976), pp. 563–76.

9 See Burton M. Sapin and Richard C. Snyder, *The Role of the Military in American Foreign Policy* (Garden City, NY: Doubleday & Co., 1954).

10 For a useful essay relevant to this point, see Allan W. Lerner, *Experts, Politicians, and Decisionmaking in the Technological Society* (Morristown, NJ: General Learning Press, 1975).

11 Much the same line of reasoning can be applied to the degree to which governments are authoritarian. This attribute can greatly facilitate or hinder the mobilization of domestic support, with authoritarian regimes having a greater capacity in this regard than democratic ones (assuming comparable degrees of internal cohesion). Presumably this relative advantage has widened as the advent of interdependence issues has increased the need for governments to win acceptance and compliance from the relevant subgroups to back up their positions on such matters. If the assumption of internal cohesiveness is relaxed, however, this attribute of political structure emerges more as an intervening than an independent variable and is thus not singled out here as a capability that has been rendered especially compelling by the growth of interdependence.

12 For a useful elaboration of this point as it applies to the United States, see Atlantic Council, "Decision-Making in an Interdependent World," *Atlantic Community Quarterly*, Vol. 13 (Summer 1975), pp. 139–57.

13 James N. Rosenau, *The Adaptation of National Societies: A Theory of Political Behavior and Its Transformations* (New York: McCaleb-Seiler, 1970).

14 For some stimulating discussions relevant to this possibility, see Marvin E. Wolfgang (ed.), "Adjusting to Scarcity," *The Annals*, Vol. 420 (July 1975), pp. 1–124.

17 The skill revolution as a dynamic process

1 This chapter was adapted from a paper originally presented at the Annual Conference of the Future Society, Washington, July 30, 2004.
2 Expressing skepticism about the future of her community in South Africa, quoted in Michael Wines and Sharon LaFraniere, "Decade of Democracy Fills Gaps in South Africa," *New York Times*, April 26, 2004, p. A1.
3 Quoted in Chadwick F. Alger, "Perceiving, Analyzing, and Coping with the Local–Global Nexus," *International Social Science Journal*, Vol. 117 (August 1988), p. 338.
4 For the most recent iteration of this formulation, see James N. Rosenau, *Distant Proximities: Dynamics Beyond Globalization* (Princeton, NJ: Princeton University Press, 2003), Chap. 10.
5 For data on enrollments of men and women between 1960 and 1985 at the elementary, secondary, and university levels that trace growth for every country in the world except North Korea, see James N. Rosenau, *Turbulence in World Politics: A Theory of Change and Continuity* (Princeton, NJ: Princeton University Press, 1990), pp. 454–60.
6 Arjun Appadurai, *Modernity at Large: Cultural Dimensions of Globalization* (Minneapolis, MN: University of Minnesota Press, 1996.), p. 7.
7 See, for example, Pippa Norris (ed.), *Critical Citizens: Global Support for Democratic Government* (New York: Oxford University Press, 1999).

18 Generational change and Internet literacy

1 This chapter was originally presented at the Annual Meeting of the American Political Science Association, Boston, August 29, 2002.
2 Quoted in Tamar Lewin, "Children's Computer Use Grows, but Gaps Persist, Study Says," *New York Times*, January 22, 2001, p. All.
3 *Ibid.*
4 George Packer, quoted in Thomas L. Friedman, "Global Village Idiocy," *New York Times*, May 12, 2002, Sec. 4, p. 15.
5 " 'Many to many' communications is the paradigm that best represents the character of communication on the Internet. Personal communication, face to face, by phone, or by fax is 'one to one' while mass media is characterized by 'one to many'. 'Many to many' communication includes the characteristics of 'one to one' as well as 'one to many', while at the same time allowing 'many to many' communications." Michael Dahan, "Internet Usage in the Middle East: Some Political and Social Implications" (http://www.mevic.org/papers/net-mena.html), p. 17, n. 6.
6 There are considerable data indicating people in the oldest age groups are increasingly mastering the rudimentary uses of the Internet. Ireland, for example, had a higher proportion (16 percent) of Internet users in the 12–17 year age group in 2001 than did any other country, but at the same time data for that country show that "the information society is not being totally confined to younger surfers": the same survey found that "Internet usage [grew] rapidly amongst 'grey' users . . ." (http:www.acnielsen.com/news/European/ie/2001/20010502.htm). In 1997, similar growth patterns were uncovered for older age groups in the United States, with a major reason for the growth being a desire "to keep in touch with their grandchildren and to learn the same things their grandchildren were learning about in regard to computers and the Internet." Joyce Philbeck, "Seniors and the Internet," *Cybersociology*, No. 2 (November 20, 1997), p. 1 (http://www.cybersociology.com). Likewise, in the United Kingdom it was found that "many elderly users are encouraged to use the net by younger relatives, and then discover they have more time available for web browsing." "UK Internet Usage Surges," *BBC News*, August 20, 2001 (http://news.bbc.co.uk/hi/english/business/newsid_1500000/1500668.stm). On the other hand, quite the opposite pattern was uncovered in a 1998 Canadian survey, with 47 percent of the 35 to 54 age group being

most likely to use the Internet and the proportion of those under 35 being nearly as high (45 percent), while the figures for the 55 to 64 and 65 and over groups were, respectively, 27 and 7 percent (http://www.statcan.ca/Daily/English/900715/ d990715a.htm). I am grateful to David Earnest, who is less than half my age, for the ten minutes of his time he devoted to helping me locate these Internet sites and those in subsequent Notes.

7 In preparing to write this chapter I initially searched the world wide web by using the key word "Internet Usage," a heading that yielded 1,194,032 citations. Stunned, I then used what I assumed would be a more manageable key phrase, "Age group Internet users," only to come upon 117,411 citations.

8 Diana Saco, *Cybering Democracy: Public Space and The Internet* (Minneapolis, MN: University of Minnesota Press, 2002), p. 41.

9 *Ibid.*, p. 189.

10 James N. Rosenau, *Along the Domestic–Foreign Frontier: Exploring Governance in a Turbulent World* (Cambridge University Press, 1997), Chap. 14. A considerable extension of the skill revolution hypothesis can be found in my *Distant Proximities: Dynamics Beyond Globalization* (Princeton, NJ: Princeton University Press, 2003), Chap. 10. For an empirical test of the hypothesis, see James N. Rosenau and W. Michael Fagen, "Increasingly Skillful Citizens: A New Dynamism in World Politics?" *International Studies Quarterly*, Vol. 41 (December 1997), pp. 655–86.

11 Lewin, "Children's Computer Use Grows, but Gaps Persist, Study Says," p. All.

12 It is interesting to note research findings indicative of "a significant physical alteration" linked to generational differences: "The thumbs of today's electronic-gadget generation of children have become more muscled, more dexterous and often more used than fingers. This is because modern youngsters grow up using hand-held gadgets where the devices are cupped in the hand and held firm by fingers, giving thumbs the pivotal role of pushing buttons." Those who undertook the research, "after studying hundreds of children in Beijing, Tokyo and other big cities, say today's youngsters have become the 'thumb generation.' " Alfred Lee, "Thumb Generation," *The Straits Times* (Singapore), March 25, 2002.

13 Saco, *Cybering Democracy*, p. 123.

14 For a cogent argument that "hackers" is an imprecise concept, that for hackers it is a term of respect, and that hackers are often helpful to those who turn to them for assistance, that they "possess qualities that serve the public," see Verna V. Gehring, "Do Hackers Provide a Public Service?" *Philosophy & Public Policy Quarterly*, Vol. 22 (Summer 2002), pp. 21–27 (quote from p. 25). See also Douglas Thomas, *Hacking Culture* (Minneapolis, MN: University of Minnesota Press, 2002).

15 Rosenau, *Distant Proximities*, Chap. 12.

16 http://www.bangalorenet.com/internetindia/

17 madans@planetasia.com

18 http://www.interasia.org/malasia/ramanathan.html

19 http://virtualchina.org/archive/archive/news/jun00/'/cgi-bin/adrotate/ad/cgi

20 http://www.mevic.org/papers/net-mena.html

21 http://www2.seasite.niu.edu/tagalogdiscuss/_0000070c.htm

22 http://www.dtmedia.lv/raksti/EN/EIT/200101/01010832.stm

23 http://www.thos.co.za/news/240498_sao.html

24 http://www.nso.gov.mt/cosnews/news02/news02102.htm

25 Michel Marriott, "Not Just Closing a Divide, but Leaping It," *New York Times*, July 18, 2002, p. E1.

26 One database lists 4,211 Internet cafés in 149 countries (http://www.cybercafe.com/). In China, for example, more than 200,000 cybercafes are spread around the country. Erik Eckholm, "Taboo Surfing . . . And Click Here for China," *New York Times*, August 4, 2002, sec. 4, p. 5.

27 While there are problems operationalizing JNDs as instruments of measurement, they

are metaphorically useful as a means of tracing phenomena marked by change. See James N. Rosenau, *Turbulence in World Politics: A Theory of Change and Continuity* (Princeton, NJ: Princeton University Press, 1990), pp. 32–3.

28 John Schwartz, "In the Tech Meccas, Masses of People, or 'Smart Mobs,' Are Keeping in Touch Through Wireless Devices," *New York Times*, July 22, 2002, p. C4, an article anticipating publication of a book by Howard Rheingold, *Smart Mobs: The Next Social Revolution* (New York: Perseus Publishing, 2002).

29 *Ibid.*

30 Jennifer 8 Lee, "Trying to Elude the Google Grasp," *New York Times*, July 25, 2002, p. E1.

31 James N. Rosenau, "The Information Revolution: Both Powerful and Neutral," in Thomas E. Copeland (ed.), *The Information Revolution and National Security* (Carlisle, PA: Strategic Studies Institute, 2000), pp. 9–27.

32 Friedman, "Global Village Idiocy." The Internet has also enabled student groups in the Middle East to launch and broaden boycotts of American goods. See Neil MacFarquhar, "An Anti-American Boycott is Growing in the Arab World," *New York Times*, May 10, 2002, p. A1.

33 For data affirming that more than a trivial number of Muslims are independent in thought and action, see Dahan, "Internet Usage in the Middle East."

19 Pre-theories and theories of foreign policy

1 This chapter was originally published in R. Barry Farrell (ed.), *Approaches to Comparative and International Politics* (Evanston, IL: Northwestern University Press, 1966), pp. 27–92, and is reprinted here by permission.

2 A third shortcoming, so obvious that it requires only brief identification, is of an organizational nature: namely, the discipline of political science is at present organized in such a way that the external behavior of national political systems does not fall within the purview of scholars who are interested in the construction of general theories. Neither group who might be expected to theorize about foreign policy – those in comparative politics and those in international politics – is drawn by conceptual necessity to find a theoretical home for the external behavior of societies. Students of comparative politics focus primarily on national political systems and the interaction processes that occur *within* them. Once a pattern of interaction moves outside a national system, therefore, the comparative politics specialist tends to lose interest in it. Of primary concern to students of international politics, on the other hand, are the processes of interaction that occur *among* national systems. Consequently, the international politics specialist tends to take internal influences on external behavior for granted and to become interested in the patterns generated by national systems only after they have crossed over into the international realm. Foreign policy phenomena, in short, are the unwanted stepchildren of political systems. They serve as outputs for one type of system and as inputs for another, but they do not constitute actions which both begin and culminate in any system that is of interest to present-day political theorists. Hence, notwithstanding their intense relevance to students of practical policy-making problems, foreign policy phenomena have been neglected by theoreticians and relegated to the residual category of systems theory known as "boundary problems." The one exception to this pattern is those theoreticians for whom the boundary between national and international systems is the core of their concern, i.e. those who specialize in the processes of supranational integration.

3 Briefly, by pre-theory is meant both an early step toward explanation of specific empirical events and a general orientation toward all events, a point of view or philosophy about the way the world is. Ideally pre-theories would be limited to the former meaning, but this requires that a field be in general agreement about the "proper" orientation toward its subject matter, a situation which the field of foreign policy research is far from even approximating.

4 A level of analysis is distinguished by the units in terms of which behavior is explained, whereas a philosophy of analysis pertains to how the units are interrelated at a given level. The same behavior, therefore, can be analyzed both at several levels and in several ways at the same level. Consider the act of blushing. This can be explained both physiologically and psychologically, but S-R and Lewinian psychologists would offer different explanations of what caused the blush (as there might, for all the author knows, be sharp differences among the physiologists). Likewise, a presidential speech at the United Nations can be explained both physiologically and politically, but some political scientists might see the behavior as the last act in a sequence fostered by a loose bipolar system and others would treat it as derived from the requirements of an oncoming election campaign. An even better example of different philosophies of analysis in the foreign policy field is provided by the role accorded to motivational variables by students of decision-making on the one hand and by "realists" on the other. Both groups attempt to explain the external behavior of societies, but the former give high priority to the motives of officials while the latter consider the examination of motives to be "both futile and deceptive" (cf., respectively, R. C. Snyder, H. Bruck, and B. M. Sapin, *Decision-Making as an Approach to the Study of International Politics* [Princeton: Organizational Behavior Section, Foreign Policy Analysis Series, No. 3, 1954], pp. 92–117, and Hans J. Morgenthau, *Politics Among Nations*, 3d ed. [New York: Knopf, 1960], p. 6).

5 Ultimately, of course, the number of pre-theories will dwindle. A large number seems plausible at present because of the undeveloped state of the field. So little systematic knowledge about the sources of external behavior is currently available that fault cannot be found with any pre-theory on the grounds that it is discrepant with observed phenomena. However, as pre-theories make theorizing possible, and as theories then facilitate more systematic observation and more incisive comprehension of how international behavior is generated, consensuses will develop about the nature of empirical reality. Accordingly, those pre-theories which prove to be most "unreal" will be abandoned. Whether the number will ever dwindle down to a single pre-theory espoused by all analysts seems doubtful. Or at least many decades will have to elapse before the mysteries of international life are fathomed to the point where widespread agreement exists on the dynamics of external behavior. More likely is a long-run future in which knowledge of empirical reality becomes sufficiently extensive to reduce the field to several major schools of thought.

6 Suffice it to note that the potency of a systemic variable is considered to vary inversely with the size of a country (there being greater resources available to larger countries, and thus lesser dependence on the international system than is the case with smaller countries); that the potency of an individual factor is assumed to be greater in less developed economies (there being fewer of the restraints which bureaucracy and large-scale organization impose on more developed economies), that for the same reason a role variable is accorded greater potency on more developed economies, that a societal variable is considered to be more potent in open polities than in closed ones (there being a lesser need for officials in the latter to heed nongovernmental demands than in the former), and that for the same reason governmental variables are more potent than societal variables in closed polities than in open ones.

7 David Easton, *The Political System: An Inquiry into the State of Political Science* (New York: Knopf, 1953), pp. 129–48.

8 Gabriel A. Almond and James S. Coleman (eds.), *The Politics of Developing Areas* (Princeton, NJ: Princeton University Press), p. 7.

9 Talcott Parsons, "'Voting' and the Equilibrium of the American Political System," in Eugene Burdick and Arthur J. Brodbeck (eds.), *American Voting Behavior* (Glencoe: Free Press, 1959), p. 81.

10 Harry Eckstein, "The Concept 'Political System': A Review and Revision," a paper presented at the 1963 annual meeting of the American Political Science Association, New York City, September 4–7, 1963, p. 4. Eckstein notes (p. 3) seven additional

definitions of a political system that can be found in the literature. Rather than digress to explain the selection of one of these – or to defend the development of still another definition – in the ensuing discussion we shall henceforth use all of the above conceptions interchangeably and assume that more or less the same phenomena are involved whenever reference is made to the authoritative allocation of values, the quest to attain legitimately determined goals, and the mobilization of support on behalf of positively sanctioned goals.

11 This incident was reported to the author by a colleague who conducted interviews in Colombia in August 1963.

12 John D. Montgomery, *The Politics of Foreign Aid* (New York: Praeger, 1962), p. 136.

13 *The New York Times*, November 27, 1961.

14 Fred W. Riggs, "The Theory of Developing Polities," *World Politics*, XVI (October 1963), p. 171.

15 Cf. US Congress, Senate, *Activities of Nondiplomatic Representatives of Foreign Principals in the United States* (Washington, DC: Hearings before the Committee on Foreign Relations, 1963), Vols. 1–12, pp. 1–782.

16 Richard E. Neustadt, *Presidential Power: The Politics of Leadership* (New York: Wiley, 1960), p. 7.

17 Philip E. Mosely, "Research on Foreign Policy," in Brookings Dedication Lectures, *Research for Public Policy* (Washington, DC: Brookings, 1961), p. 50.

18 See, for example, Chadwick F. Alger, "Comparison of Intranational and International Politics," *American Political Science Review*, LVII (June 1963), pp. 406–19; George F. Kennan, *American Diplomacy 1900–1950* (Chicago. IL: University of Chicago Press, 1951), p. 99; and Otto Klineberg, "Intergroup Relations and International Relations," in Muzafer Sherif (ed.), *Intergroup Relations and Leadership: Approaches and Research in Industrial, Ethnic, Cultural, and Political Areas* (New York: Wiley, 1962), pp. 174–6.

19 Harold and Margaret Sprout, *Foundations of International Politics* (Princeton, NJ: Van Nostrand, 1962), p. 183. Another technique for preserving the distinction, while at the same time seeming to account for the many phenomena which the distinction obfuscates, is that of moving back and forth between different levels of analysis. By stressing a readiness to analyze international events at the international level and to examine national phenomena at the national level, one can deceive oneself into believing that no sequence of interaction can go unnoticed or unexplained. Wilbur Schramm, for example, recognizes that "the national system is made up of component systems and itself belongs to a partly developed world system," but he nevertheless avoids reconceptualization and preserves the national–international distinction by reasoning that "in order to deal effectively with a system of any magnitude it is sometimes necessary to shift the level of analysis from one level to another – up and down the scale – without losing trace of what units are interacting on the particular level which is being examined" ("Communication Development and the Development Process," in Lucian W. Pye [ed.], *Communications and Political Development* [Princeton, NJ: Princeton University Press, 1963], p. 31). This procedure, however, is not sufficient to account for the breakdown of the national–international distinction. The readiness to shift back and forth between levels only serves to maintain the premise that a clear-cut differentiation can be made between them. Such a procedure is thus not likely to result in the uncovering, much less the probing, of the growing number of phenomena that occur at the unconceptualized level which fuses the national and international ones. For a general discussion of the problem of shifting the focus of analysis from one level to another, see Odd Ramsoy, *Social Groups as System and Subsystem* (New York: Free Press, 1963).

20 A noteworthy exception to this incompatibility is an undated collaborative paper, "National Political Systems and International Politics: Notes on the Need for Research," written by Harry Eckstein and Harold Sprout for the Center of International Studies of Princeton University. Even this effort, however, failed to avoid the dilemmas of the national–international distinction. Not only is the latter explicitly cited

as the basis of the paper, but, largely as the result of adhering to it, the paper is really two papers, and the reader can readily discern which parts were written by the comparative politics specialist (Eckstein) and which by the specialist in international politics (Sprout).

21 This distinction between the two fields is clearly set forth in Harold and Margaret Sprout, *Man-Milieu Relationship Hypotheses in the Context of International Politics* (Princeton, NJ: Center of International Studies, 1956), p. 75.

22 For an illuminating discussion of this point, see Harry Eckstein, "Toward the Theoretical Study of Internal War," in Harry Eckstein (ed.), *Internal War: Basic Problems and Approaches* (New York: Free Press, 1964), pp. 1–7.

23 Cf. David Easton, "The Perception of Authority and Political Change," in Carl J. Friedrich (ed.), *Authority* (Cambridge, MA: Harvard University Press, 1958), pp. 179–81.

24 This designation is non-evaluative. Although the word "penetrated" is sometimes used in connection with subversive activities, nothing invidious is intended by its use here. As will be seen, a penetrated system can be authoritarian or democratic, dynamic or static, modern or primitive. Indeed, in the ensuing discussion penetrative processes are conceived to be legitimate and authoritative for the society in which they unfold.

25 For another even more elaborate systemic creation that was at least partly designed to compensate for the weaknesses of the national–international distinction, see Fred W. Riggs, "International Relations as a Prismatic System," *World Politics*, XIV (October 1961), pp. 144–81.

26 While no other type of penetrated system can be more all-encompassing than a postwar occupation, it does not necessarily follow that all military occupations constitute penetrated systems. France during the German occupation of 1941–44, for example, would not be classified as a penetrated system, since the French did not accept German participation in their affairs as legitimate and therefore resisted being mobilized in support of values that the Germans had allocated for them. For other dimensions of the role played by military personnel in penetrated systems, see George Stambuck, *American Military Forces Abroad: Their Impact on the Western State System* (Columbus, OH: Ohio State University Press, 1963).

27 The number of these registered with the Department of Justice under provisions of the Foreign Agents Registration Act had risen from approximately 160 in 1944 to nearly 500 in 1963. See US Congress, Senate, *op. cit.*, p. 10.

28 This is not to imply, however, that the presence of nonmembers in a society marked by shortages necessarily renders a penetrated system authoritarian in structure or that their participation in its politics is necessarily based on superior–subordinate relationships. As illustrated by the Skybolt and foreign aid examples, penetrated systems can operate in open societies as well as in closed ones. Likewise, as the evolution of the Alliance for Progress demonstrates, many foreign aid programs are based on functional equality between the giving and the recipient societies. To be sure, some diffusion of the values of the nonmembers is bound to occur in the penetrated society, but such values can be as variable as their bearers and thus diffusion can lead to democratic structures as readily as to authoritarian ones.

29 For a lengthier analysis of the reasons why nonmembers are attracted to participation in the allocation of values in the United States, see US Congress, Senate, *op. cit.*, p. 10.

30 Nor is it unreasonable to contend that, for the same reasons, eventually even richly endowed closed societies are bound to experience penetrative processes. It was, after all, African students who gave Moscow its first recorded riots since the Russian Revolution of 1917.

31 One exception here would be a treaty in which one signatory agrees to allow another to participate subsequently in the allocation of its values and the mobilization of support for its goals. The treaty between France and Monaco is illustrative in

this respect, as are many treaties that victors and vanquished sign after a war. Such exceptions can be regarded as the one type of penetrated system that has a formal constitution.

32 Robert A. Dahl, *Who Governs? Democracy and Power in an American City* (New Haven, CT: Yale University Press, 1961).

33 *Ibid.*, p. 175.

34 For additional evidence that "the pattern of decision-making" varies from issue-area to issue-area in local systems, see Nelson W. Polsby, *Community Power and Political Theory* (New Haven, CT: Yale University Press, 1963), pp. 113–14, 124–8.

35 Warren E. Miller and Donald E. Stokes, "Constituency Influence in Congress," *American Political Science Review*, LVII (March 1963), pp. 45–56.

36 *Ibid.*, p. 53.

37 See Douglas A. Chalmers, *The SPD: From Working Class Movement to Modern Political Party* (New Haven, CT: Yale University Press, 1964).

38 Accordingly, henceforth we shall distinguish between horizontal and vertical political systems. A horizontal system is conceived to be a set of interdependent procedures through which a geographic unit (e.g. a city, state, or nation) or a functional institution (e.g. a party, legislature, or bureaucracy) allocates values and mobilizes support in a broad range of issue-areas. A vertical system, on the other hand, is conceived to encompass a set of interdependent procedures whereby a cluster of values within an issue-area is allocated by either a single horizontal system or a fusion of horizontal systems. The number of vertical systems operative at any one time is conceived to be quite variable and dependent on the purposes of analysis.

39 The exception is Herbert J. Spiro, "Comparative Politics: A Comprehensive Approach," *American Political Science Review*, LVI (September 1962), pp. 577–95.

40 Robert A. Dahl, *Modern Political Analysis* (Englewood Cliffs, NJ: Prentice Hall, 1963).

41 Here, the exception is Aaron B. Wildavsky, "The Analysis of Issue-Contexts in the Study of Decision-Making," *Journal of Politics*, 24 (November 1962), pp. 717–32.

42 In some cases it is more accurate to say that issue-areas are treated as unconceptualized variables in the political process. In an elaborate formulation of the legislative system and process, for example, several co-authors note the importance of issue-areas by including them among the "circumstantial variables" (p. 20), which are in turn made central to the diagrammatic presentation of their scheme (p. 18). In the diagram, however, they accompany the box that houses the circumstantial variables with the parenthetic phrase, "not conceptualized." John C. Wahlke, Heinz Eulau, William Buchanan, and Leroy C. Ferguson, *The Legislative System: Explorations in Legislative Behavior* (New York: Wiley, 1962).

43 Researchers who focus on the behavior of blocs in international organizations might be considered an exception here. Through analysis of bloc voting in the United Nations, they have turned increasingly to the question of how different issues affect the cohesiveness and functioning of blocs. See, for example, Thomas Hovet, Jr., *Africa in the United Nations* (Evanston, IL: Northwestern University Press, 1963).

44 Cf. Robert K. Merton, Leonard Broom, and Leonard S. Cottrell, Jr. (eds.), *Sociology Today: Problems and Prospects* (New York: Basic Books, 1959).

45 Exceptions, of course, can be cited. Some institutions, for example, are now offering courses in the politics of disarmament and the politics of civil liberties. As a general trend, however, political science is still organized in terms of units (local, national, and international) or institutions (party, legislative, administrative, and judicial) that process all types of issues, rather than in terms of issue-areas that activate all types of units and institutions.

46 Schramm, *op. cit.*, p. 30. The author adds that "the key words are boundary and interdependent. By interdependence we mean a relationship of parts in which anything happening to one component of a system affects, no matter how slightly, the balance and relationship of the whole system. By boundary-maintaining we mean a

state in which the components are so related that it is possible to tell where the system ends and its environment begins."

47 Conversely, the structure of vertical systems can remain just as impervious to the effects of bargaining with other units as can the structure of horizontal systems. That is, the bargaining that occurs across issue-areas need not have any greater impact on the identity, motivations, and interaction patterns of the actors who conflict over the allocation of a particular set of values than, say, treaty negotiations would have on the identity, motives, and decision-making processes of the actors in the national systems that are signatories to the treaty. The resolution of the conflict in the vertical system, i.e. the way in which the values are allocated, may be affected by the intrusion of other issues, but the distinctive behavior which forms the boundaries of the system may well continue unaltered.

48 For traces of the idea that ends-means tangibility may be a central variable in the generation of issue-area differences, see Samuel P. Huntington, *The Common Defense: Strategic Programs in National Politics* (New York: Columbia University Press, 1961), pp. 242–8; and Raymond A. Bauer, Ithiel de Sola Pool, and Lewis Anthony Dexter, *American Business and Public Policy: The Politics of Foreign Trade* (New York: Atherton Press, 1963), pp. 124–6.

49 It must be emphasized that these examples are provided only for the purpose of illustrating how an issue-area typology might be developed. The classification of data in terms of the tangibility of ends and means is clearly far more complex than this exercise implies. In each instance a case might be made for classifying these particular data in one or more of the other areas.

50 Of course, if the issue-area concept is at all valid, its implications are not confined to foreign policy research. As indicated above, for example, it would seem to provide a useful way of assessing the political stability of horizontal systems. From an issue-area perspective, a stable – though not necessarily desirable – polity is one in which the boundaries of its vertical systems are insulated from each other, whereas an unstable polity would consist of processes whereby one or more issues dominate political activity within the entire system. For other possible avenues of research opened up by the issue-area concept, see my "Foreign Policy as an Issue Area," in J. N. Rosenau (ed.), *Domestic Sources of Foreign Policy* (New York: Free Press, 1967), pp. 11–50.

20 Pre-theorizing about foreign policy in a globalized world

1 This chapter was adapted from a paper presented at a meeting of the International Studies Association, Hong Kong, July 2001.

2 James N. Rosenau, "Pre-Theories and Theories of Foreign Policy," in R. B. Farrell (ed.), *Approaches to Comparative and International Politics* (Evanston, IL: Northwestern University Press, 1966), pp. 27–92; reprinted in Rosenau, *The Scientific Study of Foreign Policy* (New York: Free Press, 1971; revised and enlarged edition, Frances Pinter Publishers, Ltd., 1980).

3 See James N. Rosenau, *Turbulence in World Politics: A Theory of Change and Continuity* (Princeton, NJ: Princeton University Press, 1990), and James N. Rosenau, *Along the Domestic–Foreign Frontier: Exploring Governance In a Turbulent World* (Cambridge: Cambridge University Press, 1997).

4 An extensive elaboration of the eight dynamics is presented in my *Distant Proximities: Dynamics Beyond Globalization* (Princeton, NJ: Princeton University Press, 2003), Chaps. 3, 10, 11, and 13. A diagrammatic outline of all eight dynamics is presented in Table 6.1.

5 See, for example, James N. Rosenau and W. Michael Fagen, "Increasingly Skillful Citizens: A New Dynamism in World Politics?" *International Studies Quarterly*, Vol. 41 (December 1997), pp. 655–86.

6 See, for example, Lester M. Salamon, "The Global/Associational Revolution: The

Rise of the Third Sector on the World Scene," *Foreign Affairs*, Vol. 73 (July/August 1994), pp. 109–22.

7 James N. Rosenau, *Distant Proximities: Dynamics Beyond Globalization* (Princeton, NJ: Princeton University Press, 2003), Chap. 11.

8 Cf. David E. Sanger, "Global Realities Redefine Bush's Agenda," *New York Times*, June 11, 2001, p. A6.

21 China in a bifurcated world: competing theoretical perspectives

1 This chapter was originally published in Thomas Robinson and David Shambaugh (eds.), *Chinese Foreign Policy: Theory and Practice* (Oxford, 1995), pp. 524–51, and is reprinted here by permission of Oxford University Press.

2 Address to the United States Congress, as reported by the *Los Angeles Times*, 22 February 1990, p. A8.

3 For a discussion of the concepts and analytic skills relevant to exploring the ways in which states and governments attempt to maintain a balance between the internal and external demands upon them, see James N. Rosenau, *The Study of Political Adaptation* (London: Frances Pinter Publishers, Ltd., 1981). For a concise summary of some major internal and external demands confronting China as an adaptive actor today, see Figure 21.2.

4 Daniel Deudney and G. John Ikenberry, "Soviet Reform and the End of the Cold War: Explaining Large-Historical Change" (Xerox, 2 May 1990).

5 For a discussion of the difficulties of expanding and integrating some of the relevant expertise, see James N. Rosenau, "CFP and IPE: The Anomaly of Mutual Boredom," *International Interactions*, Vol. 14, No. 1 (1988), pp. 17–26. Or see Chapter 11 in this volume.

6 The classic statement of realism can be found in Hans J. Morgenthau, *Politics Among Nations*, 5th ed. (New York: Alfred A. Knopf, 1978).

7 For cogent discussions of cooperation and regimes as theoretical foci in the study of IR, see Robert O. Keohane, *After Hegemony: Cooperation and Discord in the World Political Economy* (Princeton, NJ: Princeton University Press, 1984), and Stephen D. Krasner (ed.), *International Regimes* (Ithaca, NY: Cornell University Press, 1983).

8 A vigorous debate over the strengths and weaknesses of the neo-realist paradigm can be found in Robert O. Keohane (ed.), *Neorealism and its Critics* (New York: Columbia University Press, 1986).

9 While the Marxist and globalist paradigms are not identical, they have enough in common to be linked together for present purposes. For elaborations of them, see Vendulka Kubalkova and Albert Cruickshank, *Marxism and International Relations* (New York: Oxford University Press, 1989), and Immanuel Wallerstein, *The Capitalist World-Economy* (Cambridge: Cambridge University Press, 1979).

10 Perhaps the most thoroughgoing articulation of a pluralist framework can be found in Robert O. Keohane and Joseph S. Nye, Jr., *Power and Interdependence: World Politics in Transition* (Boston, MA: Little, Brown & Co., 1977).

11 A full elaboration of the bifurcationist paradigm can be found in my *Turbulence in World Politics: A Theory of Change and Continuity* (Princeton, NJ: Princeton University Press, 1990). The goals, rules, and processes whereby the two worlds of world politics interact are set forth in Chap. 10.

12 One of the parameters operates at the micro-level of individuals, one functions at the macro-level of collectivities, and the third involves a mix of the two levels. The microparameter embraces the orientations and skills by which citizens of states and members of non-state organizations link themselves to the macro-world of global politics. I refer to this set of boundary constraints as the orientational or skill parameter. The macro-parameter is designated the structural parameter, and it refers to the constraints embedded in the distribution of power among and within the collect-

ivities of the global system. The mixed parameter is called the relational one; it focuses on the nature of the authority relations that prevail between individuals at the micro-level and their macro-collectivities. See Rosenau, *Turbulence in World Politics*, Chap. 5.

13 Turbulence is defined as the onset of high degrees of complexity and dynamism with respect to all three parameters. For an elaboration of this definition and the nature of high degrees of complexity and dynamism, see Rosenau, *Turbulence in World Politics*, Chap. 3. For the analysis yielding the conclusion that some 300 years have elapsed since the previous period of global turbulence, see *ibid.*, p. 10–11.

14 For a discussion of the close link between the toppling of regimes in Eastern Europe and greater analytic skills and confidence on the part of individuals and publics, see James N. Rosenau, "The Relocation of Authority in a Shrinking World: From Tiananmen Square in Beijing to the Soccer Stadium in Soweto via Parliament Square in Budapest and Wencelas Square in Prague," *Comparative Politics*, Vol. 24 (April 1992), pp. 253–72.

15 For an earlier formulation of one dimension of China's problems as an adaptive actor, see James N. Rosenau, *Beyond Imagery: The Long-Run Adaptation of Two Chinas* (Washington, D.C.: Washington Institute for Values in Public Policy, 1985).

16 It should be noted, however, that bifurcationist theory has little to offer with respect to the salience for Chinese foreign policy of the three models depicted in Table 21.2. Bifurcationism highlights the competition from and interactions with actors in the multi-centric world with which states have to contend, but neither this competition nor the interactions it fosters are conceived to alter the structures through which states conduct their internal deliberations. A bifurcationist approach posits governments as autonomous decision-making entities enhanced or constrained by bureaucratic politics, group dynamics, and individual decision-making (or any combination of the three models outlined in Table 21.2) as their histories, cultures, and socio-economic circumstances may encourage or allow.

17 A cogent discussion of the neo-medieval alternative and other possible lines of global evolution can be found in Hedley Bull, *The Anarchical Society: A Study of Order in World Politics* (New York: Columbia University Press, 1977), Chaps. 10–13.

18 *Turbulence in World Politics*, Chap. 16.

19 Cf. Robert Axelrod, *The Evolution of Cooperation* (New York: Basic Books, 1984).

20 See Joshua Goldstein and John Freeman, *Three-Way Street: Strategic Reciprocity in World Politics* (Chicago, IL: University of Chicago Press, 1990), esp. Chap. 3.

21 An account of *Actuel*'s efforts can be found in *Europe: Magazine of the European Community* (April 1990), pp. 40–41.

22 *Ibid.* p. 41.

23 *Los Angeles Times*, May 26, 1990, p. A7.

22 Toward single-country theories of foreign policy: the case of the USSR

1 This chapter was originally published in C. F. Hermann, C. W. Kegley, Jr., and J. N. Rosenau (eds.), *New Directions in the Study of Foreign Policy* (Boston, MA: Allen & Unwin, 1987), pp. 53–74, and is reprinted here with permission of the Thomson Corporation.

2 James N. Rosenau, Philip M. Burgess, and Charles F. Hermann, "The Adaptation of Foreign Policy Research: A Case Study of an Anti-Case Study Project," *International Studies Quarterly*, Vol. 17 (March 1973), pp. 119–44.

3 Harry Eckstein, "Case Study and Theory in Political Science," in Fred I. Greenstein and Nelson W. Polsby (eds.), *Handbook of Political Science*, Vol. 7 (Reading, MA: Addison-Wesley, 1975), pp. 79–138; Alexander L. George, "Case Studies and Theory Development: The Method of Structured Focused Comparison," in Paul Gordon Lauren (ed.), *Diplomacy: New Approaches in History, Theory, and Policy* (New York: Free Press), pp. 43–68;

Arend Lijphart, "Comparative Politics and the Comparative Method," *American Political Science Review*, Vol. 65, pp. 682–93; Arend Lijphart, "The Comparable-Cases Strategy in Comparative Research," *Comparative Political Studies*, Vol. 8, pp. 158–77; and Bruce M. Russett, "International Behavior Research: Case Studies and Cumulation," in Michael Haas and Henry S. Kariel (eds.), *Approaches to the Study of Political Science* (Scranton, PA: Chandler, 1970), pp. 425–43.

4 For a cogent example of how the assumption that the Soviet system is open to investigation led to a "remarkable" finding about Soviet defense spending, see William Zimmerman, "What Do Scholars Know About Soviet Foreign Policy?" *International Journal*, Vol. 37 (1982) pp. 198–219. Indeed, Zimmerman is "convinced" that the closedness of the USSR to systematic observation can be readily reduced, that the defense-expenditure finding "is but one instance where surprising knowledge about issues or topics in Soviet foreign policy can be obtained from open sources through basic research" (p. 219). For a full presentation of this particular finding, see William Zimmerman and Glenn Palmer, "Words and Deeds in Soviet Foreign Policy: The Case of Soviet Military Expenditures," *American Political Science Review*, Vol. 77 (1983), pp. 358–67. Another example of research in open sources yielding valuable and unexpected results can be found in Peter Hauslohner, "Prefects as Senators: Soviet Regional Politicians Look to Foreign Policy," *World Politics*, Vol. 33 (1981), pp. 197–253.

5 Svetlana Alliluyeva, *Twenty Letters to a Friend* (New York: Harper and Row, 1967).

6 Strobe Talbott, *The Russians and Reagan* (New York: Vintage, 1970).

7 Arkady N. Shevchenko, *Breaking with Moscow* (New York: Knopf, 1985).

8 One study found that most analysts adhere to any one of three theories organized around three different (and competing) assessments of the motives of Soviet officials – labeled the communist expansionism model, the realpolitik expansionism model, and the realpolitik defense model – all of which are long on assertions and short on falsifiable propositions and systematic evidence. Richard K. Hermann, "Competing Analyses of Soviet Foreign Policy: A Critical Review," paper delivered at the 24th Annual Meeting of the International Studies Association, Mexico City, 1983.

9 For an exception in which an expression of hopelessness over the problem of framing systematic hypotheses about Soviet politics is followed by a playfulness with the saliency of the relevant variables, see Alexander Dallin, "The Domestic Sources of Soviet Foreign Policy," in S. Bialer (ed.), *The Domestic Context of Soviet Foreign Policy* (Boulder, CO: Westview Press, 1981), esp. pp. 380–1.

10 For an illustration of the assumption that constancy marks Soviet conduct, see virtually all the essays in the symposium edited by John J. Stremlau, "Soviet Foreign Policy in an Uncertain World," *Annals*, Vol. 481 (1985), pp. 9–171.

11 For a clear articulation of this assumption, see Dallin ("The Domestic Sources of Soviet Foreign Policy"), who notes that, "of all political systems, the Soviet seems most likely and most able to override, ignore, or distort what might otherwise or elsewhere be identified as natural or secular trends" (p. 343), even as he also attributes importance to three tendencies "identifiable in the Soviet system" that have marked other states undergoing industrialization: (1) all developing systems tend to bring an increasing part of the population into passive or active political participation; (2) such systems eventually tend to produce integration at the level of the nation-state, at the expense of both parochial and internationalist preoccupations; (3) over time, developing systems tend to focus attention, resources, and operationally relevant objectives on the domestic, rather than the foreign, arena (p. 348).

12 At some point in the process of theory development, of course, the proportion of unique to generalized dynamics that obtain in the USSR, or any country, poses empirical questions that need to be explored. Possible procedures for combining the theoretical and empirical tasks are suggested below in conjunction with the presentation in Table 22.1.

13 *New York Times*, June 27, 1985, p.1.

14 For a cogent exception that explicitly takes note of the nomothetic–idiographic distinction, see Dallin, "The Domestic Sources of Soviet Foreign Policy," p. 343.

15 For a discussion of the problem of differentiating historical breakpoints, see James N. Rosenau, "Breakpoints in History: Nuclear Weapons, Oil Embargoes, and Public Skills as Parametric Shifts" (Los Angeles, CA: Institute for Transnational Studies, 1983).

16 An interesting discussion of the emerging generation of Soviet leaders is provided by Konstantin Simis, "The Gorbachev Generation," *Foreign Policy*, No. 59 (1985), pp. 3–21.

17 A compelling analysis along these lines, replete with derived hypotheses based on explicit comparisons of the Khrushchev and Brezhnev eras, can be found in Grey Hodnett, "The Pattern of Leadership Politics," in Bialer (ed.), *The Domestic Context of Soviet Foreign Policy*, pp. 87–118.

18 Paul Hollander, *Soviet and American Society: A Comparison* (Chicago, IL: University of Chicago Press, 1978), p. 10.

19 Designed only to be illustrative of what the components of a single-country theory might consist, the entries in Table 22.1 were drawn exclusively from the compilation of essays edited by Bialer. Even as such, however, they are by no means an exhaustive list of the factors cited by the various contributors to Bialer's stimulating volume (*Domestic Context of Soviet Foreign Policy*).

20 Moreover, even in those rare instances when a Western scholar or journalist is inclined to attach credence to Soviet claims, the result is more a refutation of US contentions and evidence than an effort to reconstruct the decision rules underlying Moscow's pronouncement. Serious questions have lately been raised, for example, about the integrity of the US reaction to the downing of the Korean airliner, but at the same time the basis of Soviet decision making in the situation has not been seriously probed (Murray Sayle, "KA007: A Conspiracy of Circumstance," *New York Review of Books*, 1985, pp. 44–54; Tom Wicker, "A Disintegrating Story," *New York Times*, September 3, 1985, p. 29). On the other hand, again the work of Alexander Dallin is an exception (*Black Box: KAL 007 and the Superpowers* (Berkeley, CA: University of California Press, 1985)).

21 See two chapters in *New Directions in the Study of Foreign Policy*: Charles A. Powell, Helen E. Purkitt, and James W. Dyson, "Opening the Black Box: Cognitive Processing and Optimal Choice in Foreign Policy Decision Making," pp. 203–20, and Dwain Mefford, "Analogical Reasoning and the Definition of the Situation: Back to Snyder and Forward to Artificial Intelligence for Method," pp. 221–44.

22 Charles W. Kegley, Jr., "Decision Regimes and the Comparative Study of Foreign Policy," Hermann, Kegley, and Rosenau, *New Directions in the Study of Foreign Policy*, pp. 247–68.

23 Dallin, "The Domestic Sources of Soviet Foreign Policy," p. 315.

24 It should be noted, moreover, that by refining our theoretical sensitivities to the point where our questions may seem trivial, we would be in a position to enlist the assistance of diplomats, journalists, and others with routine Soviet contacts as data gatherers. It would have been relatively easy, for example, for a journalist to ask naively at the press conferences about how the decision to hold them was made. Conceivably the query would have generated a straightforward answer. What is trivial or commonplace to political actors, in other words, can have considerable import for the analyst who has been theoretically and explicitly creative.

25 James N. Rosenau, *The Study of Political Adaptation* (New York: Nichols, 1981).

26 James N. Rosenau, "The State in an Era of Cascading Politics: Wavering Concept, Widening Competence, Withering Colossus, or Weathering Changer?" paper presented at the 13th World Congress of the International Political Science Association, 1985.

27 For other applications of the theory, see the following papers I authored: "National and

Factional Adaptation in Central America," in R. E. Feinberg (ed.), *Central America: International Dimensions of the Crisis* (New York: Holmes and Meier, 1982) pp. 239–69; "The Adaptation of Small States," in B. A. Ince, A. T. Bryan, Herb Adoo, and R. Ramsarian (eds.), *Issues in Caribbean International Relations* (Lanham, MD: University Press of America, 1983); and "Beyond Imagery: The Long-Run Adaptation of Two Chinas" (Los Angeles, CA: Institute for Transnational Studies, 1985). At the same time it should also be noted that at least one able comparativist who specializes in the Soviet Union is dubious as to the ability of the adaptation model to "help significantly in understanding" the problem of how internal and external demands get synthesized in Moscow (Dallin, *The Domestic Sources of Soviet Foreign Policy*, p. 388).

23 National interest

1 This chapter is reproduced from *INTERNATIONAL ENCYCLOPEDIA OF THE SOCIAL SCIENCES*, edited by David Sills, Robert Merton, Macmillan © 1968, Macmillan and is reprinted by permission of The Gale Group.
2 Charles A. Beard, *The Idea of National Interest: An Analytical Study in American Foreign Policy* (New York: Macmillan, 1934), pp. 22–4.
3 *Ibid.*, p. 26.
4 Hans J. Morgenthau, *Politics Among Nations: The Struggle for Power and Peace*, 2d ed., revised and enlarged (New York: Knopf, 1954), p. 9.
5 *Ibid.*, p. 528.
6 *Ibid.*, p. 8.
7 *Ibid.*, p. 5.
8 Hans J. Morgenthau, *In Defense of the National Interest: A Critical Examination of American Foreign Policy* (New York: Knopf, 1951), p. 242.
9 Richard C. Snyder, H. W. Bruck, and Burton Sapin, *Decision-Making as an Approach to the Study of International Politics* (Princeton, NJ: Princeton University, Organizational Behavior Section, 1954).
10 Edgar S. Furniss and Richard C. Snyder, *An Introduction To American Foreign Policy* (New York: Rinehart, 1955) p. 17.
11 Hans J. Morgenthau, *Politics Among Nations: The Struggle for Power and Peace.* 2d ed., revised and enlarged (New York: Knopf, 1954), p. 5.
12 Hans J. Morgenthau, *In Defense of the National Interest: A Critical Examination of American Foreign Policy* (New York: Knopf, 1951), pp. 33–4.
13 George A. Modelski, *A Theory Of Foreign Policy* (New York: Praeger, 1962), pp. 70–2.

Index of subjects

Note: in order to facilitate reading either of the two volumes comprising The Study of World Politics, *this index combines both the subject and author indices for the entries in the two volumes by using a bold face* **1** *to indicate the entries in Volume 1 and a bold face* **2** *for those in the second volume.*

accountability **1**: 243; **2**: 99, 101, 170, 173, 176, 178, 193
accounting **1**: 31
activists **1**: 12, 77, 155, 159; **2**: 100, 154
actors **1**: 9, 16, 34, 101, 110–11, 122, 124, 125, 146, 213, 224, 230; definitions of 16; supranational actors 36, 182, 217, 253; **2**: 55, 150, 163; typology of 171–2
adaptation **1**: 117, 152–3, 180, 207, 241, 244, 280n; and co-evolution 112; **2**: 45, 86, 127, 168, 193
advocacy groups **1**: 16, 23, 202; **2**: 29, 68, 100, 172, 181, 189
Affirmative Globals **1**: 136
Affirmative Locals **1**: 136–7
Afghanistan **1**: 230, 241; **2**: women of 156
Africa **1**: 163, 184, 188, 230; **2**: 18, 44, 59, 60, 85, 156, 181, 183
agent-based modeling **2**: 70
agent-structure dynamics **1**: 23, 35, 104–5
agendas, aging **2**: 19–22, 26, 27, 28, 29; global 182
aggregations, concept of **1**: 125, 126–32; levels of 138; mobilization of 126–8, 130; unintended 126–8, 130; **2**: 117
agricultural production **1**: 129, 143, 144, 188, 201; **2**: revolution in 87
AIDS **1**: 218; **2**: 43, 114, 116, 126, 123, 163
aid workers **2**: 16
Albania **2**: 172
Al-Ibrahimi Mosque **2**: 106
Algeria **1**: 29
Alienated Cynics **1**: 137, 138
Alienated Illegals **1**: 137

Alliance for Progress **1**: 273n
alliances **1**: 90, 203; **2**: 33, 74, 130
Alliluyeva, Svetlana (Stalin's daughter) **1**: 232, 278n
Allison, Graham T. **1**: 61, 261n
Along the Domestic Foreign Frontier **1**: 64, 73, 76
ambiguities, **1**: 108–10, 119, 249; **2**: 13–14, 31, 49, 51, 121, 164
American Jewish Congress **2**: 128
American Sociological Association (ASA) **1**: 21; **2**: 68
Amnesty International **1**: 70
analogies **1**: 102–3
Andean Group **2**: 136
Angola **1**: 197
anomalies **1**: 84, 86, 88, 89, 92, 108, 117; file of 15, 62, 73; **2**: 19–22, 25, 114, 165
anthropology **1**: 20; **2**: 23, 27, 64, 73, 75
apartheid **1**: 108, 113; **2**: 156, 177
Appadurai, Arjun **1**: 259n, 260n, 264n, 268n; **2**: 67
Arab states **1**: 140–1, 163, 253
arbitration boards **2**: 155
area studies **1**: 229, 232, 234–9
Argentina **2**: 40
Armageddon **2**: 105
Armenian community **2**: 59
arms control **1**: 237, 241–3
arms race **1**: 120, 126, 144
arms trade **2**: 7
Aron, Raymond **1**: 20
Arthur, Brian **1**: 110
articulated aggregations **1**: 126–8, 130
Asahara Shoko **2**: 106
ASEAN **2**: 60

Ashley, Richard K. **1**: 62; **2**: 202n
Asia **1**: 37, 163; **2**: 39, 58, 59; cities in 133
associations **2**: 29, 41, 60, 163, 172;
    volunteer 130
atmosphere **1**: 146; pollution of 218
attitudes **1**: 99
attributes, of individuals **1**: 93; of leaders
    90
Aum Shinrikyo **2**: 106
Australia **2**: 56, 58
authoritarian societies **2**: 85, 98
authority **1**: 22, 24, 29, 36, 92, 93, 104,
    132, 147, 162, 182, 186, 216;
    compliance with 145; 222, crises of 28,
    39, 40–1, 76, 77, 100, 101, 105–6, 162,
    201, 218; disaggregation of 10, 11, 12,
    13–14, 30, 36, 45, 103, 125, 143;
    structures of 32, 119, 181, 213; **2**:
    concept of 117, 118, 122, 149, 155–6,
    173, 174, 185, 188; crises of 181, 187;
    disaggregation of 2, 18, 21, 29, 96–7,
    124, 138, 157, 163, 172, 177, 183, 186,
    193; issues of 12, 17–18, 40–3, 58,
    75–8, 95, 102; moral 22, 175;
    relocation of 24, 33, 39, 52, 111, 112,
    115, 116, 118, 119, 125–7, 181, 209n;
    structures of,: 9, 10, 23, 34–5, 36, 50,
    52, 57, 60, 68, 96, 107, 114, 116, 117,
    119, 121, 123, 124, 126, 127, 147, 149,
    151–2, 169, 170, 174, 175, 176, 179,
    185, 189
autonomy **2**: 136, 174, 188

Background **2**: 72
Baghdad **2**: 25
Bak, Per **1**: 110
balance of power **1**: 100, 103, 126, 181; **2**:
    8, 33, 113, 115
Bangladesh **2**: 44
bankers **1**: 17, 31, 90, 91, 92, 130
bargaining **1**: 35, 88, 93, 145, 149, 150,
    191, 196, 275n; **2**: 123, 185
Baruch Goldstein **2**: 106
Battle of Seattle **1**: 38, 40, 203; **2**: 74–5,
    160, 194
Bauman, Zygmunt **2**: 67, 203n, 218n
Beard, Charles A. **1**: 246–7, 280n
behavioral approaches **1**: 68
Beijing **2**: 39, 40, 42
Belgrade **2**: 39
Belgium **2**: 181
belief systems **2**: 10, 85
Berlin **1**: 108, 188, 197, 196; **2**: 7, 10, 11
Bialer, S. **1**: 240, 279n

Biersteker, Thomas J. **1**: 24
bifurcation of global structures **1**: 9–10, 12,
    14–15, 18, 28–9, 39, 40–1, 76, 119, 204,
    227; and China 206–12, 218, 224, 227;
    institutionalization of 14–15; model of
    19, 77, 202, 216, 217, 224, 226, 277n;
    sources of 219; **2**: 12, 17–18, 41–3, 44,
    58, 75–8, 148, 153, 163, 172, 173, 181,
    182, 185, 186, 218n
biological diversity **1**: 43
biology **1**: 20
biotechnology **1**: 201
bipolarity, **1**: 142, 271n; **2**: 126
birth rates **1**: 129
black box **1**: 231, 232, 241, 243
bloc voting **1**: 274n
Bosnia **2**: 44, 142, 145
Boulding, Kenneth **1**: 20
boundaries **1**: 29, 108, 118, 119, 138, 148,
    204, 270n; **2**: 36, 53, 55, 56, 85, 116,
    128, 162, 169, 171, 173; **2**: broadening
    of 85–7, 133; **1**: Canadian–US 138; **1**:
    maintenance of 190, 274n; **1**: micro-
    macro 92; **1**: of horizontal systems 191;
    1: porosity of 43, 45, 110–11; **2**: 14, 32,
    50, 51, 96, 112, 116, 117, 118, 119, 151,
    187; **2**: shifting of 23, 52, 115, 121; **2**:
    sources of 56; **1**: spanning of 110, 133; **2**:
    51, 63, 65–6, 117, 127, 151, 170
Breton Woods **1**: 90
Brezhnev, L. **1**: 236, 279n
bridge-building, **1**: 65,: 68, 70, 92
Buchanan, Patrick **2**: 86
Budapest **2**: 10
Buddha **2**: 105
budget crises **2**: 39, 127
Bulgaria **1**: 83
bulletin boards **2**: 60
bumper-sticker logic **2**: 164
bureaucracies **1**: 125, 152, 203, 210, 230; **2**:
    21; **1**: politics of 26, 88, 91, 164, 204,
    237, 238, 239, 277n; **1**: public 123, 147,
    153
Burma **1**: 216, 219; **2**: 156
Burundi **2**: 60
Bush, George W. **1**: 206, 226; **2**: 9
business **1**: 201, 202, 213; **2**: alliances in
    172, 176, 181
business executives **1**: 189, 190; **2**: 16, 75,
    158, 175
butterfly effect **1**: 113; **2**: 169
by-laws **2**: 180

cabinet system **1**: 174

Canada **1**: 29, 133, 138; **2**: 11, 40, 58, 112
capabilities **1**: 143; in interdependent world 149–53; **2**: of states 118, 166; of the US 157
capital **2**: 24, 134; accumulation of 88
capitalism **1**: 9, 91, 202, 217; **2**: 28, 130
Cardinal Fiorenzo Angelini **2**: 104
Caribbean **2**: 136
cascading sequences **2**: 85
case studies **1**: 44, 88, 229, 230; **2**: 70, 79
Castells, Manuel **2**: 24, 67; **2**: 198n, 199n
Catholic Church **2**: 41, 104
causation **1**: 7, 172, 175, 213
cell phone **1**: 43, 134, 137, 155, 156
centralization **1**: 31, 38, 112, 218–19, 222, 224; **2**: 27, 83; triumph of **2**: 88–9
certainties **1**: 100, 210
Chalmers, Douglas A. **1**: 188, 274n
change **1**: 3, 7, 11–12, 28, 35, 37–8, 39, 43, **1**: 45, 61, 70–1, 73–5, 98, 102–4, 120–3, 125, 140, 142, 164, 165, 201, 211, 218; **2**: 23, 33, 34, 49–52, 73–4, 80, 90, 111, 116, 121, 125, 127, 161, 162, 164–5, 176, 179; **1**: and technology 179; **1**: and world politics 27–33, 219; 153; **2**: breakpoint 74, 166; **2**: defined 166–8; **1**: dynamics of 123, 129, 209, 210, 213, 216, 217; **1**: in China 108, 226; **1**: in South Africa **1**: 210; **1**: in the Soviet system 217, 232–3, 242; **1**: sources of 88; defined 166–8
chaos, **1**: 26, 120, 217; **2**: 15, 17–18, 127
Chechnya **2**: 58
Chernobyl **2**: 44
children **1**: 134; **2**: 123
China **1**: 29, 83, 142, 163, 184, 185, 197, 206, 207, 211, 216, 219, 226; **2**: 21, 159, 179, 181, 194; **2**: as anomaly 20–1, 40, 94; **1**: experts in 207, 227; **1**: foreign policy of 206, 210, 212, 228, 277n; **1**: and IR theory 209, 211, 222; **1**: in a bifurcated world 219–22; **1**: market economy of: 224, 227; **1**: theorizing about 207, 224; **1**: US policies toward 188, 206–7
churches **1**: 16
Churchill, Winston S **1**: 230
Circumstantial Passives **1**: 137, 138
cities **1**: 182, 188, 274n; cities **2**: 123, 128, 165; **2**: and micro regions 132–5; **2**: city states 132
citizens **2**: 32, 38, 45, 68, 177; networks of 100–1

citizenship **1**: 28, 32, 133, 159
civic-minded **1**: 92
civil rights **1**: 132, 187, 188, 190, 191, 196, 197
civil society **1**: 14, 16, 133; **2**: 29, 51, 60, 61, 101, 118, 139, 162, 172; **2**: participation in 137
civil strife **2**: 35, 40, 85, 153
class conflicts, **1**: 124, 125, 217; **2**: 35
Clinton–Lewinsky affair **1**: 165
CNN **1**: 165
coalitions **1**: 125; **2**: 155, 186, 195; **2**: cross-border 118, 123, 128, 138–9; **2**: of the willing **2**: 33, 36, 44, 163, 172, 175
co-evolution **1**: 110
cognitive balance **1**: 89
Cold War **1**: 36, 38, 103, 113, 184, 203, 209, 210, 224; **2**: 9, 10, 14, 35, 36, 74, 89, 113, 114, 115, 135, 141; **1**: end of 17, 64, 71, 99–100, 107, 109, 113; **2**: end of 1, 7, 14, 42, 124, 126, 141–2, 145, 147, 151, 164, 200n
collective action **1**: 40, 99, 149, 155, 156, 165, 203; **2**: 39, 84, 92, 95, 100, 107, 126, 143, 164
collectivities **1**: 40, 76, 104, 118; authority of **1**: 36–7; **2**: 16–17, 28, 34, 55, 171
Colombia **1**: 178; **2**: 181
commerce **1**: 216
Common Market **1**: 254
communications, systems of **1**: 153, 162, 204; **2**: 24, 122, 130, 160, 194; revolution in **2**: 51; technologies of **2**: 26, 85, 131
communist systems **1**: 82–3, 188, 234, 254; **2**: 11; **1**: collapse of 210; **1**: ideologies of 209, 217
communities **1**: 129, 189, 193; **2**: 24, 50, 51, 53, 55, 58, 59, 69, 73, 115, 123, 130, 145, 52–6, 159; **2**: donor 172; **2**: fragmentation of 115; **2**: gated 29; **2**: imagined 49, 56–7, 60–2, 135; **2**: virtual 138
companies **2**: 32, 57, 85, 98, 114
comparative foreign policy **1**: 62, 82, 84–93, 204, 229, 230; **2**: 73
comparative politics **1**: 180, 212, 270n
comparativists **1**: 229, 234–5, 244
comparison **1**: 81, 83, 177, 235, 236; meaning of 181; methods of 205, 230
competition **2**: 126
complex adaptive system **1**: 87, 110, 111, 162, 217; **2**: 172, 179, 216n
complex humanitarian emergencies (CHEs) **2**: 36–8, 43–4

complex interdependence **2**: 32, 84, 127
complexities **2**: 13–14, 28, 39, 71, 87, 90;
    of modern life **2**: 31–2, 94, 96, 124,
    185
complexity **1**: 13, 45, 74, 100, 102, 106,
    121, 122, 157, 144, 146, 152, 154, 164,
    203, 204, 216, 242; **2**: 21, 35, 37, 52, 55,
    102, 106–7, 125, 149, 151, 159, 164,
    165, 168–9, 170, 172, 179, 194; **2**:
    networked 61; **1**: of world politics 11–12,
    76, 106, 121, 201, 209; **1**: theory of 44,
    75, 107–19; **2**: 37, 70, 79–80, 168–9,
    172, 173
Complexity: The Emerging Science at the
    Edge of Order and Chaos **2**: 79–80
compliance **1**: 145, 218; **2**: 10, 39, 40, 97,
    102, 116, 117, 118, 119, 122, 152, 155,
    170, 175, 181, 185; **2**: compliance–
    defiance continuum 174, 175; **2**: habit of
    150, 174
computer, sciences of **1**: 117; **2**: 20, 22, 39,
    80, 178; **1**: simulations in 44, 74, 110,
    111, 114, 115, 119; **2**: 70, 79; **1**: systems
    of 40, 161, 157, 162, 236
concepts, challenges of **1**: 16–19, 34; and
    equipment 101, 121; operationalized
    172
conceptual jails **1**: 11, 15–16, 61, 71, 73,
    78, 92, 123; **2**: 16–17, 33, 52, 91, 93,
    151, 187
conflict **2**: 17, 172, 184; resolution of 125
Congo **1**: 185, 186
Connally, John **1**: 148–9
connectivity **1**: 110
consensuses **1**: 164
constitutions **2**: 56, 180, 181
constructivists **1**: 11, 63, 99
consumers **1**: 30, 55, 92, 128, 147, 171,
    244, 251; **2**: 86, 87, 96, 140; **1**: boycotts
    by 128;
consumption **2**: 57, 65; as culture 114
contradictions **1**: 108–10, 117, 118, 119; **2**:
    31–2, 51, 90, 121, 165
control **1**: 92, 143; 149–53; concept of **2**:
    122; **2**: loci of 171; **1**: in an
    interdependent world, **2**: mechanisms of
    122, 123, 124–6, 127, 129, 137, 177
cooperation **1**: 143, 216
core-periphery connections **1**: 87; tensions
    of **2**: 27
corporations **1**: 16, 18, 21, 39, 90, 101, 202,
    213, 226; **1**: multinational 23, 31, 87,
    103, 120, 124, 127, 227; **2**: 23, 41, 64,
    68, 96, 98–101, 107, 128, 130, 141, 148,

150, 159, 163, 172, 174–5, 177, 181,
    186, 187
corruption **2**: 23, 158, 163, 177
cost–benefit assessments **1**: 88
coups d'état **2**: 157, 169
Court of Justice **2**: 143
credit-rating agencies **2**: 29, 118, 119, 128,
    139–40, 153, 163, 175, 186
crime **1**: 37, **2**: 23, 24, 36, 43, 65, 123, 127,
    170, 172; **1**: syndicates of 16, 18; **2**: 114,
    128, 140–1, 162, 174, 175
crisis **1**: 117, 204, 210, 235; of debt 85
critical theory **1**: 63; **2**: 22
Cuba **1**: 83, 90, 174, 184, 185; **1**: and
    missile crisis 16; **1**: Bay of Pigs invasion
    173–4; **1**: troops in Angola 85
cults **2**: 24
culture **1**: 83, 122, 277n; **2**: 16, 27, 59, 65,
    87, 156, 157, 169, 186; **2**: and
    globalization 94; **2**: and modernity 25
currencies **1**: 37; **2**: 170; **1**: crises of 29, 218,
    245; **2**: 43, 44, 112, 114, 126, 147, 157,
    163, 169; **1**: fluctuations in 129, 212
cybernetics **2**: 122
cyberspace **1**: 110, 162; **2**: 50, 157
cynicism **2**: 23, 88
Czechoslovakia **2**: 7, 58

Dahl, Robert A. **1**: 92, 187, 188, 189, 190,
    195, 262n, 274n
Darwinian analogy **2**: 25
data bases **1**: 161
De Gaulle, Charles **1**: 172, 177
decentralization **1**: 10, 31, 38, 112, 121,
    129, 147, 216, 218; **2**: 27, 33, 107, 115,
    125, 150
decisions **1**: 120, 147, 182, 241–2; **1**:
    making of 87, 88, 91, 152, 203, 223, 248,
    252, 271n; **2**: 125; **1**: models of 223; **1**:
    processes of 91, 120, 147, 179
decline, of governmental capacities **1**: 120,
    125, 130, 146, 203; **1**: of hegemons 210;
    1: of national identity 149; **1**: of US
    role 123
defense establishments **2**: 32, 73
democracy **1**: 109, 23; **2**: 17–18; 88, 136,
    144, 157, 177, 178; **2**: and globalization
    96–103; **2**: deficit 173; **2**: practices of 32,
    52, 57, 97, 99–102; **1**: trend toward 209
dependencia **1**: 87
dependent variables **1**: 212; **2**: 70, 79
deterrence systems **1**: 144, 181, 235
de-territorialization **1**: 35; **2**: 21, 161
Deutsch, Karl **1**: 74

devaluations **1**: 144
devolution **2**: 26
dialectic processes **1**: 117; **2**: 18, 165, 166
diaspora **2**: 29, 59, 172
diffusion **2**: 87
digital gap **1**: 163; **2**: 183
diplomacy **1**: 120, 131, 147, 149, 150, 152, 213, 279n; **2**: 27; **1**: historians of 229
disarmament **1**: 188, 191
disaster fatigue **2**: 44
disciplinary boundaries **1**: 91, 109
diseases **2**: 26, 64
disorder **2**: 25, 104–5, 107, 121
distances, shrinking of **2**: 32, 52, 126, 166
distant proximities **1**: 26, 60, 61, 62, 69, 73, 75, 76, 78, 135, 137; **2**: 27, 97, 104, 145
domestic analogy **2**: 96–7, 99, 102, 177
domestic opinion **1**: 91, 203, 207
domestic–foreign boundaries **1**: 35, 37, 45, 60, 73, 178, 189, 211, 212, 243, 244; **2**: 32–3, 34, 35, 36, 49, 53, 97, 171, 173, 187, 191; **2**: obsolescence of 22–3, 150–1
Drudge Report **1**: 165
drugs **2**: 26; trade in **1**: 30, 37, 218; **2**: 40, 43, 123, 126, 163, 170, 172
Dulles, John Foster **1**: 172

East Europe **1**: 82–3, 184, 219, 236, 277n; **2**: 10, 40, 85, 164
Easton, David **1**: 181, 271n, 273n
ecological processes **1**: 29; **2**: 11
economics **1**: 20–1, 23, 89, 91, 92, 93, 133, 146, 212, 244, 245; **2**: 13, 16, 68, 73, 86, 87, 88, 153, 169; **2**: and inflation 127; **1**: and power 88, 141; development **1**: 175, 188, 192, 229, 239; **2**: 157, 158; **2**: diminishing returns 120; **1**: global 29, 217, 212, 222; **2**: 28, 43, 51, 167–8; **2**: neo-liberal 183, 187; **2**: regions 56–7, 59; **2**: zones 132–5, 163
economists **1**: 229; **2**: 37, 64–5, 67, 73
Eden, Anthony **1**: 127, 174
education **1**: 154, 157, 162, 187, 190, 196; systems of 150, 153; **2**: 39
Egypt **1**: 29, 121
Einstein, Albert **1**: 231
elections **1**: 129, **2**: 102, 169; **1**: and a Polish pope 113; **1**: mandates 131; **1**: monitoring of 27; **2**: 128, 144–5
Electoral Commission **2**: 98
electronic revolution **1**: 29

elites **1**: 123, 155, 156, 159; **2**: 21, 35, 39, 152, 192; **2**: at Davos 29
El Salvador **2**: 172
e-mail **1**: 155, 161; **2**: 20, 138, 165
emergence, processes of **1**: 101, 113, 114, 218
emergent epoch **1**: 7, 36, 45, 108–9, 110, 112, 118, 123, 210, 245; sources of 8–10
emerging technologies **1**: 165
empires **1**: 103; **2**: 35, 157, 167
empowerment **1**: 12, 155, 201
energy **1**: 130, 143, 146, 147
environment **2**: 42, 63, 114, 170, 172, 183; **2**: and pollution 18, 22, 43, 126, 153, 163, 170; **2**: and regimes 158; **2**: issues of 20, 36, 57, 123, 153, 159, 186; **1**: natural 148, 150; **1**: problems of 14, 31, 201; **2**: threats to 154–5, 177; **1**: warming of 43; **2**: 19, 147, 153, 183
Episcopalian churches **2**: 105
epistemic communities **2**: 29, 34, 116, 118, 127, 128, 163, 175
epistemology **1**: 122, 208
epoch **2**: 113; emergent 11, 19–22, 26–8, 30–45, 51, 55, 59, 107, 115, 120, 182, 183, 184, 185; **2**: fragmegrative 191, 192; **2**: governance in 180; **2**: transformations of 31–45, 51, 84, 186
equilibria **1**: 108
essential structures **1**: 112
ethnic minorities **1**: 39; **2**: 34, 41, 58, 75, 127, 128, 145, 163; **1**: tensions over 22; **2**: 23, 57, 69
ethnoscapes **1**: 108; **2**: 23, 28, 50, 75, 163
Europe **1**: 97, 121, 142, 163, 209, 227, 249; Union of 10, 29
European Economic Community **1**: 181
European Union **2**: 7, 11, 36, 41, 58, 60, 86, 97, 105, 112, 116, 128, 136, 143, 153, 155, 175, 186, 212n, 218n; anti-immigrant sentiment in 13; changes in 132; four motors of 133; institutions of 97, 98, 128, 131
events, and data sets **1**: 62, 81–2; size of 101, 113–14
evidence **1**: 3, 54
evolution of human systems **1**: 113, 115; **2**: processes of 125, 128, 166
exchange rates **1**: 143, 144
Exclusionary Locals **1**: 136–7
executive–legislative relations **1**: 173, 191
executives **1**: 189, 190
experimental psychologist **1**: 231
explication **1**: 68, 69, 97–106, 208

Falun Gong **2**: 156
families **2**: 57, 87, 121
famines **1**: 124; **2**: 85
farmers **1**: 130, 147, 152
Farrell, R. Barry **1**: 73, 261n, 270n,
    275n
fax machines **1**: 8, 155; **2**: 45, 100, 116
feedback loops **1**: 9, 43, 109, 110–11, 113,
    115, 212; **2**: 21, 28, 70, 75, 79, 165, 166,
    189, 192, 194
feng shui **2**: 94
Ferguson, Yale H. **1**: 261n, 263n; **2**: 200n,
    202n
fiber optic cable **1**: 8; **2**: 45
financescapes **1**: 108; **2**: 23, 28, 75, 163
financial aid **1**: 185
Finland **1**: 179, 183, 185
food **1**: as a weapon, 144; **1**: production of,
    146, 147; **1**: shortages of 129, 130
force **1**: 144, 216
foreign aid **1**: 179, 184, 273n
foreign exchange **1**: 43
foreign offices **1**: 98, 148
foreign policy **1**: 127, 136, 173, 180, 202,
    203, 270n, 271n; **1**: formulation of 120,
    147, 181, 237; **1**: pre-theories of 87, 91,
    171–205, 270n, 271n; **1**: theories of 171,
    197, 229, 230, 234–45, 279n
fragmegration **1**: 28, 38–9, 40, 43, 44,
    45, 101, 105, 106, 107, 112, 118, 119;
    2: 2, 14, 15–18, 27–9, 34, 35, 55–6, 58,
    74–6, 79, 80, 86–7, 97, 105, 115–17,
    119, 146, 152, 153, 156, 158, 166, 173,
    176, 177, 185–6, 189, 192, 193, 194,
    195, 206n; **2**: and governance capacity
    43–5, 183; **2**: and religious
    fundamentalism 105–7; **1**: as worldview
    117; **2**: sources of 38–45; **2**: uneven form
    of 89–90, 173
fragmentation **1**: 38, 112, 109, 129; **2**: 2,
    14–15, 18, 26, 28, 32, 36, 52, 55; **1**: of
    authority 24, 125, 130, 148; **1**: theorizing
    about 105–6
France **1**: 113, 172, 177, 227, 247, 249–50,
    273n; **2**: 40, 145, 155
French journal *Actuel,* **1**: 227
fundamentalism **1**: 109; **2**: 16, 39, 104; **2**:
    spread of 32, 52

game theoretical models **1**: 98
Gell-Mann, Murray **1**: 110, 265n
General Agreement on Tariffs and Trade
    (GATT) **2**: 128, 138
generations **1**: 155, 251; **1**: changes in 156,

157, 159, 162; **2**: differences among
    65
genetic algorithm **1**: 110
Geneva Accord **1**: 14
genocide **2**: 32, 36, 60, 99, 147
geographers **2**: 64, 67, 73
geographic space **1**: 34, 109, 134, 138, 150,
    173
Germany **1**: 184, 188, 253, 273n, 279n
Giddens, Anthony **1**: 257n; **2**: 67, 203n,
    214n, 219n
global agenda **1**: 120, 131, 132, 136, 211
global governance **2**: 17–18, 33, 43, 116,
    121, 125, 127–46, 147–53, 163; **2**:
    ontology for 111–20
Global Issues Networks **2**: 195
global order **2**: 8, 9–11, 42, 150, 158, 178;
    as outcomes 7, 10
global stage **1**: 40, 121, 129, 130, 203;
    crowding of 13, 39, 77, 101, 201, 204; **2**:
    96, 126, 149, 155, 157, 159, 181, 187,
    188, 193n, 194
globalism **1**: 224; **2**: 83, 84
globalists **1**: 217
globality **2**: 61, 83
Globalization Studies Network **1**: 67
globalization **1**: 9, 10, 21–2, 23, 28, 30, 35,
    36, 37, 38, 101, 106, 112; **2**: 2–3, 14, 21,
    28, 35, 43, 49–63, 74, 101, 115, 117,
    173, 176; **1**: acceleration of 109, 202,
    218; **2**: 1, 119, 171; **2**: and democracy
    96–103; **2**: and methodology 69; **2**: as IR
    63; **2**: complexities of 83–90; **2**: defined
    1, 26, 84–6; **1**: dynamics of 200–2, 203,
    205; **2**: 16–17, 20, 33, 51, 69; **2**:
    knowledge about 161; **1**: of economies
    10, 40, 42, 109, 202; **2**: 17, 32, 52, 57,
    75–8, 126, 187; **2**: of globalization
    72–80, 159, 194; **1**: opposition to 203;
    2: 69, 159; **2**: scope of 63–7; **1**: sources
    of 75–6; **2**: 94–5; **2**: theory of 66,
    88, 91
globalized space **2**: 161–79; defined 163;
    theory of 172
global–local nexus **2**: 2, 3, 22, 23, 26–7, 28,
    29, 30, 97, 115, 126, 136; tensions in
    104, 105
GNP **1**: 90
Goa **1**: 174
Goddess of Democracy **1**: 227
Gorbachev, M. **1**: 236
governance **2**: 25, 112, 114, 116, 118,
    123–5, 145–6, 147, 148, 151, 162, 180,
    181, 182–6, 189, 192; **2**: as networks

188, 189, 190–2; **2**: bottom-up
125, 132, 135, 149, 189, 190, 191; **2**:
concept of 121–2, 179; **2**: disaggregation
of 116, 117, 159, 182 186; **2**: evolution
of 125–6, 128, 138; **2**: in corporations
152; **2**: in fragmegrated world 155–7;
2: in globalized space 158, 161–79,
194; **2**: in 21st century 121–46; **2**: on
global scale 2–3, 52, 64–5, 114; **2**:
mobius-web 2, 156, 158; **2**: of
complexity 128, 147–60, 164; **2**:
side-by-side 189, 190–2; **2**: top-down
125, 135, 149, 189, 190, 191, 219n; **2**:
typology of 189–93; **2**: without
government 123, 180
governmental variables **1**: 172, 173, 200,
203–4
governments **1**: 34, 129, 144, 153, 157,
162, 177, 204, 213, 216, 277n; **2**: 41,
44–5, 50, 52–3, 84, 85, 127, 134, 162,
208n; **1**: and collapse 37; **1**: and policy
process 114, 130, 204, 210; **2**: and states
114–15; **2**: effectiveness of 13, 40–2, 43;
2: multi-level 155, 180, 186, 193, 219n;
2: sub-national 29, 126, 127, 130, 132,
138, 145, 158, 189; **1**: weakening of 108,
123; **2**: 9, 136
Great Britain **1**: 174, 184, 186, 247,
249–50; **2**: 99
great powers **1**: 142; **2**: 33
Greek lobby **2**: 128
Greenpeace **2**: 41, 175
Gromyko, A. **1**: 243
Group of Seven **2**: 195
Group of 77, **1**: 127
groups **2**: 84, 150
guerillas **2**: 16
Gulf War **2**: 9, 25
guns-or-butter issues **1**: 244

habdaptive actor **2**: 34, 36
habits, **1**: 22–3, 31, 43, 99, 101, 118, 131,
138, 161, 175, 189, 219; **2**: 10, 19, 30, 67,
99, 125; **2**: analytic 22, 52, 68–9, 97,
187, 181
hackers **1**: 40, 162–3
Hanseatic League **2**: 116, 132
Hansen, Pauline **2**: 86
Harding, Warren **1**: 174
Havel, Václav **1**: 206, 207; **2**: 19, 26,
198n
health **2**: 65
hegemonic, **2**: decline of 136; **2**: leadership
by 124, 157, 163; **2**: orders 8, 41; 157

Held, David **2**: 24, 67, 167, 199n, 203n,
205n, 214n, 215n
Hettne, Bjorn **2**: 113, 200n, 203n, 209n,
210n, 211n
hierarchy, **2**: 42, 115, 117–19, 122, 174; **2**:
international pecking order 8, 9, 184
historic animosities **1**: 109
history **1**: 20, 23, 77, 104, 116, 117, 122,
229, 277n; **2**: 7, 9, 10, 22, 26, 69, 87,
114, 122, 162, 194; **1**: and analogies
102–3; **1**: and change 102–4; **1**: and
theory 77, 118; **1**: breakpoints in 100,
102, 104, 123, 236; **1**: continuities of
123–5; **1**: sequences of 118–19; history;
2: animosities in 32, 37, 52
Hitler, Adolph **1**: 85, 253; at Munich 247,
249–50
Hobbs, Heidi **1**: 77, 261n
Holland, John H. **1**: 110, 164n, 265n
Holsti, Ole R. **1**: 215, 223, 261n
home **2**: 50
homogenization **2**: 62
Hong Kong **1**: 27; **2**: 94
horizontal political systems **1**: 189–94, 197,
274n, 275n
hotline **1**: 15
humanitarian agency **2**: 32, 100, 142, 155,
175, 186
humanity **2**: 90, 156
human needs **2**: 86–7, 90
human rights **1**: 13, 14, 211, 226, 227; **2**:
42, 44, 57, 61, 99, 102, 114, 128, 157,
170, 172, 177, 192
human resources issue-area **1**: 193–4, 196
human systems **1**: 112, 114, 116
Hungary **1**: 174
Hussain, Saddam **2**: 7

icons **2**: 85
ideas **2**: 10, 64, 86, 87, 127
identiscapes **2**: 23, 28
identities **1**: 21–2, 28, 29, 34, 36, 136, 145,
212; **2**: 21, 51, 57–8, 61, 62, 68, 85, 89,
171; **1**: and IR 53–8, 64; **1**: and
methodology 67, 75; **1**: collective 135–6,
138, 209; **1**: crises of 135; **2**: new 29, 52,
118, 135; **2**: questions of 49, 50; **2**:
zero-sum conception of 62
ideologies **1**: 82, 153, 173, 188, 239; **2**: 41,
86, 88
ideoscapes **1**: 108; **2**: 23, 28, 50, 75, 163
idiographic inquiry **1**: 229, 241, 278n
immigrants **1**: 105–6; regulations on 127
increasing returns **1**: 110

independence **2**: 10–11, 98
independent variables **1**: 212; **2**: 70, 75, 79
India **1**: 163, 174, 179; **2**: 14
Indian tribes **1**: 121, 186
indigenous peoples **2**: 58; knowledge of 153–4
individuals **1**: 9, 12–13, 16, 23, 38, 40, 77, 99, 104, 108, 118, 125, 126, 129–30, 136, 138, 172, 177, 200, 271n **2**: 16, 28, 30, 34, 38, 55, 65, 76, 92, 107, 130, 194; **1**: as variables 85, 172–4, 175, 201, 203, 204
Indonesia **2**: 181, 184
industrialization **1**: 129, 150, 173, 218, 237, 244, 278n; **2**: 35, 87
information **1**: 101, 109, 110, 157, 217, 231–3; **2**: 122, 127, 165; **1**: neutrality of technologies 160–6; **2**: revolution 32, 35, 36, 51, 52, 57, 184
innovation **2**: 87, 124, 193
insecurities **2**: 13–14, 98
institutional structures **1**: 274n; **2**: 27, 51, 60, 125, 128; transformation of 161, 164
institutionalists **1**: 89, 91, 99
Insular Locals **1**: 136–7
insurance industry **2**: 153
insurgents **2**: 16, 40, 172
integration **1**: 38, 109, 112, 125, 224; **2**: 2, 28, 36, 55, 114, 115; **2**: of regions 32, 52
integrative complexity **1**: 12
intelligence system **1**: 242
interactive polarities **2**: 27
interagency rivalries **1**: 231
interdepartmental committees **1**: 147
interdependence, **1**: 31–2, 120–2, 124–5, 129, 130, 131, 143, 144, 145, 182, 201, 211, 213, 216, 243, 253, 274n; **2**: 10–11, 13, 35, 55, 83, 85, 99, 121, 123, 125, 127, 135, 147, 148, 181, 183; **1**: issue structures of 146–53; **2**: issues of 126, 129, 170
interdisciplinary inquiries **1**: 4, 109, 110; **2**: 67
interest groups **1**: 130
interests **1**: 216, 250, 247–8, 249; defined as power 248, 250
internal–external balance **1**: 212, 244
internal war **2**: 26, 69, 181
International Accounting Standards Board **2**: 182
international associations **2**: 98
international balances **1**: 129, 132

International Boundary Commission **1**: 133
international community **2**: 33, 43, 44
international institutions **2**: 24, 60, 65, 97, 112, 149; financial 100, 101–2; law 136, 156
internationalization **2**: 83
International Monetary Fund (IMF) **1**: 14, 85, 155; **2**: 102, 139, 160, 192, 194
international organizations **1**: 40, 127, 185, 189, 274n; **2**: 41, 93, 101, 121, 131, 136, 152, 163, 177; **2**: of governments (INGOs) 18, 21, 34, 36, 41, 43, 137, 138, 152, 155, 171, 172, 186, 189, 192
international political economy (IPE) **1**: 84–93, 212; **2**: 27
international regimes **1**: 216
international relations (IR), **1**: 60, 62, 65, 73, 104, 123, 206, 212, 217, 270n; **2**: 27, 67, 72, 150; **2**: analysts of 162, 170; **2**: and globalization 63–6, 70, 73, 161; **2**: and states 64–5, 68; **1**: entering the field 59–78; 99–100; **1**: handbook of 23–5; **1**: methodological introspection in 122–3; **1**: orthodoxy of 63; **1**: scholars of, 40, 71, **1**: study of 20–1, 23–5; **1**: textbooks in 249; **1**: theories of 209, 212–19, 222; **2**: theory challenges 169–72, 176
International Studies Association (ISA) **1**: 70–1; **2**: 64
International Studies Quarterly **2**: 72
international systems, **1**: 108, 111, 121, 172, 177, 188, 206, 207, 213, 216, 239; **2**: 32, 37, 51, 61, 157, 123, 162; **2**: anarchical structure of 33, 41
Internet **1**: 8, 13, 16, 21, 22, 40, 106, 134, 155, 259, 160, 161, 162, 166, 201; and children 156; literacy in 159–67; users of 43; **2**: 20, 45, 56, 68, 92, 100–1, 116, 176, 178, 179, 184, 186
intersubjectivity **1**: 3, 67, 68, 69, 74, 169
Inter-University Comparative Foreign Policy Project (ICFP) **1**: 81–2
intifada **2**: 11
intrastate wars **1**: 22
investments **2**: 67, 86; foreign 26
IQ **1**: 12
Iran **1**: 179, 235; **1**: seizure of embassy 90
Iraq **1**: 97, 235; **2**: 7, 25, 141, 142
Ireland **2**: 58
Islam **2**: 106; fundamentalists in 39
Israel **1**: 14, 22, 85, 141, 166; **2**: 7, 40, 69,

106, 112, 181; **1**: and Palestinian conflict 165; **2**: 13

issue-areas **1**: 10, 17, 87, 99, 121, 146, 178, 182, 187–98, 202, 217, 274n; **2**: 34, 35, 42, 50, 53, 96, 97, 114, 156, 163; **2**: and regimes 29, 118, 128, 136–8, 139, 175, 186; **1**: new issues 122, 124, 125, 143, 144, 218; **1**: socio-economic 131, 277n; **1**: typology of 192–7, 275n

Japan **1**: 142, 184; **2**: 106
Jerusalem **2**: 105
jet aircraft **2**: 13
Jews **2**: 30, 104, 106
jobs **2**: 85, 156, 186
John Paul II **2**: 104
Johnson, Lyndon **1**: 127
journalists **1**: 97–8, 127, 210, 279n; **2**: 73, 75; **2**: methods of 92–4, 95
judicial review **2**: 102
just noticeable differences (JNDs) **1**: 164–5

Kashmir **2**: 18
Kauffman, Stuart **1**: 110, 264n
Kauppi, Mark V. **1**: 215
Kelman, Herbert **1**: 20
Kennedy, John F. **1**: 174
Kenya **1**: 184
Keohane, Robert O. **1**: 63, 65, 259n, 276n; **2**: 203n, 207n, 208n
Khrushchev, N. **1**: 171, 172, 174, 177, 179, 232, 236, 279n
Kingdom of God **2**: 105
knowledge **1**: 68–9, 74, 143, 230, 235
Kobrin, Stephen J. **2**: 167, 215n
Korea **1**: 77, 103; **1**: shooting down of airliner 241–2, 243, 279n
Kosovo **2**: 25, 147, 156, 191
Krasner, Stephen D. **1**: 69, 276n, 258n; **2**: 207n, 211n
Kuhn, Thomas. **1**: 81
Kurds **2**: 25
Kyoto Protocol **2**: 153

labor **1**: 16, 89, 90, 202; **2**: and unions 100, 123
land-mine treaty **2**: 191
land owners **2**: 16
landscapes **2**: 23, 50, 75
language **2**: 65
Latin America **1**: 163, 253; **2**: 40, 59, 144
laws **2**: 56, 102
leaders **1**: 12, 86, 203, 210; **2**: 157; **1**: in

multi-centric world, 127, 203; **2**: as mobilizers 100
leadership **1**: 127, 128, 144, 236, 237, 244; **1**: and successions 232
learning **1**: 112, 117, 231
leftists **2**: 16
legislatures **1**: 188, 189, 190, 238, 274n; **2**: 51, 102; **1**: hearings in 231
legitimacy **1**: 25, 28, 86, 132, 146, 150, 181, 183, 185, 237, 272n; **2**: 10, 99, 125, 193; **2**: criteria of 40–1, 89, 174; **2**: sentiments toward 41, 42, 52
Le Pen, Jean-Marie **2**: 86, 198n
levels of analysis **1**: 173, 271n, 272n
liberalism **1**: 63, 106, 116
liberals **1**: 11, 89, 99; **2**: 18, 72, 148, 162
Liberia **2**: 142
Libya **1**: 85; **2**: 142
Lindblom, Charles E. **1**: 92, 262n
linearity **1**: 100, 108, 109, 115, 116; **2**: 21, 37, 43, 75, 79, 174
Linkage Politics **1**: 73
Lithuania **1**: 163
local circumstances **2**: 2, 30, 87, 104
local communities **1**: 22, 136, 190, 193, 202
local–global nexus **1**: 134–8
localities **2**: 24, 61
localization **1**: 10, 28, 30, 31–2, 38, 112; **2**: 35, 43, 74, 84–5, 115, 117, 173; **2**: defined 26
logrolling **1**: 190, 191
Los Angeles Times **1**: 121
loyalties **1**: 21–2, 32, 36, 101, 133, 146, 149, 182, 216; **2**: 21, 42, 57–8, 68, 69, 89

macro level **1**: 9, 89, 91, 93, 126, 212, 276n; **2**: as parameter 12, 38, 41–3
macro-micro parameter **2**: 12, 38–41
Mafia **1**: 30; **2**: 41
Maghroori, Ray **1**: 215
Malaysia **1**: 163, 254
Malta **1**: 163
Mandela, Nelson **1**: 113, 264n
markets **1**: 9, 18, 31, 37, 88, 92, 93, 165, 202, 238; **2**: 28, 29, 43, 51, 74, 85, 88, 98, 102, 134, 152, 157, 167, 170, 174, 177, 178, 182, 183, 186, 187, 189; **1**: forces of 9, 92, 212; **2**: governance of 190, 191; **2**: shares of 36, 87, 172
Marshall Plan **1**: 90
Marxism **1**: 63, 122, 124–5; and globalism 214, 216–17, 226
Marxists **1**: 89, 81, 123, 217

mass media **2**: 101, 102; **2**: and
organizations 172; **2**: governance of 152
mass publics **1**: 247
mathematical analysis **1**: 55, 74, 89, 98,
111, 114, 115, 117; **2**: 79; **1**: IR and
53–8
McCarthy era **1**: 174
Medecin Sans Frontiers **2**: 41
mediascapes **1**: 108; **2**: 23, 28, 50, 75, 163
medicine **1**: 201
Meisie Ndlovu **1**: 157
melting-pot society **2**: 69
mercantilists **1**: 89, 91
merchants **2**: 16
Meredith, James **1**: 197
methodological territorialism **1**: 43–4
methodology **1**: 26, 32–4, 38, 61, 67, 120,
122, 172, 210; **1**: and agent-based
modeling 74; **2**: 70, 75, 79–80, 91–5,
216n
Mexico **2**: 11
microelectronic revolution **1**: 218, 239; **2**:
114, 176; **1**: technologies of 21, 39, 40,
42, 156; **2**: 17, 68, 75–8, 162
micro level **1**: 9, 90, 91; **1**: actors at 76, 89,
126, 276n; **2**: as parameter 12, 13, 37–9,
123, 148
micro–macro interactions **1**: 22, 39–42, 43,
44, 45, 89–90, 125–32, 219, 238, 276n;
2: 16–17, 37–41, 74, 76–8, 79, 80, 91–4;
problems of 104–5
Middle East **1**: 14, 85, 166; **2**: 7, 16, 18, 59
migrants **1**: 77, 201; **2**: as migrations 163,
169, 170
military establishments **1**: 148, 150, 273n;
capabilities of 143–6; power of 140, 141;
strategy of 120; **2**: organizations of 117;
recruitment for 69, 182
militia groups **2**: 58
Miller, Warren E. **1**: 187, 274n
miniaturization **1**: 201
minorities **2**: 102
mobility upheaval **1**: 7, 9–10, 39, 40, 42,
76, 100, 105, 154, 201; **2**: 17–18, 20, 21,
22, 26, 51, 75–8, 85, 95, 96, 185, 187
mobius-web governance **2**: 2, 189, 190–3,
194
Moldavia **2**: 41
money **1**: 110; **2**: 16, 26, 86; **1**: stability of
85, 130, 144, 146
Mongolia **2**: 178
Moody's Investor Service **2**: 118, 139, 175
Morgenthau **1**: 247, 250–1, 271n, 276n,
280n

Moscow **1**: 185, 273n
most-favored-nation procedures **1**: 206
motives **1**: 93, 99
movements **1**: 36, 127, 155, 216; **2**: 11, 23,
24, 29, 41, 116, 118, 126, 128, 131, 155,
163, 175, 176, 178, 186
MSNBC **1**: 165
multi-centric world **1**: 14–15, 16, 17–18,
28–9, 202, 219, 222, 226, 227, 277n,
218; **2**: 42, 44, 75, 148, 153, 155, 163,
173, 174, 179, 181, 184
multi-cultural communities **2**: 37, 68, 69; **1**:
as regimes 22, 29
Multilateral Agreement on Investment
(MAI) **2**: 100–1, 102
multilateralism **2**: 142, 143, 183
multipolarity **2**: 35
music **2**: 65
Muslims **1**: 166; **2**: 104, 105, 106
Mutual Assured Boredom (MAB) **1**: 92–3

NAFTA **2**: 11, 137
narcotraffickers **2**: 16
nation state **1**: 111, 129, 138, 188, 213,
254, 274n; 251; **2**: 51, 56, 64, 89, 184;
1: adaptation of 244; **1**: as focus of
loyalties 246–7; **2**: as system 50–1, 59;
2: role of 22; **2**: crisis of 21
National Democratic Institute **2**: 144
national economies **1**: 39, 212
national interest **1**: 149, 246, 248, 252, 253
national unity **1**: 173
national–international interactions **1**:
179–87, 188, 272n, 273n; **2**: 49–50, 55,
61
nationalism **1**: 30, 134, 218; **2**: 21
nationality **2**: 61
Nature Conservancy **1**: 70
natural sciences **2**: 63, 64
Nehru **1**: 174
neighborhoods **2**: 29, 87; associations in
123, 155, 186
neo-liberal economic policies **1**: 76, 202
neo-medieval scenario **1**: 224
neo-realist paradigm **1**: 214, 216
networks **1**: 13, 22, 40, 201, 203; **2**: 24, 29,
50, 51, 55, 58, 60, 61, 65, 96, 118, 123,
138, 150, 160, 167, 175–6, 178, 178,
188, 192, 194
New Economic Order **1**: 124, 127
newspapers **1**: 98; **2**: 178
New York Times **1**: 81
NIMBY (not in my backyard) syndrome **2**:
148, 149, 152

Nixon, Richard **1**: 174; **1**: Doctrine of 90
nomothetic orientation **1**: 230, 278n
nongovernmental organizations (NGOs) **1**: 10, 16, 18, 23, 29, 36, 38, 39, 77, 100, 104, 120, 123, 125, 130, 147, 162, 276n; **2**: 16, 18, 23, 24, 29, 33–4, 36, 37, 41, 43, 45, 56, 57, 60, 75, 100–1, 107, 114, 116, 118, 128, 129–31, 137, 148, 149, 150, 152, 158, 159, 163, 170, 171, 172, 174, 175, 176, 177, 178, 179, 181, 185, 189, 191, 192; **2**: proliferation of 52, 111, 115, 116, 125, 150
nonhuman resources issue-area **1**: 193–4, 196, 197
non-interventionary rules **1**: 226
nonlinearity **1**: 44, 101, 108, 109, 113, 115, 116; **2**: 37, 165, 166; **2**: feedback mechanisms of 73; **2**: models of 22; **2**: sequences of 21, 51, 75, 79, 119–20
nonprofit organizations **1**: 18
nonrational behavior **1**: 150, 180
non-state actors **1**: 14, 25, 121; **2**: 60, 64, 98, 118, 184
Nordic region **2**: 136
norms **2**: 36, 51, 86, 114, 170, 181, 192, 212n; **2**: convergence of 33
North Atlantic Treaty Organization (NATO) **1**: 112–13, 188; **2**: 25, 191
North Korea **1**: 90, 97
North–South tensions **1**: 124
nuclear age **1**: 144, 193, 236; proliferation of weapons 76, 244; **2**: 19, 42

objective reality **1**: 150, 248, 250; **1**: national interest as 247
objectivists, as analysts **1**: 247, 248, 249, 250, 251, 252, 253
oceans **1**: 143, 146; problems of 129, 130
Odell, John S. **1**: 88, 262n
OECD **2**: 192
offshore bank deposits **1**: 43
Ogarkov, Marshall **1**: 243
oil **1**: 92, 245; reserves of 129, 150; and embargo 140–1, 145
Oklahoma City bombing **2**: 44
On the Cutting Edge of Globalization: An Inquiry into American Elites **1**: 78
ontology **1**: 34, 108; **2**: 31–2, 37, 83–4, 113–14, 118; and global governance 112–20
operational codes **1**: 91
Oppenheimer, J. Robert **1**: 69
optimism **2**: 17–18

order **2**: 10, 14, 18, 87, 127; **2**: international 167
Organization of American States (OAS) **2**: 60, 144
Organization of Petroleum Exporting Countries (OPEC) **1**: 149
organizations **1**: 89, 118, 125, 143, 238; **2**: 41, 55, 85, 88, 92, 98, 126, 151, 172, 187, 194; **1**: explosion of 7, 9–10, 12–13, 40, 76, 103, 109, 201; **2**: 16, 17, 21, 22, 26, 30, 32, 52, 75–8, 95, 100, 101, 123, 176, 184; **2**: nonprofit 20; **1**: theory of 23
orthodoxies **1**: 61, 122
outsiders **2**: 25

Pakistan **2**: 14
Palestine **1**: 14, 22, 166; **2**: 58, 69, 106
panaceas **1**: 107; search for 109–10, 111, 115, 117, 119
panarchy **2**: 33, 115
paradigms, **1**: 11, 13, 120–5; **1**: components of 124–32; **1**: jailbreak from 14–15; **2**: concept of 112–13; **2**: and change 65, 113–14
Paraguay **1**: 27; **2**: 144
parameters **1**: 118, 119; **2**: 50, 148; defined 11–12; **1**: of the global system 112
paramilitarists **2**: 16
Paris **2**: 39, 40, 145
parsimony **1**: 67, 76, 106
Parsons, Talcott **1**: 23, 93, 257n, 263n, 271n
partition **2**: 25
path-dependencies **2**: 101, 125, 146
patriots **1**: 92; **2**: 27
peace **2**: 65; keepers of 142
peasants **2**: 16
pension systems **2**: 21
Pentagon **1**: 103
people **2**: 127; **2**: alienation of 88; **2**: competence of 92
Peoples' Assembly **2**: 97–8
People Count **1**: 78
perception **1**: 88, 89, 93, 91
Peru **1**: 230; **2**: 181
phase transitions **1**: 113
Philippines **1**: 163; **2**: 20, 40, 169, 181, 184
philosophy **1**: 20, 111, 118, 119, 122; **1**: of analysis 173, 271; **2**: 20, 40, 169, 181, 184
plague **2**: 116
PLO **2**: 41
pluralism **1**: 214, 217, 222, 224, 226

polarizations **1**: 31
police powers **2**: 102
political development **1**: 229
political parties **1**: 82, 130, 187–90, 238,
    274n; **2**: 41, 172
political science **1**: 20–1, 22, 24, 34, 35–6,
    45, 61, 62, 65, 71, 248, 270n, 274n; **2**:
    73, 164, 170
political scientists **1**: 22, 188–9, 206, 229; **2**:
    37, 64, 69
politics **1**: 10, 93, 108, 133, 190, 274n;
    1: stability in 130, 275n
Politics, Economics, and Welfare **1**: 92
pollution **1**: 37, 143, 146, 147
polyarchy **2**: 33, 115
Pondering Postinternationalism **1**: 77
population growth **1**: 14, 126, 129–30, 143,
    147, 216; **2**: 19, 123
positivism **1**: 45, 65, 68
possiblism **1**: 93
post-Cold War period **1**: 108, 110, 113,
    210; **2**: 1–2, 115, 157, 166
post-industrial era **1**: 216, 217, 237
post-international politics **1**: 12, 99, 104; **2**:
    as approach 148–9
post-modernist **1**: 65, 68, 70, 72
post-positivist approaches **1**: 65
post-realists **1**: 121, 123
post-World War II **2**: 10
power **1**: 9, 22, 29, 93, 104, 123, 153, 155,
    189, 190, 248, 250; **2**: 8, 24, 28, 61, 87,
    114, 118, 119, 130, 151, 179, 184; **1**: as
    concept 140–6, 216, 248; **1**: national
    140–1, 144–6, 152, 153; **2**: sources of 24
pragmatism **1**: 116
Prague **2**: 39
pre-post modernist **1**: 67–8, 74
printing press **2**: 117
privacy **1**: 137, 165–6
private–public divide **2**: 192
probablism **1**: 93
producers **1**: 91, 92
production **1**: 29, 89; **2**: 24, 26, 86, 87,
    167
professional societies **1**: 16, 21, 39, 101,
    127, 130, 202, 210; **2**: 29, 34, 67, 68, 75,
    98, 100, 107, 148, 163, 181; *see also*
    associations
proof, politics of **2**: 101
propaganda **1**: 242
protectionists **2**: 16, 87
protests **1**: 12, 100, 103, 128, 155, 165, 219;
    2: 85, 92, 95, 101–2, 157, 181
psychic comfort **2**: 89, 90, 126

psychology **1**: 20, 72, 229, 271n; **2**: 64
public goods **2**: 43
public interest **1**: 247
public officials **2**: 101
publics **1**: 100, 108, 203, 238; **2**: 16, 28,
    31–2, 35, 45, 64, 102, 123, 149, 152,
    156, 162, 192; restlessness among 13, 38,
    92, 127
punctuated equilibria **1**: 113, 118; **2**: 165
puzzles **1**: 100, 209, 210

Quebec **2**: 40

racial tensions **2**: 39, 57
radicals **2**: 16
Ramberg, Bennett **1**: 215
random incidents **1**: 118, 121
Rangoon **2**: 39
rationality **1**: 35, 180; **2**: 21, 25, 70;
    2: and states 162; **1**: models of 35, 45,
    188
realism **1**: 11, 40, 63, 71, 75, 99, 106, 116,
    120, 122, 214, 216, 224, 226, 247, 271n;
    2: 76, 148, 162; **2**: and realists 72
reflexivity **2**: 172, 194
reformers **2**: 16
refugees **2**: 39
regimes **2**: 41, 114, 137–8; **1**: collapse of 37;
    2: 74; **2**: international 97, 114, 123, 167,
    170, 172
regionalization **2**: 57, 59, 60, 135–6
regions **1**: 134, 142, 191, 253; **2**: 23, 28, 34,
    57, 98, 128, 135–6, 186
regulatory agencies **2**: 186
relationship revolution **2**: 184
relativity theory **1**: 231
religions **2**: 24, 41, 123, 159, 172, 184; **2**:
    and fundamentalism 105–7; **2**:
    globalization of 104–5
representation **2**: 99
Resistant Globals **1**: 136
Resistant Locals **1**: 136–7
resource scarcities **1**: 126, 144, 146, 216
restored-state-system scenario **1**: 224, 226
rich-poor gap **1**: 97, 163; **2**: 17, 19, 147,
    162
Rio de Janeiro **1**: 14
risk **2**: 88
Risse, Thomas **1**: 24, 257n; **2**: 205n, 212n
rivalries **1**: 93, 152
role variables **1**: 90, 91, 132, 135, 172–4,
    177, 203, 271n; **1**: and scholars 59–60,
Romania **1**: 83
Rosenau, James N. **1**: 60, 215

Ruggie, John **1**: 72
rule systems **2**: 122, 126, 151, 155–6, 163, 173, 180, 193, 194
Russia **1**: 174, 216, 219, 232, 233, 239; **1**: revolution in, 273n; **2**: 19, 140, 181
Rwanda **1**: 29; **2**: 44, 145, 147, 169, 172

Sadat, Anwar **1**: 85
Saddam Hussein **2**: 25
Salafism **2**: 106
sanctions **1**: 206
Santa Fe Institute **1**: 44, 74, 110
Saudi Arabia **2**: 7
Save the Children **1**: 18–19
science **1**: 68, 109, 146, 147, 150; **1**: as proof 149–50; **2**: findings of 127; **1**: methods of 76, 122, 229, 230; **2**: 153–4
Scotland **2**: 58, 155
Security Council **1**: 173; **2**: 97, 141, 142
security **1**: 93, 143, 216; **1**: national 146, 147, 153, 190; **2**: 17, 32, 65, 69, 99, 167
self **1**: 135–6; **2**: and other 27
self-environment orientations **1**: 244
self-interest **2**: 44, 99, 130, 175
self-organization **1**: 110, 112; **2**: 125, 168, 215n
Seoul **2**: 39
Serbs **2**: 25
sharecroppers **2**: 16
Shiites **2**: 25
Singapore **2**: 94, 169
Sino–Soviet bloc **1**: 184, 185; **1**: and conflict 171
skill revolution **1**: 7, 9–10, 12, 28, 32, 38, 40–1, 76, 77, 119, 154–8, 162, 166, 200–2, 203, 219; **2**: 9, 52, 194; **1**: acceleration of 155, 157; **1**: as a process 150, 156; **2**: revolution, in 17–18, 37–40, 42–3, 57, 75–8, 95, 96, 100, 101, 107, 123, 126, 148, 159–60, 187
Skybolt **1**: 273n
Slovakia **2**: 20, 184
smart mobs **1**: 165
Smith, Adam **1**: 89
social psychology **2**: 73
social sciences **1**: 61, 65, 66, 109, 232; **2**: 63, 80
social systems **1**: 110–11, 135, 187; **1**: cohesion of 144, 150–2, 204
Socialist International **2**: 144
societies **1**: 21–2, 108, 133, 153, 177, 181; **2**: 25–6, 51, 65, 83, 84, 85, 120, 126 164, 190; **2**: as terminal entities 68;

2: fragmentation of 114; **1**: variables of 132, 172, 173–4, 175, 197, 200, 204, 271n
socialization **1**: 61, 175, 237
sociologists **2**: 37, 64, 67, 69, 75
sociology **1**: 20–4, 189; **2**: 68, 73; **1**: life-cycle 229, 245
Sofia **2**: 10
solar system **1**: 114, 146
Solidarity **1**: 210
Somalia **1**: 29; **2**: 44, 142, 145
South Africa **2**: 112, 177
South America **1**: 227; **2**: 136
South Korea **2**: 40
sovereignty **1**: 10, 12, 25, 29, 32, 39, 40, 108, 178, 219, 222, 226; **2**: 9, 16, 17, 32, 33, 37, 41, 115, 119, 156, 173, 181, 188; **1**: scope of 201–2; **2**: transformation of 69, 75–8, 99
sovereignty-bound actors **2**: 34, 36, 42, 43, 158
sovereignty-free actors **1**: 226, 227; **2**: 34, 36, 42, 118; **2**: 34, 36, 42, 118
Soviet Union **1**: 38, 142, 171, 177, 179, 183–4, 185, 226, 229, 232, 241; **2**: 11, 40, 74, 112; **1**: as a theoretical case 230, 236; **1**: as an adaptive system 244; **1**: collapse of 99–100, 113, 210; **2**: 8, 9, 140; **1**: foreign policy goals of 230, 233–5, 237; **1**: policy-making organization of 231, 242, 278n; **1**: theorizing about 233, 241
Soweto **2**: 39
specialist–generalist cooperation **1**: 237, 244, 245
specialization **2**: 63
Specialized Global **1**: 136
spheres of authority (SOAs) **1**: 17, 37; **2**: 21, 28, 34–6, 43, 44, 52, 97, 100, 102, 116, 117, 118, 119, 149, 155, 157, 188; **2**: and states 24; defined 29, 218n; **2**: disaggregation of 119, 150; **2**: failures of 153; **2**: proliferation of 150–1, 181, 182, 183, 184, 185, 186, 187–8, 194
Sprout, Harold and Margaret **1**: 93, 179, 263n, 272n; **1**: 273n
Sri Lanka **2**: 58
stability **1**: 119, 191; **2**: 49, 150, 157
stagnation **2**: 15
stalemate **1**: 201; **2**: 18, 40, 153, 178
Standard & Poor's Ratings Group (S&P) **2**: 118, 139
standards of living **2**: 87
Starr, Harvey **1**: 87–8, 262n

stasis **1**: 111, 113, 119; **2**: 165
state-centric world **1**: 14–15, 17–18, 28–9,
    132, 202, 216, 218, 219, 227; **2**: 16,
    41–2, 44, 59, 75, 163, 179, 181
statecraft **1**: 144, 150
states **1**: 13–14, 16, 18, 21–6, 29, 32, 40,
    73, 85, 88, 91, 125, 130, 144, 152, 202,
    208, 217, 224, 274n; **2**: 16–17, 23, 25,
    33–4, 35, 37, 40, 52–3, 55, 59, 60, 69,
    76, 85, 89, 93, 100–1, 115, 117, 123,
    131, 150, 162, 173, 188, 208n; 218; **2**:
    adversaries of 135; **1**: adaptation of 216,
    243; **2**: anarchical structure of 114, 124,
    150; **2**: and globalization 64; **2**: and
    markets 27; **2**: as anomalies 21; **2**: as
    networks 24; **2**: as system 89, 97, 99,
    181; **2**: as terminal entities 22, 26, 68,
    70; **1**: capacities of 146, 201; **2**: 9,
    97, 118, 166, 182; **2**: collapse of 25; **1**:
    concept of 15, 16, 87, 92, 101, 104; **1**:
    controls of 16–18; **2**: crises of 41, 181; **1**:
    differentiated model 120, 124, 125, 126;
    2: duration of 24; **2**: governance by
    126–7; **2**: models of 24, 26; **2**: primacy
    of 111, 116, 149; **2**: rebuilding of 25–6;
    1: role of 213; **1**: size of 85, 142; **1**:
    weakening of 10, 30, 36–7, 39, 40, 60,
    76, 101–2, 108, 109, 204, 207, 216–18;
    2: 1, 16, 22–4, 25, 29, 32, 33, 42, 43,
    50, 68, 75–8, 89, 96, 103, 111, 115,
    116, 126, 133, 151, 161, 171, 181, 182,
    183, 193
states-are-forever habit **2**: 22–5, 30
statistics **1**: 89; **2**: 79
status issue-area **1**: 193–4, 196–7
steering mechanisms **2**: 180, 184, 188,
strange attractors **1**: 101
Strange, Susan **1**: 20, 263n, 267n; **2**: 24,
    198n, 211n, 214n
strategic partnerships **2**: 29
strategists **2**: 16
strategy **1**: 120, 180
structure **1**: 93; **2**: 10; **1**: parameters of
    29; **1**: of world politics 7, 17–18, 213,
    244
subgroups **1**: 145, 146, 216, 218; **2**: 25, 34,
    41, 43, 116, 126, 170, 187, 189;
    fragmentation of **2**: 127
subjective interpretation **1**: 3, 249; **1**: of
    analysts 232, 248, 249, 251, 253
subnational groups **1**: 36, 150, 152, 182,
    218; **1**: loyalties to 145, 149
subsystems **1**: 180, 218
Suez Canal **1**: 90, 127, 174

suicide bombers **1**: 12; **2**: 13, 16, 92, 105,
    106
summit meetings **2**: 192
Sun Microsystems **2**: 176
superpowers **1**: 35, 36, 86, 103, 123, 142,
    237, 239, 244; **1**: rivalry between 113,
    226; **2**: 35, 36, 113, 115, 124, 126, 135,
    141
support, mobilization of **1**: 147, 272n
supply and demand **2**: 170, 195
supranational organizations **2**: 24, 41, 186
surveillance **2**: 45
sustainability **2**: concept of 154; **2**: and
    development 154, 158
systems **1**: 37, 173–4, 197, 200, 204, 213,
    271n, 272n; **2**: 27, 34, 74, 85, 125, 168;
    1: and co-evolution 106; **2**: bounded
    119–20; **2**: federal 155; **1**: in crisis 117; **1**:
    national 175, 191, 272n, 275n; **1**:
    penetrated **1**: 87, 177–87, 197, 273n; **1**:
    shocks to 119; **1**: transformation of 207,
    213
system–subsystem tensions **2**: 69

Taiwan **2**: 93, 94
tangibility of ends and means **1**: 195, 196,
    275n
technologies **1**: 8–9, 31, 76, 100, 134, 144,
    154, 218, 245; **2**: 35, 43, 45, 52, 59, 64,
    88, 97, 123, 126, 131, 138; **2**: and
    democracy 178; **2**: diffusion of 87; **1**:
    dynamics of 90, 109, 147, 179, 201, 243;
    2: electronic 13, 20, 101, 148, 178, 184,
    187; **2**: innovation 21, 30, 65; **2**: new 22,
    26, 114; **1**: of the Internet 165
technoscapes **1**: 108; **2**: 23, 28, 50, 75, 163
teleconferencing **1**: 155
telephone **1**: 43; **2**: 100, 117
television **1**: 143, 160, 165; **2**: 39, 45, 114,
    116, 130, 165, 178, 191; **1**: global 8, 137,
    154, 159, 162, 203
terminal entities **1**: 21–2, 24, 36–7, 101,
    102, 133; **2**: 21, 22, 25, 26, 68
terminology **2**: 32–5, 65–6
Territorial Globals **1**: 136
territoriality **1**: 39, 40, 42, 43, 108, 143,
    150; **2**: 17, 50, 51, 56, 58, 75–8, 84, 85,
    89, 112, 118, 150–1, 163, 169, 179, 187;
    1: meaning of 201–2; **2**: 166
territory **1**: 133–9, 146, 196
terrorism **1**: 11, 218, 230, 238; **2**: 39, 43,
    44, 163, 170, 172; **1**: on September 11,
    2001, 11, 71, 73, 103–4, 130, 166; **2**: 14,
    16, 17, 65

terrorists **1**: 12, 77, 130, 201
Thailand **1**: 163, 179, 184
theory **1**: 3–4, 9, 75, 76, 107, 116, 120, 208, 209, 211, 233; **1**: anti-theoretical perspectives 98, 99, 233; **1**: as imperative 97–106; **1**: building of 197, 199, 206, 229, 242, 278n; **1**: syntheses of 212; **2**: 91–5, 150
think-tanks **1**: 60
Third World **1**: 86, 126, 150
Tiananmen Square massacre **1**: 206, 226, 227
Times, The (London) **1**: 81
Tokyo Round **1**: 90
tourism **2**: 64; **1**: and tourists 105, 201
trade unions **1**: 127; **2**: 29, 41, 98, 172
trade **1**: 89, 91, 146; **2**: 86, 130, 156, 157, 186, 191; **1**: issues of 149, 181; **1**: routes 90, 124, 129; **2**: 35, 67, 167
tradition **2**: 32
traffic jams **2**: 39
transformation **1**: 71, 73–5, *see also* change
transitology, age of **2**: 164–5
transnational organizations **1**: 19, 125, 216; **2**: 41, 61, 69, 84, 90, 97, 118, 169; **1**: and advocacy groups 21, 146, 204; **2**: and norms 99; **2**: as corporations (TNCs) 34, 43, 75, 87, 131, 152, 155, 176, 189; **2**: as networks 60, 126; **2**: leaders of 101–2
transnational relations **1**: 87, 121
transparency **2**: 99–102, 178, 179, 193
Transparency International (TI) **2**: 177, 192
transportation **1**: 196, 201; **1**: and jet aircraft 8, 134; **1**: technologies of 39, 101;
travel **1**: 162; **2**: 39
treaties **1**: 186, 274n; **2**: 26; **1**: negotiation of 275n
Treaty of Westphalia **2**: 11
tribes **2**: 24
trust **1**: 109; **2**: 32, 52
truth commissions **1**: 202; **2**: 29, 153, 186
Tullis, LaMond **1**: 262, 263n
Tuned-out Passives **1**: 137
turbulence **1**: 33, 126, 64, 75, 76, 117, 11, 119; 206, 218, 277n; **2**: 57, 114, 120, 126; **1**: model of 62, 66, 76–7; **2**: 7–8, 55
Turkey **1**: 235

uncertainties **1**: 107–10, 117, 118, 119, 209, 249; **2**: 13–14, 31, 51

underdeveloped world **1**: 86
unemployment **2**: 127
UNESCO **2**: 41
uneven denationalization **2**: 88
unionists **2**: 16
unipolar system **1**: 103; **2**: 157
United Nations **1**: 173, 184, 185, 271n, 274n; **2**: 7, 8, 32, 33, 42, 97, 98, 99, 111, 123, 137, 141, 153, 157, 170; **2**: as system 121, 128, 141–3, 144, 183; **2**: decline in esteem 142; **2**: Secretary General of 141, 142
United States **1**: 9, 14, 29, 87, 103, 110, 133, 142, 163, 173, 174, 184, 230, 253; **2**: 11, 16, 27, 28, 40, 94, 157, 181, 208n; **1**: and China 206, 226; **2**: 20; **1**: and Soviet Union 107–8, 188, 191, 197; **2**: as superpower 9; **2**: borders with neighbors 134, 139; **1**: governmental institutions of 1, 15–16, 73, 90, 147, 179, 185; **1**: in Vietnam 77, 127; **1**: national interest of 252–3; **2**: nonprofit organizations in 20; **1**: power of 103, 140–1; **1**: policies of 85, 88, 142, 148–9, 257; **2**: religious right in 106; **2**: withdrawal from treaties 158; **2**: welfare programs 155
universalism **2**: 27, 83, 84
universities **1**: 16, 157, 197
urban communities **1**: 111; **2**: 17, 107; **1**: redevelopment of 187, 190, 196
urbanites **2**: 16, 27
USSR **1**: 174, 278n; **1**: as case study, 229–31, 234–45; *see also* Soviet Union

values, authoritative allocation of **1**: 181, 183, 272n; **1**: frameworks of 97, 99, 153, 196, 250
variance **1**: 76, 100
vertical systems **1**: 190–5, 197, 274n, 275n
Vietnam **1**: 103, 140, 146, 184, 185, 186, 187, 191; **1**: US intervention in 77, 127
vigilante gangs **2**: 29
violence **2**: 124
Viotti, Paul R. **1**: 215
voice mail **2**: 165

wages **2**: 32
Waldrop, M. Mitchell **1**: 44, 74, 261n, 264n; **2**: 79, 217n
Wales **2**: 155
Waltz, Kenneth N. **1**: 63, 65, 93, 258n, 263n

war **1**: 10, 22, 23, 127; **2**: 9, 64–5, 69, 124, 146, 162; **2**: factions in 172; on terrorism **1**: 11; **2**: 14, 15
Warsaw Pact **1**: 113
water shortages **2**: 18, 39
weapons **1**: 234, 244; **2**: 26; production of 144
web pages **2**: 20
Weber, Max **1**: 23, 89
Wendt, Alexander **1**: 63, 69, 257n, 263n
West Bank **2**: 39, 106
Western Hemisphere **1**: 253
West Indies Federation **1**: 254
Westphalian system **2**: 28, 29
workers **1**: 91, 123, 216; **2**: 156–7
women **2**: 156; rights of 42
World Bank **1**: 14, 155; **2**: 102, 139, 160, 192, 194, 195
World Economic Forum **1**: 15; **2**: 102, 160, 194
World Environmental Organization **2**: 149

world order **2**: 43, 104, 105, 124; **2**: as disaggregated complexity 106–7
world politics **1**: 27, 213
World Social Forum **1**: 15
world society **1**: 222, 224
world system **2**: 83, 111; **2**: consensus within 17, 98; **2**: politics in 11–12; **2**: prospects for government of 162, 163
World Trade Center **1**: 103
World Trade Organization (WTO) **1**: 14, 155; **2**: 128, 138, 149, 153, 159, 160, 194
World War II **1**: 113, 178, 184, 234, 236, 239, 247; **2**: 113
World Wide Web **2**: 178

Yugoslavia **2**: 7, 40, 58, 112, 142, 181, 191

Zaire **1**: 29
Zürn, Michael **1**: 23; **2**: 88, 89, 201n, 204n, 205n, 208n

Index of authors

Note: in order to facilitate reading either of the two volumes comprising The Study of World Politics, *this index combines both the subject and author indices for the entries in the two volumes by using a bold face **1** to indicate the entries in Volume 1 and a bold face **2** for those in the second volume.*

Adoo, Herb **1**: 279n
Agnew, John **2**: 201n, 217n
Aksu, Esref **2**: 205n
Alberts, David S. **1**: 263n
Alexander, J. C. **1**: 257n, 260n; **2**: 204n
Alexandroff, A. **1**: 265n
Alger, Chadwick F. **1**: 268n, 272n
Almond, Gabriel A. **1**: 271n
Anderson, Benedict **2**: 202n
Anderson, Walter Truett **2**: 213n
Arquilla, John **2**: 218n
Ashby, W. Ross **1**: 264n
Axelrod, Robert **1**: 277n
Aydinli, Ersel **1**: 261n

Ba, Alice D. **2**: 213n
Bache, Ian **2**: 218n
Baker, Russell **2**: 215n
Baldwin, David A. **2**: 211n
Bauer, Raymond A. **1**: 275n;
Bauman, Zygmunt **2**: 203n, 218n
Beal, Richard Smith **2**: 205n
Beilharz, Peter **2**: 218n
Benjamin, Roger **1**: 263n
Blau, Judith R. **2**: 200n
Bleeke, Joel **2**: 216n
Bohlen, Celestine **2**: 216n
Boli, John **1**: 256n, 257n; **2**: 198n, 199n, 219n
Bornstein, David **1**: 256n; **2**: 198n, 218n
Boyer, Robert **2**: 217n
Breecher, Michael **2**: 204n
Brewin, Christopher **2**: 212n
Brock, Lothar **2**: 202n
Brodbeck, Arthur J. **1**: 271n
Brooke, James **2**: 211n
Brooks, David **2**: 197n
Broom, Leonard **1**: 274n
Brown, Michael E. **2**: 212n
Brown, Seyom **1**: 267n; **2**: 200n, 207n
Bruck, Henry W. **1**: 262n, 271n, 280n
Bryan, A. T. **1**: 279n
Buchanan, William **1**: 274n
Bull, Hedley **1**: 277n

Buraway, Michael **1**: 257n
Burdick, Eugene **1**: 271n
Burgess, Philip M. **1**: 261n, 277n
Burton, John W. **1**: 265n
Buzan, Barry **1**: 259n; **2**: 204n

Camilleri, Joseph A. **2**: 201n, 205n, 210n
Caporaso, James A. **1**: 258n, 262n; **2**: 207n
Carlsnaes, Walter **1**: 257n
Carlsson, Sverker **2**: 213n
Castells, Manuel **2**: 198n, 199n
Cerny, Philip G. **2**: 200n, 201n, 207n
Cervenak, Christine M. **2**: 216n
Chernotsky, H. I. **1**: 265n
Christensen, Jon **1**: 257n
Cicourel, A. V. **1**: 257n, 260n; **2**: 204n
Clough, Michael **2**: 211n
Cohen, Roger **2**: 201n
Coleman, James S. **1**: 271n
Collins, Randall **1**: 257n
Comfort, Louise K. **1**: 264n
Commission on Global Governance **2**: 206n, 216n
Conca, Ken **2**: 207n
Copeland, Thomas E. **1**: 270n
Coplin, W. D. **1**: 265n
Corbridge, Stuart **2**: 201n, 217n
Corcoran, Elizabeth **2**: 218n
Cottrell, Leonard S., Jr. **1**: 274n
Courchene, Thomas J. **2**: 219n
Cox, Kevin R. **1**: 259n; **2**: 204n
Cox, Robert W., **1**: 264n; **2**: 200n, 207n 210n
Cruickshank, Albert **1**: 276n
Cummings, L. L. **2**: 217n
Cutler, Claire **2**: 213n, 217n
Czempiel, Ernst-Otto **2**: 208n, 213n, 215n
Czerwinsky, Thomas J. **1**: 263n

Dahan, Michael **1**: 268n, 270n
Daley, Suzanne **2**: 198n
Dallin, Alexander **1**: 278n, 279n, 280n
Dark, K. R. **1**: 259n; **2**: 204n
De Santis, Hugh **2**: 201n

Deibert, Ronald J. **2**: 205n
Der Derian, James **2**: 202n
Desai, Meghnad **2**: 206n
Destler, J. M. **1**: 262n
Dexter, Lewis Anthony **1**: 275n
Diehl, Paul E. **2**: 214n
Doerge, David **2**: 211n
Drache, Daniel **2**: 217n
Drozdiak, William **2**: 210n
Drucker, Peter F. **2**: 209n
Duchachek, Ivo D. **2**: 211n
Dunn, Ashley **2**: 205n
Dunning, John H. **2**: 215n
Dunsire, Andrew **2**: 200n, 207n
Durfee, Mary **1**: 258n; **2**: 214n
Dyson, James W. **1**: 279n

Earnest, David C. **1**: 261n, 263n, 268n
Earnest, David **2**: 199n, 216n
East, Maurice A. **1**: 262n
Eckholm, Erik **1**: 268n
Eckstein, Harry **1**: 266n, 271n, 272n, 273n, 277n
Edwards, Michael **2**: 217n
Eisenstadt, S. N. **1**: 257n
Elkin, Stephen L. **1**: 263n
Emirbayer, Mustafa **2**: 202n
Eulau, Heinz **1**: 274n
Evans, Peter B. **1**: 258n; **2**: 210n, 218n
Eyerman, Ron **2**: 217n

Fagen, W. Michael **1**: 256n, 260n, 268n, 275n; **2**: 201n, 206n, 212n
Falk, Jim **2**: 201n
Falk, Richard A. **1**: 265n; **2**: 214n
Featherstone, Mike **1**: 260n, 264n; **2**: 199n, 206n
Feinberg, R. E. **1**: 279n
Feldman, David **2**: 218n
Ferguson, Leroy C. **1**: 274n
Finger, Matthew **2**: 216n
Finkelstein, Lawrence S. **2**: 207n
Firorina, Morris P. **1**: 258n
Flinder, Matthew **2**: 218n
Frank, David John **2**: 219n
Frankel, Max **2**: 198n
Freeman, Heather **1**: 265n
Freeman, John **1**: 277n
French, Hilary **2**: 213n
French, Howard W. **2**: 216n
Friedland, Edward **1**: 267n
Friedman, Thomas L. **1**: 259n, 268n, 270n; **2**: 204n, 216n
Friedmann, John **2**: 208n
Friedrich, Carl J. **1**: 273n

Fry, Earl H. **2**: 210n
Fukuyama, Francis **2**: 197n, 202n
Furniss, Edgar S. **1**: 280n

Gaddis, John Lewis **1**: 259n, 264n
Gamble, Andrew **2**: 203n
Gambles, Ian **2**: 200n, 202n
Gapper, Gary **2**: 218n
Garber, Larry **2**: 212n
Gardner, James N. **1**: 265n
Garrett, Geoffrey **1**: 259n
Gehring, Verna V. **1**: 268n
Geller, D. S. **1**: 265n
George, Alexander L. **1**: 277n
Giddens, Anthony **1**: 257n
Gillespie, John V. **1**: 260n
Gills, Barry K. **2**: 204n
Gilpin, Robert **1**: 258n; **2**: 207n
Girard, Bruce **2**: 213n
Glassman, James K. **2**: 217n
Goizueta, Roberto C. **2**: 210n
Goldblatt, David **2**: 199
Goldstein, Joshua **1**: 259n, 277n; **2**: 204n
Goleman, Daniel **2**: 201n
Goodwin, Jeff **2**: 202n
Gordenker, Leon **2**: 201n
Gottlieb, Gidon **2**: 213n
Greenhouse, Steven **2**: 210n
Grel, Jan M. **2**: 218n
Guastello, Stephen **1**: 265n
Gusfield, Joseph, R. **2**: 217n

Haas, Michael **1**: 278n
Haas, Richard **2**: 199n
Hall, Stuart **1**: 259n; **2**: 204n
Hamlett, Bruce D. **1**: 266n
Handelman, J. R. **1**: 265n
Hannerz, Ulf **1**: 259n; **2**: 199n, 204n
Harris, Marvin **2**: 204n
Harrod, Jeffrey **1**: 265n
Harvey, Frank **2**: 204n
Haufler, Virginia **2**: 207n, 213n, 217n
Hauslohner, Peter **1**: 278n
Heidenheimer, Arnold J. **2**: 212n
Heilbronner, Robert L. **1**: 266n
Heller, H. J. **1**: 257n
Henry, Ryan **2**: 200n
Hermann, Charles F. **1**: 261n, 262n, 277n, 279n
Hermann, Richard K. **1**: 278n
Herod, A. **2**: 199n
Hewson, Martin **2**: 206n, 209n
Heyns, Terry **1**: 259n; **2**: 198n
Higgott, Richard **2**: 203n
Hironaka, Ann **2**: 219n

Hock, Dee W. **1**: 259n, 264n; **2**: 199n, 204n, 206n, 217n, 218n
Hodnett, Grey **1**: 279n
Hoffman, Stanley **1**: 267n
Hoffmann, Matthew J. **2**: 213n
Hollander, Paul **1**: 279n
Hollist, W. Ladd **1**: 262n, 263n
Holm, Hans-Henrik **2**: 200n, 201n
Holsti, Kal J. **1**: 259n, 265n; **2**: 204n
Hooson, David **2**: 202n
Horowitz, Jason **2**: 206n
Hovet, Thomas Jr. **1**: 274n
Howe, James W. **1**: 267n
Huber, Joan **1**: 257n
Huckfeldt, Robert **2**: 208n
Hulme, David **2**: 217n
Huntington, Samuel P. **1**: 275n; **2**: 201n

Ignatius, David **2**: 218n, 219n
Ince, B. A. **1**: 279n
Inotai, Andras **2**: 209n

Jackson, Robert H. **1**: 258n; **2**: 207n
Jacobson, Harold K. **1**: 258n; **2**: 210n
James, Alan **1**: 258n; **2**: 207n
Jamison, Andrew **2**: 217n
Jarvis, Anthony P. **2**: 202n
Jasanoff, Sheila **2**: 213n
Johnston, Hank **2**: 217n
Johnston, Michael **2**: 212n
Jones, R. J. Barry **1**: 259n; **2**: 204n
Jordan, Amos A. **2**: 202n
Josselin, Daphné **1**: 256n
Judge, Anthony J. N. **2**: 201n

Kakonen, Jyrki **2**: 209n, 211n
Kariel, Henry S. **1**: 278n
Katzenstein, P. J. **1**: 265n
Kaufman, R. R. **1**: 265n
Kaysen, Carl **2**: 212n
Kegley, Charles W., Jr. **1**: 262n, 277n, 279n; **2**: 197n
Kelly, Kevin **1**: 264n
Kennan, George F. **1**: 272n
Khanna, Jane **2**: 202n
King, Alexander **2**: 208n
King, Anthony D. **1**: 255n, 259n; **2**: 204n
Klineberg, Otto **1**: 272n
Knorr, Klaus **1**: 267n
Knorr-Cetina, K. D. **1**: 257n, 260n; **2**: 204n
Kober, Stanley **2**: 197n
Koehler, W. **1**: 265n
Kooiman, Jan **2**: 200n, 206n, 207n
Korany, Bahgat **1**: 262n

Korten, David C. **2**: 217n
Kotkin, Joel **2**: 211n
Kroll, J. **1**: 265n
Kruzel, J. **1**: 255n
Kubalkova, Vendulka **1**: 276n
Kuhn, Thomas S. **2**: 207n
Kuklinski, Antoni **2**: 201n

LaFraniere, Sharon **1**: 268n
Lahteenmaki, Kaisa **2**: 209n, 211n
Lakatos, Imre **2**: 207n
Landler, Mark **1**: 256n
Laqueur, S. **1**: 265n
Laraña, Enrique **2**: 217n
Larkins, Jeremy **1**: 256n
Larmanou, Marcel **2**: 198n
Lash, Scott **1**: 260n, 264n; **2**: 199n, 206n
Lauren, Paul Gordon **1**: 277n
Lawson, Stephanie **2**: 198n
Leatherman, Janie **2**: 210n
Lee, Alfred **1**: 268n
Lee, Jennifer 8. **1**: 270n
Lemann, Nicholas **1**: 255n
Lerner, Allan W. **1**: 267n
Levine, Victor T. **2**: 212n
Lewin, Roger **1**: 264n; **2**: 215n
Lewin, Tamar **1**: 268n
Lewis, Paul G. **2**: 209n
Lewis, William W. **2**: 204n
Lijphart, Arend **1**: 277n
Lincoln, Bruce **2**: 207n
Lipnack, Jessica **1**: 264n
Lipschutz, Ronnie D. **1**: 256n; **2**: 200n, 203n, 216n
Litfin, Karen T. **2**: 216n
Loya, Thomas A. **2**: 219n
Lukas, John **2**: 197n
Luke, Timothy W. **2**: 199n
Lyons, Gene M. **2**: 212n

MacFarquhar, Neil **1**: 270n
Maguire, Kevin **1**: 256n
Mahbubani, Kishore **2**: 202n
Mann, Michael **1**: 257n
Mansbach, Richard W. **2**: 200n, 202n
Maoz, Zeev **2**: 214n
Maragall, Pascal **2**: 210n
March, James G. **2**: 208n
Marin, B. **2**: 207n
Markoff, John **1**: 260n; **2**: 198n, 204n, 217n
Marriott, Michel **1**: 268n
Martello, Marybeth Long **2**: 213n
Masterman, Margaret **2**: 207n
Mathews, J. **1**: 261n
Mathews, Jessica **2**: 215n

Mathias, Albert **2**: 202n
Mayer, Judith **2**: 216n
Mayer, Peter **2**: 208n
Mayntz, R. **2**: 207n
McGowan, Patrick J. **1**: 261n
McGrew, Anthony G. **2**: 199n, 209n
McKinley, James C. Jr. **2**: 203n
McMillen, Donald **2**: 201n
Mearsheimer, John J. **2**: 199n
Mefford, Dwain **1**: 279n
Merton, Robert K. **1**: 274n, 280n
Mesjasz, Czeslaw **2**: 214n
Meyer, John W. **1**: 257n; **2**: 219n
Milner, Helen V. **1**: 259n
Minter, William **2**: 217n
Misra, K. P. **2**: 205n
Mlinar, Zdravko **2**: 201n
Modelski, George A. **1**: 259n, 280n; **2**: 204n
Monaco **1**: 273n
Montgomery, John D. **1**: 272n
Moon, Bruce **1**: 262n
Mosely, Philip E. **1**: 272n
Mueller, John **2**: 215n
Murphy, Craig **2**: 218n
Musgrave, Alan **2**: 207n
Myre, Greg **1**: 256n

Nadelman, Ethan A. **2**: 212n
Natsios, Andrew S. **2**: 201n
Neal, Fred Warner **1**: 266n
Neisser, Ulrich **1**: 256n
Neustadt, Richard E. **1**: 272n
Norris, Floyd **2**: 218n
Norris, Pippa **1**: 268n
Northedge, F. S. **1**: 265n
Nye, Joseph S., Jr. **1**: 276n

O'Leary, M. K. **1**: 265n
Ohmae, Kenichi **2**: 210n, 211n
Olsen, Johan P. **2**: 208n
Onishi, Norimitsu **1**: 256n
Ostrom, Elinor **1**: 259n

Paarlberg, Robert L. **1**: 266n, 267n
Packer, George **1**: 268n
Pagnucco, Ron **2**: 210n
Palmer, Glenn **1**: 278n
Paolini, Albert J. **2**: 202n
Pastor, Robert A. **2**: 212n
Payne, Anthony **2**: 203n
Peartree, Edward **2**: 200n
Perraton, Jonathan **2**: 199n
Peters, B. Guy **2**: 219n
Petrilla, Ricardo **2**: 210n

Pettman, Ralph **2**: 202n
Philbeck, Joyce **1**: 268n
Pierre, Jan **2**: 214n, 219n
Pierson, Christopher **2**: 214n, 219n
Plutzer, Eric **2**: 208n
Polsby, Nelson W. **1**: 274n, 277n
Pool, Ithiel de Sola **1**: 275n
Porter, Tony **2**: 213n, 217n
Powell, Walter W. **2**: 217n
Price, Richard **1**: 256n
Princen, Thomas **2**: 216n
Przeworski, Adam **2**: 214n
Purkitt, Helen E. **1**: 279n
Putnam, Robert D. **1**: 256n, 258n; **2**: 210n
Pye, Lucian W. **1**: 272n

Radebaugh, Lee H. **2**: 210n
Rai, Saritha **1**: 256n
Ramsarian, R. **1**: 279n
Ramsoy, Odd **1**: 272n
Reader, Ian **2**: 206n
Redfern, Paul **2**: 206n
Reed, Laura W. **2**: 212n
Reinicke, Wolfgang H. **1**: 260n; **2**: 213n, 219n
Rensselaer, W. Lee III **2**: 212n
Rheingold, Howard **1**: 270n
Riggs, Fred W. **1**: 272n, 273n
Riker, James **2**: 203n
Rischard, Jean-Francois **2**: 195
Rittberger, Volker **2**: 205n, 207n, 208n
Roberts, S. M. **2**: 199n
Robertson, Roland **1**: 255n, 259n, 260n, 264n; **2**: 199n, 206n
Robinson, Gillian **2**: 218n
Robinson, Thomas **1**: 276n
Robison, Richard **2**: 202n
Rogowski, Ronald **1**: 259n
Rohlem, Thomas P. **2**: 210n
Ronfeldt, David **2**: 202n, 211n, 218n
Ropp, Stephen C. **2**: 205n
Rosecrance, R. **1**: 265n
Rosell, Steven A. **2**: 208n
Rundell, John **2**: 218n
Russett, Bruce M. **1**: 277n

Sachs, Wolfgang **2**: 213n
Saco, Diana **1**: 268n
Sakamoto, Yoshikazu **2**: 197n, 206n
Salamon, Lester M. **1**: 275n; **2**: 208n, 217n
Salmore, Stephen A. **1**: 262n
Salter, Mark B. **2**: 200n, 207n
Sanger, David E. **1**: 276n
Sapin, Burton M. **1**: 262n, 267n, 271n, 280n

Saravanamuttu, Johan **2**: 202n
Sassen, Saskia **1**: 258n; **2**: 210n
Sayle, Murray **1**: 279n
Sbragia, Alberta **2**: 212n
Schacter, Harvey **2**: 215n
Scheff, Thomas J. **1**: 257n
Schemo, Diana Jean **2**: 210n
Schmemann, Serge **1**: 263n
Schneider, Bertrand **2**: 208n
Schofer, Evan **2**: 219n
Scholte, Jan Aart **1**: 256n, 260n; **2**: 199n, 203n, 210n, 213n, 219n
Schrage, Michael **2**: 218n
Schramm, Wilbur **1**: 272n, 274n
Schwartz, John **1**: 270n
Sciolini, Elaine **2**: 212n
Seaburg, Paul **1**: 267n
Sewell, James P. **2**: 200n, 207n
Seybolt, Taylor B. **2**: 216n
Shambaugh, David **1**: 276n
Shapiro, Ian **1**: 258n
Shapiro, Michael J. **2**: 202n
Shaw, Martin **1**: 257n
Sherif, Muzafer **1**: 272n
Shermer, Michael **1**: 265n
Shevchenko, Arkady N. **1**: 278n
Sikkink, Kathryn **2**: 205n, 210n, 216n, 217n
Sills, David **1**: 280n
Simai, Mihaly **2**: 206n
Simis, Konstantin **1**: 279n
Simmons, Beth **1**: 257n
Simon, Herbert A. **1**: 265n
Sinclair, Timothy J. **2**: 206n, 207n, 208, 211, 213n, 216n
Singer, J. David **1**: 260n, 263n; **2**: 204n
Siochrú, Seán Ó **2**: 213n
Skolnikoff, Eugene B. **1**: 258n; **2**: 207n
Smith, Craig S. **2**: 206n
Smith, Jackie **2**: 210n
Smith, R. David **1**: 265n
Snyder, Richard C. **1**: 262n, 267n, 271n, 280n
Soja, Edward W. **2**: 209n
Soldatos, Panayotis **2**: 210n
Sorenson, George **2**: 200n, **2**: 201n
Sparks, Allister **1**: 265n
Speth, James Gustave **2**: 214n
Spiro, Herbert J. **1**: 274n
Sprague, John **2**: 208n
Stamps, Jeffrey **1**: 264n
Staniland, Martin **1**: 263n
Staw, Barry M. **2**: 217n
Stein, Arthur **2**: 211n
Stocker, J. **1**: 265n

Stokes, Donald E. **1**: 187, 274n
Stone, Webster **1**: 256n
Stremlau, John J. **1**: 278n
Stripple, Johannes **2**: 213n
Szymborska, Wislawa **2**: 201n

Tai, Susan H. C. **1**: 260n; **2**: 206n
Talbott, Strobe **1**: 278n
Tarrow, Sidney **2**: 217n
Taylor, Bron Raymond **2**: 216n
Taylor, Charles **1**: 266n
Tharoor, Shashi **2**: 198n
Thiele, Leslie Paul **2**: 209n
Thomas, George M. **1**: 256n; **2**: 219n
Thorup, Cathryn L. **2**: 211n, 217n
Tilly, Charles **1**: 258n
Tonn, Bruce E. **2**: 218n
Triandis, Harry C. **2**: 200n
Tuathail, Gearóid Ó **2**: 199n
Tucker, Robert W. **1**: 267n
Tuma, Nancy Brandon **2**: 219n

Urry, John **1**: 263n; **2**: 203n

Van Evera, Steven **2**: 199n
Vasquez, J. A. **1**: 265n
Vayrynen, Raimo **2**: 213n
Vogler, John **2**: 209n, 211n

Wahlke, John C. **1**: 274n
Walker, R. B. J. **2**: 209n
Wallace, William **1**: 256n
Wallerstein, Immanuel **1**: 257n, 276n
Waltz, Kenneth N. **2**: 207n
Wang, Hongying **2**: 219n
Wapner, Paul **2**: 216n
Waters, Neil L. **1**: 255n
Webber, Alan **2**: 217n
Weiss, Thomas G. **2**: 201n, 217n,
Wendt, Alexander **2**: 213n, 218n
Wicker, Tom **1**: 279n
Wildavsky, Aaron B. **1**: 267n, 274n
Willetts, Peter **2**: 216n, 217n
Williams, Phil **2**: 212n
Wines, Michael **1**: 268n
Wittkopf, Eugene **1**: 262n
Wolfgang, Marvin E. **1**: 267n
Wong, Y. H. **1**: 260n; **2**: 206n

Young, Oran R. **2**: 208n

Zacher, Mark W. **2**: 197n, 213n
Zartman, I. William **2**: 203n
Zimmerman, William **1**: 278n
Zinnes, Dina A. **1**: 260n